The Nature of Desire

# The Nature of Desire

*Edited by* FEDERICO LAURIA
AND JULIEN A. DEONNA

Oxford University Press is a department of the University of Oxford. It furthers the University's objective of excellence in research, scholarship, and education by publishing worldwide. Oxford is a registered trade mark of Oxford University Press in the UK and certain other countries.

Published in the United States of America by Oxford University Press
198 Madison Avenue, New York, NY 10016, United States of America.



Library of Congress Cataloging-in-Publication Data
Names: Lauria, Federico, author. | Deonna, Julien A., author.
Title: The nature of desire / Federico Lauria & Julien Deonna.
Description: New York : Oxford University Press, 2017. |
Includes bibliographical references and index.
Identifiers: LCCN 2017008872 (print) | LCCN 2016047086 (ebook) |
ISBN 9780199370962 (cloth : alk. paper) | ISBN 9780199370979 (pdf) |
ISBN 9780199370986 (online course)
Subjects: LCSH: Desire (Philosophy)
Classification: LCC B105.D44 L38 2017 (ebook) | LCC B105.D44 (print) |
DDC 128/.3—dc23
LC record available at https://lccn.loc.gov/2017008872

9 8 7 6 5 4 3 2 1

Printed by Sheridan Books, Inc., United States of America

# CONTENTS

## ACKNOWLEDGMENTS

The project of this book took shape in 2012 as we organized the conference *The Nature of Desire* at the University of Geneva, which most of the contributors to this volume participated in. While Federico was writing his dissertation on this topic, it had become apparent that there was no serious contemporary debate on what desires are. Hence the conference. To our eyes and ears, it was a great success: the papers presented were challenging, exemplified very different perspectives, and revealed that there was much more to desire than lots of stale dogmas receiving cursory treatment in the literature. This naturally spurred us to collect the papers for a special volume and add a few more to the mix, forming an ensemble that would bring fresh insight and stimulate further explorations on the nature of desire. We were delighted that Oxford University Press shared our enthusiasm, and we feel elated today to finally have our desire for the finished product gratified.

This project would not have been possible without the assistance, expertise, and support of several people. First, we wish to express our gratitude to the contributors to this volume for their precious work and perseverance. The help and patience of Lucy Randall from Oxford University Press was crucial; we are very grateful to her. This book is an achievement of the Swiss National Science Foundation Project "Desire, Emotion, and the Mind," and we thank the Foundation for its support. We thank the Swiss Center for Affective Sciences, the interdisciplinary center for the study of emotions of the University of Geneva, which hosted this project. We owe a word of appreciation also to *Thumos*, the Genevan research group on emotions, values, and norms, to all its members, friends, and many visitors. Finally, our most important debt is to the following three persons: Kevin Mulligan, who taught us what philosophy is about and how it should be done ; Gianfranco Soldati, for his incisive questions and friendship ; and Fabrice Teroni, our best philosopher friend.

# CONTRIBUTORS

**Maria Alvarez** is a reader in philosophy in the Department of Philosophy, King's College London. Her research focuses on the philosophy of action, including the nature of agency, the metaphysics and explanation of actions, choice and moral responsibility. She has also published widely on the nature of reasons, especially practical reasons and normativity. She is the author of *Kinds of Reasons: An Essay in the Philosophy of Action* (Oxford University Press, 2010).

**Lauren Ashwell** is an associate professor of philosophy in the Department of Philosophy at Bates College. Her areas of specialization include metaphysics, epistemology of mind, and feminist philosophy. Her published work includes articles in *Philosophical Studies*, the *Australasian Journal of Philosophy, Philosophy Compass*, and *Social Theory and Practice*.

**Julien A. Deonna** is an associate professor of philosophy at the University of Geneva and a project leader at the Swiss Centre for Affective Sciences. His research interests are in the philosophy of mind, in particular the philosophy of emotions, moral emotions, and moral psychology. In addition to many articles in the area, he is the co-author of *In Defense of Shame* (Oxford University Press, 2011) and *The Emotions: A Philosophical Introduction* (Routledge, 2012). He is the co-director of Thumos, the Genevan philosophy research group on emotions, values, and norms.

**Sabine A. Döring** is the chair of practical philosophy at Eberhard Karls Universität Tübingen. Research interests are (meta)ethics and the theory of agency with an emphasis on the emotions. Recent publications include "Expressing Emotions: From Action to Art," in *Art, Mind, and*

*Narrative: Themes from the Work of Peter Goldie*, edited by Julian Dodd (Oxford University Press, in print); "What's Wrong with Recalcitrant Emotions? From Irrationality to Challenge of Agential Identity," in *Dialectica* (2015); "What Is an Emotion? Musil's Adverbial Theory," in the *Monist* (2014); and (with Eva-Maria Düringer) "Being Worthy of Happiness: Towards a Kantian Appreciation of Our Finite Nature," in *Philosophical Topics* (2013).

**Bahadir Eker** is a PhD student at Eberhard Karls University Tübingen.

**Daniel Friedrich** works as a data analyst. He did his PhD at the Australian National University. He has published articles on desire, motivation, promises, and the ethics of adoption.

**Alex Gregory** is a lecturer in philosophy at the University of Southampton. He works mostly in ethics and meta-ethics, and more specifically on the role that desires play in explaining and justifying behavior and related questions about moral motivation and reasons for action.

**Federico Lauria** is a postdoctoral researcher in the Philosophy Department and Swiss Center for Affective Sciences of the University of Geneva. He was recently associate researcher at Columbia University. His work is at the intersection of philosophy of mind, ethics, and aesthetics. More specifically, he is interested in issues in philosophy of desire and emotions, such as self-deception, musical emotions, and epistemic emotions.

**Olivier Massin** is a lecturer at the University of Geneva. His research lies at the confluence of metaphysics, philosophy of mind, and value theory. He has published several papers on perception, pleasure and pain, effort, and willing.

**Graham Oddie** is a professor of philosophy at the University of Colorado at Boulder. He has broad interests in the theory of value, metaphysics, and epistemology, about which he has written a number of articles and books, including *Value, Reality and Desire* (Oxford University Press, 2005).

**Peter Railton** is the Kavka Distinguished University Professor and Perrin Professor of Philosophy at the University of Michigan. His research has been in meta-ethics, normative ethics, philosophy of science, and philosophy of psychology. A collection of some of his papers can be found in *Facts, Values, and Norms* (Cambridge University Press, 2003), and he is a co-author of the recent interdisciplinary book *Homo Prospectus* (Oxford University Press, 2016).

**Timothy Schroeder** grew up on the Canadian prairies, an environment that afforded him plenty of time for philosophical speculation. He received his BA from the University of Lethbridge and his PhD from Stanford University and is now a professor of philosophy at Rice University. He is the author of *Three Faces of Desire* (Oxford University Press, 2004) and, with Nomy Arpaly, of *In Praise of Desire* (Oxford University Press, 2014).

**G. F. Schueler** is Professor of Philosophy Emeritus at the University of Delaware. He is the author of *Desire* (MIT Press, 1995) and *Reasons and Purposes* (Oxford University Press, 2003) as well as articles on ethics, philosophy of action, and philosophy of mind in various philosophy journals.

**David Wall** was most recently a lecturer in philosophy at the University of Northampton. His research interests lie in philosophy of mind, epistemology, philosophy of action, and moral psychology. In particular he is interested in theories of desire, introspection and self-deception, Moore's Paradox, akrasia, and animal ethics, and has published articles on some of these subjects.

# The Nature of Desire

# Introduction

## *Reconsidering Some Dogmas about Desires*

FEDERICO LAURIA AND JULIEN A. DEONNA

OUR LIFE IS imbued with desire. While some people desire to see the ocean, others want to live in New York. While some people want to understand the laws of the universe, Juliet simply aspires to kiss Romeo. Some desires are stronger than others. Some last longer than others. Sometimes we are happy because one of our desires is gratified; on another occasion, we may cry due to the frustration of a desire. These are among the many platitudes of the life of desire. One may wonder: What is this thing called 'desire'? What is the essence of desire? This is the main question addressed in this volume.

Desires play an important role in our lives. Yet contemporary philosophy has neglected the issue of the nature of desire as compared with investigations of perception, belief, emotion, intention, and other types of mental states. Although there are some notable exceptions to this neglect (Marks 1986; Stampe 1986, 1987; Schroeder 2004; Oddie 2005; Tenenbaum 2007; Friedrich 2012; Arpaly and Schroeder 2013), it is fair to say that no live debate on the nature of desire is presently taking place (see Schroeder 2015 for a similar diagnosis). The aim of this volume is to redress this imbalance by bringing together scholars who adopt different perspectives on the subject. The volume aspires to draw a taxonomy of the main conceptions of desire and to create a fruitful debate about this under-explored topic. But why is it important to understand desire, and what does the philosophy of desire consist of? In what follows, this question is answered from three distinct angles.

## Beyond the Dogma of the Motivational Conception of Desire

The lack of a real debate about desire is perplexing. The central explanation for this fact is, we believe, that one intuitive view of desire is often taken for granted in the philosophical literature. It is, we conjecture, the main dogma of desire. Since Hume, most philosophers have assumed that desire is essentially a motivational state (Armstrong 1968; Stampe 1986; Stalnaker 1984 Smith 1994; Dretske 1988; Dancy 2000; Millikan 2005). In this "hydraulic" view of desire (McDowell's 1998 expression), desire is the spring of action *par excellence*. To desire, for example to listen to a symphony, is nothing but being inclined to do so—end of story. The motivational conception of desire is rarely defended in detail, but it is presupposed in numerous debates. Most interpretations of the notion of direction of fit rely on it; functionalist accounts of desire often mention it in passing; standard views of action and decision making in philosophy and economics build on it; and disagreements about whether desires can be reasons for acting often revolve around it. From this perspective, action and motivation are key to understanding desire. But is motivation all there is to desiring?

There are reasons to doubt it. To start with, our folk concept of desire appears much richer. When we acknowledge our desires, are we merely talking about our motivations to act? Intuitively, professing my desire to see Juliet seems to go beyond conveying the motivation to act so as to see her; it seems to express something deeper. Furthermore, looking at the history of philosophy or the contemporary literature, there is another approach to desire that deserves special attention. On this conception, to desire something is to evaluate it in a positive light. Desiring to swim in the river is to represent this state as good in some way or other. According to this evaluative conception, which can be traced back to Aristotle at least and which has found new advocates recently, goodness is the crux around which desire revolves.[1] Given their historical pedigree, we shall call the motivational and evaluative conceptions the "classical views of desire." On the face of it, they seem very different. The evaluative view is centered on goodness, while the motivational view concentrates on motivation. Now, goodness and motivation seem to be distinct concepts despite the intimate relations that exist between them. As the debate on moral motivation has taught us, it might be that one could positively evaluate a state of affairs without being motivated to realize it. It is thus fair to ask which one of the two conceptions captures desire best. Is desire essentially a motivational state? Is it a positive evaluation? Is it both? Or is it neither? Most of the essays in this collection explore the classical views of desire. This is one way of going beyond the dogma that desiring is the state of being motivated and of adopting a more critical stance on the nature of desire.

## Revisiting Other Philosophical and Empirical Dogmas of Desire

The philosophy of desire touches on many other issues, however. A survey of the philosophical literature reveals that several principles about desire are often taken for granted and are rarely put into doubt. In other words, there are other dogmas of desire. This book aims to discuss these dogmas too, covering more minutiae than is usually the case, from the perspective of the nature of desire. A brief presentation of these dogmas is thus in order.

Desires are often contrasted with beliefs in terms of their direction of fit. According to this metaphor or figurative way of talking, beliefs are supposed to fit the world, while the world is supposed to fit our desires.[2] In the case of a mismatch between the world and our beliefs, our beliefs should change—not the world. Changing the world so as to fit a belief would be inappropriate. Consequently, beliefs have the *mind-to-world* direction of fit: they aim at truth. In contrast, when the world does not correspond to some desire, the *world* should change. Changing a desire simply because it is frustrated would be wrong. Desires thus have the *world-to-mind* direction of fit: they aim at satisfaction. There is an important debate about the meaning of this notion (see Smith 1994; Humberstone 1992; Zangwill 1998; Gregory 2012; Archer 2015). Despite these controversies, the standard interpretation of the *world-to-mind* direction of fit of desire is motivational in spirit: in the case of a mismatch between desire and the world, subjects should *act* to bring about the satisfaction of the desire. This common interpretation fits well the motivational view of desire. Is it correct? Does the *world-to-mind* direction of fit reveal that desires are essentially motivations (see Gregory, Lauria, Railton *this volume*; for detractors of the metaphor, see Sobel and Copp 2001; Milliken 2008; Frost 2014)?

In addition to aiming toward satisfaction in the way explained, desires are often said to aim at the good, just as beliefs aim at the truth (De Sousa 1974; Velleman 2000; Hazlett *unpublished*). One way of understanding this slogan is to interpret it as follows: one cannot desire something without "seeing" some good in it. Call this the "guise of the good" thesis. The "guise of the good" thesis has an important historical pedigree: it can be traced back to at least Plato, was at the heart of the scholastic conception of desire in the Middle Ages, and is often referred to in the contemporary literature.[3] Although friends of the evaluative conception of desire naturally embrace this thesis, other views are compatible with it: that desiring involves a positive evaluation does not imply that it *is* a positive evaluation. Can we not desire something without seeing any good in it? If so, what does this teach us about desire (see Oddie, Massin *this volume*; for detractors of this thesis, see Stocker 1979; Velleman 1992; Döring and Eker *this volume*)?

Another dogma that is less often examined concerns a form of impossibility in desire. Since Plato, it is common to think that one cannot desire what one already has. Consider that I want to climb Mount Etna. The intuition is that as long as I have a desire to climb Mount Etna, I have *not* climbed it. As soon as I have, my desire extinguishes itself. Desires are for absences, or, less metaphorically, they are about what is not actual.[4] Although some scholars disagree about the formulation of the principle (see Boghossian 2003; Oddie 2005; Lauria *this volume*), some version of the principle is often taken for granted. What does this reveal about desire (see Oddie, Lauria, Massin *this volume*)? And is it true (for detractors, see Heathwood 2007; Oddie *this volume*)?

Finally, leaving armchair philosophy, it is uncontroversial in the neurosciences that desires are strongly implicated in the reward system and are closely connected to the neurotransmitter dopamine (Schultz 1997; Schultz, Tremblay and Hollerman 1998; Schroeder 2004). According to the standard neuroscientific picture, desire involves the anticipation of reward and the encoding of prediction errors: in desiring something, one anticipates some reward (say, a banana) and then compares the expected reward with the actual obtaining of the reward. In this way, desires are crucial for learning in the sense of adapting one's behavior to one's environment. How can this help us understand the nature of desire (see Schroeder, Railton, Lauria *this volume*)? Examining these four dogmas is another way of questioning the received wisdom about desire and has the potential to shed new light on its essence.

## Beyond the Philosophy of Desire

The issue of the nature of desire is important *per se*, but it can also illuminate other philosophical puzzles—controversies in which desires are frequently mentioned and their role examined without sufficient attention being paid to what they are. In the absence of a clear conception of desire, these debates are on shaky ground. This is especially so given that the motivational view of desire is often simply assumed. Let us present three examples of important debates featuring desires in, respectively, philosophy of mind, ethics, and meta-ethics, which could benefit from a deeper understanding of what they are. This will reveal the wider philosophical significance of this book.

The direction of fit of desire is often considered an essential feature of desire, but it has broader ramifications in the philosophy of mind and of language (Searle 1983). In the philosophy of mind, it is used as a tool to contrast conations or states meant to modify the world (e.g. desires, intentions, needs) from cognitions or states meant to represent the world (beliefs, perceptions, etc.). This Humean picture of the mind is at the heart of traditional philosophical accounts of agency and the main models of decision making in economics. If our exploration into the nature of desire can elucidate the metaphor of direction of fit, it will *eo ipso* clarify the general issue of the taxonomy of the mental and of other types of representations suggested by the metaphor. This has far-ranging implications, since it can help to put in perspective traditional accounts of agency in philosophy and economics (see Railton *this volume*).

In ethics the most significant line of research about desire concerns its role in the explanation and justification of action. Can desires be reasons for acting in a certain way? If they can, are they motivating reasons, normative ones, or both? Although scholars disagree on how to answer these questions, they often rely on implicit and varying conceptions of desire—most of the time presupposing that desiring is nothing but the motivation to act. Addressing the issue of the nature of desire should thus help to solve the puzzle of their practical role. How can one determine whether desires are reasons for acting without knowing what they are? Four contributions in this volume attest to the fact that one's stance on the nature of desire has relevant implications for this investigation (Döring and Eker, Alvarez, Friedrich, Gregory *this volume*).

Finally, in meta-ethics desires appear in the debate about the very nature and definition of value. According to the mainstream fitting attitude analysis of value, what is good is just what is worth desiring (Broad 1930). *Prima facie*, this debate seems disconnected from the question of desire's essence and seems to rest on an intuitive grasp of what counts as a desire. Yet, as Oddie's essay reveals, the question of the nature of desire can contribute to this meta-ethical puzzle as well.

A more detailed examination of what desires are can thus lead to a better understanding of important and various philosophical concerns. We have focused here on established controversies where desires surface, but it goes without saying that more neglected issues will also benefit from this inquiry (see the second part of this volume).

With these clarifications in mind, the aim of this volume can be further specified as follows. In addition to examining the classical views of desire, this collection of essays purports to explore the dogmas about desire one finds in the literature. And it does so with an eye to the implications the nature of desire has with regard to wider controversies.

The book is divided into two parts. The first tackles directly the question of the essence of desire; the second addresses unexplored issues in the philosophical literature that bear on conceptions of desire. In the remainder of this introduction, we summarize each contribution and raise questions that connect each with other essays in the volume. This should convince the reader that a fruitful and rich debate about the nature of desire has begun.

## I. Conceptions of Desire

Are desires positive evaluations? Are they motivations? Are there alternative conceptions? What does the empirical evidence suggest about the nature of desire?

This section is divided into four subsections corresponding to each question raised.

### Evaluative Views: Desire and the Good

Is goodness the key for understanding desire? In their contributions, Oddie and Friedrich, elaborating on previous work, answer this question affirmatively. To desire, they argue, is to be struck by the goodness of certain things. Imagine a person who is disposed to switch on any radio she encounters (Quinn 1993). She is not doing this because she enjoys it or thinks there is something good about turning on radios (e.g. she considers it a means to listen to music). Rather she does not see any good whatsoever in the action she is performing. Does she desire to turn on radios? Quinn's (1993) intuition, which is shared by Oddie and Friedrich, is that this person does not desire to switch on radios precisely because she does not see any good in it. Hence a desire should involve a positive evaluation. Ultimately it might be that desire is essentially a positive evaluation. Which type of evaluation? Both contributors agree that the evaluation that is crucial to desire does not amount to desires being evaluative judgments.

In his contribution "Desire and the Good: In Search of the Right Fit," Oddie defends the "value appearance view." In this conception, to desire something is for this thing to appear good. Juliet's longing for Kyoto is the same thing as Kyoto appearing good to her. More specifically, Oddie expounds on the idea that desire and goodness fit like hand in glove, defends the view against objections, and presents a new argument in its favor. If we conceive of desires as value appearances, we may hope to fruitfully address issues surrounding the nature of values. The argument proposed concerns chiefly the fitting-attitude analysis of value: the thought that goodness is what is fitting to favor, in particular, what is fitting to desire. This analysis has been criticized on the grounds that it cannot account for "the wrong kind of reasons" to favor something (Rabinowicz and Rønnow-Rasmussen 2004) and for the existence of "solitary goods" (Bykvist 2009). Oddie elegantly specifies *desiderata* for the positive attitude that is part of the analysis so as to make it immune from these problems and to find the right fit between goodness and desire. The positive attitude should be a representation of a value and should neither entail a belief about goodness nor the presence of this value outside the mind of the favorer. Moreover, Oddie stresses that value judgments should stem from an experiential source that is not an evaluative belief and that entails desire. Desires, he argues, can fit this bill provided they are value seemings, i.e. representations of values. As the experiential source of value, they imply neither beliefs about goodness nor the existence of the value represented. And they entail desires.

Friedrich defends another variant of the evaluative conception in his "Desire, Mental Force and Desirous Experience." His approach is original in that he addresses the issue by means of the distinction between mental force and mental content. Consider the contrast between asserting p and ordering p. Intuitively, both representations involve the same content, p, but they differ in their linguistic force. Friedrich's proposal is that desires are positive evaluations in the sense that they involve a mental force that is evaluative in nature. Desiring is thus the representing of a state of affairs with the mental force of goodness. In this picture, desire differs from evaluative beliefs and value appearances: it is not a cognitive state but consists in a *sui generis* evaluation. What is this evaluation and evaluative mental force? Building on a similar proposal for the case of pleasure, Friedrich proposes to account for evaluative mental force in *phenomenal* terms. Desiring, in this view, involves a distinctive feeling—the 'desirous experience'—consisting of the feeling of felt need. When desiring a cup of coffee, one represents having coffee *as good*, in that one feels the *need* for coffee and that one *must* have it. This captures the phenomenal tone of desire and can in turn explain desire's special motivational power.

The intuition that desires are evaluative representations is compelling. The authors do a great job of exploring it and rebutting several objections to the evaluative conception. Still, some questions remain and other contributions in the volume help to frame them.

Is it enough to represent a state of affairs in a positive way to desire that state of affairs? There are reasons to doubt it. For instance, one might positively evaluate that Mozart lived a longer life yet not desire this: one would rather *wish* that he lived longer (Döring and Eker *this volume*). Similarly, one can evaluate positively the fact that Obama was elected without desiring so, as one is aware that this state of affairs has obtained (Döring and Eker *this volume*). And, having lost hope, Pollyanna could believe that being in jail is after all a good thing without desiring to be there (Döring and Eker *this volume*). Or consider that Othello is clinically depressed: he represents Desdemona's well-being as a good thing but, because of his depression, fails to desire that she fare well (Lauria *this volume*). Aren't these possible scenarios? Strictly speaking, the evaluative conception does not entail that all positive evaluations are desires; some might be other phenomena such as emotions or long-standing affective states that involve desires only indirectly (see Oddie *this volume*). But isn't, then, the evaluative conception too modest as an account of desire? The appeal to the feeling of felt need might be helpful, since it seems to go beyond mere positive evaluation. But does this not amount to giving up on an evaluative account of desire and switching to a deontic approach like the one explored by Lauria and Massin in this volume?

The second question that we can raise about the evaluative conception of desire is more dramatic: Do all desires involve a positive evaluation? Do we desire everything under the "guise of the good"? This question is answered negatively by Döring and Eker, who open the exploration of the motivational conceptions of desire.

### Motivational Views: Desire and Action

Desires bear a special relation to action and are usually thought of as explaining intentional actions. The fact that you are reading this book, say, can be explained by your desire to do so. This explanatory role is often understood in terms of two further features of desire. The first is that desires explain intentional actions in virtue of being *dispositional* states.

The second is that they explain intentional action because they involve an *evaluative* component. In their respective contributions, Döring and Eker and Alvarez examine this explanatory role of desire and, in particular, the two facets just mentioned.

In "Desires without Guises: Why We Need Not Value What We Want," Döring and Eker approach the issue of desire's role in the explanation of actions by questioning the guise of the good thesis. They retrace the motivation for thinking that we desire only what seems good to us to the intuition that desires explain action through the evaluative component they involve, as Radioman-type scenarios are meant to reveal. However, in an original manner, they argue that Radioman's scenario does not support the evaluative view. Indeed, Radioman's behavior is not made more intelligible by appealing to his positive evaluation of switching on radios; quite the reverse. For such an evaluation is puzzling in itself. And this seriously undermines the main motivation for the evaluative picture. More generally, the authors argue that the evaluative conception, whether in its doxastic or appearance version, is inadequate. As has already been pointed out, evaluation might not be sufficient for desiring. The authors go as far as to argue that evaluation is not a necessary feature of desire: one might desire to tell a joke despite being aware that it is a bad thing, desire to go to the kitchen to have a drink without any positive representation of this state taking place, or want to watch a movie without having made up one's mind about its value. Desires thus do not involve the guise of the good. This is not to say that they are just dispositions to act, however. The authors propose a more holistic motivational conception of desire: desires might involve wider agential dispositions, such as the disposition to form long-term plans or agential policies. This, they suggest, is absent in Radioman's case while he undergoes an urge to switch on radios. Agential dispositions might thus suffice to make sense of his behavior without reference to the "guise of the good."

Döring and Eker's contribution is very challenging, as it casts doubt on one of the main dogmas of desire and does so by disputing the classical lesson drawn from Radioman's scenario. They rightly point out that appealing to evaluation would not help make Radioman's behavior less bizarre. Yet doesn't a desire provide *pro tanto* justification for some action, irrespective of how strange the desire is (see Oddie *this volume*)? Consider that Radiowoman desires to switch on radios because she represents this action as good. Would it not be irrational to refrain from turning on radios given her state of mind? Isn't the oddness of an action distinct from its justification? And would the appeal to a policy of switching on radios make

Radiowoman's behavior less puzzling? This touches on the vexed question of whether desires justify actions and how they could do so.

In her contribution, "Desires, Dispositions and the Explanation of Action," Alvarez tackles this issue from an unexplored angle. She agrees that desires figure into action explanation in virtue of being dispositions. She thus proposes to explore the role of desire in action explanation by investigating the dispositional nature of desire. Dispositions can exist at some point in time without being manifested at that time: a sugar cube can be soluble even if it does not dissolve now. Similarly, I can desire something, at some point in time, even if I do not manifest my desire at this time. Desires are thus dispositions. But *to what* are they dispositions? In other words, how are we to characterize their manifestation? The traditional answer to this question is that desires are dispositions to act. By contrast, Alvarez argues that the manifestations of desire constitute a much richer set: it encompasses behaviors (e.g. actions), expressions (e.g. linguistic acts), and inner mental states (e.g. anticipated pleasure). By exploring the variety of desire's manifestations, Alvarez proposes an integrative approach to desire that reconciles rival accounts of desire (e.g. the hedonic and the motivational conceptions of desire). In addition, investigating further the relation between desires and their manifestations sheds new light on how desires explain action. Desires differ from physical dispositions such as fragility and solubility. A glass is still fragile even if it *never* breaks or manifests its fragility in some way; what is needed is that it *would* do so in some circumstances. Desires are not like this: one cannot desire something without manifesting the disposition in some way or other, i.e. being disposed to act or expect some pleasure, etc., as is attested by the fact that we do not attribute a desire for holidays to a person who never thinks about holidays, never expects pleasure from a holiday, or never considers taking one. It appears that desires are dispositions that cannot exist without at least one of their manifestations taking place. This invites us to think about the way desire explains action in a more holistic fashion than is usually the case.

At this junction we may wonder how the dispositional profile of desire relates to the classical views of desire. For instance, does the fact that desires are dispositions admitting of various manifestations go against the thought that they are essentially evaluations? Is the evaluative nature of desire not one way of unifying their manifold manifestations? We begin to appreciate how complex the relations between the different conceptions of desires and the various perspectives we may have on them can become.

Another question concerns the intuitive distinction between dispositional or standing desires, on the one hand, and occurrent or episodic ones, on the other (see Döring and Eker *this volume*). Some desires, like Romeo's desire that Juliet fares well, are dispositional or standing: they typically last longer than others (Romeo desires this his whole life long); they still exist when they are not conscious (e.g. when Romeo is sleeping); and they admit future manifestations (every time Juliet is suffering, Romeo's desire that she fare well manifests itself). Other desires, like Sam's desire to smoke a cigarette right now, are episodic or occurrent: they are short-lived, typically conscious, and do not admit of reiterated manifestations. How does this distinction connect with the thought that desires are essentially dispositions? Isn't there a tension between the view that desires are dispositions and the distinction between episodic and dispositional desires that is standard in the literature? Are there two senses of dispositionality involved here? This important ontological question will be left open here.

## The Deontic Alternative: Desires, Norms, and Reasons

So far we have concentrated our attention on the classical views of desire and have briefly presented more holistic conceptions that build on them. Very recently an alternative perspective on desire has emerged: the appeal to deontic entities such as norms or reasons as opposed to values and motivation.

In his contribution "The 'Guise of the Ought to Be': A Deontic View of the Intentionality of Desire," Lauria criticizes the classical pictures of desire and proposes the deontic view. In this conception, which can be traced back to Meinong (1917), to desire a state of affairs is to represent it *as what ought to be* or *as what should be*. Desiring to see the ocean is representing this state *as what ought to be*. Desires involve a specific *manner* of representing content: a *deontic* mode. Lauria provides three arguments for this picture, which correspond to the dimensions of desire that the classical views cannot accommodate: the arguments of direction of fit, of death of desire, and of explanatory relations. This is not to say that there is no grain of truth in the classical conceptions. Lauria suggests that desires are grounded in evaluations and, in turn, ground motivations. In other words, it makes sense to explain my desire to see the ocean by my positive evaluation of such a landscape. And desiring to see the ocean can explain why I am disposed to do so. This explanatory profile of desire is illuminated by the deontic view as follows. Some states of affairs (say, that people don't die of cancer) ought to be *because* they are good, and subjects ought to bring them about *because* these states of affairs ought to be. If desires are deontic representations, it is not surprising that they are explained by evaluations and, in turn, explain motivations. For this is the mental counterpart of the meta-ethical explanatory relations already mentioned. The deontic view can thus accommodate the intuitions that drive classical views of desire. Yet as far as desire is concerned, these conceptions slightly miss their target.

Lauria's contribution brings a new perspective to the classical views. One line of criticism raised by other contributors to this volume concerns the "death of desire" principle—one of the dogmas of desire. Lauria assumes that a desire ceases to exist when one represents that its content obtains. And he argues that this is satisfactorily explained by the deontic view, because norms cease to exist when they are satisfied: a state of affairs, say, that it rains, cannot be such that it ought to obtain and is obtaining at the same time. Yet both the *explanandum* and the *explanans* are questionable. Consider that Hillary wants to be the first female president of the United States and that at some point she becomes president (Oddie's example in this volume). Can she not still desire to be the first female president of the United States despite knowing that she has won the election? Moreover, can she not believe that things are exactly how they should be and rightly so (Massin *this volume*)?

Another question concerns the degree of sophistication that desires end up having in the deontic view. It seems that babies and non-human animals have desires. Do they really represent things as what ought to be? *Prima facie*, this seems a quite complex representation compared to evaluations or motivations. This worry is reminiscent of the objection often raised against doxastic views of desire (see Friedrich, Döring and Eker *this volume*) and examined by some contributor (see Gregory's reply).

Adopting a similar approach in his "Desire, Values and Norms," Massin argues that the formal object of desire is better construed as being deontic than evaluative. In other words, desiring something implies representing it under the guise of the ought-to-be or of the ought-to-do (the "guise of the ought" thesis). Unlike Lauria, Massin appeals to norms in general, not only norms of the ought-to-be type. Moreover, he considers that the "guise of the ought" thesis is necessary but not sufficient to desire. The argument he proposes focuses on the polarity of desire. Aversion is the polar opposite of desire, as hate is the polar opposite of love. Still, the two pairs of opposites differ. The opposition between desire and aversion, argues Massin, is best understood in deontic rather than evaluative terms, and this contrasts with love and hate. A detour in deontic logic reveals why. Logic teaches us that obligation and interdiction are interdefinable: they define each other with the help of negation. Something is forbidden (say, stealing) if, and only if, it is obligatory that this thing does not happen (it is obligatory not to steal); something is obligatory (say, stopping at the red traffic light) if, and only if, it is forbidden that this thing does not happen. Goodness and badness, however, aren't interdefinable in the same way. A state's being good is not equivalent to its negation being bad. It might be elegant to wear a hat, but this does not mean that not wearing it is bad: not wearing it might be neutral. Now, Massin argues, desires and aversions are interdefinable, just as obligation and interdiction are. Desiring something is equivalent to being averse to its negation, and being averse to something is to desire it not to happen. Desiring to wear a hat is equivalent to being averse to not wearing it: it is incompatible with being indifferent to not wearing it. In contrast, liking something is not equivalent to disliking its negation: liking cheesecake is compatible with indifference toward not eating cheesecake. Therefore, desire is to aversion what obligation is to interdiction, and love is to hate what goodness is to badness. The "guise of the ought" thesis thus fares better than the "guise of the good."

Massin's approach sheds light on the polar opposition characteristic of desire by appealing to polarity in meta-ethics, two issues that are rarely discussed. It can be put in perspective with the help of two questions.

The first concerns the restriction to obligation. Does a desire for something involve representing this thing as being obligatory? The other deontic accounts defended in this volume appeal to deontic entities like what ought to be (Lauria) or reasons (Gregory) without putting an emphasis on obligation. How are we to capture the deontic entity that is relevant for understanding desire?

The second issue concerns the relation between the polarity of desire and the essential features of desire. As observed, one might divorce the two features: that the polar opposition of desire is best understood in deontic terms is *prima facie* neutral with regard to desires being essentially deontic representations. This, however, contrasts with what other of our contributors assume. From the perspective of the evaluative view, it is natural to think that the polar opposite of desire, i.e. aversion, is a negative evaluation precisely because desiring is a positive one (Oddie, Railton *this volume*). What is the relation between polarity and the essence of desire?

In his contribution "Might Desires Be Beliefs about Normative Reasons for Action?," Gregory defends another type of deontic view: the desire-as-belief view. He argues that desires are beliefs about reasons to act. Desiring to drink coffee is to believe that one has a normative, defeasible reason to do so. This claim differs importantly from all others, since desire is understood as a kind of *belief* rather than an appearance (Oddie *this volume*) or a non-cognitive attitude (e.g., Friedrich, Döring and Eker, Lauria *this volume*). As mentioned earlier, there are some difficulties in accounting for desire in terms of beliefs. Gregory's contribution goes a long way toward rebutting a number of objections. He considers worries concerning desires' direction of fit, appetites, and objections about the sufficiency and necessity of the view. Let us mention two examples that tightly connect with other key issues in the volume. We already mentioned that desires differ from beliefs in terms of direction of fit. How, then, could a desire be a belief? Gregory argues that desires have both directions of fit and that the same is true of beliefs about practical reasons. More importantly, it is common to think that desires cannot be assimilated to beliefs on the grounds that non-human animals have desires but lack beliefs (Friedrich, Döring and Eker *this volume*). Against this objection, Gregory considers the possibility that non-human animals have a minimal grasp of reasons to act and thus, in a sense, have normative beliefs. Alternatively, it might be that non-human animals have drives rather than desires. Finally, Gregory argues that his account is superior to the appearance view, i.e. the idea that desires are appearances of the good (Oddie *this volume*) or of reasons (Scanlon 2000). Appearances, he argues, are unlike desires in that they fall outside our rational control.

Gregory does a great job at undermining the main difficulties associated with the desire-as-belief account. The objections examined are reminiscent of the ones that have been raised against the view that desires are evaluative beliefs and that have often been used to dismiss it without being carefully examined. This similitude raises the following question: Should desires be understood in terms of beliefs about *reasons* rather than in terms of beliefs about *values* or other normative entities such as norms? Are we to identify values with reasons, in which case the two proposals would boil down to the same thing? This is where the philosophy of desire meets vexed meta-ethical issues.

From another perspective, one might wonder whether identifying desire with belief is supported by empirical evidence. Lewis famously argued that reducing desire to belief cannot accommodate the regulation of desire and belief predicted by Bayesian models of decision making, which is the main empirical model in economics (Lewis 1988). It is also an open question whether reducing desire to belief is compatible with neuroscientific studies in this area. The next section touches on these questions.

## Empirical Perspectives: Desire, the Reward System, and Learning

The nature of desire can also be approached with the help of the empirical evidence on the subject, in particular through the lens of neuroscientific findings on the reward system and models of decision making in economics. Given the importance of these perspectives, an exploration of the nature of desire would be incomplete without taking this literature into consideration.

Drawing on previous work, Schroeder's contribution, entitled "Empirical Evidence against a Cognitivist Theory of Desire and Action," is mainly inspired by neuroscientific findings on desire, motivation, and action. His aim is to assess Scanlon's (2000) view of desire and motivation by confronting it with the neuroscientific evidence. Scanlon claims that motivation stems from judgments about reasons for action and that desires, in the wide sense of the term, are judgments about reasons for actions. Scanlon's proposal shares interesting connections with that of Gregory. More generally, let us call "cognitivism" the view that some judgment or cognition about reasons or values is the source of motivation. Schroeder's question is whether cognitivism is in line with the available empirical evidence. The relevant literature in neurobiology, he argues, suggests a negative answer. Importantly, it appears that the neural structures relevant for motivation are distinct from the ones involved in cognitions like perception, memory, and belief. Cognitivism is thus in serious tension with the empirical evidence. And none of the ways that cognitivism may try to accommodate the empirical evidence, Schroeder argues, is likely to succeed. These attempts to reconcile cognitivism with the empirical findings might explain alienated actions, like Tourette syndrome, or habitual actions. Yet they cannot be the whole story about motivation and action. Schroeder then warns against philosophical analysis that lacks proper empirical guidance.

In a similar spirit, in "Learning as an Inherent Dynamic of Belief and Desire," Railton builds on neuropsychological findings about desire and affect as well as on models of human behavior to be found in economics. As observed, it is common in philosophy and economics to think of belief and desire as the main determinants of human behavior. This Humean picture is partly motivated by the directions of fit of belief and desire. But is it compatible with learning in the realm of desire, i.e. the thought that we can improve our desires as we can improve our beliefs and cognitions? Learning comes with tracking facts. The direction of fit metaphor suggests that learning is the purpose of belief only, since beliefs aim to represent the world, unlike desires. Against this skepticism, Railton offers a model of learning for desire that is inspired by the way beliefs are regulated and, ironically, exploits Hume's account of belief as a feeling. In a nutshell, the thought is that learning in belief is made possible by the expectations and feelings of confidence that come with believing. Subjects learn what to believe by confronting their expectations and feelings of confidence with the facts that are presented to them. Similarly, desires are regulated by means of comparisons between the positive anticipation they are associated with (the "liking" aspect of desire) and the actual satisfaction of the desire. When desiring something, unlike when experiencing an urge, one is not merely disposed to act in a certain way: one sees the thing in a positive light. Studies on the reward system, at least for non-pathological cases, reveal that desires involve positive anticipation of reward. Now, this provides room for learning in desire as the positive anticipation can be compared with one's actual experience of desire satisfaction. With the help of feedback afforded by experience, one will learn what to desire, as one does for belief, by reducing discrepancy and by testing one's expectations and positive evaluations in the arena of life.

These findings and the philosophical considerations they elicit provide important insights for understanding desire. They raise ontological and metaphysical issues that are particularly relevant for the theories of desire explored in this volume.

For example, we may wonder whether Railton's proposal implies that desires are motivational states grounded in evaluation, in which case the proposal would be a variant of the motivational conception. Alternatively, we may think that the picture favors a compound view, in which desire is a whole made of evaluation and motivation or, more simply, that desires are multitrack dispositions, as one contribution in this volume suggests. This touches on the important ontological question of how types of mental states should be individuated.

Similarly, one question that is relevant to Schroeder's essay concerns the commonsense interpretation of the idea that desires are representations of rewards. Does it favor the evaluative view of desire or the motivational conception? Does it provide support for an alternative account of desire? In previous work (Schroeder 2004) and in his present contribution, Schroeder argues that the literature on the reward system does not favor the hedonic, evaluative, or motivational pictures of desire. How, then, are we to translate these findings into folk psychological terms?

## II. Desiderative Puzzles

As outlined earlier, a better understanding of the nature of desire has wide-ranging significance. In the second part of this volume, three puzzles pertaining to practical rationality are addressed and approached from the perspective of the nature of desire. They concern, respectively, the philosophy of mind, ethics, and epistemology. These issues are analogous to hotly debated questions on theoretical rationality. Yet the practical side of the inquiry is often left untouched. The first topic examined is desire inconsistency. Some desires are inconsistent. Is this to be understood along the same lines as inconsistency between beliefs? Does it teach us something about desire? The second issue is the direct practical analogue of theoretical reasoning. Desires, it is commonly thought, figure into the process of deliberating about what to do. They are commonly viewed as the first premise of practical reasoning. How are we to understand this feature? What should desires be to play such a role? The last puzzle concerns self-knowledge. Self-knowledge has been widely discussed in the case of belief. How are we to understand self-knowledge of one's desires? What does it reveal about the nature of desire? The last contributions aim to fill these lacunas in the philosophical literature. Let us briefly summarize how.

Juliet desires to be faithful to her partner while also desiring to have an affair. Something is wrong with this combination. Why is it so? This is the main question addressed by Wall's contribution, "Desiderative Inconsistency, Moore's Paradox, and Norms of Desire." More specifically, Wall discusses Marino's contention that there is nothing especially or necessarily problematic with desiderative inconsistency (e.g. Marino 2009). What goes wrong pertains to the subject's well-being—one of her desires is not satisfied—and thus has no special connection to desire inconsistency. Moreover, desiderative inconsistency is not necessarily bad, since some desires are better not satisfied. By contrast, Wall argues that there is something especially and necessarily wrong in having inconsistent desires: the subject violates a constitutive norm for desire. It is common to think that beliefs are constituted by the norm of believing the truth. Wall extends this approach to the case of desire so as to shed light on desiderative inconsistency. To do so he makes use of Moore's Paradox, the well-known puzzle of belief. Asserting "p and I do not believe that p" or believing *that p and I do not believe that p* is an odd thing to say or to believe (Moore's Paradox). This can be explained by the violation of the norm of belief: one should believe the truth. *Mutatis mutandis*, this norm explains what is wrong with inconsistent beliefs. If a similar paradox for desire can be found, it will reveal the existence of a constitutive norm for desire. Elaborating on previous work (Wall 2012), Wall proposes that the desire *that p and I do not desire that p* is such a case. The oddness of this desire suggests that desires are constituted by the norm of avoiding frustration. Having inconsistent desires violates this norm and is thus necessarily wrong irrespective of the subject's well-being or other considerations. This is analogous to the case of belief.

Wall's use of constitutive norms in approaching the issue of the nature of desire is promising. Yet proponents of the evaluative conception of desire have argued that desires are constituted by the norm of the good and have thus proposed cases of Moore's Paradox along evaluative lines, for instance, "I desire that p and p does not seem good to me" (Stampe 1987; see Oddie 2005 for another proposal). How does Wall's candidates for Moore's Paradox and norms of desire connect with the ones inspired by the conceptions of desire examined in this volume? Is the norm of avoiding frustration compatible with them, or is it to be preferred over them? This is where the normative approach of the mental that appeals to constitutive norms meets the approach of the mind adopted so far in this volume, which focuses on the intentionality or functional role of desire understood in descriptive terms.

Desire seems to play an important role in practical deliberation. According to the traditional understanding, desires appear as the first premise of the reasoning. Discussions on the nature of deliberation are often focused on the result of the deliberative process. In "Deliberation and Desire," Schueler's pioneering approach aims to question the role of desire in such a process and, by doing so, to shed light on the nature of desire. We do not deliberate about everything we desire. For instance, I do not deliberate about my whim of seeing my neighbor's front lawn filled with wildflowers even if I favor this state of affairs. Consequently, it would appear that the 'favoring' view does not accommodate the role of desire in practical deliberation. That is why Schueler argues that desires can play this role only if they are conceived as being representations of aims or purposes. But do desires *qua* representations of aims actually figure in the first premise of practical deliberation, as the traditional picture has it? Since practical deliberation is a kind of reasoning, the first premise must be understood as being a *belief* about one's desire. Now, this belief can be false: Othello can believe that he desires something, when in fact he does not. It thus appears that one can deliberate from a desire that one does not have, and so, contrary to received wisdom, desires do not play a significant role in practical reasoning. This being said, subjects who intentionally did something resulting from a process of deliberation *eo ipso* wanted to do so. For intentionally bringing about something entails having this thing as an aim, i.e. desiring it. This is puzzling. On the one hand, it appears that deliberation doesn't involve actual desire; on the other hand, desire is necessarily involved in deliberation when the latter results in intentional action. How are we to disentangle this puzzle? Schueler proposes distinguishing between two kinds of practical reasoning. We sometimes reason from our beliefs about what we desire and determine the action that suits their satisfaction. In this case, desire can be absent from the process, since the belief about desire does not imply the presence of the desire. But we sometimes deliberate differently, starting with our intentions. As soon as I have formed the intention to go for coffee, I might deliberate about the best means of doing so and settle on the appropriate actions. In this case, the starting point is the intention itself—not a belief. This is what happens when we act out of deliberation. The goal of an intention is something we want, so it appears that this type of deliberation requires a desire. Desires, however, do not figure into the content of this sort of deliberation: they are constituted by the actions based on deliberation. The puzzle is thus dissolved.

At least two issues that connect with other pieces in this volume are worth noting. Schueler argues that we do not deliberate from our desires when the latter are understood as states of favoring. Is it to say that desires cannot be the starting point of deliberation insofar as they are understood as evaluations? Turning to the case of Radioman, one might be inclined to think that the evaluative nature of desires is what provides them with the power to explain action. Is it not the case, then, that the evaluative dimension of desires is also the key for understanding their contribution to deliberation?

The second issue concerns the extent to which intentions are immune to the type of error desires are liable to. Can't we be wrong in our beliefs that we have some intentions (even when we act on them), in the same way that we can falsely believe that we desire something? This raises the issue of self-knowledge that is the focus of the final contribution.

In "Introspection and the Nature of Desire," Ashwell explores desire from the viewpoint of self-knowledge. We can know other people's desires by observing their behavior. In contrast, we have direct access to our own desires: we do not need to observe them; we can introspect them. While the question of how we know our own beliefs is familiar, its desiderative counterpart is more rarely investigated. The originality of Ashwell's contribution lies in the way her account of desire introspection is informed by various views of desire. She argues that desires are not evaluations but are better viewed as motivations. Indeed, we commonly attribute to ourselves evaluative beliefs without attributing corresponding desires. For instance, in the case of weakness of will, I can introspect my belief that going to the gym would be a good thing while being aware that

I do not desire to go to the gym. If that is the case, desires cannot be evaluative beliefs, as the self-attribution of the latter can be rightly separated from that of the former. The appearance view of desire—that desires are seemings of value—fares better in this respect, however. In being weak-willed, going to the gym might not appear good to me, hence I neither desire to go nor do I introspect this desire. This being said, the appearance view does not provide the right phenomenological picture of desire. While experiencing my desire to have another glass of wine, I do not only experience this state of affairs as good; I am also aware that I am drawn to act in a certain way. These feelings of motivation are an integral part of desire and the basis on which we introspect them. The weak-willed person does not introspect any feelings of motivation and hence does not attribute to herself a desire. Consequently, one condition for a reliable introspective access to our desires is that desires be motivational rather than evaluative states.

Comparing Ashwell's picture to other contributions in the volume brings them into sharper focus. Her argument relies on the assumption that weakness of will comes with absence of desire. But is it so? Gregory argues that weakness of will involves a failure of motivation rather than a failure of desire: one lacks the motivation to realize a desire that one has. How best to capture the nature of weakness of will, then?

This in turn touches on the question of whether feelings of motivation are necessary features of desire and thus of desire introspection. Famously Strawson has argued that we can conceive of creatures having desires without any motivation: Weather Watchers desire sunshine without being motivated to act in any way (Strawson 2009). Leaving this thought experiment to one side, some contributors to this volume discuss actual cases of desiring subjects who are not motivated to act. Being weak-willed, in one description, is such a case (Gregory *this volume*); being severely depressed is another (Lauria *this volume*). These conditions might impair one's motivational system and feelings without affecting one's desire and presumably one's knowledge of them. This is one way of making the question of whether motivation is the essence of desire particularly salient—which is this volume's starting point.

In conclusion, it is fair to say that this collection creates the ground for a more systematic debate on the nature of desire. It is high time that contemporary philosophers paid more attention to desire and put into question the dogmas associated with it. In exploring various conceptions of desire from different perspectives, and in examining how these conceptions can illuminate many issues in several domains, we hope that this volume makes a first step toward reinstalling desire at the heart of our philosophical preoccupations.

## Notes

1. See Stampe 1987; Oddie 2005; Tenenbaum 2007; Friedrich 2012.

2. The thought behind the intuition is already present in Hume 2000, but the metaphor has been introduced into the philosophy of mind by Anscombe 1963 and Searle 1983.

3. See, for instance, Plato 1953b; Aristotle 1962; Aquinas 1920–1942; Kant 1997; Oddie 2005; Raz 2008; Tenenbaum 2013.

4. See Plato 1953a, Aquinas 1920–1942; Descartes 1989; Locke 1975; Hobbes 1994; Sartre 1984; Kenny 1963; Dretske 1988.

## References


Anscombe, G. E. M. (1963). *Intention*. Oxford: Blackwell.

Aquinas, T. (1920–1942). *Summa Theologica*. London: Burns, Oates & Washburne.

Archer, A. (2015). 'Reconceiving Direction of Fit', *Thought*, 4 (3), 171–180.

Aristotle. (1962). *Nicomachean Ethics*, tr. M. Oswald. Indianapolis: Bobbs-Merrill Co.

Armstrong, D. M. (1968). *A Materialist Theory of the Mind*. London: Routledge.

Arpaly, N., and Schroeder, T. (2013). *In Praise of Desire*. Oxford: Oxford University Press.

Boghossian, P. (2003). 'The Normativity of Content', *Philosophical Issues*, 13, 32–45.

Broad, C. D. (1930). *Five Types of Ethical Theory*. New York: Harcourt Brace.

Bykvist, K. (2009). 'No Good Fit: Why the Fitting Attitude Analysis of Value Fails', *Mind*, 118, 1–30.

Dancy, J. (2000). *Practical Reality*. Oxford: Oxford University Press.

Descartes, R. (1989). *The Passions of the Soul*, tr. S. H. Voss. Indianapolis: Hackett.

De Sousa, R. (1974). 'The Good and the True', *Mind*, 83, 534–551.

Dretske, F. (1988). *Explaining Behavior: Reasons in a World of Causes*. Cambridge, Mass.: MIT Press.

Friedrich, D. G. (2012). 'The Alluringness of Desire', *Philosophical Explorations: An International Journal for the Philosophy of Mind and Action*, 15 (3), 291–302.

Frost, K. (2014). 'On the Very Idea of Direction of Fit', *Philosophical Review*, 123 (4), 429–484.

Gregory, A. (2012). 'Changing Direction on Direction of Fit', *Ethical Theory and Moral Practice*, 15 (5), 603–614.

Hazlett, A. (*unpublished*). 'Belief and Truth, Desire and Goodness'.

Heathwood, C. (2007). 'The Reduction of Sensory Pleasure to Desire', *Philosophical Studies*, 133, 23–44.

Hobbes T. (1994). *Leviathan*, ed. E. Curley. Indianapolis: Hackett.

Humberstone, I. L. (1992). 'Direction of Fit', *Mind*, 101 (401), 59–83.

Hume, D. (2000). *A Treatise of Human Nature*. Oxford: Oxford University Press.

Kant, I. (1997). *Critique of Practical Reason*, ed. M. Gregor. Cambridge, UK: Cambridge University Press.

Kenny, A. (1963). *Action, Emotion and Will.* London: Routledge.
Lewis, D. (1988). 'Desire as Belief', *Mind*, 97 (418), 323–332.
Locke, J. (1975). *An Essay Concerning Human Understanding*, ed. P. H. Nidditch. Oxford: Clarendon Press.
Marino, P. (2009). 'On Essentially Conflicting Desires', *Philosophical Quarterly*, 59 (235), 274–291.
Marks, J. (1986, ed.). *The Ways of Desire: New Essays in Philosophical Psychology on the Concept of Wanting*. Chicago: Precedent.
McDowell, J. H. (1998). *Mind, Value and Reality.* Cambridge, Mass.: Harvard University Press.
Meinong, A. (1917). *On Emotional Presentation.* Translation (1972). Evanston, Ill.: Northwestern University Press.
Millikan, R. G. (2005). *Language: A Biological Model.* Oxford: Oxford University Press.
Milliken, J. (2008). 'In a Fitter Direction: Moving beyond the Direction of Fit Picture of Belief and Desire', *Ethical Theory and Moral Practice*, 11, 563–571.
Oddie, G. (2005). *Value, Reality, and Desire.* Oxford: Oxford University Press.
Plato. (1953a). *Symposium*, in *The Dialogues of Plato*, tr. B. Jowett, 4th ed. Oxford: Clarendon Press.
———. (1953b). *Meno*, in *The Dialogues of Plato*, tr. B. Jowett, 4th ed. Oxford: Clarendon Press.
Quinn, W. (1993). *Morality and Action.* Cambridge, UK: Cambridge University Press.
Rabinowicz, W., and Rønnow-Rasmussen, T. (2004). 'The Strike of the Demon: On Fitting Pro-attitudes and Value', *Ethics*, 114 (3), 391–423.
Raz, J. (2008). 'On the Guise of the Good', *Oxford Legal Studies Research*, 43, 1-34.
Sartre, J.-P. (1984). *Being and Nothingness*, tr. H. E. Barnes. New York: Washington Square Press.
Scanlon, T. M. (2000). *What We Owe to Each Other.* Cambridge, Mass.: Harvard University Press.
Schroeder, T. (2004). *Three Faces of Desire*. Oxford: Oxford University Press.
———. (2015). 'Desire', *The Stanford Encyclopaedia of Philosophy* (Summer 2015 Edition), Edward N. Zalta (ed.), URL = <https://plato.stanford.edu/archives/sum2015/entries/desire/>.
Schultz, W. (1997). 'A Neural Substrate of Prediction and Reward', *Science*, 275 (5306), 1593–1599.
Schultz, W., Tremblay, L., and Hollerman, J. R. (1998). 'Reward Prediction in Primate Basal Ganglia and Frontal Cortex', *Neuropharmacology*, 37 (4–5), 421–429.
Searle, J. R. (1983). *Intentionality. An Essay in the Philosophy of Mind.* Cambridge, UK: Cambridge University Press.
Smith, M. (1994). *The Moral Problem.* Oxford: Blackwell.
Sobel, D., and Copp, D. (2001). 'Against Direction of Fit Accounts of Belief and Desire', *Analysis*, 61 (1), 44–53.
Stalnaker, R. (1984). *Inquiry.* Cambridge, Mass.: MIT Press.
Stampe, D. W. (1986). 'Defining Desire', in J. Marks (ed.), *The Ways of Desire. New Essays in Philosophical Psychology on the Concept of Wanting*. Chicago: Precedent.
———. (1987). 'The Authority of Desire', *Philosophical Review*, 96 (3), 335–381.

Stocker, M. (1979). 'Desiring the Bad: An Essay in Moral Psychology', *Journal of Philosophy*, 76 (12), 738–753.

Strawson, G. (2009). *Mental Reality*. Cambridge, Mass.: MIT Press.

Tenenbaum, S. (2007). *Appearances of the Good: An Essay on the Nature of Practical Reason*. Cambridge, UK: Cambridge University Press.

———. (2013). 'The Guise of the Good', in *The International Encyclopaedia of Ethics*, ed. H. LaFollette, 659, 1-9. Oxford: Wiley-Blackwell.

Velleman, J. D. (1992). 'The Guise of the Good', *Noûs*, 26 (1), 3–26.

———. (2000). *The Possibility of Practical Reason*. Oxford: Clarendon Press.

Wall, D. (2012). 'A Moorean Paradox of Desire', *Philosophical Explorations*, 15 (1), 63–84.

Zangwill, N. (1998). 'Direction of Fit and Normative Functionalism', *Philosophical Studies*, 91 (2), 173–203.

# PART I | Conceptions of Desire

## *Evaluative Views: Desire and the Good*

# CHAPTER 1 | Desire and the Good

## *In Search of the Right Fit*

GRAHAM ODDIE

[In] the [pull] of the will and of love, appears the worth of everything to be sought or to be avoided, to be esteemed of greater or lesser value.

—AUGUSTINE 1982[1]

WHAT IS THE relation between desire and the good? In this paper I elaborate and defend an account of the nature of desire that deems the connection between these two concepts to be very tight indeed. It is a version of the evaluative theory of desire, that desires are essentially evaluative in nature. There are two possibilities within this approach: that desires are value judgments (doxastic value seemings) and that desires are value appearances (non-doxastic value seemings).[2] I defend the second of these, the *value appearance thesis*.[3] To desire something is for it to appear, in some way or other, good. To be averse to something is for it to appear, in some way or other, bad. To be indifferent to something is for it to appear lacking in either positive or negative value.

Augustine, in the passage above from *The True Meaning of Genesis*, is clearly articulating a version of the value appearance thesis. But while the thesis is by no means novel, it has been given a new lease of life in recent work on the metaphysics and epistemology of value.[4]

If desires are value appearances, then, under the right conditions, they amount to perceptions of value. If a desire is a perception of value, then it is no mystery how, in addition to being involved in the causal explanation of action, desires play a role in the rational explanation of action. An agent who perceives a state of affairs as good has a reason to act to bring it about. If, in addition, her perception is accurate, then her reason for so acting may well be a good one.

It is a virtue of the value appearance thesis that it is neutral among a wide range of metaphysical stances on value. It is quite compatible with the idealist thesis that facts about value entirely reduce to or supervene upon desires—that value supervenes on the value appearances. But it is also compatible with the realist thesis that facts about value are not reducible to desires, that they enjoy a robust independence from the value phenomena, that value appearances and value reality can come apart. Finally, it is also compatible with the nihilist thesis that nothing at all is of value. Our desires might present as valuable things that have no value at all.

While the value appearance thesis is metaphysically quite neutral, it is a powerful epistemological thesis. If there were no value appearances, then we would be stuck with excogitating value facts *a priori* from constraints of reason alone, or perhaps postulating a faculty of "value intuition" that somehow connects us to, and mysteriously delivers, value judgments. Value appearances would provide reasons, albeit defeasible reasons, to accept the corresponding value judgments, in roughly the same way that perceptual appearances provide defeasible reasons for accepting perceptual judgments. And since desire and aversion are ubiquitous, the thesis that desires are value appearances promises a rich source of value data.

The value appearance thesis thus has a number of nice features, but it has also attracted some serious criticisms.[5] It has been faulted for rationalizing bizarre actions, for denying desires to human neonates and nonhuman animals, and for entailing that one can desire what one already knows to be the case. While my main aim is to present a new line of argument for the thesis, one that draws on work on fitting attitudes, I also hope to answer some of the critics.

## 1 The Objects of Desire and the Bearers of Value

In what follows I take *desire* and *want* to be synonyms that denote what might be called a *thin* concept, a determinable of which there are various thick determinates. We have quite a rich vocabulary for different determinates of desire: *crave, hanker, yearn, wish, hunger, long*, and *fancy*, among others. There are also closely related concepts, such as *like* and *love*, that may involve desire, although it is not immediately clear that they are just determinates of desire. They may, however, be concrete realizations of desire. That is, they may be constituted by desire together with additional contingent features. Any claim that involves either the thin determinable *desire* or one of its thick determinates or realizations I call a *desire claim*.

One fundamental question that a complete theory of desire should answer is this: What type, or types, of entity can serve as the objects of desire? The surface grammar of desire claims suggests there are many different types of object. For example: Harry has a hankering for a *hokey-pokey ice-cream*; Joan fancies *a picnic in the mountains*; Basho longs for *Kyoto*; Martha desires *happiness* above all else; Grace yearns for *the war to be over*; Count Kaiserling would like *the Goldberg Variations*. The types of objects apparently desired include small material particulars (*a hokey-pokey ice-cream*); large sprawling particulars (*Kyoto*); possible states (*the war's being over*); types of episodes (*a picnic in the mountains*); properties of individuals (*being happy*); musical works (*the Goldberg Variations*). Despite the apparent diversity of types it is widely presumed that the objects of desire, like the objects of belief, all hale from some uniform ontological category. And the prevailing view is the objects of desire (and of belief) are *propositions*, or closely related entities like *states of affairs*.[6]

The propositional view, although widely held, sits unhappily with the surface grammar of desire claims. However, one can usually recast such claims, framing their objects as propositions. Whenever a desire seems directed at something non-propositional—like *a hokey-pokey ice-cream, Kyoto*, or *happiness*—what one really wants is a certain interaction with that thing: to *eat* a hokey-pokey ice-cream, to *be in* Kyoto, to *instantiate* happiness. So *Basho longs for Kyoto* should be parsed as *Basho longs for it to be the case that Basho is in Kyoto*.

Despite the popularity of the propositional view, it is at least as natural to take the objects of desire to be *states of being*—such things as *eating a hokey-pokey ice-cream, hearing the Goldberg Variations performed, being happy*. What makes it true that one wants this or that is that one wants to stand in some appropriate relation to this or that.[7] The case of desiring a state of affairs, like *the war's be over*, is a special case—what is desired is *being in circumstances in which the war is over*. However, we can take the propositional view to be a reasonable first approximation of the property view, and the differences between the propositional and the property view do not materially affect the arguments presented here. From now on I will call the objects of desire *states*.

In addition to being suitable objects of desire, states are apt subjects of value.[8] Of course, not all potential bearers of value are states. Other kinds of entities can have value: a hokey-pokey ice-cream, Kyoto, the *Goldberg*

*Variations*, persons, species, and ecosystems are all apt subjects for evaluation. Perhaps the value of these objects is reducible to or derives from the value of states in which they feature. It may be that the *fundamental* value bearers are states and the fundamental value facts consist in states bearing value. But we need not explore this possibility here. It is necessary for the value appearance thesis that the objects of desire are potential bearers of value properties. But it isn't necessary that all value bearers be objects of desire. The converse of the value appearance thesis—that all appearances of value are desires—would require that all value bearers be objects of desire. But that is obviously a logically independent claim, and it isn't plausible. Certain objects might well bear value (perhaps derivatively) but are objects of desire only indirectly at best. Certain emotional states—like loving, cherishing, or taking delight in—might be the appropriate responses to such entities. And while it is possible, it is by no means obvious that these are either desires or reducible to desires.

## 2 The *Per se* Authority of Desire

The value appearance thesis, or at least various close neighbors, has an ancient pedigree. If we interpret both the *pull of the will* and the *pull of love* as desiderative states, then Augustine, in the quote with which we began, may be affirming not only that desires are appearances of value but also that value appearances are desires.

A widely noted scholastic saying—"Sicut enim nihil desiderat appetitus nisi sub ratione boni, ita nihil fugit nisi sub ratione mali"—is often called *the guise of the good* thesis.[9] That we do not desire anything except under the "guise" of the good might be considered a version of the value appearance thesis.[10] There is, however, an interpretation of the "guise of the good" that aligns it with the doxastic version of the evaluative theory: that one cannot desire *S* without believing or judging *S* to be good.[11] But the doxastic version is implausible—one can desire what one doesn't believe to be good, or what one believes to be bad, or about which one harbors no evaluative beliefs at all.[12]

Perhaps neither Augustine nor Aquinas is unambiguously committed to the value appearance thesis. For a clear and unequivocal statement we must turn to a remarkable paper by Stampe:

> The view I shall take is this: Desire is a kind of perception. One who wants it to be the case that *P* perceives something that makes it seem to that person

as if it would be good were it to be the case that *P*, and seem so in a way that is characteristic of perception. To desire something is to be in a kind of perceptual state, in which that thing seems good.[13]

The value appearance thesis is, in Stampe's view, the best available explanation for what he calls the *per se* authority of desire—the idea that a desire for *S* provides, through itself, a reason to pursue *S*. If desires are brute dispositions to bring about *S*, this authority would be mysterious. However, if a desire were a kind of *perception* of the goodness of *S*, then desire would carry with it the authority of perception.

> Because it is a form of perception, desire is autonomous in its authority, as is any perceptual modality, not requiring legitimation by the representations of the intellect. A desire is certified a reason to act by its perceptual content; being a state in which it seemed to one as if it would be good were a certain state of affairs to obtain, it is a state in which the thing wanted is represented as such that it would be good were that state of affairs to obtain.[14]

Here is what I take Stampe to be arguing: On the standard belief-desire account of reasons, one has a reason to do *A* just in case there is some state *S* that one desires, and one believes that doing *A* is a way of bringing about *S*. What would desires have to be like for the standard story to be plausible?

Consider the dispositional theory of desire, that desires just *are* states that mesh with beliefs to cause actions. Or, as Stalnaker puts it, "To desire that *P* is to be disposed to act in ways that would tend to bring it about that *P* in a world in which one's beliefs, whatever they are, were true."[15] Stampe argues that such dispositions are not reason generating. To see this, imagine that a malevolent demon plants a chip in Radioman's brain so that whenever he believes of any radio within reach that he can turn it on, he turns it on. *Ipso facto*, on the dispositional account he desires radios within his reach to be on. Two questions: First, does Radioman have a reason, even a weak one, to go around turning on radios? No, he just finds himself turning the damn things on. He finds he can no more stop doing this than someone with a social anxiety disorder can stop blushing every time she comes to believe she has become the center of attention. Second, does Radioman even have a desire that radios within reach be on? If we ask Radioman whether he wants radios to be on, he denies it. He doesn't like the sound of radios blasting, and he would be just as happy if radios didn't exist at all. And he has no desire to have radios within reach so that he can have them blasting away. Not only does he not enjoy radios in his vicinity being on, he doesn't like turning them on. But he has found that his attempts to stop doing it make no difference to his disposition. Radioman's disposition not only doesn't fill the reason-generating role demanded of desire on the standard account, but Radioman himself denies he has any such desire. So it seems a bit perverse to say that he has such a desire simply in virtue of having that pesky disposition. So there must be more to desire than a behavioral disposition. But what, exactly?

Consider Radiowoman. She has the same behavioral disposition as Radioman, but this is because the radio's being on seems good to her, she feels drawn to the prospect, it is alluring. And when she hears the radio come on she feels satisfied by that. Radiowoman, unlike her male counterpart, wants the radio to be on. Radioman sees no difference in value between radios being on and radios being off. By contrast, Radiowoman does, and this helps explain both her disposition to turn radios on and her acting on that disposition.[16] It makes sense for her to turn radios on, given the way things seem to her. So if desires are perceptions of value, Radiowoman's desire gives her some kind of reason to turn radios on, while Radioman's disposition does not.

How good is Radiowoman's reason?[17] Suppose that the demon foisted on Radiowoman her desire for radios to be on, just as he foisted on Radioman his disposition to turn them on. How can having this rather bizarre desire foisted on her give her a genuine reason for going around turning on radios, whereas having the related *tic* foisted on Radioman doesn't give him any reason? Suppose Radiowoman were to find out about the etiology of her desires. Then she would know that they are not reliable indicators of goodness. Rather they are systematic illusions of goodness. They are like the Mueller-Lyer illusions that, once you know about them, give you no reason at all to believe that the lines that appear unequal really are unequal.[18] And even if she knows nothing of the peculiar etiology of her desire, Radiowoman's desires are defective (assuming that it is not actually good for radios in Radiowoman's vicinity to be on). It follows from the value appearance thesis itself that desires can be misleading, and the reason-generating power of value appearances may be destroyed by their inaccuracy.

There is certainly something very suggestive about Stampe's claim that desires are reason-generating, but this power seems to be a conditional one. For example, if nihilism is right, it is not clear that desires do generate genuine reasons, as opposed to the illusion of reasons.

## 3 Value Data and the Magnetism of the Good

In an earlier work I argued that two considerations weigh in favor of the value appearance thesis.[19] The first appeals to the necessity for value data. The second appeals to the apparent magnetism of the good.

For value theorizing to get off the ground we need more than purely formal constraints on value, like universalizability or the transitivity of the better-than relation. Such constraints provide no reasons for rejecting the nihilist thesis that nothing is more valuable than anything else. What we need, in addition to such formal constraints, is some source of data that provides evidence for substantive value claims, such as that *pleasure is good* or *pleasure is better than pain.* Quite generally, *X's seeming F* is defeasible evidence for the judgment *that X is F*. And *S's seeming good* would be defeasible evidence for the judgment that *S is good.* Value seemings could thus play the same role in value knowledge that perceptual appearances play in regular knowledge of the world. We don't have to *postulate* value seemings. Seeming good, bad, and indifferent are ubiquitous features of everyday experience. We are *bombarded* with value appearances all the time. The only question is this: What kind (or kinds) of mental states are appearances of value?

Let's say that a representation of *X as F* is belief-entailing if it entails the belief that *X* is *F*. Believing that *X* is *F*, knowing *X is F* are, trivially, belief-entailing representations. Perceptual experience is not belief-entailing. One can visually experience a rose as pink without believing that it is pink. One might be having the visual experience while believing that one is looking at a white rose through rose-tinted glasses. It is only because they are not just more beliefs that perceptual experiences might halt the regress of justification of beliefs. So perceptual seemings, to play a role in the justification of beliefs, must be non-belief-entailing representations of things. By analogy the appearance of *S* as good would also have to be a non-belief-entailing representation of the goodness *of S*, if it is to serve as evidence for the non-inferentially justified belief that *S* is good. A state can appear good to one without that entailing that one believes or judges that it is good. (One might be quite aware that certain value appearances are being systematically distorted in some way, perhaps through intoxication or bias.) Additionally, one can believe that a state is good without its appearing good. (For example, one might take the word of someone one trusts about such matters, such as the recommendation of a reliable critic.) Since value seemings and value beliefs can come apart at both seams, whatever the value seemings are they should be non-belief-entailing.

Desires have this feature. That one desires *S* does not entail that one believes that *S* is good, nor does the belief that *S* is good entail that one desires *S*. By satisfying the non-belief-entailing requirement, desires are, in this respect, good candidates for the role of value data.

This argument still seems to me to provide some support for the value appearance thesis, although it is clearly not decisive. There are, for example, other candidates for the role of value appearance that are not belief-entailing (for example, certain emotions).

I gave another argument for the value appearance thesis that now strikes me as less good:

> When I desire *that P*, *P* has a certain magnetic appeal for me. It presents itself to me as something needing to be pursued, or promoted, or preserved or embraced. Now the good just *is* that which needs to be pursued, promoted, or preserved or embraced. So my desire that P certainly involves *P*'s seeming good.... It is but a small step from there to identifying the desire that *P* with the experience of *P*'s seeming good.[20]

This has two defects. First, it appears to commit an intentional fallacy. Even if *X* appears to be $\varphi$, and $\varphi$ is $\phi$, it does not follow that *X* appears to be $\phi$.[21] (The morning star appears to be the brightest celestial body in the morning sky, and the brightest celestial body in the morning sky is the brightest celestial body in the evening sky, but it does not follow that the morning star appears to be the brightest celestial body in the evening sky.) This kind of objection might be blocked if the identity in question—that the good just *is* that which needs to be pursued—is taken to be analytically true. But treating it as analytically true is problematic. *Need* here is clearly some kind of deontic notion. The idea is that *S* is good if and only if it *ought* to be pursued (etc.). But if this is right, then the argument assumes a deontic version of the fitting attitude analysis of value that—as we will see in section 5—isn't plausible.

Despite this, I think the seeds of a decent argument are buried here. The magnetism of the good, or of the apparent good, has seemed somewhat mysterious. As non-cognitivists have long urged, if there are truth-evaluable propositions about goodness, then it would be possible to judge that *S is good* without feeling in the least bit moved to pursue, welcome, appreciate, or embrace *S*. A purely cognitive apprehension of the goodness of *S* might leave one completely unmoved about the prospect of *S*, or even *averse* to *S*. And there is nothing to prevent this disconnect between judgment and desire being systematic and all-pervasive.

The non-cognitivists are right about this, but contrary to what they have claimed, this gap between value judgment and desire is not only possible but a fairly common feature of experience. In itself it doesn't seem particularly puzzling at all. What would be deeply puzzling, however, would be if genuine *acquaintance* with goodness were to be accompanied by such systematic indifference or aversion. If a cognitivist cannot block that possibility, then she has a problem. It should not turn out to be a matter of sheer chance or preestablished harmony that those who know what's good, through an awareness of that goodness, feel moved by what they know to be good.

Now, suppose that there are certain *ubiquitous* appearances of goodness and that these kinds of appearances either are or entail associated desires. Then the magnetism of the apparent good would lose its mystery. For those who become aware of the goodness of things through such value appearances would *ipso facto* have the relevant desires. Call this the *desire-entailing* desideratum on value appearances.

Let's summarize the desiderata so far. First, value data must come in the form of *non-belief-entailing* representations (i.e. *appearances*) of goodness, badness, and betterness. Second, to explain the magnetism of the apparent good, value appearances have to be *desire-entailing* and *ubiquitous*. If desires are value appearances, then these desiderata are satisfied. They are desire-entailing (trivially); they are non-belief-entailing representations of goodness; and they are ubiquitous.

## 4 The Fittingness of Attitudes

The fitting attitude thesis provides independent support for these desiderata, but to show this requires some work.

There is a tight conceptual connection between certain evaluative properties and certain attitudes. This is especially clear in the case of the so-called thick evaluative properties. Consider the pairs: *being delightful* and *taking delight in, being admirable* and *admiring*. The fitting attitude account tells us that the delightful is not just what people happen to take delight in or what people typically take delight in, but in what it is *fitting* to delight in.[22] And for each thick value attribute (e.g. *admirable, precious*) there will be suitable attitudes (e.g. *admire, cherish*) that stand in this fittingness relation. A number of value theorists maintain that the same kind of relation holds between the thin evaluative attribute of *goodness* (or *desirability*) and *desire*. The idea can be traced back to Brentano and receives a clear if characteristically guarded statement here by C. D.

Broad: "I'm not sure that 'X is good' could not be defined as meaning that X is such that it would be a fitting object of desire to any mind which had an adequate idea of its non-ethical characteristics."[23] Quite generally, the fitting attitude account of value posits the following schema for the connection between value *V* and an associated attitude *F(V)*:

> (FA schema) *X* has value *V* if and only if it is *fitting* to take attitude *F(V)* to *X*.

For the schema to be universally applicable, with each value attribute *V* there must be an associated attitude *F(V)* (or perhaps class of attitudes) for which the biconditional holds.[24] The fitting attitude reduction of value consists in (i) an endorsement of the general schema for all values and (ii) the claim that instances of the schema provide a reduction of facts about *V* to facts about the fittingness of *F(V)*. According to the reduction thesis, the right-hand side (a fact about fittingness) is fundamental; the left-hand side (a value fact) is reducible. If the biconditional schema fails, then the reduction also fails. But even if the biconditional schema succeeds there remains a question about which of these two kinds of fact are fundamental. One can endorse the schema without buying into the reductive claim that the LHS holds in virtue of the RHS.

Here I am only concerned with the success of the *FA* schema, not the reductive claim, which I think fails. The *FA* schema is successful only if there is a suitable notion of *fittingness*, and for each value attribute there is an associated attitude that generates a true instance of the schema. While *F(V)* is an attitude connected to *V* in the *FA* schema, it may or may not be the case that *F(V)* has evaluative *content*. On some *FA* accounts it will; on others it won't. (For example, the attitude of *judging X to be precious* can be specified only by means of evaluative content. But some at least might consider the attitude that consists in *cherishing X* to be specifiable without invoking that content.)

What does fittingness amount to? In a recent survey of neosentimentalist theories of value, Tappolet distinguishes two fundamentally different accounts of the *appropriateness* of emotional attitudes: "There are two main ways to understand the concept of appropriateness at stake. The first, which is now standard, is to take this concept to be normative. An appropriate emotion is one that satisfies a normative requirement; the emotion *ought* to be felt, in some sense of *ought*."[25] Tappolet notes that there are two different normative conceptions of fittingness that are worth distinguishing: "*Normative* is used in its narrow sense, which is equivalent to 'deontic' and excludes the evaluative. If one takes the normative to encompass both the deontic and the evaluative, this would make for two sub-possibilities one of which is being that appropriate is evaluative. Given the circularity involved, this might not seem a very tempting suggestion."[26] We can commandeer Tappolet's typology by identifying *appropriateness* with *fittingness* and expanding the class of attitudes. She thus identifies two broadly normative notions of fittingness:

(*Deontic FA*) *X* is *V* if and only if one *ought* to take attitude *F(V)* to *X*.

(*Axiological FA*) *X* is *V* if and only if it is *good* to take attitude *F(V)* to *X*.

Where *favoring* is a placeholder for *F(good)*, the latter schema yields:

*X* is *good* if and only if it is *good* to *favor X*.

This biconditional clearly cannot underwrite a reduction of goodness, since *good* appears ineliminably on the right-hand side, in the fittingness slot. Nevertheless, Axiological *FA* might conceivably be a necessary truth about goodness, without underwriting the possibility of a reduction of good. The Deontic reading, on the other hand, is not subject to this circularity and might also provide a reduction of evaluative properties to deontic properties.[27]

The alternative to a normative reading of fittingness is what Tappolet calls the *descriptive* reading. Tappolet motivates it by appealing to the idea that emotions are value appearances: "An alternative conception . . . is that the appropriateness of emotions is a matter of representing things as they are. In the relevant sense, appropriate emotions are emotions that are correct from an epistemic point of view."[28] With some terminological shifts, I will call this the *Representational* notion of fittingness:

(*Representational FA*) *X* is *V* if and only if it is representationally accurate for one to take attitude *F(V)* to *X*.

On this reading, fittingness depends on the fact that the attitude *F(V)* involves a representation of the object *X* as having the associated value attribute *V*. At a first pass, a representation of an object *X as V* is accurate if and only if *X* has the value attribute *V* that it is represented as having.

Note that accuracy here need not be deemed a normative concept. There is of course a large literature that argues truth is a "norm" of belief. But it is difficult to spell this out satisfactorily.[29] One can take truth and accuracy to be purely descriptive concepts and hold that it is a matter of substantive value theory whether or to what extent truth and accuracy are valuable features of representations generally or of cognitive states in particular. It is by no means obvious, for example, that a true belief is in general better than a false belief.[30] In any case, I am not interested here in the viability of a reduction of value but only in whether or not some version of the biconditional generally holds. What notion of fittingness and what kinds of attitudes would we need for the schema to hold?

I outline two objections to the *FA* biconditional: the well-known *Wrong Kinds of Reason* objection (WKR) and the less well-known *Solitary Goods* objection (SG). The WKR objection, if successful, shows that the *FA* biconditional fails from right to left if the notion of fittingness is one or other of the two normative notions. So that leaves us with the representational reading of fittingness if the biconditional is to succeed. What kinds of representations? The SG objection, if successful, shows that the schema fails from left to right if fitting attitudes are either state-entailing or belief-entailing.

If both objections are on the right track, we end up with one constraint on fittingness that dovetails with the requirement that there be value seemings or value appearances and another constraint on the fitting responses to value that dovetails with the requirement that such appearances be neither belief-entailing nor state-entailing.

## 5 Right-to-Left Failure of the *FA* Biconditional: The Wrong Kinds of Reason

Start with the Deontic version of the *FA* schema. If an evil demon threatens the world with some terrible outcome unless you admire him, then you ought to admire him. But he isn't admirable. If successful, this shows that the RHS of Deontic *FA* can hold, while the LHS fails. Such counterexamples can also be constructed against Axiological *FA*. If the demon threatens to bring about the worst outcome unless you desire that outcome, and will spare us the worst outcome if you do so desire, then it is clearly better for you to desire the worst outcome than not. Desiring the worst outcome may be good. But that does not make the worst outcome itself desirable or good.[31]

Olson, following Ewing, suggests that the *FA* theorist distinguish two notions of *ought*: the moral ought and the ought of fittingness.[32] Morally you ought to admire the demon—because there would be disastrous consequences if you didn't. However, the ought of fittingness doesn't apply here, since the demon is contemptible. In addition Ewing maintains that whether or not your response is morally correct is a matter of what response it is fitting for the *rest of us* to have to your response to the demon. Moral obligation is a matter of certain moral emotions (praise and blame, resentment, etc.) being a fitting response to an agent's actions or choices. It would be entirely fitting for you to despise the demon, for he is despicable, but it would also be fitting for us to condemn your despising him as morally blameworthy. Even though it would not be at all fitting for you to admire the demon, it would be fitting for us to praise your admiration.

The Ewing-Olson response can deflect the WKR objection, but it houses a residual tension. The Representational *FA* theorist can deflect the objection without the tension. The representationalist can say, "It isn't fitting for you to admire the demon, because it is simply inaccurate to represent the demon as admirable. He isn't; he's contemptible. But you ought to do what you can to avert the disaster even though it involves taking an attitude toward the demon that isn't accurate. So in order to do what you ought to do you must take an attitude to him that misrepresents him." The representational account may or may not allow disvalue to accrue to inaccurate attitudes, but that is irrelevant to the fittingness of those attitudes. It is unfitting to admire the demon because the fellow simply isn't admirable. The normative aspects of your attitudes (whether or not they are good or obligatory) can be prised apart from their accuracy. So it may be that it is good or obligatory to admire the demon, although quite unfitting to do so.

We can thus rescue what is intuitively compelling about the *FA* schema from the WKR counterexamples, provided we go representational with the notion of fittingness and embrace evaluative content in the fitting attitudes themselves. This delivers a constraint on fitting attitudes (namely that they be capable of being representationally accurate) that will narrow the range and nature of the fitting responses to evaluative attitudes in general and to the thin evaluative attribute of goodness. The fitting response to a state's being good must be a presentation of that state *as good.*

## 6 Left-to-Right Failure of the *FA* Biconditional: Solitary Goods

Berkeley hoped to reduce physical objects to congeries of experiences. According to Berkeley, there is a tree in the quad just in case experiencers have suitable tree-in-the-quad experiences. But a tree in the quad that goes unexperienced is a problem: no tree experiences, no tree. Berkeley posited an omni-experiencer to make up for a possible dearth of experiences. Phenomenalists, unwilling to appeal to supernatural beings, retreat to counterfactual experiences. There is a tree in the quad if suitably placed observers would have appropriate tree-in-the-quad experiences. But suppose it would be *impossible* for anyone to have the appropriate experiences. Berkeley invites us to contemplate the following object: *an object not conceived by anyone.* He claims it is impossible to conceive of an object that is not conceived by anyone (cf. *experience a tree that is not experienced by anyone*). If this is right, Berkeley had already disposed of the phenomenalist fix even before it was proposed.

A strict value idealist would, like Berkeley, hold that something has a certain value attribute only if some valuers actually take the associated valuing attitude to it. No attitudes, no value. But some things have value in the absence of actual responses. Absent an infallible omni-valuer, the value idealist might well retreat from actual responses to merely possible but fitting responses. That is, a thing is good if valuers would respond to it favorably were they suitably placed and responding fittingly. The fitting attitude schema can thus be construed as a version of value phenomenalism.

Bykvist argues that the *FA* schema suffers from analogues of the unexperienced tree.[33] *Solitary goods* are those that exist without anyone's being around to respond to them fittingly. Such goods should surely be deemed possible by all but strict value idealists.

Let's dub the fitting attitude for goodness *favoring*. Favoring is that attitude, if there is one, that underwrites the *FA* biconditional schema for the thin evaluative property of goodness: *S* is good if and only if favoring *S* is fitting. I will take it that favoring covers both *favoring positively* and *favoring negatively* (i.e. *disfavoring*) and that it admits of degrees, just as goodness admits of degrees.

Bykvist assumes that even if no one actually favors *S*, for *S* to be good it must be both *logically possible* and *rationally coherent* for some valuer to favor *S*. So *S's being good* cannot logically preclude the favoring of *S* (call this the logical constraint), nor can it preclude the coherence of favoring *S* (call this the coherence constraint).

Let's say that an attitude or relation is *state-entailing* if one cannot bear that relation to *S* without *S* obtaining. So *bringing S about, knowing that S*, and *taking pleasure in the fact that S* are all state-entailing. Consider an apparently good state, **E**, that *happy egrets exist.* Conjoin **E** with the state **F**: that *there are no past, present, or future favorers.* Suppose that the conjunctive state **E&F** is also good. Then we can show that if the *FA* schema holds, favoring cannot be state-entailing.

> Proof: By assumption **E&F** is good. Suppose favoring is state-entailing. Assume (for the sake of a *reductio*) that someone favors **E&F**. Then **E&F** obtains; so there are no past, present, or future favorers. Contradiction. Hence **E&F**'s being good logically precludes anyone's favoring **E&F**, violating the logical constraint.

Being state-entailing is a rather stringent requirement on an attitude. Call a relation between an individual and a state *S belief-entailing* if an individual's bearing the relation to *S* entails that he believes *S* obtains. Suppose Moe and Joe are competing for Olympic gold, and Moe is listening for the announcement of the winner. What he hears over the crackly speaker is "Moe won the gold!". He delights in winning, and since winning is delightful his response is entirely fitting. But suppose it was in fact *Joe* who won, and Moe misheard. Moe can still delight in winning the gold, so delight is not state-entailing. But Moe soon discovers his error. He learns he's a loser after all. Whatever attitude Moe now takes to winning the gold he can no longer *delight* in it. He cannot delight in winning if he doesn't believe he won. So taking *delight in* is belief-entailing, as are some other attitudes that fitting attitudes theorists invoke.

We can now show that favoring cannot be belief-entailing.

> Proof: By assumption **E&F** is good. Suppose favoring is belief-entailing. Assume (for the sake of a *reductio*) that someone *X* favors **E&F**. So *X* believes **E&F** obtains. But **E&F** entails that no one favors anything. So *X*'s favoring **E&F** entails *X* believes something logically incompatible with *X*'s favoring **E&F**. So it would be incoherent for *X* to favor **E&F**, violating the coherence constraint.

One problematic feature of these arguments is that **E&F** is assumed to be good. That doesn't follow from the assumption that **E** is good. Whether **E&F** is good depends both on the degree of goodness of **F** and the way in which the value of compound states depends on the value of the components. It might be that the non-existence of fitting responders to value is a defect of the universe. If it is bad enough, then **E&F** wouldn't be good after all. Suppose **F** isn't bad but merely an indifferent state of affairs (neither good nor bad). Then if value is additive, **E&F** has the same value as **E**. But value may not be additive over conjunction, in which case all bets on the goodness of **E&F** are off. So whether or not value is additive, the goodness of **E** doesn't guarantee the goodness of **E&F**.

It would be better if we could run the argument without having to settle substantive issues in value theory. And we can. For **E&F** must have *some* degree of value. It may not be better than **E**, and it may well be worse than **E**, but it lies *somewhere* on the spectrum of thin value (*V*), and, as such, according to the *FA* schema, there must be *some* degree of favoring *F(V)* that fits. But if *F(V)* is state-entailing it will violate the logical constraint, and if it is belief-entailing it will violate the coherence constraint. So favoring can be neither state-entailing nor belief-entailing.

The obvious way for a defender of the *FA* biconditional to block the argument is to abandon the idea that any fitting attitudes are state-entailing or belief-entailing. (It is Bykvist's intention to narrow down the range of admissible fitting attitudes until there are no good candidates left.) But that seems hasty. Surely taking delight is the fitting response to what's delightful, if anything is, and taking delight is belief-entailing. So there may be certain thick values the fitting responses to which are belief-entailing. But how could there be such values if the second SG argument is sound?

It is instructive to try to extend the SG argument to the delightful. We have to find a *delightful* state that it would be impossible or incoherent for anyone to take delight in. Suppose **D** is a delightful state. Let **B** be the eternal non-existence of beings capable of taking delight in anything at all. If **D&B** were delightful, then we would have the required state. But there is no reason to judge **D&B** delightful. Embedding a delightful state within some larger state doesn't guarantee that the larger state is delightful. **B** certainly isn't delightful, and there is no reason to think that the conjunction of a delightful state with a decidedly non-delightful state is delightful. The parallel argument thus stalls.

What we had to assume for the SG argument is that the state **E&F** has *some determinate of the thin value of goodness*. That is to say, we have to assume that **E&F** can be placed somewhere on the scale of goodness and badness. Where *V* is the value of **E&F**, the *FA* biconditional assures us there is some attitude, *F(V)*, some determinate of the *favoring-disfavoring* determinable, that it is fitting to take to **E&F**. So the *reductios* apply to thin value because every state is assumed to lie somewhere on that scale. However, it is not clear that all states have some degree or other of delightfulness, encompassing both positive and negative degrees, and that delighting in is a determinable that embraces both positive degrees and negative degrees of delight. If there are any such thick values, then the argument would, of course, apply to them as well, precluding the possibility that fitting responses to them are belief-entailing or state-entailing.

What we can conclude from the SG argument about thick attributes is this: If the only fitting responses to some thick value *V* are (say) belief-entailing, then that value cannot be exemplified by any state that necessitates the non-existence of beings capable of taking attitude *F(V)*. So if delight is the only fitting response to the delightful, and delight is belief-entailing, then no state that entails the non-existence of delighting beings can be delightful.

Whatever the fate of the *FA* schema for thick values, as far as the thin values go fitting responses can be neither state-entailing nor belief-entailing.

## 7 Inference to the Best Explanation: Desire = the Fitting Response to the Good

We now have two desiderata for value data and two desiderata for fitting responses to value.

(i) *Non-belief-entailing*: The basic value data must be appearance-like rather than belief-like; they must be non-doxastic value appearances.
(ii) *Desire-entailing*: To explain the magnetism of the apparent good a significant subset of the value data have to be desire-entailing.

There are also two desiderata governing fitting responses to values:

(iii) *Representation:* The fitting response to an object's having a particular value is a representation of that object as having that value (from WKR).
(iv) *Non-state- and non-belief-entailing*: The fitting response to the goodness of a state cannot be state-entailing or belief-entailing (from SG).

These four desiderata fit together rather nicely. (iii) and (iv) entail that fitting responses to the thin values must be non-belief-entailing, non-state-entailing representations of those values—that is, they must be appearances of value. And (i) and (ii) tell us that the *value data* must also be value appearances and that a significant subset of those value appearances must be desire-entailing. One simple hypothesis that unifies and explains all four is the value appearance thesis. For suppose desires are appearances of value. Since they are non-belief-entailing, desire-entailing, and ubiquitous they satisfy constraints (i) and (ii). Since desires are also non-state-entailing they also satisfy (iv). Finally, if the desire for *S* is an appearance of *S* as good, then that desire will clearly be a fitting response to the goodness of *S* on the representational notion of fittingness. The simplest hypothesis that explains and unifies these is that *F(good)* = *desire*.

Are there other possible responses to value that satisfy all the desiderata? Suppose attitude *A* is a candidate for the role of fitting response to degree of value *V*, and that *A* is not a determinate of desire/aversion. Attitude *A* will have to be (i) non-state-entailing and non-belief-entailing, (ii) desire-entailing, (iii) as ubiquitous as desire, and (iv) an appearance of value. Since *A* to *S* is desire-entailing without being the desire that *S*, it will have to be a somewhat more complex attitude than desire, which suggests that the hypothesis that *A* = *F(good)* is not as simple as *desire* = *F(good)*. Further, since *A* entails desire without being entailed by desire, instances of *A* will almost certainly be *less ubiquitous* than instances of desire, perhaps much less ubiquitous. The only way to ensure that instances of *A* are as ubiquitous as instances of desire would be to require that *A* be necessarily coextensive with desire. But then it is hard to see what would set *A* apart from desire. So, *ceteris paribus*, any hypothesis other than that *desire* = *F(good)* is going to violate ubiquity.

## 8 The Death of Desire

A powerful criticism that has been leveled against the value appearance thesis rests on what Lauria calls *the death of desire* principle.[34] It is a widely held thesis—one that dates back at least as far as Plato but is also embodied in contemporary subjective decision theory—that one cannot desire what one already has, or at least what one thinks one has. The idea is that the desire for *S* must vanish once one comes to believe that *S* already obtains. Hence the *death* of desire through the acquisition of belief. By contrast the appearance of *S* as good need not disappear when one comes to believe that *S* obtains. So desires and appearances of the good come apart.

Consider Hillary's obsessive desire to become the first female president of the United States. To fulfill her desire she labors tirelessly for two years campaigning for the office. Around midnight on the first Tuesday in November 2016 she learns that her desire has been fulfilled, albeit by a very narrow margin. When her rival, Trump, concedes victory, it tastes very, very sweet to her. So becoming the first female president of the United States still seems good to her. But surely the prospective desire to *become* the first female president of the United States will cease once it is clear to her that she has in fact already achieved that goal. She won't say "I *still* want to become the first female president of the United States," and she will stop campaigning for the office. Moreover, her desire won't fade gradually. It will be *completely extinguished* as soon as the vote count is settled in her favor. If this is an endemic feature of desire, then the value appearance thesis cannot be right—or so the argument goes.

Strictly speaking, the *death of desire* principle doesn't clash with the modest value appearance thesis: that desires are value appearances. Rather it clashes with the converse thesis, that appearances of value are either desires or desire-entailing. If there are value appearances that are not desires, then the desire that *S* can be extinguished even while *S* continues to appear good. However, as Lauria points out, this defense leaves the evaluative theory without any explanation for the death of desire in that range of cases (and perhaps the Hillary case is one) in which it seems to hold.[35] Nor does it explain how, if the appearance is initially sustained by a desire, by what mechanism it is sustained when the desire disappears.

The death of Hillary's desire to *become* the first female U.S. president may be explained by the fact that one *cannot* become the *first* female president of the United States a second time. After she has already become the first president of the United States it would be very odd for her to say "I still want to *become* the first female president of the United States." This is a case in which a certain kind of desire should die with belief. What about Hillary's desire to *be* the first female president of the United States? It doesn't seem odd for her to say, after learning that she now *is* the first female president of the United States, "I am now the thing I most want to be: the first female president of the United States." She doesn't find it an unexpectedly disappointing thing to be. Quite generally, the following doesn't seem odd: "For a long time I have wanted things to be thus-and-such, and now things are *exactly as I want them to be*."[36] The following haiku by Basho is a rather more striking expression of this:

> Even in Kyoto—
> hearing the cuckoo's cry—
> I long for Kyoto.[37]

But perhaps this is striking precisely because it trades on the intuition that one cannot really desire, let alone long for, what one already knows obtains.

Fortunately there is an irenic resolution to this debate within reach. There are rival sets of intuitions concerning the connections between desire and belief. When this happens we often resort to distinguishing different concepts. The downside of this strategy is that it often seems *ad hoc*—especially when there is no obvious connection between the concepts—but in this particular case the concepts are clearly linked, the relation being that of a thick determinate to its thin determinable.

The thin concept of desire (the all-encompassing notion required by the value appearance thesis) can be characterized in terms of the more fundamental notion of preference. To desire$^t$ *S* is simply to *prefer S* to not-*S*. On the value appearance thesis, *preferring S to* not-*S* is a case of *S*'s *appearing better than* not-*S*. Clearly one can maintain such a preference even as one's credence in *S* and not-*S* change. Imagine that Héloise starts out as a complete agnostic about God but strongly prefers God's existence to God's non-existence. In her troubled uncertainty she yearns for a divinely infused universe; she lives in hope. Then one day Héloise chances upon Anselm's ontological argument (*Proslogion* 3) and becomes convinced not only that God exists but that this is knowable *a priori*. She retains her strong preference for God's existence, but for the first time her deepest desire is *satisfied*. Later, she chances upon Lactantius's *Treatise on the Anger of God*, with its pithy summary of Epicurus's devastating argument from evil. She is now convinced that the ontological argument is a sham and that the universe is Godless. She retains her preference for God's existence (things would be so much better!) and feels frustrated that God does not exist.

Throughout these swings in belief Héloise unwaveringly retains her desire (or preference) for God's existence. But there are certain changes on the broadly desiderative side of her nature. She starts out affirming "I hope God exists," moves to "I am deeply satisfied that God exists!," and ends up with "My desire for God is frustrated!"

The desire$^t$ for *S* can be combined with various different credal attitudes to *S*. These different combinations of desire and belief yield different thick concepts of desire. One *prospectively* desires *S* if one desires$^t$ *S* and is more or less uncertain about whether *S* is or will be the case, investing less than complete credence in both *S* and not-*S*.

When we talk of desire we are often talking about prospective desires. One often begins in a state of prospectively desiring something, unsure of whether or not the desire will be fulfilled. Prospective desires are those that, in conjunction with beliefs about one's causal powers with respect to *S*, can give rise to actions. If one desires$^p$ *S* and believes of some action *A* that it could help bring about *S*, one may well decide to do *A*. If one does *A* and this brings *S* about, then, provided one has epistemic access to this, one's uncertainty about *S* will be replaced by a firm belief in *S*, and (by its very nature) the prospective desire for *S* dies. This is what happens to Hillary. Her prospective desire to become the first female president of the United States dies when she becomes certain that that desire is fulfilled. But her desire$^{t}$ to be the president of the United States does not die. That (thin) desire, her preference for being the president of the United States rather than not, survives the change in belief intact.

Suppose, then, that one prospectively desires *S*, comes to believe *S*, and retains the preference for *S*. In this case one is *satisfied that S*. But again the thin desire does not die. Desire is still a constituent of satisfied desire: call it *desire*$^{s}$. To be satisfied that *S* one must desire$^{t}$ *S* and be convinced that *S* obtains. Desire$^{t}$ is a necessary condition of desire$^{s}$.

Satisfaction is the subjective correlate of desire *fulfillment*—of the combination of desiring$^{t}$ *S* and *S*'s *actually* obtaining. Having a fulfilled desire and having a satisfied desire are, of course, logically independent states, and they play important roles in different value theories. (Some maintain that what is good for one is desire fulfillment, others that it is desire satisfaction.) But note how strange it would be to insist that well-being hangs on fulfilled desires and satisfied desires if there were really no such desires at all. On the present account fulfilled and satisfied desires are a genuine species of desire. Note also that there is a big difference in the psychological state of one who abandons his desire$^{t}$ for *S* as soon as he becomes certain that *S* and one who retains his desire$^{t}$. The latter is enjoying a state of desire satisfaction; the former is probably experiencing disappointment about *S*.

Consider the state of desiring$^{t}$ *S* and becoming certain that not-*S* obtains. If the desire$^{t}$ for *S* survives the change in belief, then one enters the state of *desire frustration*. One is frustrated that not-*S* (or desires$^{f}$ *S*) if one desires$^{t}$ *S* and is certain that *S* does not obtain, that that desire is unfulfilled. Frustration is the subjective correlate of desire non-fulfillment (desiring$^{t}$ *S* while *S* does not in fact obtain). Frustrated and unfulfilled desires are still desires.

According to the value appearance thesis, all desires, all determinates of desire$^{t}$, are appearances of value. Desire$^{t}$ is clearly compatible with the many different credal relations that one can bear to the object of desire. As one's credal state changes from uncertainty about the prospect to certainty, one's prospective desire dies, to be replaced by a satisfied desire or a frustrated desire. So this account does entail the death of a certain species of desire—that is, of *prospective* desire—whenever one acquires a belief in the fulfillment or the non-fulfillment of the prospective desire. But in such cases the desire$^t$ need not lose its grip, and often it will persist.

## 9 Experience and Concept Possession

Tim Schroeder articulates a common objection to the value appearance thesis:

> One puzzle for [good-based] theories might be to explain the relationship of desires to non-human animals. On the one hand, it would seem that rats desire to get away from cats, desire to be around other rats, and the like. On the other hand, it would seem that rats do not represent anything as good (they would both seem to lack the concept of goodness and to lack a perceptual-style representation of goodness that would be well poised to generate such a concept). But if rats can desire without representing the good, then why would people be different? The options available for solving such puzzles have not yet been explored.[38]

Schroeder's objection assumes something like the following general *concept possession principle: X* cannot appear *F* to one who does not possess the (or a) concept of *F*.

Suppose propositions are structured entities that contain concepts as constituents, and that to grasp a proposition one must grasp its constituent concepts. Suppose, in addition, that desire is an attitude that takes structured propositions as object, and that bearing such an attitude to a proposition involves grasping it. Then if human neonates (babes) and non-human animals (brutes) cannot grasp concepts, they cannot have any desires (or indeed beliefs). But it is implausible that human neonates or non-human animals lack *desires*, whether or not they also lack beliefs. Cloudy (my cat) surely enjoys perceptual states, states that represent the world as being a certain way. If the food bowl that he is staring at is empty, it appears empty to him. And such perceptual states combine with desires (like hunger) to dispose him to carry out various antics (meowing plaintively in my direction), which he is rightly confident will secure the filling of the bowl. Whatever else is true about cats, I think we have to agree both that Cloudy gets hungry and that his bowl sometimes appears disappointingly empty to him.

Does Cloudy possess the concept of *emptiness*? This of course depends on a theory of concepts, something that is rather controversial. But we can make some progress here without resolving that. Suppose we concede, for the sake of the argument, that Cloudy doesn't possess any concepts—at least not the kind of concepts that feature as constituents in propositions. It follows that the concept possession principle is false: in general one doesn't have to have the concept of *F* for *X* to appear *F*. So the argument fails, but we are still owed an account of how something can appear *empty* or *good* to Cloudy.

There are two quite different but promising tacks to take here. One would be to embrace the possibility of the non-conceptual content of perceptual experience. We experience a far richer palette of colors, for example, than we have the conceptual tools to characterize. Our grasp of various color concepts presumably emerges from such color experiences, together with the powers of perceptual discrimination that they presuppose and the relationships of similarity and betweenness that obtain among the constituents of those experiences.[39] But we do not have to possess those concepts prior to having the experiences. Now suppose desire and aversion bear the same relation to the concepts of good and bad that color experiences bear to color concepts. They are the basic elements of (evaluative) experience that we have to have to enable us to get a grip on evaluative concepts. Of course, just as in the case of color, one can have the relevant desiderative experiences before one grasps the associated concepts. Thus it is that Cloudy can experience both the emptiness of the bowl and the unsatisfactoriness of that emptiness without having to grasp the concepts of emptiness or unsatisfactoriness.

But there is a quite different tack that may be just as promising. This has been developed by both Friedrich and Lauria in their preferred theories of desire, but Stampe also hinted at it.[40] A ball might *look* round, *feel* round, or (if you perceive by means of echo location) *sound* round. Each of these is a way for the ball to appear round. These are different kinds of appearance—the first is visual, the second tactile, and the third is auditory—but they are all presentations of the ball as round. One might try to locate the difference between these appearances in the *content* of the presentation, but another way is to locate the difference not in the content but in the *mode* of the presentation. Similarly, one can argue that there are different modes of presentation of a state of affairs. In the perception of *S*, *S* is presented *as being the case*. In the desire for *S*, *S* is presented *as being good*. One and the same state can be presented in these two different ways. The perception that *S* and the desire that *S* take the same object but present *S* in different ways.

This idea of distinct modes of presentation of one and the same object of presentation can be traced back to Brentano. According to Brentano, every mental state involves a presentation of something, but there are two (and only two) different modes of presentation. In the one mode the object is presented as existing, and judgment consists in either accepting or rejecting the existence of the object. In the other, the mode of interest, the object is presented as being good, and acceptance or rejection consists in either loving (desiring) or hating (being averse to) the object presented. Being presented *as existent* is one mode; being presented *as good* is the other. Brentano did not countenance states of affairs as the object of presentations, but the basic idea can be transferred. For a state *S* to *seem good* one does not need to grasp the concept of goodness and judge that it applies to *S*. Rather one just has to accept the presentation of the object in the mode of interest. If, in addition, one can master and apply concepts, including the concept of goodness, then such presentations would provide a reason to embrace the associated judgment.

Both non-conceptual content and mode of appearance are sufficient to ensure that babes and brutes enjoy a rich life replete with a full range of desires.

## 11 Conclusion

The value appearance thesis unifies and explains a wide range of phenomena, including the need for value data, the magnetism of the apparent good, and the immunity of fitting attitudes to both the wrong kinds of reason and the paradoxes of solitary goods. It also suggests that other aspects of value and our responses to value may be illuminated by the analogy with perception. Consider the fact that experiences in general are highly perspectival. One always perceives the world from a particular location within the world. It would be absurd to require that all perceivers should "ideally" have exactly the same experiences of a perceiver-independent world. One's perceptions depend not just on the properties of perceiver-independent states but on the different relations each perceiver bears to those states. This is not a bug in perception but a necessary feature of the fact that perceivers are differently situated in the world. Perception is always perception of how things appear from where one stands in relation to them. So, if desires are perceptions of value, the heavily perspectival nature of perception in general provides a powerful resource for explaining and legitimizing the subject-relativity of desire, even if and when desires are responses to subject-independent value.[41]

## Notes

1. I would like to thank the participants of the Nature of Desire conference in Geneva in the summer of 2012 for numerous comments on an early version of this paper. I owe a special debt of gratitude to Federico Lauria who read, commented on, and helped me considerably improve the paper through several drafts.

2. See also Friedrich *this volume.*

3. Sometimes this is called "the guise of the good" thesis, but one must be careful here. For the guise of the good is often understood as the thesis that desires are or involve value judgments. That is both implausible and no part of the value appearance thesis. For "the guise of the good," see Döring and Eker, Massin, Lauria *this volume.*

4. Stampe 1987; Oddie 2005.

5. See Friedrich 2008; Lauria 2014, *this volume*; Döring and Eker *this volume.*

6. See Döring and Eker, Alvarez *this volume.*

7. Lewis 1979.

8. I also think, and argue elsewhere (Oddie *forthcoming*) that on the property view the objects of desire are even better candidates for bearers of value.

9. See Tenenbaum 2007, and Döring and Eker, Massin, Lauria *this volume.*

10. Aquinas 1975: lib. 3 cap. 62 n. 7. Thanks to Bob Pasnau, who tracked this down for me. The usually quoted formulation—quoted in Kant—does not appear to be anywhere in Aquinas.

11. The thesis has been the focus of a good deal of technical work stemming from Lewis (1988, 1996), who claims that the thesis is incompatible with the most basic elements of subjective decision theory. See Oddie (1994, 2001) for two different analyses of Lewis's argument. Whether or not desires might *be* beliefs about goodness, it is at least possible for the two to covary, contrary to the conclusion of Lewis's argument.

12. See Döring and Eker, Gregory (*this volume*) for the desire as belief thesis.

13. Stampe 1987: 381. See also Oddie 2005. While Stampe obviously takes propositions to be the objects of desire, his overall position does not hinge on this. One could easily generalize his formulation to properties, simplifying it in the process: "One who wants to be φ perceives something that makes it seem to that person that it would be good to be φ."

14. Stampe 1987: 377.

15. Stalnaker 1984: 15.

16. Lauria (2014, *this volume*) makes the point that one can explain a disposition to behave in terms of salient desire, something that is ruled out by the dispositional account.

17. See the extended criticism by Döring and Eker (*this volume*) in their searching analysis of the evaluative theory of desire. They also criticize the evaluative theory for conflating standing desires with occurrent desires. For a response to this kind of objection see Oddie (2005: 55–57).

18. Stampe (1987) maintains that the assumption that desires are at least *fairly* reliable indicators of goodness is a necessary condition for them to count as perceptions at all.

19. Oddie 2005.

20. Ibid., 55.

21. See Lauria 2014.

22. The idea has a long history: Brentano 1889; Broad 1930; Ewing 1939, 1948, 1959; Chisholm 1986; Lemos 1994; Mulligan 1998; Scanlon 1998; Tappolet 2000; D'Arms and Jacobson 2000; Zimmerman 2001.

23. Broad 1930: 283.

24. If *F(V)* is a class of fitting attitudes, then the schema should be this: *X* is *V* if and only if it is fitting to take any member of *F(V)* to *X*. We could restore the uniqueness of *F(V)* by taking the disjunction of members of *F(V)* to be a single attitude.

25. Tappolet 2011: 119.

26. Ibid.

27. This was precisely why Ewing (1939: 14) endorsed it.

28. Tappolet 2011: 119.

29. See Bykvist and Hattiangadi 2007.

30. See Oddie (2014a) for an extended discussion.

31. Rabinowicz and Rønnow-Rasmussen 2004.

32. Olson 2009; Ewing 1959.

33. Bykvist 2009.

34. See Lauria 2014: 50–54, *this volume*. Döring and Eker (*this volume*) and Massin (*this volume*) make similar claims.

35. Lauria *this volume*.

36. See Heathwood (2007) for a defense of this claim.

37. Basho, in Hass 1994: 11. I am indebted to Bradford Cokelet for alerting me to this wonderful example of the undying nature of real desire.

38. Schroeder 2014.

39. See Gärdenfors 2000.

40. Friedrich 2008, *this volume*; Lauria 2014, *this volume*; Stampe 1987.

41. Some of these are sketched in Oddie (2005, 2010) and further developed in Oddie (2014b, 2016).

## References


Augustine. (1982). 'The Literal Meaning of Genesis', in J. Quasten, W. J. Burghardt, and T. C. Lawler (eds. and trans.), *Ancient Christian Writers*. Vol. 1, book 4. Mahwah, N.J: Paulist Press.

Aquinas, T. (1975). *Summa contra gentiles*, tr. A. C. Pegis et al. South Bend, Ind.: University of Notre Dame Press.

Brentano, F. (1889). *Vom Ursprung sittlicher Erkenntnis*. Leipzig: Duncker & Humblot.

Broad, C. D. (1930). *Five Types of Ethical Theory*. London: Kegan Paul.

Bykvist, K. (2009). 'No Good Fit: Why the Fitting Attitude Analysis of Value Fails', *Mind*, 118, 1–30.

Bykvist, K., and Hattiangadi, A. (2007). 'Does Thought Imply Ought?', *Analysis* 67, 277–285.

Chisholm, R. M. (1986). *Brentano and Intrinsic Value*. Cambridge, UK: Cambridge University Press.

D'Arms, J., and Jacobson, D. (2000). 'Sentiment and Value', *Ethics* 110, 722–748.
Ewing, A. C. (1939). 'A Suggested Non-Naturalistic Analysis of Good', *Mind*, 39, 1–22.
———. (1948). *The Definition of Good*. London: Routledge and Kegan Paul.
———. (1959). *Second Thoughts in Moral Philosophy*. London: Routledge and Kegan Paul.
Friedrich, D. G. (2008). 'An Affective Theory of Desire', PhD dissertation, Australian National University.
Gärdenfors, P. (2000). *Conceptual Spaces*. Cambridge, Mass.: MIT Press.
Hass, R. (1994, (ed. and trans.). *The Essential Haiku: Versions of Basho, Buson and Issa*. New York: Harper Collins.
Heathwood, C. (2007). 'The Reduction of Sensory Pleasure to Desire', *Philosophical Studies*, 133, 23–44.
Lauria, F. (2014). 'The Logic of the Liver: A Deontic View of the Intentionality of Desire', PhD dissertation, University of Geneva.
Lemos, N. M. (1994). *Intrinsic Value: Concept and Warrant*. Cambridge, UK: Cambridge University Press.
Lewis, D. (1979). 'Attitudes *De Dicto* and *De Se*', *Philosophical Review*, 88, 513–543.
———. (1988). 'Desire as Belief', *Mind* 97, 323–332.
———. (1996). 'Desire as Belief II', *Mind* 105, 303–313.
Mulligan, K. (1998). 'From Appropriate Emotions to Values', *Monist*, 81, 161–188.
Oddie, G. (1994). 'Harmony, Purity, Truth', *Mind* 103, 451–472.
———. (2001). 'Hume, the BAD Paradox, and Value Realism', *Philo* 4 (2), 109–122.
———. (2005). *Value, Reality and Desire*. Oxford: Oxford University Press.
———. (2010). 'Experiences of Value', in C. R. Pigden (ed.), *Hume on Motivation and Virtue*. New York: Palgrave Macmillan.
———. (2014a). 'Truthlikeness', in E. N. Zalta (ed.), *The Stanford Encyclopedia of Philosophy* (summer 2014 edition), URL = <http://plato.stanford.edu/archives/sum2014/entries/truthlikeness/>.
———. (2014b). 'Thinking Globally, Acting Locally: Partiality, Preferences and Perspective', *Les Ateliers de l'Éthique/the Ethics Forum*, 9 (2), 57–81.
———. (2016). 'Fitting Attitudes, Finkish Goods, and Value Appearances', in R. Shafer-Landau (ed.), *Oxford Studies in Metaethics*, vol. 11. Oxford: Oxford University Press, 74–101.
———. (forthcoming). 'Value Perception, Properties, and the Primary Bearers of Value', in A. Bergqvist and R. Cowan (eds.), *Evaluative Perception*. Oxford: Oxford University Press.
Olson, J. (2009). 'Fitting Attitude Analyses of Value and the Partiality Challenge', *Ethical Theory and Moral Practice*, 12, 365–378.
Rabinowicz, W., and Rønnow-Rasmussen, T. (2004). 'The Strike of the Demon: On Fitting Pro-Attitudes and Value', *Ethics*, 114 (3), 391–423.
Scanlon, T. M. (1998). *What We Owe to Each Other*. Cambridge, Mass.: Harvard University Press.
Schroeder, T. (2014). 'Desire', in E. N. Zalta (ed.), *The Stanford Encyclopedia of Philosophy* (spring 2014 edition), URL = <http://plato.stanford.edu/archives/spr2014/entries/desire/>.

Stalnaker, R. (1984). *Inquiry*. Cambridge, Mass.: MIT Press.
Stampe, D. W. (1987). 'The Authority of Desire', *Philosophical Review*, 96 (3), 335–381.
Tappolet, C. (2000). *Emotions et Valeurs* Paris: Presses Universitaires de France.
———. (2011). 'Values and Emotions: Neo-Sentimentalism's Prospects', in C. Bagnoli (ed.), *Morality and the Emotions*. Oxford: Oxford University Press.
Tenenbaum, S. (2007). *Appearances of the Good: An Essay on the Nature of Practical Reason*. Cambridge, UK: Cambridge University Press.
Zimmerman, M. (2001). *The Nature of Intrinsic Value*. Lanham, Md.: Rowman & Littlefield.

# CHAPTER 2 | Desire, Mental Force and Desirous Experience

DANIEL FRIEDRICH

## I

Desire, it is often said, is a *pro-attitude*. This is sometimes understood in the sense that desiring p disposes us to act in ways designed to realize p. On another understanding desire is a pro-attitude in the sense that desiring p entails a positive evaluation of p. Some theorists of desire have focused exclusively on the first reading, apparently assuming that the evaluative dimension reduces to the causal-functional one or that it can be dispensed with.[1] This is a mistake. As has been forcefully argued by Warren Quinn, the mere fact of being drawn in one practical direction rather than another is not sufficient to yield evaluation; an agent can be drawn to turn off radios, to swear, or to find her left hand undoes the work of her right hand without seeing any good whatsoever in turning off radios, swearing, or the work of her left hand.[2] Hence the futility of trying to reduce the evaluative dimension of desire to desire's propensity to move us toward action. Nor can the evaluative dimension be dispensed with, as it explains a crucial platitude about desire's role in rationality, namely, that desiring p and believing X-ing to promote that p makes it at least minimally rational for one to X.[3] If desiring p entails a positive evaluation of p, we can explain why desiring p and believing X-ing to promote p does make it at least minimally rational to X, since it shows that as a result of desiring p and believing X-ing to promote p, there was at least something to be said for X-ing from the agent's point of view. Yet if we dispense with the evaluative dimension, we will be at a loss to explain why it is always minimally rational to act in pursuit of one's desired ends.[4]

A common strategy to explain the evaluative dimension of desire has been in terms of evaluative belief. On this view, desiring p entails a positive evaluation of p because desiring p entails believing p to be good.[5] This view faces a number of counterexamples, e.g. Nina the nihilist and Pablo the pervert. Nina is convinced nothing has any value whatsoever, but she desires to have some fries. Pablo has pedophile desires but also believes that there is nothing good whatsoever about realizing his pedophile desires; he believes acting out his desires would be a moral abomination, would be prudentially unwise (as he would rot in hell), and wouldn't even give him any momentary pleasure (as he would instantly be struck by fear and shame).[6]

Perhaps more telling, there are also a number of theoretical problems with the attempt to account for the pro-attitudinal character of desire in terms of evaluative belief. I will briefly highlight two. First, evaluative belief seems to presuppose a higher degree of cognitive sophistication than desires. We think that dogs, cats, and young children lack the cognitive sophistication required for evaluative belief. Even so, it seems that dogs, cats, and young children can have certain desires, such as a desire to be fed, to be comforted, or to have a glitzy toy.[7]

One may, of course, insist that animals and young children can hold evaluative beliefs. This does come at a high cost, though. After all, believing something to be good involves deploying evaluative concepts. It is not just a matter of wanting or liking it. It involves thinking that there are reasons for people to desire or like it. Yet it seems really quite implausible to suppose that animals or toddlers think about their world in these terms.[8] The response that animals and young children aren't capable of desires, on the other hand, seems plainly *ad hoc* and contrary to everyday experience. At the very least, the proponent of the evaluative belief account owes us a good reason for thinking that the natural ascription of certain kinds of desires to animals and young children should be confused.

Second, beliefs are subject to the norm of truth. They represent things as being a certain way and as such are subject to an assessment in terms of whether things really are the way they are represented to be. If belief represents things as being other than they actually are, belief manifests some kind of failing. This does not mean that one always ought to rid oneself of those beliefs, but it does mean that the belief manifests a failing and falls short of an inbuilt ideal. If you imagine there is an elephant in the room, you do not fall short of any inbuilt standard if there isn't. But if you believe that there is an elephant in the room, your belief falls short of an inbuilt ideal if the closest elephant is in the zoo three miles away.

Now take any evaluatively *neutral* state of affairs—e.g. that there is an elephant in the room or that there are flowers on one's grave. Believing these evaluatively neutral states of affairs to be good is falling short of an inbuilt standard. If believing the desired object to be good were part of desire, then in desiring these things one would also have to fall short of an inbuilt standard. Yet desiring these states to obtain does not exemplify any shortcoming whatsoever. Desires directed at the evaluatively neutral do not fall short of any inbuilt standard and are as correct and wholesome as any other desire fairly and squarely directed at the most valuable state of affairs.[9]

Here is another way to make this point. You can put epistemic pressure on someone who believes that having flowers on one's grave is desirable, but you cannot put the same epistemic pressure on someone who desires to have flowers on her grave. Someone who has this desire can shrug her shoulders and simply retort, "Sure, but this is what I want." There is an important analogy with liking here (to which I shall return). One can like something without thereby believing that it is valuable. And one can desire those things one likes (e.g. flowers on one's grave) without thereby believing that this would be valuable.[10]

In light of counterexamples à la Pablo the pervert or the objection from (a lack of) cognitive sophistication, a number of philosophers have tried saving the spirit of the view that desiring p entails believing p to be good by claiming instead that desiring p entails a *perception* of p as being good.[11] This view, however, is also subject to the present objection. Perceptions, like beliefs, purport to represent things the way they really are. In virtue of this they too are subject to an assessment in terms of whether things really are the way these states represent them to be. If you perceive there to be an elephant in the room, then this perception falls short of an inbuilt standard if there is no elephant in the room; you have a hallucination or are experiencing an illusion. If you perceive there being flowers on your grave as good, then this perception manifests some kind of failing, but the corresponding desire does not.

## II

Let us call a state that represents things as purported facts a cognitive state. Beliefs and perceptions are cognitive states by this definition; imaginations, for example, are not. We can give a simple and straightforward account of evaluation in terms of cognitive states: to evaluate something is to represent it as a purported fact that it has an evaluative property. Put differently, on this account, evaluation is a matter of a cognitive state with an evaluative content.

Is all evaluation cognitive in this sense? If so, we cannot both accept the conclusion of the previous section and continue to hold that desiring p and believing X-ing to promote p makes it minimally rational to X. For some, this is incentive enough to insist that there must be a way to save an account of desire as a pro-attitude in terms of evaluative belief, perception, or some other cognitive state no matter what. Here I shall consider instead whether there is an alternative to cognitive evaluation.

Non-cognitivists usually help themselves to the notion of evaluation, but they have arguably not provided an intelligible model of non-cognitive evaluation. According to one popular account, for example, cognitive states give us a map of the world, whereas non-cognitive states provide us with motivation; cognitive states lay out the territory, non-cognitive states push us across it. However, as pointed out earlier, being disposed to move in certain practical directions is one thing, evaluation another. An alternative account of non-cognitive evaluation is needed, and I believe the roots to such an account lie in a distinction (originally due to Brentano) between mental content and mental force.[12] In the following, I will try to explain this distinction and how it affords a framework for non-cognitive evaluation.

Some, perhaps all mental states are about things. For example, thinking that Shakespeare wrote *Hamlet* is about Shakespeare writing *Hamlet*. What a mental state is about constitutes one dimension of its content. The other dimension concerns its mode of presentation. Thus, there is one sense in which thinking that Shakespeare wrote *Hamlet* differs in content from thinking that the Bard wrote *Hamlet*, but not because these thoughts are about different things but rather because they involve different modes of presentation. These two dimensions—aboutness and modes of presentation—exhaust mental content.

The cognitivist models evaluation in terms of evaluative content. An evaluative mental state is a state with an evaluative content. It is a state that is about the world being a certain, evaluatively shaped way. Indeed, how else could a state evaluate an object if not by having an evaluative content? This reasoning betrays the assumption that a mental state's overall representational character is wholly fixed by its content; that is, it betrays the assumption that the way something is given in thought is entirely fixed by content. In contrast, I think the overall representational character of a mental state also involves the phenomenon of mental force. To explain what

I mean by mental force, it will be helpful to consider an analogy from the philosophy of language. Sentences that have the same extension and the same intension can nonetheless differ in a significant way if they have been put forward with different force (Dummett 1993). Contrast the assertion "Sam smokes habitually" with the command "Sam, smoke habitually." The two sentences have the same extension and the same intension—they refer to the same person, predicate the same property, and do so under the same mode of presentation. Nonetheless, different things are being conveyed by the two sentences. If you knew only the content of a sentence but did not know with what force it had been put forward, you would be missing an essential element. Something very similar occurs in the case of mental states. Contrast, for example, believing that Shakespeare wrote *Hamlet* with entertaining that proposition in thought. While the two mental states have the same content, believing that Shakespeare wrote *Hamlet* involves representing that content with a certain force, namely as a purported fact.

There is a difference in the way the proposition that Shakespeare wrote *Hamlet* is given in thought depending upon whether this proposition is believed or merely entertained. This difference, however, is not a difference in *content* but a difference in *force*. This shows that explaining evaluation in terms of evaluative content is not the only option. There is also the distinct theoretical possibility of accounting for evaluation in terms of *evaluative mental force*. Thus, the non-cognitivist can say that just as there is a distinctively cognitive manner in which content can be given in thought (a cognitive mental force), there also is a distinctively evaluative manner in which content is given in thought (an evaluative mental force). Just as there is a way in which a content is presented to the subject as a purported fact, so there also is a way in which a content is presented to the subject in a positive or negative light.

## III

A common response at this point is to object that speaking of mental force is just an unusual way of speaking of propositional attitudes, that propositional attitudes can be reduced to causal-functional profiles, and that, therefore, the current proposal hasn't effectively advanced over the initial (and inadequate) attempt to cash out non-cognitive evaluation in terms of dispositions to act.

Given the distinction between mental content and mental force, two ways of accounting for evaluation exist in logical space: one in terms of cognitive force + evaluative content and the other in terms of evaluative force. Yet this theoretical richness would be a mere chimera if mental force really reduces to causal-functional profiles, since evaluation cannot be explicated in terms of the latter. Hence we would be back where we started. Cognitive evaluation would remain the only game in town. However, the objection is too quick to assume that speaking of mental force must be shorthand for causal-functional profiles. An alternative is to account for mental force in terms of phenomenal character. I will introduce this alternative in the context of hedonic experiences in this section. In the next section, I will extend the argument of this section to the case of desire.

Consider the case of liking, enjoying, or taking pleasure in something. These states are paradigmatic pro-attitudes; they necessarily involve a certain kind of positive evaluation of their object. To enjoy the scent of a blooming flower or to take pleasure in the taste of chocolate necessarily involves some kind of positive evaluation of the sensations involved. As in the case of desire—and for similar reasons[13]—this positive evaluation is ill-captured in terms of cognitive evaluation. Consider, instead, that their evaluative dimension is a function of them involving a distinctive evaluative mental force, that to take pleasure in something involves a distinctive evaluative manner in which the object of one's pleasure is given to the mind. But to be in these hedonic states is also to be in a distinctive phenomenal state; there is a distinctive character to what it is like to be in those states. Moreover, it is very natural to think that the positive evaluation involved in hedonic states is ineliminably tied to the distinctive phenomenal character of that hedonic state; that the pro-ness of hedonic states is ineliminably tied to the way one feels about the objects of hedonic states when one is in these states.

Admittedly this contradicts much theorizing about the nature of hedonic experience. Many philosophers think there is something quite flawed in the attempt to understand hedonic states as feelings, preferring instead a desire-based analysis or an account that treats them as *sui generis* attitudes. It is instructive to consider why these philosophers think that "pleasure is not a feeling" (Feldman 1997: 463). Their standard argument begins by highlighting that the phenomenal character of pleasure differs in kind from the phenomenal character of sensuous qualities of experience, such as the phenomenal character of seeing red, tasting something sweet, or feeling a sharp pain. Whereas we can strip away those sensuous qualities from the overall experience, the same does not apply to pleasure, as

Sidgwick famously pointed out. That is to say, whereas we can look at a car and notice the same reddish quality that was present in our experience of a tomato at the supermarket, we can't in the same way detect a pleasure quality shared between our joy of driving the car and eating the tomato. And on this basis it is concluded that hedonic experience has no distinctive phenomenal character.[14] But this doesn't follow. What follows is just that if there is a distinctive phenomenal character to hedonic experience, it can't be a sensuous quality but must be, as we might put it, a *feeling tone*—"a mode of consciousness distinct in nature and conditions from all sensations" (McDougall 1911: 312); in other words, it would have to be the kind of phenomenal character apt to characterize evaluative mental force rather than a property of the represented content.[15]

There are good reasons to think that hedonic experience involves a distinctive feeling tone.[16] First, there is clearly a world of a difference between what it is like to enjoy something and what it is like to find displeasure in it. These experiences differ in their phenomenal character. This raises a problem for those who want to deny that hedonic experience is marked by a distinctive feeling tone. How do they purport to explain this platitude? They must argue that the difference between taking pleasure and displeasure in something lies in a difference in what one takes pleasure and displeasure in. Yet this has the queer consequence that it is impossible that one and the same thing may be the object of pleasure and displeasure, or, to put it differently, that pleasant or unpleasant objects are necessarily pleasant or unpleasant.

Second, a pleasant experience is an intrinsically good experience,[17] and it is so in virtue of its pleasantness. An unpleasant experience is an intrinsically bad experience, and it is so in virtue of its unpleasantness. Indeed, this is why hedonic experiences have ethical significance. To account for hedonic experiences being good or bad in virtue of their pleasantness or unpleasantness we must talk about the way those experiences feel: pleasant experiences are good because they feel good, and unpleasant experiences bad because they feel bad. We shall be at a loss to make sense of this if we deny that hedonic experience has a distinctive phenomenal character.[18]

Third, the popular alternatives to feeling-based analyses of pleasure are untenable. Consider desire-based accounts, such as the theory that an experience is pleasant in virtue of a desire for it to continue and the theory that a pleasant experience is the upshot of satisfied desire.[19] There are counterexamples to both claims. Against the first claim, we can point out that there can be too much of a good thing. "There are," as Kenny (1963: 135) reminds us

> so many cases where the prolongation or repetition of what was enjoyed would ruin the enjoyment. The sweetest last to make the end most sweet might not be sweet were it not also last. Enjoying a play does not mean wishing that it had six acts instead of five, and one can enjoy the first movement of a symphony without being distressed that it is followed by the second.

With respect to the second proposal, on the other hand, we can ask what of those cases in which we "run into" a pleasure we did not know to exist before we found it. Children, for instance, discover all sorts of pleasures that they then hold onto or seek again. Surely the pleasure could not have been caused by the success of the very desire that the pleasure itself had initiated (Duncker 1941: 394). This points to a more general problem, namely, that pleasure is *simpler* than desire insofar as desire has certain logical presuppositions that pleasure lacks. Desire, for example, requires the capacity to conceive of a gap between the way the world is and how it could be.[20] Pleasure does not. Consider a simple organism that lacked the capacity to represent past, future, or merely possible states and whose conception of things was strictly limited to its present perceptual input. It would seem possible for this organism to take pleasure in its perceptual states, but it could not possibly desire anything. Since pleasure has fewer logical presuppositions than desire, the attempt to analyze the former in terms of the latter must fail.

The alternative theory that is prominent among those who deny the phenomenal nature of hedonic phenomena is that pleasure is constituted by a *sui generis* attitude of liking.[21] There is, I think, nothing wrong with this as long as one also maintains that our grasp of this attitude is anchored in distinctive phenomenal episodes. But since this is being denied, proponents of this approach must, it seems, have either of two things in mind. They must either think that our conception of pleasure is ultimately grounded in its being a state with a certain causal-functional profile or that there is simply nothing whatsoever that gives substance to our conception of pleasure—neither its phenomenal nature, nor its relation to desire, nor its causal-functional properties. The latter option makes pleasure objectionably mysterious. The former option seems scarcely more credible. What exactly is this functional-causal property supposed to be? It can't be the causal power to give rise to a desire for the experience to continue, but this would have seemed to be the most plausible candidate. At the very least, therefore, someone favoring this option faces the serious challenge of specifying the functional causal property that supposedly determines the nature of pleasure and hedonic states more generally.

So while it is true that the phenomenal character of hedonic experience differs from the phenomenal character of sensuous qualities of experience, we shouldn't conclude that the pleasantness of an experience doesn't add anything to the phenomenal character of the experience. Intuitively it clearly does. As such it lends credence to the idea that the evaluative dimension of hedonic states can be accounted for in terms of their distinctive evaluative force, where this notion of evaluative force is ineliminably tied to a distinctive phenomenal character that is part of hedonic experience.

## IV

In the previous two sections, my general aim has been to explicate an intelligible model of non-cognitive evaluation. Non-cognitive evaluation, I have argued, should be understood in terms of evaluative mental force. The notion of evaluative mental force is in turn tied to the distinctive feeling tone of certain experiences. In this section, my aim is to relate these ideas to desire.

An extension of these ideas to desires requires that there is a feeling tone distinctive of desire. Yet the dominant view in modern analytic philosophy is that although desire can be caused by phenomenal states (e.g. pangs of hunger) and can cause phenomenal states (e.g. suffering if the fulfillment of the desire is continually thwarted), there is nothing that can reasonably be labeled the phenomenology of desire itself; there are conscious states contingently associated with desire, but there is no genuinely desirous consciousness, no way for desire (or a constitutive part of desire) itself to be part of our conscious experience.[22]

I think this influential position gains much of its attraction from two assumptions. First, it is observed that there can be standing desires, that desiring something does not imply being in an experiential state. And from this it is inferred that there is no phenomenology of desire. This, however, falsely assumes that only essentially conscious states can be characterized by a distinctive phenomenology. Loving someone, for example, does not imply being in an experiential state. Yet there clearly is something like a phenomenology of love; there are conscious episodes in which love manifests itself in consciousness.[23]

Second, it is observed that there is no bodily sensation essential to desire and apt to constitute the phenomenology of desire. From this it is concluded that there is no phenomenology of desire. However, why should we grant the implicit assumption that the phenomenology of desire would have to consist of a bodily sensation? After all, the phenomenal character of experience does not in general reduce to bodily sensation nor, I have argued, to mental content alone. So we should remain open to the possibility that there is a phenomenology of desire that is tied to its mental force.

Modern analytic philosophy aside, thinking of a desire as involving a distinctive phenomenal character has been popular. Attempts to explicate the distinctive phenomenal character of desire in terms of hedonic experiences have been particularly prominent.[24] These attempts have come in two broad flavors: as pleasure-based theories of desirous experience and as displeasure-based accounts of desirous experience. Pleasure-based accounts hold that taking pleasure in the thought that p is sufficient for desirous experience, whereas displeasure-based accounts hold that taking displeasure in the thought that not-p is sufficient for the conscious manifestation of a desire for that p.

Neither provides a satisfactory account of the phenomenology of desirous experience. As noted earlier, taking pleasure in something does not entail a desire for the experience to continue. Similarly, taking pleasure in the thought of p does not entail a desire for p to occur. As Mark Johnston (2001: 225) observes,

> Suppose that I feel pleased at the thought of my working in the local soup kitchen. Even so, I need not find my working in the soup kitchen appealing. I might only find the thought of it appealing. I could be a self-indulgent dreamer, one who particularly enjoys the costless contemplation of himself in a good moral light. I might be pleased at the thought of my working in the soup kitchen while knowing that I would not find my working there appealing.[25]

*Mutatis mutandis* for having a *desire* to work in the soup kitchen. Consider another case. Suppose I am reading a work of fiction and take pleasure in the description of a particular scene. Does this mean that I must have some desire for this scene to exist in actuality? Surely not. These two examples point to a more general problem with the claim that pleasure in the thought of p suffices for desirous experience: If you desire something, you want it to be the case. You do not just entertain it, but you entertain it in a way that includes a kind of demand that it should come to obtain. Not so in the case of pleasant thoughts. Our pleasant thoughts can exemplify a contentment with the way things are, that wanting something to be the case must necessarily lack.

Displeasure-based accounts do not fare better. Just as being pleased by the thought of p does not entail a desire for p to obtain because being pleased by p can lack any direction beyond itself, so too being displeased by the thought of not-p does not entail a desire for p to obtain because being displeased by the thought of not-p can also lack all engagement with anything beyond itself. To illustrate, consider the case of severely depressed people. It is part of their condition that they find most things unpleasant. At the same time, severely depressed people can lack any desire for things to change. They are so focused on their misery, so engulfed in their displeasure, that they don't conceive of, let alone desire, any alternative.[26]

What emerges from this discussion is that desirous experience involves a certain dynamic dimension inasmuch as in desirous experience one entertains the desired end in a way that includes a kind of demand for it to become reality. In desiring something one does more than *conceive* of something that is not, but could be, the case. One also conceives of it as *having to become the case*. Consider this passage by John Locke (1975: bk. 2, ch. 21, §32):

> Who is there that has not felt in desire . . . that it being "deferred makes the heart sick"; and that still proportionable to the greatness of the desire, which sometimes raises the uneasiness to that pitch, that it makes people cry out, "Give me children." Give me the thing desired, "or I die." Life itself, and all its enjoyments, is a burden that can't be borne under the lasting and unremoved pressure of such an uneasiness.

Locke himself took this to be reason to conclude that desire is "nothing but an uneasiness in the want of an absent good" (§31). However, this evocative passage also serves well to bring an alternative explication of desirous experience into focus. For we can note that in Rachel's cry "Give me children or else I die," she does not just express her frustration with a world that continually stymies the satisfaction of her innermost desire. She also gives expression to her *felt need* for the world to be a certain way. She *feels* that she *must* have children. This aspect is missing from hedonic theories of desire. Pleasure and displeasure are evaluative states, but they do not essentially involve the felt need for something to be a certain way. Desirous experience is different. In desirous experience, the desired end is given to the mind under a feeling tone of felt need; it is given to the mind as something that must be realized.

Let me try to clarify the idea of a felt need. (i) We are creatures with biological needs, and our desires are often linked with our biological needs. In fact, it is presumably because of this link with biological needs that we evolved to have desires in the first place. But despite the important connection between felt needs and biological needs, a felt need is not a biological need. A felt need is an experience; a biological need is not. Moreover, to have a biological need for x implies that the organism will be seriously harmed unless x is secured in a timely fashion. Having a felt need does not imply any such thing. (ii) Felt needs can differ in intensity. Often the most natural expression of a felt need will be "This must become reality," but at other times this exclamation will have too much of a sense of urgency to capture the phenomenal character of the experience, in which case the experience may be better expressed by saying "Would only that this state become reality." (iii) Felt needs often can be given linguistic expression. For example, "This must become reality" is a natural linguistic expression of paradigmatic felt needs. However, felt needs are not linguistic phenomena, and every linguistic expression will at times be somewhat inadequate. (iv) A felt need is not a prediction of some kind. To give expression to a felt need by saying "This must become reality" is not to imply that being in that state involves some conviction that the phenomenally needed thing will become reality. We come closer to the truth if we say it involves regarding the needed thing as something that must come about in the sense that it *ought* to come about. But while there is certainly some kind of affinity between felt needs and normative claims, it would also be a mistake to think that feeling that something must become reality implies believing that it ought to obtain.[27]

I have argued that there are experiences in which the desire for an end can manifest itself in consciousness. These experiences involve a distinctive mental force that is anchored in a distinctive phenomenology that can be articulated in terms of the notion of a felt need inasmuch as in these experiences the desired end is given to the mind as something that has to become reality. I finally wish to argue that desirous experience is essential to desire. I can think of at least three plausibly weak specifications of this claim: (i) desiring p entails that the subject from time to time has a desirous experience of p; (ii) desiring p entails being disposed to be in a state of desirous consciousness of p given appropriate triggering conditions; or (iii) desiring p entails that the desire could *in principle* become an occurrent one and that it would then manifest itself in a desirous experience of

p. I am sympathetic to the first, but for my current purposes I will stay neutral toward these three specifications. Any given specification of the idea that desirous experience is essential to desire suffices for my current purpose. Why, though, think that desirous experience should be essential to desire at all? Or, as Braddon-Mitchell and Jackson (1996: 139) put it, "What can be so important about the capacity to become occurrent?" The answer is that desirous experience anchors the notion of a distinctive mental force involved in desire. It is thus central to a non-cognitive explanation of the pro-attitudinal character of desire and its role in practical rationality. It is in virtue of the desired end being given to the mind as something that has to become reality that acting in ways one believes to promote the desired end is minimally rational.[28] This non-cognitive account avoids the objections against the cognitive evaluation accounts surveyed in the first section. For example, it is entirely consistent with p being presented to the mind as something that has to become reality that one lacks the belief that p is good. Indeed, since p being presented to the mind as something that has to become reality is a matter of p being presented under a distinctive evaluative mental force, it is also consistent with the desiring agent lacking the cognitive sophistication required for evaluative belief. Moreover, because the analysis avoids reference to representations of purported fact, it avoids making desire subject to the norm of truth. In short, if desirous experience is essential to desire there is a credible explanation of the role of desire in rationality. We can explain why desiring p makes the pursuit of p minimally rational without having to appeal to an unsatisfactory cognitive analysis. This explanatory virtue is the best reason for thinking that desire stands in an essential relation to desirous experience.

## V

According to a deep-seated intuition, there is something special about desire's motivational power, and it may be thought the current position cannot do justice to this intuition. For example, consider the thesis that all action can be explained in terms of desire. This, it might be said, is a problem for the current position because not all states explaining action stand in an essential relation to episodes of desirous consciousness.

There are two possible responses to this objection. The first response charges that the objection involves an equivocation. There are, the response runs, a generic and a specific sense of desire. According to the generic sense of desire, any mental state that motivates intentional action counts as a desire. To say “He X-ed because he wanted to X” is only an alternative way of saying “He X-ed intentionally.” Desire in this generic sense needs to be distinguished from desire proper, that is, desire as a mental state distinct from other kinds of mental states such as belief. The objection runs these two senses together because while all action can be explained in terms of desire in the generic sense, not all action can be explained by desire proper.[29]

Not everyone is convinced by this line of thinking, pointing to a range of arguments designed to show that desire (proper) is the only spring of motivation. Here the second response comes into play, which is that the seeming implausibility of all states explaining action standing in an essential relation to episodes of desirous consciousness is itself an artifact of considering an overly strong relationship between desire and desirous consciousness. Is it really so implausible, for example, to maintain that all states that play the requisite role in action explanation also dispose the agent to experience an episode of desirous consciousness or that they could all at least in principle manifest themselves in an episode of desirous consciousness? In fact, the current account seems congenial to staunch Humean thinking that only desire can motivate action (Hume 2003). If one thinks that cognitive states cannot in principle motivate action, then one cannot endorse a cognitive account of the pro-attitudinal character of desire.[30] But I have argued the best non-cognitive account of the pro-attitudinal character of desire will make desirous experiences essential to desire.

So rather than being a problem for the current account, that only desire motivates action would actually further strengthen the present view because it would provide a strong additional reason for endorsing a non-cognitive account of the pro-attitudinal character of desire. But the current account also sits well with weaker explications of the intuition that there is something special about desire’s motivational powers. Even if one merely wants to retain the claim that only desire necessarily motivates or that motivation by desire is distinct from motivation by other states, one needs a non-cognitive account of desire to retain a clear-cut contrast to motivation by cognitive states. By highlighting the difference between cognitive and non-cognitive evaluation, the current account provides the resources to account for motivational differences between motivation by desire and motivation by cognitive states—differences that can be traced to the differing properties of cognitive and non-cognitive evaluation. In contrast, if one embraces a cognitive account of the pro-attitudinal character of desire, it is far from obvious how one can do justice to the intuition that there is something special about the role of desire in the motivation of action.

I have argued that acting in ways believed to promote the desired end is always at least minimally rational and that in order to vindicate this role of desire in practical rationality we need to offer an account of desire that explains the pro-ness with which the desired end is apprehended in desire. Attempts to do so in terms of evaluative cognition, I argued, are unsatisfactory. Instead I have explored the possibility of developing a thoroughly non-cognitive account of the pro-ness of desire by drawing upon the notion of a distinctive mental force and distinctive episodes of desirous consciousness, specifically episodes of felt need. *En passant*, I have tried to show that many objections to giving desirous consciousness a central role in a theory of desire—e.g. the possibility of standing desires, that there is no genuine phenomenology to desire, that there is no theoretic role for desirous consciousness to play, that all action is motivated by desire—are overblown. Finally, I have suggested that a surprising auxiliary benefit of the account championed in this paper may be that it allows for a better understanding of what underlies desire's special motivational power.

## Notes

1. Cf. Armstrong 1968; Smith 1994; Stalnaker 1987.

2. Quinn 1993. See also Dancy 2000; Scanlon 1998; Raz 2001. Though see Döring and Eker (*this volume*) for a dissenting view.

3. No claim is being made about what an agent has *reason* to do or about what would be more than minimally rational for the agent to do.

4. In particular we will be at a loss to explain this if we assume that desiring p involves nothing but a disposition to act in ways designed to realize p. For why should the *mere fact* that one was disposed to move in a certain direction make it at all rational to do so?

5. E.g. Anscombe 1976; Dancy 2000; Quinn 1993; Raz 2001. See also Oddie, Döring and Eker (*this volume*) for critical discussions of this view. See Gregory (*this volume*) for a defense of the related position that for an agent to desire p is for the agent to believe that she has a normative reason to promote p.

6. Those who are convinced that desires entail evaluative beliefs are unlikely to be swayed by such examples. They will insist that people who deny that there is anything good about p and who assert that p is not good in any way still also believe that p is good if they desire that p; that someone desires p is all the evidence one needs to know that she also believes that p is good. That a theory commits one to ascribing beliefs to agents that they explicitly disavow, however, is a cost we should strive to avoid. All other things being equal, if an alternative theory could explain the evaluative dimension of desire without incurring such costs, then we should prefer this alternative theory.

7. See also Döring and Eker *this volume*. Though see Gregory (*this volume*) for a dissenting view.

8. Notice too that it is not enough to argue that animals or toddlers can believe that securing the object of their desire will be pleasant. I can believe that something is pleasant without thereby believing that there are reasons for people to desire or promote it. To believe that there are reasons for people to desire something, for example, requires some kind of understanding of other people as agents that can be swayed by reasons as well as some ability to be guided by reasons oneself. Neither this understanding nor this ability seems to be present in, say, infants. (I thus disagree with Gregory's deflationary claim that "seeing an action as being called for in some respect"—something I would agree is part of desiring and will try to elucidate in section IV—is the same as believing that there is a reason to perform the action (Gregory *this volume*). Nonetheless, as any parent can attest, infants can surely still desire things.

9. This is not to deny that desire is subject to various norms—e.g. moral and prudential norms. It is only to point out that it is not subject to the norm of truth, that there are, as one may also put it, strictly speaking no correctness conditions for desire.

10. It might be said that desiring the evaluatively neutral does not fall short of an inbuilt standard because desires invest their objects with significance for the good of the agent. In virtue of desire the (hitherto evaluatively neutral) desired state acquires value for the agent; the agent will be better off if the desired state comes to obtain. I want to stay clear of the question if desire can invest its objects with significance for the good of the agent and only point out that it is implausible to suppose that desire satisfaction always makes an agent better off. For example, it seems implausible to suggest that there being flowers on one's grave makes one better off. (But doesn't even this kind of desire lend some comfort to the agent and is thus at least to some extent good for the agent? Perhaps, but in order to avoid the objection it needs to be shown that the desired end is good, not that having the desire is good.). Yet even in these cases, in having these desires one is not falling short of an inbuilt standard. (Note too that this argument does not rely on the view that an agent's life cannot be made better or worse after her death. It may even be that the satisfaction of desires that are suitably central to an agent's life can affect an agent's welfare after her death. The argument here only needs to highlight that it is implausible to think that the satisfaction of every desire—no matter its content or time of satisfaction—adds to an agent's welfare).

11. E.g. Stampe 1986; Oddie 2005, *this volume*. See also Döring and Eker, Lauria, Gregory (*this volume*) for further discussions of this view.

12. Cf. Brentano 1902, 1911. While Brentano's thesis that intentionality is the mark of the mental has generated wide interest, his discussion of the present distinction has been mostly ignored in the contemporary literature (though see e.g. Lauria *this volume* for a related proposal. See also Deonna and Teroni 2012, whose interesting account of the nature of mental attitudes, though different in detail from the one presented here, can also be seen to be inspired by Brentano's distinction between mental content and mental force).

13. We can enjoy things even if we believe that nothing has value. We can also enjoy things that we believe are bad. Indeed, we can even believe that the pleasure we derive from enjoying these things is itself bad. What is more, even cognitively quite simple animals seem capable of pleasure. At the same time, these animals seem to lack the requisite degree of cognitive sophistication to be able to hold evaluative beliefs. While an account in terms of evaluative perceptions would avoid these objections, it would still entail that

liking or taking pleasure in something is subject to the norm of truth. This is quite implausible indeed. One does not fall short of any inbuilt standard if one takes pleasure in something evaluatively neutral (e.g. the wall being red).

14. Sidgwick 1981: 127. See also Alston 1967b; Broad 1962; Feldman 1997; Parfit 1987.

15. See also Broad 1962; Schlick 2002. Moore (1988: 13), another eminent proponent of an account of hedonic phenomena in terms of conscious experience, was less careful, at one point even writing that "it is enough for us to know that 'pleased' does mean 'having the sensation of pleasure.'" Part of the problem may lie in the common but flawed assumption that pleasure and pain are opposites (for critical discussion see McCloskey 1971; Penelhum 1957; Trigg 1970).

16. To be more precise, there are good reasons to think that hedonic experiences involve at least two kinds of distinctive feeling tones: a feeling tone distinctive of positive hedonic experiences and a feeling tone distinctive of negative hedonic experiences. (Some may argue that fine-grained distinctions can and should be made. I remain neutral on this point.)

17. Note that saying that a pleasant experience is intrinsically valuable (valuable in and of itself) is distinct from claiming that it is necessarily valuable (valuable in all possible contexts).

18. It is not good enough to argue that we desire pleasant experiences and that this explains their ethical significance. Pleasant experiences would be of ethical significance even if they would not be desired (e.g. even if the creature lacked the ability to desire. See below for the argument that this is possible). But note too that in any case this option isn't open for most critics of the view that pleasure is a feeling, as they also deny that desire has any ethical significance (e.g. Feldman 1997; Parfit 1997).

19. See Alston (1967a), Armstrong (1968), and Sidgwick (1981) for the first kind of analysis. See Heathwood (2006) and Schroeder (2004) for the second kind of analysis.

20. See also Döring and Eker, Oddie, Massin, Lauria (*this volume*) for discussion of the related claim that one cannot desire that which one believes to be the case.

21. Feldman 1997. See also Broad 1962; Trigg 1970.

22. See e.g. Anscombe 1976; Braddon-Mitchell and Jackson 1996; Dancy 2000; Kenny 1963; McGinn 1997; Ryle 1984; Shoemaker 1980; Smith 1994. See also Döring and Eker *this volume*.

23. Or consider being afraid of death. One can have this fear even when one is asleep and not subject to any conscious episode. Yet from this it does not follow that there is no distinctive phenomenology of fear.

24. To be more precise, analyzing desire in terms of hedonic states has commonly been attempted. Often, but not always, this attempt has been carried out via an explication of desirous experience. For some proponents of hedonic accounts of desire or desirous experience see Duncker 1941; Ehrenfels 1982; Ewing 1944, 1953; Fehige 2001; Hobbes 1994; Locke 1975; Mill 1991; Moore 1988; Schlick 2002; Strawson 1994. For an illuminating historical overview see Fehige 2005.

25. As I have argued, hedonic states are *simpler* than desire inasmuch as desire requires (but hedonic states do not) the capacity to conceive of a gap between the way the world is and how it could be. This also poses a problem for any position that holds that a hedonic state is sufficient for desire or desirous experience.

26. There is also something theoretically odd about the attempt to understand desire in terms of displeasure, because desire is a *pro*-attitude, whereas displeasure is a *con*-attitude. The response that a con-attitude toward a proposition is the same as a pro-attitude toward its negation isn't convincing either. Taking pleasure in something is not the same as taking displeasure in its absence or negation, and these states do not necessitate each other. I can enjoy a movie without finding not watching the movie displeasurable. I can take displeasure in the thought of an accident without taking pleasure in the thought of there being no accident. See also Massin *this volume*.

27. Massin (*this volume*) and Lauria (*this volume*) distinguish between evaluative and deontic theories of desire. Given this distinction, my discussion may seem confused. While I speak of providing an account of the evaluative dimension of desire, I seem to end up with an account that falls into the deontic camp. Now while I do not deny that the realm of values can be distinguished from the realm of reasons, requirements, and norms, and while I also do not deny that there is a difference between evaluative beliefs and normative beliefs, I am not sure that this distinction is fruitfully applied to the case of non-cognitive mental force and desirous experience. Thus, I would say that desirous experience is both *related* to normative claims and to evaluative claims and that it, strictly speaking, does not exactly involve representing the desired object "as that which ought to be" (Lauria, Massin, *this volume*) nor "as good." These are descriptions that are best suited for the rich inferential and fine-grained relations between mental contents, but they are not entirely suitable to exactly capture the nature of non-cognitive mental force and desirous experience. In any case, these are really minor details (and there is thus, for example, a great deal of overlap between the position advocated here and the view defended by Lauria, *this volume*). The main point I am making is that the pro-attitudinal character of desire—that which allows desire's role in rationalization—should be understood in terms of non-cognitive mental force, which in turn should be explicated in terms of a distinctive kind of desirous experience. Whether this pro-attitudinal character should then be understood as purely evaluative or purely deontic or, as I would maintain, as containing elements of both is interesting but of secondary importance.

28. This brings out a stark contrast to the position defended by Döring and Eker *this volume*. Both Döring and Eker and I agree that desires can rationalize action without these desires necessarily involving any conscious episode when the desire motivates action. However, whereas Döring and Eker infer that no conscious episode can be essential to the rationalizing the power of desire, the present argument holds that (non-conscious) desires can rationalize action only because they are linked in the right way to episodes of desirous consciousness; their rationalizing unfolds against the background idea of the agent being in a state that relates the agent in the appropriate way to seeing the desired state in a certain light. (Döring and Eker also argue that because an agent need not endorse any desirous experience of an object, no such experience can rationalize an action. However, this objection seems to conflate minimal rationalization with some more demanding notion of rationalization). See also Lauria (*this volume*) for a closely related view about desires.

29. Cf. Nagel 1978; Schueler 1995.

30. This assumes that the motivational power of desire is mediated by its evaluative dimension, that is, that desire disposes an agent to act in ways believed to promote the desired end because of the positive light in which the desired end is presented to the

agent. This view has a number of benefits: it fits well with the intuition that we try to get what we desire because of the way the object of our desire is presented to us; it can vindicate the intuition that in acting on the basis of desire, agents can be guided by and display minimal rationality; it makes sense of the idea that the more alluring the desired end appears to the agent, the greater desire's motivational impact; and so forth. In addition, Humeans have another strong reason for thinking that the motivational power of desire is mediated by its evaluative dimension. For suppose instead that desire's motivational power were independent of its evaluative dimension. Then we might ask: Why should it not be possible for a cognitive state to have this motivational power as well?

## References


Alston, W. (1967a). 'Emotion and Feeling', in P. Edwards (ed.), *The Encyclopedia of Philosophy*. New York: Macmillan, Free Press.

———. (1967b). 'Pleasure', in P. Edwards (ed.), *The Encyclopedia of Philosophy*. New York: Macmillan, Free Press.

Anscombe, G. E. M. (1976). *Intention*. Ithaca, N.Y.: Cornell University Press.

Armstrong, D. M. (1968). *A Materialist Theory of the Mind*. London: Routledge & Kegan Paul.

Braddon-Mitchell, D., and Jackson, F. (1996). *Philosophy of Mind and Cognition*. Oxford: Blackwell.

Brentano, F. (1902). *The Origin of the Knowledge of Right and Wrong*. Westminster, UK: Archibald Constable.

———. (1911). *Von der Klassifikation der psychischen Phänomene*. Leipzig: Von Duncker & Humblot.

Broad, C. D. (1962). *Five Types of Ethical Theory*. London: Routledge & Kegan Paul.

Dancy, J. (2000). *Practical Reality*. Oxford: Oxford University Press.

Deonna, J., and Teroni, F. (2012). *The Emotions: A Philosophical Introduction*. London: Routledge.

Dummett, M. (1993). *Frege: Philosophy of Language*. Cambridge, Mass.: Harvard University Press.

Duncker, K. (1941). 'On Pleasure, Emotion, and Striving', *Philosophy and Phenomenological Research*, 1 (4), 391–430.

Ewing, A. C. (1944). 'Subjectivism and Naturalism', *Mind*, 53 (210), 120–141.

———. (1953). *Ethics*. New York: Macmillan.

Fehige, C. (2001). 'Instrumentalism', in E. Millgram (ed.), *Varieties of Practical Reasoning*. Cambridge, Mass.: MIT Press.

———. (2004). 'Wunsch', in J. Ritter, K. Gründer, and G. Gabriel (eds.), *Historisches Wörterbuch der Philosophie*, vol. 12. Basel: Schwabe.

Feldman, F. (1997). 'On the Intrinsic Value of Pleasures', *Ethics*, 107 (3), 1077–1085.

Heathwood, C. (2006). 'Desire Satisfactionism and Hedonism', *Philosophical Studies*, 128 (3), 539–563.

Hobbes, T. (1994). *Leviathan*. Indianapolis: Hackett.

Hume, D. (2003). *A Treatise of Human Nature*, ed. D. F. Norton and M. J. Norton. Oxford: Oxford University Press.

Johnston, M. (2001). 'Is Affect Always Mere Effect?', *Philosophy and Phenomenological Research*, 63 (1), 225–228.
Kenny, A. (1963). *Action, Emotion, and Will*. New York: Routledge and Kegan Paul.
Locke, J. (1975). *An Essay Concerning Human Understanding*, ed. P. H. Nidditch. Oxford: Oxford University Press.
McCloskey, M. A. (1971). 'Pleasure', *Mind*, 80, 542–551.
McDougall, W. (1911). *Body and Mind: A History and Defence of Animism*. London: Methuen.
McGinn, C. (1997). *The Character of Mind*. Oxford: Oxford University Press.
Mill, J. S. (1991). 'Utilitarianism', in *On Liberty and Other Essays*, ed. J. Gray. Oxford: Oxford University Press.
Moore, G. E. (1988). *Principia Ethica*. New York: Prometheus Books.
Nagel, T. (1978). *The Possibility of Altruism*. Princeton, N.J.: Princeton University Press.
Oddie, G. (2005). *Value, Reality, and Desire*. Oxford: Clarendon Press.
Parfit, D. (1987). *Reasons and Persons*. Oxford: Clarendon Press.
———. (1997). 'Reason and Motivation', *Proceedings of the Aristotelian Society Supplementary Volume*, 71, 99–130.
Penelhum, T. (1957). 'The Logic of Pleasure', *Philosophy and Phenomenological Research*, 17 (4), 488–503.
Quinn, W. (1993). *Putting Rationality in Its Place*. Cambridge, UK: Cambridge University Press.
Raz, J. (2001). 'Incommensurability and Agency', in *Engaging Reason*. Oxford: Oxford University Press.
Ryle, G. (1984). *The Concept of Mind*. Chicago: University of Chicago Press.
Scanlon, T. M. (1998). *What We Owe to Each Other*. Cambridge, Mass.: Harvard University Press.
Schlick, M. (2002). *Fragen der Ethik*. Frankfurt a.M.: Suhrkamp.
Schroeder, T. (2004). *Three Faces of Desire*. Oxford: Oxford University Press.
Schueler, G. F. (1995). *Desire: Its Role in Practical Reason and the Explanation of Action*. Cambridge, Mass.: MIT Press.
Shoemaker, S. (1980). 'Functionalism and Qualia', in N. Block (ed.), *Readings in Philosophy of Psychology*, vol. 1. Cambridge, Mass.: Harvard University Press.
Sidgwick, H. (1981). *The Methods of Ethics* (7th ed.). Indianapolis: Hackett.
Smith, M. (1994). *The Moral Problem*. Oxford: Blackwell.
Stalnaker, R. (1987). *Inquiry*. Cambridge, Mass.: MIT Press.
Stampe, D. W. (1986). 'Defining Desire', in J. Marks (ed.), *The Ways of Desire*. Chicago: Precedent.
Strawson, G. (1994). *Mental Reality*. Cambridge, Mass.: MIT Press.
Trigg, R. (1970). *Pain and Emotion*. Oxford: Clarendon Press.
Von Ehrenfels, C. (1982). 'System der Werttheorie I', in *Werttheorie: Philosophische Schriften Band 1*, ed. R. Fabian. Munich: Philosophia Verlag.

## *Motivational Views: Desire and Action*

# CHAPTER 3 | Desires without Guises

## *Why We Need Not Value What We Want*

SABINE A. DÖRING AND BAHADIR EKER

## 1. Introduction

Few would deny that our desires and our evaluations are closely linked. Normally, we desire to achieve or promote the things that we value. Beyond that, it is often the case that our desires lead us to evaluate things one way or another and that our evaluations, in turn, give rise to novel desires. Suppose, for instance, that you are looking for a new car and desire one with an especially large boot. This will surely have an impact on how you evaluate the alternatives you have. Or suppose you evaluate a movie very positively. This might produce a desire in you to see it again. It thus seems plausible that desires and evaluations do interact in a significant and thoroughgoing way. This much is, we take it, uncontroversial. However, one could advance a much more ambitious thesis about the extent and nature of this patent interaction. One could claim, in particular, that there is a *necessary* link between desires and positive evaluations because desires *just are*, or at least *necessarily involve*, evaluations of their object as good—one can desire something only *sub specie boni*, that is, *under the guise of the good*, as Scholastic philosophers used to put it.[1] We shall call this view *evaluativism about desire*.

Let us clarify somewhat how we understand the key evaluativist idea—for talk of "necessary involvement" is a bit too vague even for our purposes. We shall assume that the claim that desires involve evaluations as a matter of metaphysical necessity implies that token desires ontologically depend on token evaluations. More precisely, we shall assume that the basic evaluativist thesis implies, at a minimum, the following:

> (ME) Necessarily, for any agent *a*, any proposition *p*, any time *t*, if, at *t*, *a* desires that *p*, then, at *t*, *a* evaluates *p* positively (as good).[2]

(ME) rules out that an agent can have some token desire that *p* at some specific time, while not evaluating *p* positively (whatever that amounts to) at that time. (ME) is relatively weak, because it is silent about whether desires *essentially* depend on corresponding positive evaluations, whether positive evaluations are part of the essence of corresponding desires. Note, however, that (ME) is stronger than some sort of *generic* dependence claim according to which, roughly, any token desire necessitates some evaluation or other in general but none in particular. We shall also assume that the core evaluativist claim is not simply a claim about the *ontogeny* of token desires to the effect that any token desire that *p* is formed or acquired on the basis of a token positive evaluation of *p*, even though the desire that *p* can persist without the positive evaluation of *p*. (ME) defines a *permanent* rigid existential dependence and not merely a *past* one; thus it commits the evaluativist to something stronger than a merely ontogenic claim.[3]

Evaluativism is a popular view in contemporary theorizing about desire, and versions of it have been endorsed by a number of philosophers.[4] Our aim in this paper is to argue that evaluativism about desire overstates and mischaracterizes the connection between desires and evaluations. We begin section 2 by laying some preliminary groundwork that will be useful for the discussion to come. Section 3 concentrates on the typical motivation for evaluativism: a well-known worry about the role desires are supposed to play in the explanation of intentional action. We then discuss in sections 4 and 5 the two main varieties of evaluativism and demonstrate why neither of them can establish a plausible account of desire. Finally, in section 6, we argue that one can handle the worry discussed in section 3 without appealing to any kind of evaluativism and that the basic idea behind evaluativism is therefore not even well-motivated in the first place.

## 2. Desire: Some Preliminaries

*Desire* is sometimes used by philosophers as a generic term for many different conative states (or "pro-attitudes," as they are also called), referring to as diverse mental phenomena as wishes, hopes, intentions, appetites, preferences, urges, cravings, and longings.[5] Of course, such imprecision can be observed in everyday discourse as well. It is clear that desires, properly so called, should be carefully distinguished from these other conative attitudes, but we are not interested in taking on this very general task here.[6] Instead, we shall simply assume that the intuitive distinction between desires and the other conative states is not too obscure.

It is a platitude that desires are intentional mental states: a desire is always directed at something, it is always a desire *for* something. So one basic question about the nature of desire is what *sort* of things a desire can be directed at. Most philosophers agree that desires are propositional attitudes; they think that having a desire is a matter of having some specific mental attitude with a propositional content that represents or expresses some state of affairs.[7] To be sure, in many contexts, desire reports with transitive verbs or *to* infinitive phrases ("I want a nice cold beer" or "I want to drink a nice cold beer") sound more natural than the corresponding construction with an explicit *that* clause ("I want that I drink a nice cold beer"). Still, we shall assume that the former two forms are elliptical for the latter. So when you want a nice cold beer, what your desire is really directed at is not a nice cold beer *per se* but rather the state of affairs that you drink a nice cold beer.[8] Note that the assumption that desires are propositional attitudes does not imply anything substantial about what it is for a person to have such an attitude. It is not our purpose here to give a fully developed answer to that latter question, but the following discussion will roughly indicate the kind of answer we favor.

Our ordinary notion of desire is not just ambiguous between different sorts of conative attitudes but also fails to discriminate between mental phenomena that are, in fact, ontologically distinct. However one separates desires from other conative attitudes, a distinction remains to be made between *standing* and *occurrent* desires.[9] You probably desire, like most people, to live a long and healthy life. This desire will play a role in the explanation of several other elements of your psychology as well as some of your actions (your intention to lose weight or attempts at quitting smoking, for instance). However, presumably, the desire rarely, if ever, occupies your consciousness. Still, you have it not only on those rare occasions when you undergo a conscious experience of desiring to live a long and healthy life but also when your conscious attention is drawn elsewhere. Indeed, you have it even when you temporarily lose consciousness, when you are dreamlessly sleeping, for instance; you do not cease to desire to live a healthy life just because you fell asleep watching television and then acquire this desire once again when you wake up.

The desire to live a long and healthy life, which we can attribute to many people and suppose them to have it incessantly over very long periods of time, is a standing desire. Now contrast this with the following case. You are walking home from work, and you see a woman with her two daughters on the street. They remind you of your nieces who live in a different country, and you suddenly feel a strong desire to be with them. As you continue walking, you start to think about visiting them during the upcoming Christmas, trying to figure out how long the flight would take. The desire to be with your nieces that you felt (and that led you to think about the flight) is an occurrent desire, a phenomenally conscious mental episode. It is of course very plausible to think that you have a standing desire to be with your nieces as well (which would also explain, at least in this particular case, why the sight of the children led you to have the relevant occurrent desire), but this is importantly distinct from the occurrent desire you have just had.[10] If you have the standing desire to be with your nieces, you probably had it well before you saw the children, and you continue to have it even as you are making travel plans. Your occurrent desire, by contrast, came into existence right after you saw the children and ceased to exist once your attention was directed away from your nieces and you started thinking about the duration of the flight.

Standing desires and occurrent desires belong to fundamentally different ontological categories.[11] Your occurrent desire to be with your nieces is something that *happens*—it is an *occurrence*, a mental *event* that takes up a certain (typically short) amount of time. By contrast, your standing desire to live a long and healthy life neither happens nor occurs; rather, it is a mental state of yours that consists in your instantiating a certain mental property (however complex). You may of course be in this state over a very long period of time, which means that standing desires can *persist* through time (as they typically do). Unlike occurrent desires, however, they do not *unfold* over time.[12]

An occurrent desire is, as already indicated, a phenomenally conscious episode of desiring; there is something it is like having this sort of experience.[13] Standing desires, by contrast, are not phenomenally conscious phenomena. Of course, it is possible for you to be conscious *of* your standing desire that *p* (or to be conscious *that* you desire that *p*), in the sense of consciously "monitoring" your standing desire that *p*, but although this does not require an occurrent desire that *p*, it does require an occurrent, conscious thought (or judgment) that you desire that *p*.[14] It is also possible for your standing desire that *p* to "surface" in your consciousness.[15] Yet this does not mean that, when this happens, your standing desire somehow transforms itself into a phenomenally conscious attitude (and then back into an unconscious one, when its "manifestation" is over); it means only that you experience an occurrent desire that has the same content as your standing desire. However, as already noted, the occurrent desire that *p* is not simply the conscious version of the standing desire that *p*; that is, it is not simply the standing desire that *p* plus consciousness.[16]

So standing desires are not phenomenally conscious mental events. What exactly are they, then? Here we cannot offer more than a very rough answer, though one that is located within a familiar theoretical framework. On our view, standing desire is a *dispositional profile* of a distinctive kind (let us call this *the desiderative dispositional profile*); accordingly, having some standing desire that *p* consists in having some specific dispositional profile of that distinctive kind.[17] We shall not attempt here to give a full characterization of the desiderative dispositional profile that we identify with standing desire; we shall, however, briefly address some features of it that we take to be crucial.[18]

The core idea behind dispositionalism about standing attitudes is that the fact that you now have some such attitude does not consist in what is now going on in your conscious mind but rather in the fact that you now have a complex disposition to act and/or react in certain ways under certain circumstances. What sorts of disposition might having a standing desire involve? One very widespread thought is that desiring that *p* necessarily involves an inclination to act in ways that one takes to be conducive to the realization of *p*. We can spell out this idea a bit more formally as follows:

> (D1) Necessarily, for any agent *a*, any proposition *p*, any time *t*, and any act type $\varphi$, if, at *t*, *a* desires that *p*, then *a* is disposed at *t* to $\varphi$ in circumstances where *a* takes[19] her $\varphi$-ing to be conducive to *p*'s being the case.[20]

We think that (D1) is true: the sort of multitrack disposition it specifies is partly constitutive of any desiderative dispositional profile. We shall elaborate on a few points in order to make clear what our endorsement of (D1) does and does not imply.

First, we do not think that having the kind of disposition specified in (D1) is *sufficient* for having a standing desire—our claim is merely that it is necessary for it. There are other dispositions that are plausibly typical, though perhaps optional, elements of particular desiderative profiles. Moreover, there might be other necessary components of the desiderative dispositional profile.[21] Second, we take "act type $\varphi$" in (D1) to refer not just to overt bodily actions but also to speech acts as well as mental acts.[22] Given these two caveats, it should be clear that (D1) does *not* commit us to what is sometimes called "the motivational/action-based theory" of desire; the dispositionalism we favor does not focus exclusively on dispositions to engage in observable overt behavior and is openly "holistic" in spirit.[23]

Some philosophers oppose the idea that a desire that *p* necessarily disposes one to act in ways one takes to be conducive to *p*'s being the case; they think that cases where a person (allegedly) desires something that is (logically, metaphysically, or merely nomologically) impossible for her to bring about by doing something constitute counterexamples to (D1).[24] It will be instructive to address this issue at some length, because this will allow us to introduce two further crucial features of desire.

Timothy Schroeder has us imagine a mathematician in Ancient Greece (let us call him Pythagoras) who does not know the value of π but (allegedly) has a strong desire that it turn out to be an irrational number (which it already is).[25] There is nothing Pythagoras could do to determine the value of π, and he himself does not believe there is. So he has a desire, despite not being disposed to do anything, or so the argument seems to go.

Galen Strawson presents a scenario that is quite a bit more fanciful:

> The Weather Watchers are a race of sentient, intelligent creatures. They are distributed about the surface of their planet, rooted to the ground, profoundly interested in the local weather. They have sensations, thoughts, emotions, beliefs, desires. They possess a conception of an objective, spatial world. But they are constitutionally incapable of any sort of behavior.... They lack the necessary physiology. Their mental lives have no other-observable effects. They are not even disposed to behave in any way.[26]

Strawson imagines that the Weather Watchers are also incapable of performing any mental acts: although they can passively experience many different sorts of mental episodes, they cannot actively initiate them. They are also under no illusion that they can change the weather. Strawson claims that these beings can have desires that the weather be this or that way, although they are not disposed to act in any way.[27]

Our diagnosis will eventually be that neither Pythagoras nor the Weather Watchers, as they are described originally, have the relevant desires. The important point is, however, that this is not so because they fail (D1): they *can* have the relevant dispositions all right, but it is still wrong to say that they have the relevant desires.

Let us first focus on the case of Pythagoras, who, we are told, desires $\pi$ to be an irrational number and believes that there is nothing he can do to contribute to that result. The question is whether, for any $\varphi$, he is now disposed to $\varphi$ in circumstances where he comes to think that his $\varphi$-ing is conducive to $\pi$'s being an irrational number. Any such thought would be incorrect, of course, but that is not to the point; what matters is only whether Pythagoras would $\varphi$, *ceteris paribus*, if he came to form some such thought, and we see no reason to think that he would not. We will argue in what follows that Pythagoras should not be described as having a desire, but assuming that he has one, there is no reason to think that he fails (D1).

To be fair, Schroeder presents this argument against a much cruder rendering of the idea that desires necessarily involve dispositions to act and then concedes that a more refined formulation of it, which is more similar to our (D1), would not be affected by cases like this. However, he believes that such more refined versions would still be vulnerable to counterexamples of the following kind:

> Suppose I desire that a committee make up its mind in my favor without my intervention. This is a state of affairs I might want very much, yet because of the very nature of the desire it makes no sense to try to act as to satisfy it. What I want is that the committee make a certain decision without my needing to do anything.[28]

We fail to see how this is supposed to constitute a counterexample to (D1), however. It is simply false that your desire that a committee decides in your favor without any interference on your part is not satisfiable through *any* agential contribution of yours. If you have that desire, then there will be (under normal circumstances) plenty of actions that you take to count as interfering with the committee's decision process, and you will also think that refraining from performing them is conducive to satisfying your desire. (D1) predicts, correctly, that if you desire that the committee decides in your favor without your intervention, you will be disposed to refrain from performing any acts that you regard as interfering. Besides, this desire will involve not just dispositions to "perform" intentional omissions but also dispositions to perform "positive" actions. Suppose that it came to your attention that your uncle, who is a particularly well-connected individual, heard about the committee and is going to make some phone calls to increase your chances. (D1) predicts, again correctly, that, given your desire, you would, *ceteris paribus*, ask your uncle not to intervene in any way.[29]

The case of the Weather Watchers is certainly more complicated. First, it is not clear whether these creatures are even capable of taking their performance of some act to be conducive to fulfilling their desires; they might simply lack the cognitive resources to form such thoughts, to represent themselves as acting.[30] But even if they could, they would not act in any way, simply because they are "constitutionally" incapable of acting.[31] This sort of inability to act would certainly be ruled out by the *ceteris paribus* clause in (D1); that is, a general ability to act is one of the things that have to be equal for the disposition to manifest.[32] So the question is, in any case, whether we can ascribe to the Weather Watchers dispositions to act in certain ways that cannot possibly manifest—that is, unmanifestable dispositions.[33] We think that we can and should, and here is why.

Since we employ (though are not committed to) the conditional analysis here, the issue can be framed in terms of counterpossible conditionals, that is, conditionals with impossible antecedents. Now, according to the standard Lewis-Stalnaker semantics, all counterpossible conditionals are trivially true.[34] But if there are to be any non-trivial unmanifestable dispositions, some counterpossibles must have non-trivial truth values. We reject the triviality of counterpossibles in general, but we shall illustrate this point with a specific example that is more relevant to the discussion here.[35] Suppose that Wendy the Weather Watcher has a very strong conative attitude toward there being a snow shower; in fact, this is the only positive conative attitude she has.[36] By contrast, she feels positively averse to there being a rain shower. We think that Wendy now has a disposition to make herself visually imagine a snow shower in circumstances where she thinks her imagining a snow shower is conducive to there being a snow shower and she is capable of making herself imagine something. Accordingly, we think that the following counterpossible is non-trivially true:

> (W1) If Wendy were to think that her imagining a snow shower is conducive to there being a snow shower, and if she were capable of making herself imagine something, she would make herself imagine a snow shower, *ceteris paribus*.

To see why it makes sense to think that (W1) is non-trivially true, contrast it with another counterpossible about Wendy:

> (W2) If Wendy were to think that her imagining a rain shower is conducive to there being a rain shower, and if she were capable of making herself

imagine something, she would make herself imagine a rain shower, *ceteris paribus*.

Given what we know about Wendy's current psychology, (W2), unlike (W1), seems clearly and non-trivially false, even though the antecedents of both (W1) and (W2) are necessarily false, as, *ex hypothesi*, Wendy cannot make herself imagine anything.[37] Wendy may be necessarily incapable of acting, but this does not, by itself, suffice to trivialize all of the truths about how she would behave in certain conditions that are impossible to obtain; given her present conative states, she would act only in certain specific ways, and not others, if she were, *per impossibile*, capable of acting.[38]

The upshot of this is that an agent can be *inclined* to act in a certain way under certain circumstances, even if she is necessarily *incapable* of acting in that (or any) way; the incapability in question may necessarily prevent the inclination from manifesting without completely extinguishing it.[39] What make (W1) non-trivially true and (W2) non-trivially false are certain facts about Wendy's current conative psychology, the unmanifestable dispositions she now has or lacks.[40]

But if the Weather Watchers can have dispositions to act despite their incapability of acting, and thus can in principle satisfy (D1), why do we still insist that they do not have any desires? The reason is that their situation, as described by Strawson, seems to conflict with another necessary constraint on desire:

(D2) Necessarily, for any agent $a$, any proposition $p$, any time $t$, if, at $t$, $a$ desires that $p$, then there is at least one act type $\varphi$ such that, at $t$, $a$ does not think her $\varphi$-ing not to be conducive to $p$'s being the case.

Notice how weak a constraint (D2) introduces: (D2) does not require that, in order to have a desire at all, one must think that there is some act type such that one's performing it is conducive to satisfying one's desire. You can desire that $p$ even if you do not think of any particular act that it will be conducive to $p$'s being the case, and this is perfectly compatible with (D2). (D2) merely rules out that you can desire that $p$, while thinking that nothing you could do in any possible situation would be conducive to $p$'s being the case. You may be undecided whether any act on your part would contribute to satisfying some desire of yours, but you cannot be clear that nothing would make some such contribution.

(D2) captures the familiar idea that the object of a desire must be taken by the person who has it to be "attainable, in the sense of being a possible future outcome."[41] Note also that (D2) does not apply to mere wishes and thus serves to distinguish them from desires.[42] This is why we believe that both the Weather Watchers and Pythagoras are best described as having wishes rather than desires: they believe that nothing they could do would in any way contribute to satisfying their respective conative attitudes. Wishes involve an inclination to act in certain ways, just as desires do, yet the latter type of conative attitude is subject to further restrictions, such as (D2).[43]

The thought that the object of a desire must be regarded as an attainable, possible future outcome by the person who has it has a further implication that we would like to briefly clarify:

> (D3) Necessarily, for any agent *a*, any proposition *p*, any time *t*, if, at *t*, *a* desires that *p*, then, at *t*, *a* does not think *p* already to be the case.[44]

(D3) is compatible with one's being undecided about whether *p* is the case, while desiring that *p*; it only rules out that one can desire that *p*, while clearly thinking that *p* already is the case. For if you think that *p* already is the case, then you cannot even be undecided about whether some act of yours is conducive to *p*'s being the case; nothing can be conducive (in the relevant sense) to *p*'s being the case if *p* already *is* the case.[45] Thus, you cannot desire something you take to already obtain. So (D2) entails (D3), but the converse entailment does not hold: (D3) applies to wishes as well, for instance, whereas (D2) does not.[46]

This concludes our preliminary discussion of certain key features of desires. In what follows, we shall take for granted the admittedly rough picture outlined in this section. It will prove useful to take a closer look at the principal motivation for evaluativism in the next section, before we go on to critically examine the two main variants of it.

## 3. Motivating Evaluativism

Why think that evaluativism about desire is true? The view is typically motivated by focusing on the issue of the explanation of intentional action.[47] Actions are usually understood as belonging to the ontological category of events, though they are clearly not just any old event. An action is not something that simply *happens* to the agent but rather something that is *performed* by the agent. Moreover, intentional action makes up a special subclass of behavior performed by an agent. Involuntary reflex movements, for instance, are certainly not intentional actions. Intentional actions are *purposeful* and *goal-oriented*: they are performed with a purpose in mind and some sense of how to achieve that purpose—they are, in short, actions performed *for a reason*.[48]

This contrast is also reflected in the respective ways in which mere events or non-intentional behavior, on the one hand, and intentional actions, on the other hand, are supposed to be explained. When we pose a question of the form "Why did *x* happen?," where *x* is an event that is not an action, the sort of explanation that is called for is a merely causal one. By contrast, questions of the form "Why did the agent $\varphi$?" are supposed to be answered, roughly, by citing the reason for which the agent $\varphi$-ed, by specifying what purpose she took her $\varphi$-ing to serve—that is, by giving a *teleological* explanation.[49]

Teleological explanations of actions make reference to certain psychological states of the agent, and here desires are supposed to play a crucial role. This should hardly come as a surprise, since, as we have seen in section 2, desires necessarily involve practical inclinations, dispositions of an agent to act in certain specific ways under certain specific circumstances. When a desire figures in a correct teleological explanation of an agent's $\varphi$-ing, the propositional content of her desire encodes what she seeks to bring about, the goal she pursues. When this picture is supplemented with the agent's beliefs encoding information about possible ways of bringing about the desired outcome, we get a sense of what motivated her $\varphi$-ing, what led her to perform this particular action. The action is explained, in other words, not just as a mere effect of certain causal processes but essentially as the pursuit of a goal.[50]

A teleological explanation of an action, then, cites the agent's propositional attitudes (some desire of hers, along with a means-end belief) in order to make sense of her overt behavior as the pursuit of a goal. Explaining actions in terms of reasons by appeal to certain elements of the agent's psychological setup is commonly thought to have a further important implication: it *rationalizes* or *subjectively justifies* the action, at least in the minimal sense of making her behavior intelligible as the pursuit of a goal. Whether the action is *objectively justified* (relative to whatever system of norms), whether the reason for which the agent acted is in fact a *good* reason, is, of course, a different issue. The claim that someone $\varphi$-ed for a reason need not be *genuinely normative*: it does not necessarily entail that this person did what she has normative reason to do or *ought to* do.[51] But once we understand the reason for which she acted, we can at least see what, from the agent's perspective, counted in favor of performing the action, what the *point* of what she did was, at least in her eyes.

This precisely is the point at which evaluativists typically launch their distinctive claim. They agree, first, that intentional action is action done for a reason and also that action done for a reason implies rationalization or subjective justification in the sense explained earlier. They then go on to argue, third, that the relevant sort of rationalization is not to be had if desires are understood as non-evaluative phenomena.[52] An intentional action is motivated by a desire of the agent that encodes a goal, but if such behavior is to be considered rational (even in the aforementioned minimal sense), desires must, so the story goes, also involve an evaluation of that goal as something *worth* pursuing. Here it is useful to consider Warren Quinn's influential example of a man who feels an urge to turn on each and every radio he sees:

> Suppose I am in a strange functional state that disposes me to turn on radios that I see to be turned off. Given the perception that a radio in my vicinity is off, I try, all other things being equal, to get it turned on. Does this state rationalize my choices? Told nothing more than this, one may certainly doubt that it does. But in the case I am imagining, this is all there is to the state. I do not turn the radios on in order to hear music or get news. It is not that I have an inordinate appetite for entertainment or information. Indeed, I do not turn them on in order to *hear* anything. My disposition is, I am supposing, basic rather than instrumental.[53]

Quinn then raises the question whether ascribing to the agent this bare disposition to turn on radios suffices to rationalize and render intelligible his behavior, and answers it negatively. This is not to simply deny that desires can minimally rationalize actions; but, Quinn maintains, they can only do so if they accommodate "some kind of evaluation of the desired object as good."[54] From this evaluativists draw the moral that Radioman has no genuine desire because he does not value turning radios on in any sense. They think the example shows that "we do not get a proper intentional explanation of an action, or even a proper motivating reason or desire, if we cannot understand how the agent saw the object of his desire or action as good in some way."[55]

The basic idea behind evaluativism about desire and what typically motivates it should now be clear. There are two main versions of evaluativism, which differ in how they construe the evaluative element that desires are supposed to incorporate. We shall designate them as *doxastic evaluativism* and *perceptual evaluativism*. In the following two sections, we will discuss these two versions in turn. Some of the arguments we will present against them overlap, but these accounts are different enough to merit separate address.

## 4. Doxastic Evaluativism

According to doxastic evaluativism, the desire that *p* either just is or, at least, necessarily involves the belief that *p* is good.[56] Doxastic evaluativism is a radical view, as it runs counter to, and indeed threatens to collapse, the intuitive conceptual distinction between desires and beliefs as entirely disparate mental states (or, in Humean parlance, as 'distinct existences' without any necessary connections between them), either by identifying desires with evaluative beliefs or by establishing a necessary link between the two.[57] This does not quite show that doxastic evaluativism is false, but given its radical consequences, it is particularly in need of a substantial defense.

One general worry about this variety of evaluativism is that the picture it presents seems "overintellectualizing" in the extreme. Desires are closely connected to goal-directed behavior, and while goal-directed behavior is clearly observed in creatures with psychological apparatus less complex than that of adult humans, conceptual evaluation seems to require a considerable degree of cognitive sophistication. We normally ascribe desires to many non-human animals as well as to human infants and toddlers, but, as many have noted, doxastic evaluativism appears to entail that only more mature humans who have a sufficient grasp of and competence with evaluative concepts can have desires. This is indeed very counterintuitive, for it seems perfectly sensible to think that a dog or a human infant can want to play ball, for instance, even if we would hesitate to say that a dog or an infant can have a fully fledged belief that playing ball is good.[58]

Some caution is advised in pressing this objection, however. First, the objection seems to presuppose both a particular (broadly Fregean) conception of propositional content and a particular (rather restrictive) understanding of what it takes for a creature to possess concepts or to have some mental attitude with propositional content. Second, it could be transformed into an objection against the much more general view that desires are propositional attitudes. For if propositional content is conceptual in general, and if non-human animals and human infants can have desires although they do not possess any concepts, then it might seem fundamentally misguided to understand desires as propositional attitudes.[59] Still, it seems that doxastic evaluativism faces a particularly serious challenge here, because evaluative concepts are acquired in much later stages of cognitive development.[60] Moreover, if standing desires and standing beliefs are to be analyzed in terms of dispositional profiles, then one could argue that, whereas the doxastic dispositional profile necessarily involves dispositions to perform certain mental and linguistic acts that require fairly complex conceptual capacities, the desiderative dispositional profile does not, which would explain why very young humans and many non-human animals can have a desiderative profile, while it is at least questionable that they can have a doxastic one.[61]

Doxastic evaluativism has implausible implications even if we put aside this particular objection, however. First of all, it seems quite clear that the belief that *p* is good does not suffice for desiring that *p*. Recall the constraint we called (D2): you cannot desire that *p* if you think that nothing you can do would be conducive to *p*'s being the case. But no constraint of this sort applies to evaluative beliefs; states of affairs that a person takes to be unattainable can very well be believed to be good by that person. Suppose that you have the evaluative belief that the state of affairs that Mozart lived until his late seventies and produced a host of great masterpieces after his forties is valuable. But this state of affairs cannot be the object of a desire of yours, even if it can be the object of a wish, given your belief that nothing you can do would contribute to prolonging Mozart's life and/or boost his creativity.

Moreover, the objects of our evaluative beliefs are in most cases states of affairs that we think already obtain. However, as argued earlier, (D2) entails another constraint, namely (D3), that rules out desires directed at states of affairs that one takes to already obtain. Thus, while you can now believe that Obama's being president is good, you cannot now desire (nor even wish, for that matter) Obama's being president, because this is a state of affairs you already know to obtain (though you can, of course, desire that he remain in his post).

Yet quite apart from these two constraints on desire, it is in general implausible that belief in the goodness of that state of affairs implies that one desires it. Take, for example, Pollyanna, the famous diehard optimist. Suppose that she is falsely accused of stealing milk and, after an unfair trial process, is sentenced to six years in prison. Still, being a hopeless Pollyanna, she somehow manages to believe that it is good that she will be incarcerated (because, say, she will have plenty of time for reading). Does this mean that she genuinely wants to be sent to jail? Surely not. The same reasoning goes for less pathological cases of post hoc rationalization and occasional sugarcoating of prospective misery.[62]

But even if an evaluative belief is clearly insufficient for a corresponding desire, it is perhaps necessary for it. It is difficult to see, however, why this should be the case. As both Michael Stocker and David Velleman point out, having "perverse" desires, that is, desiring some state of affairs that one believes to be bad in every respect, and even desiring it precisely *because* it is so bad, seems perfectly possible.[63] Stocker and Velleman mention in their discussions quite exceptional cases (Milton's Satan, agents who are depressive or self-destructive), but desiring something that you believe to be bad is possible even in more mundane, ordinary situations. Suppose that, at the beginning of a long business meeting with your colleagues, you suddenly remember a joke that a friend told you some time ago. You do not think there is anything good about telling the joke during the meeting; not only would it be generally inappropriate, but the joke would in fact be extremely offensive to some participants and is not even slightly funny. Still, it seems possible that you desire to tell it, even if that desire is fortunately too weak to actually influence your behavior.

Doxastic evaluativism is incompatible not only with cases in which a person desires $p$ while believing $p$ to be bad in every respect, but also with cases in which a person desires $p$ but does not have *any* opinion about the value of $p$, either because she has not considered it or because, having considered it, she suspends (or withholds) judgment about it. Let us focus first on cases of the former sort, which we believe are ubiquitous: the vast majority of our everyday desires are such that we just have not even considered the value of their object and formed an opinion about it. This becomes especially salient when one considers extrinsic (or instrumental) desires. Suppose that Thomas is reading this paper. He plans to have a short break in about an hour and desires to go to the kitchen to brew some coffee. Is it really plausible to say that Thomas now literally believes that going to the kitchen in fifteen minutes is (instrumentally) good? Fair enough; we can plausibly ascribe to Thomas the means-end belief that he can brew coffee by going to the kitchen, but the belief that $\varphi$-ing is a means of bringing it about that $p$ is not the same as the belief that $\varphi$-ing is instrumentally valuable; thinking of $\varphi$-ing as conducive to the obtaining of some state of affairs is one thing, and thinking of it as promoting something valuable is quite another.

It might be thought that we can also ascribe to Thomas the *disposition to believe* that going to the kitchen is (instrumentally) good: the disposition to take this standing attitude or, perhaps, the disposition to have an occurrent belief (a conscious thought) to that effect. We can imagine that these dispositions would manifest (so Thomas would form the standing or the occurrent belief that going to the kitchen is good), for instance, if he were asked what good he sees in going to the kitchen. These specific doxastic dispositions are, however, importantly distinct from the standing belief that going to the kitchen is (instrumentally) good, itself understood as a doxastic dispositional profile.[64] You may, at *t*, have a mere disposition to form the standing belief that *p*, or a disposition to occurrently judge that *p*, without having, at *t*, the standing belief that *p*, without having the *p*-related doxastic dispositional profile, that is. Now we do not think that desiring *p* necessarily involves being disposed to believe that *p* is good, but even if this were true, doxastic evaluativism would not be any less wrong. Any version of doxastic evaluativism is committed to (ME), which rules out that one can, at *t*, desire that *p*, although one does not believe, at *t*, that *p* is good. Suppose that, between $t_0$ and $t_1$, Thomas desires to go to the kitchen. During that time interval, he also has the disposition to form both the standing and the occurrent belief that going to the kitchen is good. It is perfectly possible that, although Thomas has those doxastic dispositions between $t_0$ and $t_1$, these dispositions do not manifest between $t_0$ and $t_1$. But if so, then during that period of time, Thomas has the desire that *p*, although he has neither a standing nor an occurrent belief that *p*. But this result is incompatible with any form of doxastic evaluativism.[65]

Turn now to cases where a person desires that *p* yet does not believe that *p* is good because she is suspending judgment about the value of *p*.[66] This can happen, for example, when one cannot form an opinion about the value of something that one desires *in advance, before* the state of affairs one's desire is directed at actually obtains. Suppose that there is a new French film coming out. Pauline is a dedicated cinephile and a true fan of the classic art house movies. However, over the past few months, she has seen some recent French films that she regarded as appallingly pretentious and derivative. In the present case, she is very uncertain about what to expect. The film is a directorial debut, so there is no information on the director's directing ability or style. She read conflicting reviews in the media: it is one of those controversial, love-or-hate kind of films that has already divided critics. For all she knows, in short, it could be a masterpiece or a complete fiasco. Being a true cinephile, she is curious, and she has a strong desire to watch the movie. Despite her curiosity, however, she knows very well that she will absolutely regret watching the movie if it turns out to be bad: she will not, for instance, feel any satisfaction at fulfilling her "duty" as a cinephile. So she wants to watch the movie and to find out whether it is any good, but, in her eyes, whether her watching it (and her finding out about its value) is good or bad depends entirely on the value of the movie itself, about which she has absolutely no idea right now. Therefore, she suspends judgment about the value of her watching it and her finding out about its value: if the movie turns out to be enjoyable, then she will regard her watching it as good; if, on the other hand, the movie turns out to be bad, she will regard her watching it as a terrible waste of time. Pauline's case constitutes another counterexample to doxastic evaluativism: she wants to watch the movie and find out about its value at some specific time *t*, but she suspends judgment about the value of her watching the movie and her finding out about its value at that time.

Here is a final worry about doxastic evaluativism: Consider once again Quinn's Radioman. The evaluativist's point has been that we cannot quite understand Radioman's behavior unless we ascribe to him a positive evaluation of his pursued goal. Doxastic evaluativists interpret the required evaluation as an evaluative belief. Now, let us suppose that Radioman has the belief that turning on all the radios in his vicinity is intrinsically good. Our question is: Is there any sense in which Radioman's action is even slightly more intelligible or less bizarre now that we imagine him as someone who thinks that turning radios on is a worthwhile activity in itself? We think not! Despite having ascribed to him the evaluative belief in question, we are still puzzled as to why he acts as he does; in fact, now that we assume him to be committed to the idea that turning radios on is intrinsically valuable, the case is even more perplexing, if anything. Note that we need to imagine Radioman as believing his goal to be valuable for its own sake; we cannot simply attribute to him the belief that turning radios on is good *for* listening to music, for instance, because Quinn explicitly stipulates that Radioman's desire to turn on radios is intrinsic, not instrumental.[67] It seems, then, that if Radioman's intrinsic desire cannot provide a minimal rationalization for his action, neither can his belief that the object of that desire is intrinsically good: Quinn's condition that Radioman's desire is to be understood as non-instrumental already excludes from the case everything that could make the corresponding evaluative judgment intelligible and leaves us with the deeply puzzling belief that turning radios on is good for its own sake. It is therefore redundant to ascribe the relevant evaluative belief to Radioman, as this falls short of making the air of bizarreness surrounding his action disappear.

## 5. Perceptual Evaluativism

As we have seen, the doxastic route to evaluativism is not really viable. But perhaps the alleged evaluative dimension of desires could be modeled on perception instead. This indeed has been the strategy recently followed by many evaluativists.[68] On such views, desires are generally conceived of as involving both a representational content and a rich phenomenal dimension, and sometimes they are understood as analogous to or even simply as a special kind of *emotion*.[69] According to one currently predominant view, emotions are (analogous to) perceptions, though they differ from ordinary sensory perceptions in that their representational content is evaluative: to fear a lion is to experience it as fearsome or dangerous; to admire it is to experience it as admirable; and so forth.[70] Despite (sometimes important) differences among them, perceptual evaluativists all share the core idea that, analogously, desiring *p* is a matter of *p*'s being experienced as good or seeming good. Thus, Dennis Stampe argues:

> Desire is a kind of perception. One who wants it to be the case that *p* perceives something that makes it seem to that person as if it would be good were it to be the case that *p*, and seem so in a way that is characteristic of perception. To desire something is to be in a kind of perceptual state, in which that thing seems good. . . .[71]

A variation on this basic idea is found in Thomas Scanlon's attention-based account of desire.[72] According to Scanlon, "A person has a desire in the directed-attention sense that P if the thought of P keeps occurring to him or her in a favorable light, that is to say, if the person's attention is directed insistently toward considerations that present themselves as counting in favor of P."[73] One clear advantage of perceptual evaluativism over doxastic evaluativism is that the former, unlike the latter, does not require that a person who desires *p* have a fully fledged evaluative belief that *p* is good. What perceptual evaluativists demand is only that the state of affairs *p seems* good to this person. This allows them to avoid the "over-intellectualizing" conception of agents' psychology that doxastic versions of evaluativism seems to entail.[74] However, there are a number of serious difficulties with this variety of evaluativism as well.

Perceptual evaluativists typically *identify* a person's desiring *p* with *p*'s seeming good to that person.[75] But the claim that something's seeming good suffices for desiring it is just as implausible as its doxastic variant. To see this, we need only adjust and reapply the counterexamples from section 4. Suppose that you are confident that Obama is president, and also that nothing you could do would be conducive to Mozart's leading a longer and more productive life than he actually did. When you think about these states of affairs, they may very well seem good to you; however,

(D2) and (D3) rule out that you can desire them. Similarly, consider once again the case of Pollyanna, who, being a diehard optimist, may regard the time she will spend in prison as good, and her attention may be constantly directed toward considerations that seem to count in favor of her being incarcerated (to the prospect of having plenty of time for reading or writing her memoirs, for instance). Still, it is very implausible to conclude that Pollyanna genuinely desires to be sent to jail.

It thus seems that something's appearing in a favorable light is not sufficient for desiring it. Is it at least necessary for it? Again, the arguments against doxastic evaluativism we presented earlier apply to perceptual evaluativism as well. Recall, for instance, the case of Pauline the cinephile. Pauline has a strong desire to watch the movie and find out about its value, yet when she thinks about watching the movie and finding out about its value, these states of affairs do not seem good to her—if her desire involves any evaluative experience at all, then, plausibly, it is an experience of those states of affairs' seeming to her to be evaluatively ambivalent. Hence the case of Pauline constitutes a counterexample to the perceptual version of evaluativism as well.

There is, however, a more pressing difficulty with perceptual evaluativism, a difficulty that reveals what is fundamentally wrong with this approach to desire. Recall the distinction between standing and occurrent desires. Here is how this distinction spells trouble for perceptual evaluativism. On the face of it, perceptual evaluativism seems applicable only to occurrent desires since it associates desire with some sort of conscious episode in which the desired object is experienced as good. So even if it is established that occurrently desiring *p* just is, or necessarily involves, experiencing *p* as good, this leaves it entirely open how standing desires are to be understood. Since the standing desire that *p* can be had even when you are not conscious at all, it can neither just be nor necessarily involve experiencing *p* as good. Therefore, perceptual evaluativism cannot pretend to be a general theory of desire; at best, it can account only for occurrent desires.[76]

To appreciate how severe this problem is, note that a huge number of the mental phenomena we normally call desires are standing desires, not occurrent ones. Besides, it is standing desires that take center stage in many debates in meta-ethics and the philosophy of action. This is quite unsurprising, given that the vast majority of our intentional actions are not preceded by any occurrent desires but are rather motivated by our standing desires.[77] So restricting the account to occurrent desires is not much of an option for the evaluativist, at least not within the context of the debate about the explanation of intentional action.

Can the perceptual evaluativist extend his analysis to standing desires? The perceptual evaluativist might propose that the standing desire that *p* necessarily involves the disposition to occurrently desire that *p*, which, in turn, is identified with (or is taken to necessarily involve) experiencing *p* as good.[78] It is plausible that dispositional profiles of the desiderative kind typically involve a disposition to have occurrent desires with the relevant content, though we do not think that such dispositions are necessary constituents of desiderative profiles. But let us suppose, for the sake of argument, that the standing desire that *p* necessarily involves the disposition to undergo experiences of occurrently desiring that *p* in circumstances where, for instance, one occurrently thinks about *p* and so on. Does this solve the perceptual evaluativist's problem with standing desires? It does not, and to see why, consider once again the case of Thomas from section 4. Between $t_0$ and $t_1$, Thomas has the standing desire to go to the kitchen. We are supposing that, during this period, he also has the disposition to occurrently desire to go to the kitchen. However, this disposition might not manifest between $t_0$ and $t_1$, and if it does not, then Thomas has a standing desire between $t_0$ and $t_1$, without having any corresponding positive evaluation. But this is incompatible with (ME), to which any form of evaluativism is committed.[79] So the perceptual evaluativist cannot account for standing desires simply by claiming that desiderative profiles necessarily involve a disposition to have corresponding occurrent desires.[80]

Here is a further worry about perceptual evaluativism. As we have seen in section 3, the principal motivation for evaluativism is that desires cannot have the minimal justificatory function they are supposed to have if they do not somehow imply that the goal they encode is a goal that is worth pursuing. But it is in fact dubious whether evaluative experiences can have this sort of justificatory force (if, that is, we are to suppose that non-evaluative conative attitudes cannot), even in those cases in which an agent actually undergoes them. After all, perceptual evaluativists require only that the pursued goal *seems* good to the agent, not that the agent really *accepts* that goal as good in any sense. As many have argued, a desired goal may continue to seem good to the agent although he judges that this goal is in fact not worth pursuing. That is, desires may prove *recalcitrant* to the agent's better judgment. Scanlon gives the example of a person who continues to desire a new computer even when her better judgment is that she in fact has no reason to buy a new computer.[81] The perceptual evaluativist's explanation of such recalcitrant desires is that they must be more like perceptions of value, not like value judgments—for otherwise we would have to attribute to the person two contradictory judgments, which is very implausible.[82] As Scanlon puts it, "Desires are unreflective elements in our practical thinking."[83] We take this to imply that the evaluations involved in desires differ from those involved in beliefs in that they are not regarded as true by the agent. They have "the *appearance* of truth, whether or not [the agent] would *affirm*" their truth.[84] While this nicely explains the phenomenon of recalcitrant desires (it is only the content of his better judgment that the agent regards as true, whereas the content of his desire merely appears to be true[85]), it would seem that this comes at the price of depriving desires of their capacity to rationalize actions. For why think that an evaluation that the agent does not even affirm, or regard as true, can rationalize his action if his non-evaluative conative attitude cannot? While Scanlon seems to think that desires cannot even *motivate* action if their content is not affirmed by the agent,[86] Mark Johnston insists, on the contrary, that desires can directly rationalize action "without going by way of the evaluative beliefs."[87] This comes as a surprise, considering that Johnston adopts Scanlon's perceptual evaluativism about desire and connects it with perceptual theories of emotion.[88] Whatever Johnston's reasons for that thesis, it is our view that evaluative experiences that perceptual evaluativists ascribe to agents fail to rationalize actions because experiencing a desired goal as good does not imply that the agent affirms this evaluation.[89]

Finally, consider how the perceptual evaluativist's suggestion applies to the case of Radioman, setting aside the problems we canvassed earlier. Let us assume that Radioman's behavior is motivated by an occurrent desire that consists in his experiencing turning radios on as good for its own sake. Remember that we are not allowed to suppose that this course of action appears instrumentally good to him. So the question is once again whether the assumption that Radioman experiences turning radios on as intrinsically valuable makes his action any less bizarre than it was before, and the answer is once again no. His action is still very odd, and it is even more puzzling that turning radios on should seem intrinsically valuable to him.

We thus conclude that neither version of evaluativism can provide us with a plausible theory of desire: as the arguments we presented in this section and section 4 show, a positive evaluation of the desired object, be it doxastic or perceptual, does not suffice for desiring something; nor is it, in fact, necessary for it. Moreover, it seems that, as far as examples like Radioman's go, which are supposed to be the main motivation for evaluativism about desire, turning desires into evaluative beliefs or experiences does not produce any gains. This means that the bizarreness of the case of Radioman is due not to his lack of some positive evaluation of turning radios on but to something else. In section 6, we shall sketch out some ideas on what that something else might be and try to explain why evaluativism about desire is an overreaction to whatever challenge the case of Radioman poses.

## 6. Demotivating Evaluativism

Let us recapitulate what we know about Radioman. We know that he desires to turn radios on, at least in the sense that he is disposed to turn on any that catch his eye. Call this particular conative state of Radioman DESIRE. We know that DESIRE is intrinsic. We also know that DESIRE does not involve any evaluation of its object as good.

Suppose now Radioman enters a room and spots a radio at the other end of the room. He then steadily walks across the room and turns the radio on. Call this particular event ACTION. The question now is whether ACTION can be rationalized or explained by DESIRE as an instance of pursuing a goal. Quinn and evaluativists of all stripes give a negative answer: they think that rationalization is impossible because DESIRE lacks the evaluative element that is responsible for making actions intelligible as the pursuit of some goal. We think, on the contrary, that no evaluative element is in principle necessary for such rationalization, though we also believe that we do not know enough details to make a final decision about this particular case. It may be objected that ACTION strikes one as bizarre even before we are given more information about Radioman's psychology and the circumstances of ACTION. We agree that there is something odd about ACTION, but we think that two issues should be distinguished here. On the one hand, there is the question whether ACTION can be understood as Radioman's pursuing some goal, given the facts about his psychology. Suppose that it can be so understood. This is compatible, on the other hand, with Radioman's goal being an extremely bizarre one. Indeed, turning radios on is a very odd thing to desire intrinsically, and, as we have seen, the oddness of it does not simply go away when we ascribe to Radioman the corresponding positive evaluations, because those evaluations themselves would be every bit as odd as DESIRE itself, if not odder. DESIRE is quite unlike the typical intrinsic desires most people have: the desire to be happy, the desire to be healthy, the desire to be free from pain, and so on. Compared to being healthy or free from pain, turning radios on seems far too trivial to want for its own sake. One might also be tempted to say that Radioman intrinsically desires something he has no objective, normative reason to desire. It is controversial in general whether normative reasons can be given for intrinsic desires, but we can safely bypass this controversy because *that* has never been our question.[90] Our question was, and still is, whether DESIRE (together with relevant means-end beliefs) can explain ACTION as Radioman's pursuit of some goal. We would probably insist that the goal he pursues is absurd, but pursuing an absurd goal is still pursuing a goal.

As already pointed out, it is difficult to give a decisive answer to the question whether DESIRE rationalizes (in the relevant minimal sense) ACTION, because the example is, as originally presented, fatally underdescribed.[91] One might imagine Radioman, for instance, as someone who compulsively runs from one radio to another, utterly possessed by a mechanical urge to turn them on. It might be, for instance, that this urge to turn on radios regularly gets into the way of his efforts to satisfy his desires, to realize his intentions and plans. He might also be completely alienated from this urge, feeling that the actions produced by it are not really *performed* by him but merely *happen* to him.[92] If this is the correct description of the case, then it clearly does not make much sense to say that Radioman genuinely pursues some goal in turning the radio on; in fact, it becomes highly questionable whether his behavior can still count as an intentional action.

The point to be emphasized is, however, that this enriched version of the story does not give us any reason to endorse evaluativism about desire.[93] It is assumed in Quinn's discussion (and in many subsequent treatments by others) that non-evaluativists are committed to the view that desires just are simple dispositions to act in certain ways. If this were true, then it would perhaps be difficult for non-evaluativists to draw a distinction between desires and compulsive urges such as the one we might suppose Radioman to have. But non-evaluativists have no such commitment.[94] Indeed, as we argued in section 2, the desiderative dispositional profile does not exhaust itself in the disposition to act in ways that you take to be conducive to satisfying your desire, even if that disposition is a necessary element of the desiderative profile. A more detailed characterization of the desiderative profile would distinguish it from the dispositional profile associated with compulsive urges, and this would allow non-evaluativists to respond to (the enriched version of) Quinn's example by denying that Radioman has a standing desire to turn radios on. So if his conative attitude does not minimally rationalize the way he behaves, then this does not quite show that a desire, understood non-evaluatively, cannot rationalize actions, but rather merely that compulsive urges cannot rationalize actions.

What other kinds of dispositions might the desiderative profile necessarily or typically involve? Here we can do no more than point to one kind of disposition that would be useful for distinguishing desires from compulsive urges. What we have in mind are, very roughly, dispositions that link desires to other agency-related psychological phenomena such as intentions, general agential policies, or long-term plans, and spotlight their place within the broader context of diachronic or 'temporally extended' agency.[95] It seems plausible, for instance, that the desiderative dispositional profile necessarily includes, roughly, dispositions to form long-term intentions to achieve the object of the desire, to integrate such intentions into more general and complex plans the agent already has, and to form agential policies that encode general patterns of action in certain specific situations. Of course, many or even most desires we have do not actually lead us to engage in such higher agential activities, but they all dispose us to do so under certain suitable conditions. By contrast, urges and compulsions plausibly do not involve such dispositions: although urges and compulsions of which the agent is conscious are also relevant for the shape her overall agency takes, they are more like external limiting factors than mediators of potential goals. One can take into account one's compulsive urge to do something that one does not want to do when intending or planning to act, yet one does not really intend or plan to act *on them*. So if desires and compulsive urges can thus be contrasted in terms of their different dispositional connections with intentions and plans, for instance, then the non-evaluativist can spell out why acting *out of an urge* does not quite count as an instance of pursuing a goal, while acting *on a desire* does.[96]

Given the lack of detail, we cannot tell whether DESIRE fits the desiderative profile, understood as including the sort of agency-related dispositions roughly sketched above, and thus qualifies as a genuine desire, or whether it is just a compulsive urge. But if it is a genuine desire, it is difficult to see why it should fail to rationalize ACTION in the relevant minimal sense. Again, this need not prevent us from regarding DESIRE as very unusual or even downright outlandish and Radioman himself as quite eccentric. It does not follow from this, however, that we need to ascribe to him an evaluation of the object of his desire in order to understand him as pursuing a goal.

There still remains, of course, the further, independent question of whether Radioman's agency-related attitudes make up the kind of coherent whole that can be seen as the trademark of a stronger, more robust form of agency, that is, *ideally autonomous agency*. Again, we need to know much more about Radioman in order to decide to what extent he is an autonomous agent in general and to what extent ACTION is an instance of autonomous agency. Does he, for instance, have certain general, higher-order attitudes aiming at self-regulation? If so, how sensitive are the particular action-related elements of his mental setup to these self-governing policies? More specifically, how does he behave when DESIRE comes into conflict with other action-related elements of his psychology? These are some of the questions we need to be able to answer before we can tell whether Radioman can be evaluated as an autonomous agent, or whether ACTION can be understood as an instance of autonomous agency.[97] Note that failure to comply with forms of autonomous self-regulation, which surely comes in degrees, need not mean that the agent cannot be understood as pursuing a goal. We can still make sense of an agent's behavior as an instance of pursuing a goal or acting for a reason, even if we think that it falls short of the ideal of autonomous agency.[98]

## Notes

1. See Massin (*this volume*) for a similar characterization. Evaluativists typically do not specify whether the necessity in question is a conceptual or metaphysical sort. The metaphysical claim that attitudes of desiring are identical to, or at least necessarily involve, attitudes of positive evaluation need not have any conceptual implications, but we shall assume that the claim that the concept DESIRE is identical to, or necessarily involves, the concept POSITIVE EVALUATION has the metaphysical implication that attitudes of desiring are identical to, or at least necessarily involve, attitudes of positive evaluation. Thus, we assume that the metaphysical claim is weaker than the conceptual one, and this is why we shall focus on the former (though without making any precise distinction).

2. Note that there are various different relations of ontological dependence (for helpful overviews, see Correia 2008; Koslicki 2013; Lowe 2013; Tahko and Lowe 2015); the one appealed to in (ME) is commonly called *rigid existential dependence*.

3. See esp. Correia 2008: 1016 on this.

4. Proponents of evaluativism include Anscombe 1963; Davidson 1980a, 1980c (on one reading, at least); de Sousa 1974; Stampe 1987; Scanlon 1998, 2002; Raz 1999, 2010; Wallace 1999; Helm 2001; Johnston 2001; Chang 2004; Oddie 2005, *this volume*; Tenenbaum 2007; Hawkins 2008; Schapiro 2009; and Schafer 2013. Evaluativism is sometimes developed as a claim about intentions instead of desires (see, e.g., Raz 2010), but here we will put aside this complication. Another related view, *deonticism about desire*, is that desiring that *p* entails its seeming to one that *p* ought to be the case or at least that there are normative reasons in favor of *p*'s being the case; see, e.g., Gregory (2013, *this volume*), Lauria (*this volume*), and Massin (*this volume*). Some of those who prefer to talk of reasons hold that values are somehow reducible to reasons, and this move makes evaluativism and deonticism basically equivalent (this is most clear in Scanlon

1998, but compare also Schapiro 2009; Schafer 2013). However, depending on precisely how it is fleshed out, deonticism about desire can potentially differ from evaluativism in crucial respects; therefore, we shall ignore in what follows any form of deonticism that is clearly distinct from evaluativism, although some of the arguments we present would equally apply to some versions of the former view.

5. This usage is mainly due to Davidson (1980a). Compare also Davidson 1980c; Schueler 1995: ch. 1.

6. Though later on in this section and in section 6, we shall hint at some of the respects in which desires differ from wishes and urges.

7. Exceptions do exist, though; see, e.g., Ben-Yami 1997; Thagard 2006. See Sinhababu (*forthcoming*) for a defense of propositionalism about attitudes in general.

8. Graham Oddie (*this volume*) explicitly rejects this and argues that the primary objects of desires are properties: when you want a nice cold beer, your desire is not directed at some state of affairs but rather at the property of drinking a nice cold beer. Now, if this is supposed to be a genuine alternative, a desire with that property as its object must be distinct from the desire directed at the state of affairs that you drink a nice cold beer. It is difficult to see how this could be, however. As Oddie himself seems to acknowledge, it makes little sense to say that you desire the property of drinking a nice cold beer *per se*; what you desire is *having* that property or, equivalently, the *state of affairs* that you have (or instantiate) that property. But if this is correct, then what Oddie calls "the property view" simply collapses into the picture proposed earlier.

9. For discussions of this, see, e.g., Goldman 1970: 86–88; Mele 2003: 30–33; Strandberg 2012; Schroeder 2014: sect. 2.4; Alvarez (*this volume*). Note, however, that the way these authors use *occurrent* and *standing* diverges from ours; our understanding of the distinction parallels the way Tim Crane (2001: 102–108, 2013) distinguishes between dispositional beliefs and occurrent, conscious thoughts.

10. Note, however, that you can have an occurrent desire that *p* at *t*, even if you did not have a standing desire that *p* at any point before *t* or have it at *t*. Suppose, for instance, you have a strong aversion to wearing perfume; you disliked all the perfumes you have tried up until now, and you would not even consider buying one. Then, one day, you smell a perfume on a colleague at work, which, to your own surprise, instantly fascinates you, and suddenly you feel a strong desire to find out more about this perfume, to buy it and wear it yourself. You may then go on to adopt this as a standing desire, but this is not necessary. So occurrent desires need not correspond to some already existing standing desire, and they do not necessarily inaugurate a corresponding standing desire.

11. See, e.g., Crane 2001: 103, 2013: 163–166.

12. More precisely, "mental states *obtain* over, and throughout, intervals of time, and at times; whereas mental events and processes *occur/happen/unfold* over time and/or at times. The idea here is that even when a mental state and a mental event (or process) have the same temporal extension—even when they occupy the same interval of time—they won't have the same temporal character. They will fill that interval of time in quite different ways" (Soteriou 2013: 27). See also Soteriou 2007; Steward 1997.

13. It is a further question whether occurrent desires have a *non-derivative* phenomenal character—that is, whether there is a *conative phenomenology* of a distinctive sort, independent from the phenomenology of other mental episodes they may involve or be accompanied by (mental imagery, bodily sensations, sensory perceptions and so on); see,

e.g., Kriegel 2013, 2015: ch. 2; Friedrich *this volume*. We remain silent on this, but note that the analogous question about cognitive phenomenology has attracted a fair amount of attention recently; see, e.g., Bayne and Montague 2011; Smithies 2013a, 2013b.

14. There is another sense in which one might be said to be "conscious" of one's standing desire that *p*: you may have a standing belief that you have that desire. Being in this state may constitute a form of self-knowledge, but it does not accord phenomenal consciousness (or conscious "monitoring") of your standing desire, for the standing belief in question is just as unconscious as the standing desire itself: you can have both of these attitudes while you are dreamlessly sleeping and have no phenomenal consciousness at all.

15. Thus, when we call standing desires unconscious, we do not thereby mean that they are all unconscious in a Freudian sense. Indeed, most standing desires (well, except for Freudian ones) will also have what Ned Block (1995, 2002) dubbed *access consciousness*. As Block makes clear (1995: 232), access consciousness is an entirely functional notion; an attitude can be access-conscious, without actually figuring in the subject's stream of consciousness. Crane (2013) suggests that access consciousness should be understood in terms of a mental state's disposition to "manifest" itself in consciousness via some conscious, occurrent state.

16. This is why Crane (2001: 105–108, 2013) thinks that "occurrent belief" is a misleading label for conscious episodes of entertaining some proposition in the doxastic mode. This would also apply, *mutatis mutandis*, to "occurrent desire," but we will not worry about it here.

17. See esp. Schwitzgebel 2002, 2013. Our approach is in general quite similar to Schwitzgebel's, though we seem to have some disagreements over the details. As will become clear shortly, we think that kinds of attitudinal dispositional profiles have some necessary features, whereas Schwitzgebel (2002: 252) seems to deny this, conceiving of attitude concepts as strictly cluster concepts. Then again his focus is largely on attitude ascriptions and their appropriateness; so there is reason to think that our approach may be reconcilable with his. However, although he does not quite endorse evaluativism, Schwitzgebel (2013: 89–90) explicitly downplays the differences between desiring something and believing it to be good, saying that they amount to nothing more than a "nuance" (90). We are in general sympathetic to the idea that dispositional profiles of different kinds can overlap to some degree, but we shall argue that the contrast between the conative state of desiring that *p* and the cognitive state of believing that *p* is good is quite a bit more significant than Schwitzgebel seems to think. For further discussion of the dispositional conception, see, e.g., Smith 1987, 1994: ch. 4; Ashwell 2014; Hyman 2014. See also Alvarez (*this volume*).

18. Note that even this rough first approximation entails that, just as the occurrent desire that *p* is not simply a conscious version of the standing desire that *p*, the standing desire that *p* is not simply a dispositional version of the occurrent desire that *p*—that is, not simply the *disposition to have* the occurrent desire that *p*. The standing desire that *p* is a complex desiderative dispositional profile that includes many different dispositions, even though it is plausible that token desiderative profiles typically include a disposition to have the relevant occurrent desire (indeed, one might even regard this as necessary).

19. We formulate the stimulus condition this way because we do not want to rule out that a cognitive attitude somewhat weaker (less committal) than outright belief (such as

mere acceptance; see Cohen 1992; Bratman 1992) can also be sufficient to trigger the manifestation.

20. Ascriptions of dispositional properties are usually analyzed in terms of counterfactual conditionals; accordingly, (D1) can be reformulated as follows:

> (D1*) Necessarily, for any agent $a$, any proposition $p$, any time $t$, and any act type $\varphi$, if, at $t$, $a$ desires that $p$, then, if, at $t$, $a$ took her $\varphi$-ing to be conducive to $p$'s being the case, $a$ would $\varphi$, *ceteris paribus*.

According to the standard Stalnaker-Lewis semantics (Stalnaker 1968; Lewis 1973), the truth value of the counterfactual conditional in (D1*) is determined by what goes on in the closest possible worlds in which its antecedent is true: the counterfactual is true iff $a$ performs $\varphi$ at those closest antecedent worlds. The counterfactual approach has quite a bit of intuitive appeal; as is well known, however, a number of counterexamples have been offered against it: dispositions can be "finked," masked, or mimicked due to the presence of certain interfering factors (there is a huge literature on these issues—see, to name just a few, Johnston 1992; Martin 1994; Bird 1998); hence the *ceteris paribus* clause in (D1*). Critics argue that this move faces a dilemma: either one attempts to specify what other things have to be equal for the manifestation to occur in the stimulus conditions, or one does not. Leaving the *ceteris paribus* clause unspecified seems to render the whole analysis vacuous: it is as if one were saying that the manifestation would occur in the stimulus conditions *unless* it did not. On the other hand, a comprehensive specification of all the things that have to be equal seems rather unlikely in the case of most dispositions. Responses to this dilemma fall broadly into two categories: Some (e.g., Lewis 1997; Choi 2008; Manley and Wasserman 2008; Contessa 2013) seek to provide a general but non-vacuous formula for specifying the *ceteris paribus* clause. Others (e.g., Schwitzgebel 2002, 2013; Steinberg 2010) deny that accounts with unspecified *ceteris paribus* clauses are *ipso facto* vacuous. Here we shall not take a stand on these issues since we are not committed to (any particular version of) the counterfactual approach (though we shall deploy it in the following, for convenience).

21. Some philosophers (e.g., Strawson 1994) seem to think, for instance, that having a desire that $p$ necessarily involves being disposed to feel pleasure upon its seeming that $p$. This is surely false; one can have a strong desire to attend the funeral of a close relative without being disposed in any sense to feel pleasure upon attending it (compare Smith 1998: 453–454). Consider a different affective disposition instead:

> Necessarily, for any agent $a$, any proposition $p$, any time $t$, if $a$ desires that $p$ at $t$, then $a$ is disposed at $t$ to feel relief (to some non-zero degree) when it seems to $a$ that $p$.

This is more plausible as a necessary element of the desiderative profile, yet we cannot pursue this any further here. See also Hyman 2014: 85; Friedrich *this volume*.

22. So the dispositional account we have in mind has no "reductive" aspirations.

23. Compare the taxonomy in Schroeder (2014). We state this explicitly because evaluativism is commonly supposed to be an alternative to the so-called motivational/action-based theory; so committing ourselves to the latter view at the outset would seem to be dialectically illicit. Neither dispositionalism about standing desire in general nor the particular version of it we outline here is in principle incompatible with evaluativism, however—so no question is begged against the evaluativist.

24. See, e.g., Strawson 1994: ch. 9; Schroeder 2004: 16–20; Arpaly and Schroeder 2014: 113–116. See also Lauria (*this volume*).

25. See Schroeder 2004: 16.

26. Strawson 1994: 251.

27. See ibid., 251–258.

28. Schroeder 2004: 17. See also Strawson 1994: 287, 1998: 473.

29. See also Smith (1998: 450–451), Wall (2009), and Ashwell (2014: 473) on this issue.

30. Both options seem fine by Strawson (1994: 252–253).

31. It is not clear whether this implies metaphysical impossibility. The Weather Watchers' complete practical incapability may be "constitutional" by virtue of being grounded in their intrinsic features, without being grounded in essential properties of them. In that case, their cognitive capacities could be enhanced, for instance, by neurochemical means so that they could at least perform mental acts. In what follows, we shall ignore these complications and assume that it is metaphysically impossible for the Weather Watchers to act.

32. Alternatively, one could extend the stimulus conditions in (D1) so as to require explicitly that the agent be capable of performing the act in question.

33. See Jenkins and Nolan (2012) for a recent defense of unmanifestable dispositions.

34. Since the antecedent is not true at any possible world, any antecedent world is trivially the consequent world, for any consequent.

35. The standard way of providing counterpossible conditionals with non-vacuous truth values is to extend the Lewis-Stalnaker semantics by introducing impossible worlds; see Nolan 1997; Berto 2013; Brogaard and Salerno 2013; Bjerring 2014.

36. Whether this attitude is a desire depends on other features of Wendy's psychology, as we shall shortly explain.

37. Here is a more "mundane" example: Suppose that John is a huge fan of the Belle Époque and has a very strong conative attitude toward having a firsthand experience of the period. By contrast, he has no interest whatsoever in the Early Medieval Period. If John thought that he can have a firsthand experience of the Belle Époque or the Early Middle Ages by traveling back into one of the periods, and if backward time travel were possible, he would travel back into the Belle Époque rather than the Early Medieval Period, *ceteris paribus*. So John is now disposed to travel back into the Belle Époque under certain circumstances, although this disposition is unmanifestable, as backward time travel is (*ex hypothesi*) impossible. By contrast, it would be wrong to ascribe to John any disposition to take time travel back into the Early Medieval Period, even if that disposition too would be just as unmanifestable as the former.

38. Michael Fara (2008: 849–853) seems to contend this, though his focus is slightly different than ours.

39. This also highlights the fact that "dispositional properties come in different flavors. For example, there are tendencies, capacities, liabilities, and pronenesses, each differing in modal profile" (Schwitzgebel 2013: 79). Being capable of $\varphi$-ing can be glossed, very roughly, as the disposition to $\varphi$ in circumstances where one tries to $\varphi$. We claim that one can have an inclination to $\varphi$ even if one is not, or even cannot be, capable of $\varphi$-ing, although of course being capable of $\varphi$-ing is a necessary condition for the manifestation of the inclination. However, it sounds odd to say that you

can have the capacity to $\varphi$ even if that capacity cannot manifest, because its stimulus condition cannot be fulfilled—because, that is, it is (perhaps even merely psychologically) impossible for you to even try to $\varphi$. (Incidentally, this might be all that Fara wants to argue, and if so, we agree with him on this score; see n37 above.) This suggests that there is a significant contrast between *practical inclinations* (inclinations to act in some way) and *practical capacities* (capacities to perform some act): whereas one can possess a practical inclination that is unmanifestable, a practical capacity is essentially manifestable. (On this and related issues about practical capacities, see Maier 2014, esp. sect. 2-3.)

40. Alvarez (*this volume*) argues that desires are not just essentially manifestable but even essentially *manifested* dispositions. It might seem that this contradicts our verdict that there can be unmanifestable practical inclinations, but this is illusory. On our view, having some standing desire is having a particular desiderative dispositional profile that consists of various different dispositions. (Alvarez herself accepts a similarly "pluralist" picture.) The inclination to "act" in ways that one takes to be conducive to satisfying one's desire is just one (though necessary) element of such a profile. Alvarez claims that one cannot be said to *have* some particular desiderative profile between $t_0$ and $t_1$, if *none* of the constituent dispositions of that dispositional profile is manifested at least once between $t_0$ and $t_1$, though she is clear that it is not required for having that desire between $t_0$ and $t_1$ that *any particular* constituent disposition be manifested between $t_0$ and $t_1$. This is perfectly compatible with what we have said about unmanifestable inclinations, which are, after all, not themselves desires but rather necessary elements of desiderative dispositional profiles.

41. Velleman 1992a: 17. As already pointed out, however, (D2) is a fairly weak, less controversial rendition of that basic idea.

42. Drawing the distinction between desires and wishes this way is not just intuitively plausible; there is also some linguistic evidence for it:

(1) I wish that I had been there.
(2) I wish that he were here too.
(3) *I want/desire that I had been there.
(4) *I want/desire that he were here too.

In (1)–(4) the use of past perfect and past subjunctive signals the perceived unattainability of the object of the relevant conative attitude, and, unlike (1) and (2), (3) and (4) are clearly ungrammatical. This is not to deny, of course, that the verb *want* can sometimes be used to report wishes rather than desires: an utterance of "I want him back!" by someone in grief sounds perfectly natural, for instance.

43. In fact, it seems plausible that having an inclination of the type specified in (D1) is something that *all* (positive) conative attitudes have in common, or perhaps even what makes conative attitudes conative in the first place—the essence of (positive) "conativity," as one might put it. Compare Velleman 2000: 260–263.

44. (D3) corresponds to what Lauria (*this volume*) calls "the death of desire principle." See also Massin (*this volume*) and Oddie (*this volume*) for discussion.

45. Importantly, (D3) does not rule out that you can think that $p$ already is the case and desire that it *continues* to be the case because the former thought is compatible with thinking that (or being undecided about whether) something you could do would be conducive to its *continuing* to be the case that $p$. See Hyman 2014: 86.

46. Lauria (*this volume*) disputes that (D3) is entailed by (D2). He gives the example of a person who believes that *p*, and also believes that he can change the past. He then goes on to suggest that it will be likely that this person can believe her performing of some acts to be conducive to *p*'s being the case. However, Lauria's discussion leaves it unclear why believing that one can change the past might lead you to believe that you can contribute to *p*'s being the case, *despite* already believing that *p*. Here is a concrete example that one might take to challenge the idea that (D2) entails (D3). Between $t_0$ and $t_1$, John desires to be a father. At $t_1$, he becomes a father and forms the belief that he is one. It follows from (D3) that, at $t_1$, John no longer desires to be a father (though, of course, he may desire to continue to be a father). Suppose now that, at $t_1$, John also believes that he can change the past and make it the case that he is not a father at $t_1$. It might seem plausible that, in such a case, John, at $t_1$, might also believe that his refraining from changing the past in such a way that he is not a father at $t_1$ is conducive to his being a father at $t_1$. But if so, John, at $t_1$, believes both that he is a father at $t_1$ and that his "performing" a particular act is conducive to his being a father at $t_1$—and this would be a counterexample to the claim that believing that *p* implies believing that nothing can be conducive to *p*'s being the case. Besides, if we suppose that John, at $t_1$, is disposed to refrain from changing the past in such a way that he is not a father at $t_1$, a disposition that is manifested (let us suppose) at $t_1$, it might seem, *contra* (D3), that he, at $t_1$, *desires* to be a father *despite* believing, also at $t_1$, that he already is a father. We believe that this description of John's case is mistaken. Given his belief that he is a father, John cannot simultaneously believe that something is conducive to his being a father—that is, he cannot take something to be contributing to bringing it about that he is a father, while he is convinced that his being a father is *already brought about*. However, given his belief that he can change the past, he might believe, at $t_1$, that his refraining from changing the past in such a way that he is not a father at $t_1$ is conducive to its *continuing* to be the case that he is a father. Now if we suppose that John, at $t_1$, is disposed to refrain from changing the past in such a way that he is not a father at $t_1$, this disposition would be explained by the desire that John has at $t_1$ to continue to be a father. Further, John might also believe that his changing the past in such a way that he is not a father at $t_1$ would be detrimental to his being a father at $t_1$. If so, then we can also explain John's disposition to refrain from changing the past in terms of his being glad at $t_1$ that he is a father at $t_1$, for it seems plausible that being glad that *p* necessarily involves both believing that *p* and being disposed to refrain from performing actions that one takes to be detrimental to *p*'s being the case. Hence, neither the idea that believing that *p* implies believing that nothing is conducive to *p*'s being the case nor the idea that (D2) entails (D3) are threatened by the possibility of believing that one can change the past.

47. See, e.g., Stampe 1987; Quinn 1993; Wallace 1999; Johnston 2001; Tenenbaum 2007: 9–16; Hawkins 2008; Schapiro 2009; Friedrich 2012, *this volume*; Schafer 2013.

48. The thesis that intentional action is action performed for a reason is widely endorsed in contemporary philosophy of action. Davidson (1980a: 6) writes, for example, that we can define "an intentional action as one done for a reason." Compare also Davidson 1980b: 264; Anscombe 1963: 9; Goldman 1970: 76; Mele 1992.

49. Whether teleological explanations are just a special form of causal explanations or constitute an independent, irreducible type of explanation is a matter of ongoing debate, but nothing hinges on this in the present context. For further discussion, see, e.g., Smith 1987, 1994: ch. 4; Sehon 1994; Schueler 2003; Mele 2003: ch. 2. See also Alvarez (2007) for a nice overview.

50. Note that the view outlined here is a theory of the explanation of intentional action; it does not imply anything substantial about the nature of desire (or any other attitudes, for that matter), let alone the so-called motivational/action-based theory. Indeed, as we shall see soon, most evaluativists motivate their view broadly within the framework of this theory of the explanation of intentional action.

51. This contrast is sometimes explicated by distinguishing between *motivating* and *normative* reasons (see esp. Smith 1987, 1994: ch. 4). Motivating reasons are not necessarily normative, but they "render an agent's action intelligible" by "specifying what there is to be said for acting in the way in question" (Smith 1994: 95).

52. One important exception is Scanlon (1998: 35), who thinks that "the only source of motivation lies in [one's] taking certain considerations . . . as reasons." So desires must involve some positive evaluation not just in order to rationalize actions, but also (or perhaps rather) in order to be motivationally efficacious at all.

53. Quinn 1993: 236–237. For similar examples, see Anscombe 1963: 70ff.; Helm 2009: 250.

54. Quinn 1993: 247.

55. Tenenbaum 2013: 3.

56. Doxastic evaluativists include Anscombe 1963; Davidson 1980a, 1980c (on one reading at least); de Sousa 1974; Raz 1999, 2010.

57. This distinction is commonly cashed out in terms of the different 'directions of fit' beliefs and desires are supposed to have; see esp. Smith 1987, 1994: ch. 4. See also Anscombe 1963: 56; Searle 1983; Humberstone 1992; Gregory 2012, *this volume*; Lauria *this volume*; Railton *this volume*. Compare David Lewis's (1988, 1996) treatment of this issue within the framework of formal decision theory.

58. See, e.g., Velleman 1992a: 7; Copp and Sobel 2002: 258; Friedrich 2012: 292, *this volume*.

59. See Thagard (2006) for an argument to this effect.

60. See Hawkins (2008) on this point.

61. Compare Baker 2014: 5–6, n8.

62. Compare Ruth Chang's (2004: 68) discussion of "rationalizers."

63. See Stocker 1979: 747–749; Velleman 1992a: 17–21. See also Watson 1975: 210–211.

64. This point is argued extensively in Audi (1994). See also n18 above.

65. We should also keep in mind that the principal motivation for doxastic evaluativism is to explain how desires can rationalize actions. But why think that a mere disposition to believe that $p$ is good can rationalize or subjectively justify any action, if the (non-evaluative) desire that $p$ cannot? After all, it is possible that, at the time of the action, the agent has the disposition to form the relevant belief without actually having that belief.

66. We take suspending judgment about $p$ to be a distinct doxastic attitude; see, e.g., Friedman (2013) on this.

67. See Quinn 1993: 236–237.

68. Defenses of perceptual evaluativism include Stampe 1987; Scanlon 1998; Wallace 1999; Helm 2001; Johnston 2001; Chang 2004; Oddie 2005, *this volume*; Tenenbaum 2007; Hawkins 2008; Schapiro 2009; Schafer 2013. According to Friedrich (2012, *this volume*), desires necessarily involve episodic experiences with a distinctive

phenomenology. Friedrich is clear that these experiences are not "evaluative seemings"; they do not have an evaluative representational content. However, he argues that their distinctive phenomenal character presents the desired object as something that must obtain, and claims that this amounts to a form of "non-cognitive evaluation." Now, as already announced (see n13), we do not intend to take a stand on the question of whether occurrent desires have a distinctive phenomenal character, but it is not clear to us why Friedrich calls the distinctive phenomenology of occurrent desires *evaluative*, or why, in general, he takes his view to be a form of evaluativism. It seems that one can have an experience with the phenomenal character he describes without the desired object seeming *good* or in any *evaluative* way. So, whatever the merits of his view about the phenomenal character of occurrent desires, it does not, as far as we can see, constitute a version of evaluativism at all. On the other hand, Friedrich's thesis that desires in general necessarily involve phenomenally conscious, episodic experiences falls prey to our main argument against perceptual evaluativism; see n78 below for more on this.

69. This is particularly conspicuous in e.g., Helm 2001; Johnston 2001; Chang 2004.

70. See, e.g., Goldie 2000; Helm 2001; Roberts 2003; Döring 2003, 2007.

71. Stampe 1987: 359. Similarly, Oddie (2005: 42) writes: "The desire that P is P's seeming good (or P's being experienced as good)."

72. See, e.g., Copp and Sobel (2002), Schapiro (2009), and Gregory (*this volume*) for critical discussion.

73. Scanlon 1998: 39. This is roughly equivalent to the view that desiring *p* is experiencing *p* as good, because, for Scanlon, "counting in favor of P" is roughly synonymous with "being a reason for P" (17), and, according to his famous buck-passing account, values reduce to reasons. Note, however, that Scanlon specifies here only a sufficient condition for having a desire. This is a bit odd, given his intention "to capture an *essential* element in the intuitive notion of (occurrent) desire" (39, emphasis added).

74. Again these advantages depend on a certain, nontrivial conception of perceptual content. See Hawkins (2008) on this issue.

75. This is observed by Baker (2014: 3, n6) as well. Note, however, that Oddie (*this volume*) explicitly denies that *p*'s seeming good is sufficient for desiring that *p*.

76. Does an analogous argument apply to doxastic evaluativism? After all, doxastic evaluativists claim that the desire that *p* necessarily involves the belief that *p* is good, and this does not seem to be applicable to occurrent desires. Well, doxastic evaluativists have an easy solution here: they can simply claim that while the standing desire that *p* necessarily involves the standing belief that *p* is good, the occurrent desire that *p* necessarily involves the occurrent judgment (or thought) that *p* is good. By contrast, it seems that perceptual evaluativists seek to characterize both standing and occurrent desires in terms of mental phenomena that are essentially occurrent and do not have any "standing" counterparts.

77. Incidentally, Quinn (1993: 235) states explicitly that Radioman is to be understood as having a standing desire.

78. This seems to be what Scanlon (1998: 39) has in mind when he writes, "What is generally called a desire involves having a tendency to see something as a reason." Friedrich (*this volume*) also mentions this sort of extension as a possible solution to the problem at hand.

79. Friedrich (*this volume*) suggests a stronger link between standing and occurrent desires: if, between $t_0$ and $t_1$, *a* has a standing desire that *p*, then not only must *a* have,

during that time, the disposition to occurrently desire that *p*, but that disposition must also *manifest* at some point or another between $t_0$ and $t_1$. But this does nothing to bypass the objection above, for even if we suppose that the disposition manifests frequently, at multiple points between $t_0$ and $t_1$, there would at least be some points between $t_0$ and $t_1$ at which Thomas does not occurrently desire to go to the kitchen, yet his standing desire persists.

80. To reapply yet another point from the previous section (see n64 above), here too it is unclear how a mere disposition to experience something as good should rationalize any action. After all, the agent can have the disposition to experience something as good without actually undergoing any evaluative experience before or during his performance of the action.

81. Scanlon 1998: 43. See Gregory (*this volume*) for a critical discussion of this example.

82. Compare Patricia Greenspan's (1988: 18) influential argument against doxastic analyses of recalcitrant emotions. See also Schapiro 2009; Friedrich 2012: 293.

83. Scanlon 1998: 39.

84. Roberts 2003: 92. Compare the notion of the "appearance of good" in Tenenbaum (2007).

85. See Döring 2010.

86. Scanlon (1998: 41) writes, "Desire . . . characterizes an important form of variability in the motivational efficacy of reasons, but it does this by describing one way in which the thought of something as a reason can present itself rather than by identifying a motivating factor that is independent of such a thought."

87. Johnston 2001: 206.

88. For more details, see Döring 2007: 387–388, n19.

89. This is not necessarily to deny that the experience of *p*'s seeming good to one can justify the belief or judgment that *p* is good, rather in the way that perceptions justify perceptual beliefs. The claim is rather that evaluative experiences cannot play the justificatory role that perceptual evaluativists suppose them to play because they themselves cannot justify actions directly.

90. Smith (2012b) makes this point very clearly. Note that Quinn (1993: 253) appears to conflate the two issues.

91. For similar complaints, see Copp and Sobel 2002; Smith (2012a).

92. This is a familiar theme in the philosophy of action. See, e.g., Frankfurt 1971; Watson 1975; Velleman 1992b; Bratman 2000a, 2000b, 2003, 2007.

93. Compare Baker (2014: 14–22). This is not to deny that evaluativism may also be compatible with this more detailed picture; the point is rather that it is not *uniquely compatible* with it. If this is true, if, that is, the enriched version can just as well be accounted for within a non-evaluativist framework, then the central motivation for evaluativism is undermined.

94. This is also pointed out by Copp and Sobel 2002: 261; Smith 2012b: 80–83.

95. These broader agency-related phenomena have been discussed most elaborately in Michael Bratman's work. See, e.g., 1987, 2000a, 2007.

96. This is roughly analogous to Smith's (2012a: 394) response to the example of Radioman.

97. For more on these issues, see esp. Bratman 2007.

98. An earlier draft of this paper was presented at the Graduate Colloquium in Practical Philosophy at University of Tübingen; we thank Mitchell Green and all of the participants for helpful questions and discussions. We are especially grateful to Julien Deonna and Federico Lauria for their detailed and insightful comments on the penultimate version.

## References

Anscombe, G. E. M. (1963). *Intention*, 2nd ed. Oxford: Blackwell.

Alvarez, Maria. (2007). 'The Causalist/Anti-Causalist Debate in the Theory of Action: What It Is and Why It Matters', in Anton Leist (ed.), *Action in Context*. Berlin: Walter de Gruyter.

Arpaly, Nomy, and Schroeder, Timothy. (2014). *In Praise of Desire*. Oxford: Oxford University Press.

Ashwell, Lauren. (2014). 'The Metaphysics of Desire and Dispositions', *Philosophy Compass*, 9, 469–477.

Audi, Robert. (1994). 'Dispositional Beliefs and Dispositions to Believe', *Noûs*, 28, 419–434.

Baker, Derek. (2014). 'The Abductive Case for Humeanism over Quasi-Perceptual Theories of Desire', *Journal of Ethics and Social Philosophy*, 8, 1–29.

Bayne, Tim, and Montague, Michelle. (2011, eds.). *Cognitive Phenomenology*. Oxford: Oxford University Press.

Ben-Yami, Hanoch. (1997). 'Against Characterizing Mental States as Propositional Attitudes', *Philosophical Quarterly*, 47, 84–89.

Berto, Francesco. (2013). 'Impossible Worlds', in Edward N. Zalta (ed.), *The Stanford Encyclopedia of Philosophy* (winter 2013 edition), URL = <http://plato.stanford.edu/archives/win2013/entries/impossible-worlds/>.

Bird, Alexander. (1998). 'Dispositions and Antidotes', *Philosophical Quarterly*, 48, 227–234.

Bjerring, Jens Christian. (2014). 'On Counterpossibles', *Philosophical Studies*, 168, 327–353.

Block, Ned. (1995). 'On a Confusion about a Function of Consciousness', *Behavioral and Brain Sciences*, 18, 227–247.

———. (2002). 'Concepts of Consciousness', in David J. Chalmers (ed.), *Philosophy of Mind: Classical and Contemporary Readings*. Oxford: Oxford University Press.

Bratman, Michael E. (1987). *Intention, Plans, and Practical Reason*. Cambridge, Mass.: Harvard University Press.

———. (1992). 'Practical Reasoning and Acceptance in a Context', *Mind*, 101, 1–16.

———. (2000a). 'Reflection, Planning, and Temporally Extended Agency', *Philosophical Review*, 109, 35–61.

———. (2000b). 'Valuing and the Will', *Philosophical Perspectives*, 14, 249–265.

———. (2003). 'A Desire of One's Own', *Journal of Philosophy*, 100, 221–242.

———. (2007). 'Planning Agency, Autonomous Agency', in *Structures of Agency*. Oxford: Oxford University Press.

Brogaard, Berit, and Salerno, Joe. (2013). 'Remarks on Counterpossibles', *Synthese*, 190, 639–660.

Chang, Ruth. (2004). 'Can Desires Provide Reasons for Action?', in R. Jay Wallace, Philip Pettit, Samuel Scheffler, and Michael Smith (eds.), *Reason and Value: Themes from the Moral Philosophy of Joseph Raz*. Oxford: Oxford University Press.

Choi, Sungho. (2008). 'Dispositional Properties and Counterfactual Conditionals', *Mind*, 117, 795–841.

Cohen, Jonathan L. (1992). *An Essay on Belief and Acceptance*. Oxford: Clarendon Press.

Contessa, Gabriele. (2013). 'Dispositions and Interferences', *Philosophical Studies*, 165, 401–419.

Copp, David, and Sobel, David. (2002). 'Desires, Motives, and Reasons: Scanlon's Rationalistic Moral Psychology', *Social Theory and Practice*, 28, 243–276.

Correia, Fabrice. (2008). 'Ontological Dependence', *Philosophy Compass*, 3, 1013–1032.

Crane, Tim. (2001). *Elements of Mind: An Introduction to the Philosophy of Mind*. Oxford: Oxford University Press.

———. (2013). 'Unconscious Belief and Conscious Thought', in Uriah Kriegel (ed.), *Phenomenal Intentionality*. Oxford: Oxford University Press.

Davidson, Donald. (1980a). 'Actions, Reasons, and Causes', in *Essays on Actions and Events*. Oxford: Clarendon Press.

———. (1980b). 'Hempel on Explaining Action', in *Essays on Actions and Events*. Oxford: Clarendon Press.

———. (1980c). 'Intending', in *Essays on Actions and Events*. Oxford: Clarendon Press.

de Sousa, Ronald. (1974). 'The Good and the True', *Mind*, 83, 534–551.

Döring, Sabine A. (2003). 'Explaining Action by Emotion', *Philosophical Quarterly*, 53, 214–230.

———. (2007). 'Seeing What to Do: Affective Perception and Rational Motivation', *Dialectica*, 61, 363–394.

———. (2010). 'Why Be Emotional?', in Peter Goldie (ed.), *The Oxford Handbook of Philosophy of Emotion*. Oxford: Oxford University Press.

Fara, Michael. (2008). 'Masked Abilities and Compatibilism', *Mind*, 117, 843–865.

Friedman, Jane. (2013). 'Suspended Judgment', *Philosophical Studies*, 162, 165–181.

Friedrich, Daniel. (2012). 'The Alluringness of Desire', *Philosophical Explorations*, 15, 291–302.

Frankfurt, Harry. (1971). 'Freedom of the Will and the Concept of a Person', *Journal of Philosophy*, 68, 5–20.

Goldie, Peter. (2000). *The Emotions: A Philosophical Exploration*. Oxford: Oxford University Press.

Goldman, Alvin. (1970). *A Theory of Human Action*. Englewood Cliffs, N.J.: Prentice-Hall.

Greenspan, Patricia S. (1988). *Emotions and Reasons: An Inquiry into Emotional Justification*. London: Routledge.

Gregory, Alex. (2012). 'Changing Direction on Direction of Fit', *Ethical Theory and Moral Practice*, 15, 603–614.

———. (2013). 'The Guise of Reasons', *American Philosophical Quarterly*, 50, 63–72.

Hawkins, Jennifer. (2008). 'Desiring the Bad under the Guise of the Good', *Philosophical Quarterly*, 58, 244–264.

Helm, Bennett. (2001). *Emotional Reason: Deliberation, Motivation, and the Nature of Value*. Cambridge, UK: Cambridge University Press.

———. (2009). 'Emotions as Evaluative Feelings', *Emotion Review*, 1, 248–255.

Humberstone, I. Lloyd. (1992). 'Direction of Fit', *Mind*, 101, 59–83.

Hyman, John. (2014). 'Desires, Dispositions and Deviant Causal Chains', *Philosophy*, 89, 83–112.

Jenkins, C. S., and Nolan, Daniel. (2012). 'Disposition Impossible', *Noûs*, 46, 732–753.

Johnston, Mark. (1992). 'How to Speak of the Colors', *Philosophical Studies*, 68, 221–263.

———. (2001). 'The Authority of Affect', *Philosophy and Phenomenological Research*, 63, 181–214.

Kriegel, Uriah. (2013). 'Understanding Conative Phenomenology: Lessons from Ricœr', *Phenomenology and the Cognitive Sciences*, 12, 537–557.

———. (2015). *The Varieties of Consciousness*. Oxford: Oxford University Press.

Koslicki, Kathrin. (2013). 'Ontological Dependence: An Opinionated Survey', in Miguel Hoeltje, Benjamin Schnieder, and Alex Steinberg (eds.), *Varieties of Dependence: Ontological Dependence, Grounding, Supervenience, Response-Dependence*. Munich: Philosophia Verlag.

Lewis, David. (1973). *Counterfactuals*. Oxford: Basil Blackwell.

———. (1988). 'Desire as Belief', *Mind*, 97, 323–332.

———. (1996). 'Desire as Belief II', *Mind*, 105, 303–313.

———. (1997). 'Finkish Dispositions', *Philosophical Quarterly*, 47, 143–158.

Lowe, E. Jonathan. (2013). 'Some Varieties of Metaphysical Dependence', in Miguel Hoeltje, Benjamin Schnieder, and Alex Steinberg (eds.), *Varieties of Dependence: Ontological Dependence, Grounding, Supervenience, Response-Dependence*. Munich: Philosophia Verlag.

Maier, John. (2014). 'Abilities', in Edward N. Zalta (ed.), *The Stanford Encyclopedia of Philosophy* (fall 2014 edition), URL = <http://plato.stanford.edu/archives/fall2014/entries/abilities/>.

Manley, David, and Wasserman, Ryan. (2008). 'On Linking Dispositions and Conditionals', *Mind*, 117, 59–84.

Martin, C. B. (1994). 'Dispositions and Conditionals', *Philosophical Quarterly*, 44, 1–8.

Mele, Alfred R. (1992). 'Acting for Reasons and Acting Intentionally', *Pacific Philosophical Quarterly*, 73, 355–374.

———. (2003). *Motivation and Agency*. Oxford: Oxford University Press.

Nolan, Daniel. (1997). 'Impossible Worlds: A Modest Approach', *Notre Dame Journal of Formal Logic*, 38, 535–572.

Oddie, Graham. (2005). *Value, Reality, and Desire*. Oxford: Oxford University Press.

Quinn, Warren. (1993). 'Putting Rationality in Its Place', in *Morality and Action*. Cambridge, UK: Cambridge University Press.

Raz, Joseph. (1999). *Engaging Reason: On the Theory of Value and Action*. Oxford: Oxford University Press.

———. (2010). 'On the Guise of the Good', in Sergio Tenenbaum (ed.), *Desire, Practical Reason, and the Good*. Oxford: Oxford University Press.

Roberts, Robert C. (2003). *Emotions: An Essay in Aid of Moral Psychology*. Cambridge, UK: Cambridge University Press.

Schafer, Karl. (2013). 'Perception and the Rational Force of Desire', *Journal of Philosophy*, 110, 258–281.

Scanlon, Thomas M. (1998). *What We Owe to Each Other*. Cambridge, Mass.: Harvard University Press.

———. (2002). 'Replies', *Social Theory and Practice*, 28, 337–358.

Schapiro, Tamar. (2009). 'The Nature of Inclination', *Ethics*, 119, 229–256.

Schroeder, Timothy. (2004). *Three Faces of Desire*. Oxford: Oxford University Press.

———. (2014). 'Desire', in Edward N. Zalta (ed.), *The Stanford Encyclopedia of Philosophy* (spring 2014 edition), URL = <http://plato.stanford.edu/archives/spr2014/entries/desire/>.

Schueler, George F. (1995). *Desire: Its Role in Practical Reason and the Explanation of Action*. Cambridge, Mass.: MIT Press.

———. (2003). *Reasons and Purposes: Human Rationality and the Teleological Explanation of Action*. Oxford: Oxford University Press.

Schwitzgebel, Eric. (2002). 'A Phenomenal, Dispositional Account of Belief', *Noûs*, 36, 249–275.

———. (2013). 'A Dispositional Approach to the Attitudes: Thinking Outside of the Belief Box', in Nikolaj Nottelmann (ed.), *New Essays on Belief: Constitution, Content and Structure*. Basingstoke, UK: Palgrave Macmillan.

Searle, John L. (1983). *Intentionality: An Essay in the Philosophy of Mind*. Cambridge, UK: Cambridge University Press.

Sehon, Scott R. (1994). 'Teleology and the Nature of Mental States', *American Philosophical Quarterly*, 31, 63–72.

Sinhababu, Neil. (*forthcoming*). 'Advantages of Propositionalism', *Pacific Philosophical Quarterly*.

Smith, Michael. (1987). 'The Humean Theory of Motivation', *Mind*, 96, 36–61.

———. (1994). *The Moral Problem*. Oxford: Blackwell.

———. (1998). 'Galen Strawson and the Weather Watchers', *Philosophy and Phenomenological Research*, 58, 449–454.

———. (2012a). 'Four Objections to the Standard Story of Action (and Four Replies)', *Philosophical Issues*, 22, 387–401.

———. (2012b). 'Scanlon on Desire and the Explanation of Action', in R. Jay Wallace, Rahul Kumar, and Samuel Freeman (eds.), *Reasons and Recognition: Essays on the Philosophy of T. M. Scanlon*. Oxford: Oxford University Press.

Smithies, Declan. (2013a). 'The Nature of Cognitive Phenomenology', *Philosophy Compass*, 8, 744–754.

———. (2013b). 'The Significance of Cognitive Phenomenology', *Philosophy Compass*, 8, 731–743.

Soteriou, Matthew. (2007). 'Content and the Stream of Consciousness', *Philosophical Perspectives*, 21, 543–568.

———. (2013). *The Mind's Construction: The Ontology of Mind and Mental Action*. Oxford: Oxford University Press.

Stalnaker, Robert. (1968). 'A Theory of Conditionals', in Nicholas Rescher (ed.), *Studies in Logical Theory (American Philosophical Quarterly Monograph Series, vol. 2)*. Oxford: Blackwell.

Stampe, Dennis W. (1987). 'The Authority of Desire', *Philosophical Review*, 96, 335–381.

Steinberg, Jesse R. (2010). 'Dispositions and Subjunctives', *Philosophical Studies*, 148, 323–341.

Steward, Helen. (1997). *The Ontology of Mind: Events, Processes, and States*. Oxford: Oxford University Press.

Strandberg, Caj. (2012). 'Expressivism and Dispositional Desires', *American Philosophical Quarterly*, 49, 81–91.

Strawson, Galen. (1994). *Mental Reality*. Cambridge, Mass.: MIT Press.

———. (1998). 'Replies to Noam Chomsky, Pierre Jacob, Michael Smith, and Paul Snowdon', *Philosophy and Phenomenological Research*, 58, 461–486.

Stocker, Michael. (1979). 'Desiring the Bad: An Essay in Moral Psychology', *Journal of Philosophy*, 76, 738–753.

Tahko, Tuomas, and Lowe, E. Jonathan. (2015). 'Ontological Dependence', in Edward N. Zalta (ed.), *The Stanford Encyclopedia of Philosophy* (spring 2015 edition), URL = <http://plato.stanford.edu/archives/spr2015/entries/dependence-ontological/>.

Tenenbaum, Sergio. (2007). *Appearances of the Good: An Essay on the Nature of Practical Reason*. Cambridge, UK: Cambridge University Press

———. (2013). 'Guise of the Good', in Hugh LaFollette (ed.), *The International Encyclopedia of Ethics*. Oxford: Wiley-Blackwell.

Thagard, Paul R. (2006). 'Desires Are Not Propositional Attitudes', *Dialogue*, 45, 151–156.

Velleman, David J. (1992a). 'The Guise of the Good', *Noûs*, 26, 3–26.

———. (1992b). 'What Happens When Someone Acts?', *Mind*, 101, 461–481.

———. (2000). 'On the Aim of Belief', in *The Possibility of Practical Reason*. Oxford: Oxford University Press.

Wall, David. (2009). 'Are There Passive Desires?', *Dialectica*, 63, 133–155.

Wallace, R. Jay. (1999). 'Addiction as Defect of the Will: Some Philosophical Reflections', *Law and Philosophy*, 18, 621–654.

Watson, Gary. (1975). 'Free Agency', *Journal of Philosophy*, 72, 205–220.

# CHAPTER 4 | Desires, Dispositions and the Explanation of Action

MARIA ALVAREZ

WE OFTEN EXPLAIN human actions by reference to the desires of the person whose actions we are explaining: "Jane is studying law because she wants to become a judge." But how do desires explain actions? A widely accepted view is that desires are dispositional states that are manifested in behavior. This view can be traced back to Davidson's influential 1963 paper "Actions, Reasons, and Causes," which opens with this question: "What is the relation between a reason and an action when the reason explains the action by giving the agent's reason for doing what he did?" (685). Davidson's answer, which subsequently became the orthodoxy in action theory, is that the relation between the reason that explains an action and the explained action is that of cause and effect and that, therefore, explanations that give the agent's reason for acting, which he called "rationalizations," are "a species of causal explanation" (685). A reason why an agent did something, according to Davidson, consists of a belief and a desire; specifically, he claimed, "Giving the reason why an agent did something is often a matter of naming the pro-attitude (a) or the related belief (b) or both; let me call this pair the primary reason why the agent performed the action" (686). *Pro-attitude* is a semitechnical term intended by Davidson to include, among other things, "desires, wantings, urges, promptings, . . . in so far as these can be interpreted as attitudes of an agent directed toward actions of a certain kind" (686).

Davidson's characterization of desires is not precise, but he implicitly endorses the view that desires are dispositional states and that, like other dispositions, they are causal conditions of the actions they explain. This is evident in his response to the objection that a primary reason "consist of attitudes and beliefs, which are states or dispositions, not events; therefore they cannot be causes" (693): "It is easy to reply that states, dispositions, and conditions are frequently named as the causes of events: the bridge collapsed because of a structural defect; the plane crashed on takeoff because the air temperature was abnormally high; the plate broke because it had a crack" (694). The gist of this response is, then, that desires and beliefs *are* states or dispositions, but that doesn't imply that they are not causes, since states and dispositions are often named as causes of events. Perhaps, Davidson goes on to say, such states and dispositions are causes only on the assumption that there was a triggering event (*the* cause), but again, that does not impugn their status as causes or, more precisely, causal conditions of the events they explain.[1]

The view that desires, and indeed many psychological states, are dispositional states is now widely accepted; in fact it is often taken as obvious.[2] And so is the view that dispositions are causes (or causal conditions) of their manifestations: fragility is often cited as the cause of a fragile object's breaking, solubility as the cause of the dissolving of soluble things, malleability of the change in shape of malleable things, etc.[3] In this paper I examine this view of desires. While I do not reject it, I argue that, if desires are dispositions, they are dispositions with a distinctive feature that sets them apart from ordinary physical dispositions, such as fragility or conductivity. And I suggest, in my concluding remarks, that this feature of desires favors a particular model for how desires explain actions when they feature in action explanations, namely the "context-placing" model.

The structure of the paper is as follows. In section 1, after some preliminary clarifications, I outline the idea that desires are dispositional states. I then examine in section 2 the various ways in which desires are manifested, and in section 3 I turn to the question of how that manifestation relates to the presence of a desire. I suggest that the nature of that relationship shows that desires are what I call "manifestation-dependent" dispositions. My concluding remarks relate this feature of desires to the question of how desires explain actions.

## 1. Desires as Dispositional States

In ordinary contemporary usage *desire* is more often reserved for desires related to the natural appetites: desires for food, warmth, comfort, sleep, etc., and, in particular, for sexual desire. By contrast, in philosophy the term normally covers any state of wanting or desiring (but see Schueler

1995). Some philosophers sometimes use *desire* interchangeably with *pro-attitude*, while others restrict it to refer to states that form a species within that genus. In this latter usage, desires are sometimes contrasted with, say, wishes, hopes, longings, or cravings. Each of those four concepts (and there are others) differs somewhat from the others as well as from the concept of desire with which they are contrasted. The first two overlap with desire in involving a positive evaluation of their object but differ from it in that they are not tied to behavior, or not as closely as desire is. The last two terms are less clearly linked to positive evaluation. But all of them, as well as related concepts, are generally regarded as sufficiently close to each other that they tend to be brought together under umbrella terms such as Davidson's *pro-attitude*.

In this paper I shall be concerned primarily with desires in the semi-technical and somewhat restricted philosophical sense just outlined. So I shall leave aside for the most part other pro-attitudes such as wishes, hopes, longings, and cravings and shall not be concerned with whether what I say about desires is also true of any of these pro-attitudes, or indeed of other psychological states.

A further clarification about my focus is needed. It is a familiar point that the term *desire*, like *belief, conviction, statement*, and many similar psychological terms, suffers from what might be called a "state/object ambiguity." So "my desire" may be used to talk about my desiring something or about what I desire; for instance, to talk about *my desiring* to carry the vote at a meeting, or about what I desire, namely *to carry the vote at the meeting*. This paper is concerned with desires understood in the first sense, as *my desiring* something.

So what is it to desire something? A common answer in the philosophical literature is that desiring something, like believing something, is or consists in *being in a state*, namely a state of desiring.[4] However, if desiring is being in a state, it is not a state that need be manifested throughout the time when it is true that one desires that thing. For instance, a person may desire financial security over a period of time, and yet at some times in that period she may not manifest the desire in any way: that is, she may not talk or think about it, or do anything related to that desire, etc. at those times. Because of this, because desires are states that may be manifested in a variety of ways but that need not, at any one time, be manifested in any of those ways, it seems plausible to think of desires as *dispositional* states: states that, perhaps together with other dispositional states such as the subject's beliefs, dispose the agent to certain forms of behavior, thoughts, mental images, emotional reactions, sensations, feelings, etc.

Thus, many philosophers today think of desires as belonging to the category of dispositions, in particular of "multitrack" dispositions: dispositions that can be manifested in a variety of ways. This view of desires raises the question: How are desires manifested?

## 2. Desires and Their Manifestation

Let me start with a point about the notion of the manifestation of a disposition. When we talk about the manifestation of a disposition, we tend to think of the occurrence of certain sorts of physical changes or processes that are related to the disposition (indeed are defining of the disposition)—changes or processes that are in principle "perceivable" through the senses.[5] However, although this may be right for inanimate things, human psychological dispositions are different in that they may be manifested both in perceivable occurrences that include, but are not limited to, purposive behavior,[6] and also in "purely mental" phenomena, such as thoughts, sensations, feelings, emotional reactions, etc. that need not have any outward or publicly perceivable expression. Accordingly psychological dispositions can be manifested, as we might say, "externally" or "internally."[7]

Desires are manifested externally in what seem to be two categorically different types of manifestation. First, they are manifested in *behavior*, which may be purposive or simply expressive.[8] Second, desires are manifested in *physiological changes* in the agent that has the desire—changes that do not amount to behavior. The categorical distinction between behavior and mere physiological changes is drawn on the basis of the fact that there are things that we do that are, in principle and to some extent, under our direct control even if their occurrence is not intentional on a particular occasion, while others are never under our direct control. To illustrate: grabbing and cursing are, on this characterization, behavioral manifestations; sweating and salivating are not—they are mere physiological changes.

The behavior that manifests desires may, in turn, be of two kinds: purposive or merely expressive ("merely expressive" because purposive behavior may also be expressive). A desire is manifested in purposive behavior when the agent who has the desire engages in goal-directed behavior: the agent acts so as to bring about what the desire is a desire for and adapts its behavior to that end. The adaptation of behavior is shaped by the agent's exercise of its cognitive abilities; that is to say, the agent directs its behavior according to its cognition of the circumstances—cognition that may be perceptual or of some other kind (for instance, inferential) and may or may not involve the manipulation of concepts. In cases where the agent is not capable of concept manipulation, cognition shapes behavior through the discriminatory capacities of the agent. In cases of agents capable of concept manipulation whose desires are manifested in purposive action, cognition can shape behavior in several ways: in the conceptualization of the object of desire, in reasoning about whether and how to satisfy the desire, and in the exercise of the range of cognitive capacities (perceptual, inferential, perhaps intuitive, etc.) required to guide the agent's behavior toward the intended goal. In such cases, purposive behavior is not only goal-directed but also typically guided by reasons (see Döring and Eker *this volume*).

Accordingly, the desire to eat can be manifested in eating but also in food searching and grabbing behavior, both of which are *purposive* behavior; in the case of humans, the desire to eat can also be manifested in linguistic expressions—which may be purposive or merely expressive (see below). Likewise, a desire to buy a car may be manifested in buying a car, but it can also be manifested in actions conducive to doing so, for instance, in finding out about the different virtues of various cars; saving money to buy a car, perhaps by forgoing other purchases; and so on.

Desires are also manifested in behavior that is not purposive but is, as I noted earlier, merely *expressive*. For example, the desire to eat may be manifested in crying (for instance, in babies), meowing (in cats), and, for adult humans, in linguistic behavior, such as the exclamation "I'm hungry!". Similarly, the desire to buy a car may be manifested in talking about cars; expressions (e.g. linguistic or facial expressions) of disappointment when finding out that car taxes have gone up, such as looking sad, or cursing; or in expressions of joy, such as smiling, laughing, or cheering, when realizing that one can now afford the desired car or that one is about to buy it.

A distinctive feature of desires is that, at least for humans (I leave aside whether this is also true of any other animals), it is often possible to *suppress* what would be a behavioral manifestation of a desire one has—for instance, by choosing not to act in ways that would lead to the satisfaction of the desire, by suppressing its linguistic expression and even voicing a contrary desire, or by suppressing the expression of the associated emotions: hiding one's disappointment or anger, pretending or declaring that one feels the opposite emotion, and so on. In other words, agents can sometimes choose whether to manifest their desires behaviorally.

Desires also have, as I suggested, external but non-behavioral manifestations—which are manifestations that are not typically under our control: we can neither bring them about nor suppress them at will, though we can often do things at will that will result in the occurrence of those sorts of changes. These manifestations may be purely physiological changes, or they may be changes tied to emotions such as fear, joy, anxiety, etc. For example, desires may be manifested in bodily changes such as salivation or tummy rumblings (purely physiological) or in trembling (with fear), blushing (in anger), or getting flushed (with excitement) at the thought or sight of what one wants, or of getting it, or of losing it, and so on.

So much for the external manifestations of desires. The internal manifestations of desires include thoughts (contemplative, imaginative, calculative, etc.), emotional reactions (Strawson 1994), mental images, and sensations and feelings of various kinds. The sensations that manifest a desire may be those that accompany related thoughts and emotions, such as feelings of fear, anticipation, or delight, or sensations associated with bodily appetites, etc. And the thoughts, mental images, or daydreams that constitute manifestations of a desire may be of the kind that come unbidden, or they may be the result of intentional mental activity, such as purposeful deliberation or imagining. Thus, engaging in deliberation about how to achieve something and the relative costs of doing so, etc. and deliberately imagining satisfying the desire can also be manifestations of a desire, as can be emotional reactions and feelings to these. (See Schueler *this volume* on deliberation concerning desires.)

When desires are manifested in this internal way, they may also be manifested externally, and so the desire may be attributed to the agent on the basis of those external manifestations. But regardless of whether or not desires are externally manifested, these internal phenomena may constitute manifestations of a desire, if only to oneself: my well-concealed feelings of envy on hearing of a friend's professional success may make me realize that, contrary to what I thought, I do want to achieve professional recognition. In such cases, I may then see some of my past actions in a new light, e.g. see them as directed at achieving such recognition and hence as manifestations of my desire. But it is also possible that the feeling of envy should be the first manifestation of my desire. Because of this it is possible that sometimes only its possessor may be in a position to recognize that she has a certain desire, although this is by no means always the case. Indeed, often the opposite is true: others can be in a position to tell us about unacknowledged desires by witnessing their various external manifestations. And of course sometimes oneself and others may misinterpret manifestations of a desire for A as those of a desire for B. And so on.

Desires have this range of internal and external manifestations partly because desires are linked to pleasure and pain in various ways. So desiring is a state that often brings with it pain or displeasure, whether in the form of a sensation or a negative psychological state, such as frustration, fear, annoyance, etc., which may arise from the as yet unsatisfied desire or from the frustration of the desire. The satisfaction of desire typically brings with it (a degree of) pleasure, as does the anticipation of satisfaction. To be sure, sometimes the satisfaction of a desire is disappointing (for instance, less pleasant than one expected); distasteful (one may be disgusted after having given in to a desire to eat three cream doughnuts; or after doing something one felt one had to do and in that sense wanted to do but also found repugnant to do); or regarded by the agent as an outright disaster (perhaps very little pleasure and much pain comes from the satisfaction of the desire). Still, there is often some pleasure in getting what one wants even if it is very short-lived and even if the pleasure merely consists in the assuaging of the discomfort or frustration of desiring; and repugnance or distaste may be mixed with the pleasure of having done one's duty, or having got an unpleasant task out of the way, and so on. Moreover, even when there is very little and short-lived pleasure, there tends to be some pleasure in the anticipation of satisfaction. So desires cause and are caused by pleasure, pain, or displeasure (physical or psychological), which is itself often linked (causally or expressively) to purposive behavior (toward or away from the object), emotional reactions, feelings, thoughts, etc.

Thus, we have seen that desires can be manifested externally in purposive behavior (including in actions done for reasons), in expressive behavior, or in physiological changes, and also internally in certain patterns of thoughts, sensations, emotional reactions, etc., which may, in turn, be externally expressed.

It could be objected that, although in a sense of the word *manifestation* that means simply "making evident" these are all possible ways in which desires are manifested, they are not all manifestations of a desire in the sense of manifestation relevant to dispositions. For dispositions, the objection would go, are defined by their manifestations: what the bearer of the disposition *does*, so fragility is the disposition to break in certain circumstances, and solubility is the disposition to dissolve, etc. And similarly, what defines a desire is what the person who has the desire *does*: characteristic behavior, and in particular characteristic desire-satisfying behavior.[9] The objection is unconvincing. First, dispositions, such as fragility and solubility are what Ryle (1949: 44) calls "single-track dispositions." But, as he notes, there are also multi-track dispositions, "the exercises of which are indefinitely heterogeneous" (44), and psychological dispositions such as desires, beliefs or character traits, belong in this group. To illustrate the point, Ryle says:

> When Jane Austen wished to show the specific kind of pride which characterised the heroine of *Pride and Prejudice*, she had to represent her actions, words, thoughts and feelings in a thousand different situations. There is no one standard type of action or reaction such that Jane Austen could say "My heroine's kind of pride was just the tendency to do this, whenever a situation of that sort arose." (44)

It may be true that actions, and among them "overt" actions (i.e. those involving bodily behavior), are a central way in which desires are manifested, and are analogous to the manifestation of simple physical dispositions, e.g. breaking or dissolving. But this is no reason to deny that the range of phenomena described above can also be genuine manifestations of a desire.

Because of this, it should now be clear that our initial question about how desires explain actions will be illuminated by examining the nature of the relationship between desiring something and the whole range of "external" and "internal" manifestations of that desire, since the range includes intentional actions. I turn to that question in section 3, where I argue that there is a feature of the relationship between desires and their manifestations that sets them apart from the ordinary physical dispositions often discussed in the literature, such as solubility, elasticity, fragility, etc.[10]

## 3. Desires as Manifestation-Dependent Dispositions

The *SEP* entry for dispositions says that "in general, it seems that nothing about the *actual* behavior of an object is ever necessary for it to have the dispositions it has" (Choi and Fara 2016). This is clearly intended as a claim about dispositions in general and the term *actual behavior* is meant to include not just the current or past actual behavior but the actual behavior of an object over its lifetime. So a particular thing may have a disposition such as fragility or solubility even if the thing itself never has and never will manifest it. For instance, a particular lump of sugar or pinch of salt is said to be soluble (have a disposition to dissolve in certain conditions) and a particular glass vase or a ceramic tile is said to be fragile (disposed to break under certain kinds of stress) even if they never have and never will dissolve or break. Typically these dispositions have a categorial basis as well as conditions for their manifestation (conditions that enable the disposition to be manifested); in addition many require a stimulus or trigger that brings about their manifestation—[11]though it has proved singularly difficult to specify what these conditions and triggers are, even for fairly simple dispositions, such as fragility, as is shown by the failures so far of attempts to provide a satisfactory conditional analysis of dispositions.[12] The problem is that an object or portion of stuff can have a disposition that is not manifested even when the trigger occurs because of the presence of masks, antidotes, or finks; and, in such cases, the failure of manifestation does not imply the absence of the disposition. The recent literature on dispositions is full of such examples: fragile glasses wrapped in Styrofoam that do not shatter when struck, poisonous pills that do not poison if ingested together with an antidote (Bird 1998), "finked" live wires that don't conduct electricity when electric currents are applied (Martin 1994), and so on (Mumford 1998).[13] So a particular may have a disposition it never manifests, either because it is never in the required conditions (enabling conditions, plus trigger) or perhaps because it is, but something blocks or otherwise prevents its manifestation. The important point for my purposes is that a particular thing may have a disposition that it never manifests.

By contrast, there seem to be dispositions that are what might be called "manifestation-dependent": the absence of the manifestation over the lifetime of the object implies the absence of the disposition. That is, contrary to what the *SEP* entry says, there are dispositions that an individual has only if it has already manifested it at some point over its lifetime or is now manifesting it. And this dependence of the disposition on its manifestation is not epistemic; that is, it is not that in the absence of the manifestation we cannot know whether the object has the disposition. Rather, the dependence is constitutive: certain types of disposition are not present if they are not manifested. It is part of the concept of a disposition of this kind that its presence implies its manifestation at some point in the past. The attribution of such dispositions imply not just that its possessor would do certain things or undergo certain changes or has the power to do so in certain circumstances but that it *has done or is doing* those things or *has undergone or is undergoing* those changes. Being a smoker and being generous, for example, are such dispositions: a smoker is someone who has a disposition to smoke even while he's not smoking, but someone who has never smoked is not a smoker, just as someone may be generous without now manifesting that character trait in any way, but someone who has never had a generous reaction, thought, or feeling or has never performed a generous deed is not generous.[14] The point about these dispositions is not that they are frequently manifested but rather that, unlike other dispositions, attribution of the disposition depends (logically) on their having been manifested.

I want to suggest that desires are dispositions of this kind. My claim is that it is part of the concept of desire that someone has a desire at time *t*, only if the desire has been manifested in any of the various ways I described above at some point up to and including time *t*. So I have the desire to eat spinach or to become a lawyer, only if at some point up to the present I have manifested that desire in any of the ways described above (but of course not necessarily in behavior). Desires are dispositions such that someone who has a desire is someone of whom it is true not just that she would or can do certain things but that she has done or is doing certain things: has had or is having certain thoughts, feelings, and emotions, or has behaved or is behaving in certain ways, etc.

Note that I am not suggesting that desires are dependent on any one of the possible ways in which they are manifested, whether internally or externally, for they clearly are not: someone can have a desire in the absence of a manifestation of any one or several of those kinds. So one may have the desire to eat without acting on the desire; but not without at least thinking about it, or having certain feelings, sensations, etc. Or one may want to put out the washing without feeling particularly emotionally engaged in the issue, or one may want to become a dentist without really thinking about it at the time or experiencing any sensations relating to it; but in both cases there must still be some other way in which the desire has been or is being manifested. The literature is full of examples where a desire is plausibly claimed to be present in the absence of one or several of these sorts of typical manifestations; this has in fact led to competing views about what is essential to the concept of desire.[15] But my point is that a desire is in fact intrinsically connected to the range of phenomena that constitute its possible manifestations and, therefore, that an agent cannot (conceptually) have a desire in the absence of *all* of those manifestations over the agent's lifetime: the range of possible manifestations is constitutive of what it is to have the corresponding desire. Moreover, the various manifestations of a desire are criteria for the *strength* of desire: the more one feels inclined to satisfy a desire (i.e. the harder it is to suppress the relevant purposive behavior), the stronger the associated sensations, emotions, the more acute the physiological changes, the more frequent related thoughts about it, and relatedly, the harder it is to suppress the associated expressive behavior, the stronger the desire. Desires are, then, a kind of manifestation-dependent disposition.

It might be objected that this alleged difference from ordinary dispositions is only apparent. For, it might be argued, just as an object may have an ordinary physical disposition but not manifest it because it is not in the right conditions, or because of the presence of a mask, antidote, fink, etc., that blocks its manifestation, a person may have a desire that she has never manifested because of the presence of a mask or antidote, for instance because of injury, paralysis, physical coercion, perhaps contrary desires, etc. And therefore, as with other dispositions, the failure of manifestation does not imply the absence of the disposition, i.e. of the desire, but rather the presence of impediments to its manifestation.

There is truth in these remarks, for sometimes a desire is present even though a particular form of its manifestation is prevented in the ways just outlined. However, there is an important difference concerning the possibility of preventing the manifestation of the disposition between the two types of case: physical dispositions and desires. For it is true that one can prevent some types of manifestation of desires, for example by physically paralyzing a person. But even then, it will still be possible for the desire to be manifested in thoughts, emotions, etc. And, in order to prevent or block all possible manifestations of a desire, the person must be rendered incapable of movement, thought and feeling, and so she must be either totally unconscious (i.e. in a coma) or dead. The dead have no desires,[16] and while a comatose person may still have the desires she had before entering that state, those desires will be attributed to her on the basis of her having manifested them somehow in the past. On the other hand, it is implausible to argue that she can acquire new desires during her coma. To be sure, she could express a new desire on waking up, but there's no ground for saying that she had the desire but did not manifest it while in a coma, rather than that she acquired the desire and expressed it on waking up. In other words, it is implausible to argue that a person can be in a state that makes it impossible for her to manifest her desires in any way but can, during that time, acquire new desires. Thus the objection fails: although preventing the *external* manifestation of a desire in whatever way (physical injury, paralysis, etc.) does not imply its absence, the fact that a desire has never been manifested in any internal or external way does: that is simply part of the concept of desire.[17]

This may seem unconvincing, for surely, it might be argued, it is possible for one to discover that one had a desire one didn't know about. For instance, mention or perception of the object of desire may elicit certain reactions, internal or external, which evince the presence of a desire that, until then, perhaps no one, including the agent herself, knew she had. And surely the right way to construe such cases is to say that these reactions (internal or external) are evidence for its antecedent presence: the desire was there all along, and the reactions simply reveal its existence. But this is also implausible. First, if the object of desire is something the agent was not at all familiar with, then it is wholly implausible to suggest that the agent's reaction is a manifestation of a desire that was there all along. It is true that a person may desire something, say, to have peace of mind, and discover that something else, say, retiring, is just what she'd always wanted because it brings peace of mind. That, however, is not discovering a desire she has always had but never manifested. It is instead discovering that a desire she had and had manifested (perhaps in certain feelings of unhappiness or thoughts and actions about how to get peace of mind) could be satisfied in ways she didn't know about. If, by contrast, the object of desire is something already familiar to the agent, then it is also implausible to say that in the absence of any previous relevant thoughts, emotions, behavior, etc., the agent already had the desire for that thing because, again, there seem to be no grounds for attributing an antecedent desire rather than a newly acquired desire. To be sure, reflection on some already familiar object of desire may help one to remember or perhaps *recognize* past emotional and thought patterns as manifestations of a desire for that thing, but then that is a desire that *had* already been manifested. So desires do seem to be manifestation-dependent dispositions.

This feature of desires does not impugn the dispositional nature of desires, since a desire that has been manifested in one way can still be regarded as a dispositional state that can be further manifested in other ways.[18] But, and this is the point I want to emphasize, the feature does distinguish desires (along with some other psychological states) from dispositions such as fragility, solubility, or conductivity, which may be present in an object despite the object's never having manifested them in any way. For in the case of desires, the presence of the acquisition of a desire, the disposition, coincides with at least one of its manifestations. This may seem odd because, at least among physical dispositions, there do not seem to be any that are acquired only at the point at which they are first manifested. But that is grist to the mill: if desires are dispositions, they, together with at least some other psychological states, have some peculiar features that seem to set them apart from familiar physical dispositions.

## Conclusion

As I noted at the beginning, a widely accepted view about how desires explain actions, closely associated with Davidson, is that they do so just as dispositions in general explain their manifestations. And dispositions are said to explain their manifestations causally: dispositions are antecedent causal conditions that, when triggered by a stimulus, cause their manifestations to occur. We have seen, however, that desires are a distinctive kind of disposition, what I have called "manifestation-dependent" dispositions, where the attribution of the disposition depends constitutively on their manifestation.

I shall finish with a sketch of an answer to the question posed at the beginning of this paper. The feature of desires I have described suggests that an illuminating way to understand how desires explain actions is in terms of "context-placing" explanations: explanations that place the action in the context of the manifestation pattern that is characteristic of the desire in question.[19] Accordingly, an action is explained by a desire when we see the action as part of an intelligible pattern formed by the agent's past and future behavior, thoughts, feelings, emotions, etc. in the context in which the agent acted—a complex pattern that we regard as the characteristic manifestation of the desire in question. Because of this, *which* desire should be attributed to an agent as explanatory of her action is constrained in important ways by whether the action fits best into one or another of the patterns of manifestation of the different desires that the agent can be plausibly thought to have, given the context.

This talk of patterns of explanation echoes another passage in Davidson's 1963 paper, where he defends his answer to the question of how desires explain actions and issues a challenge to dissenters: "One way we can explain an event is by placing it in the context of its cause; cause and effect form the sort of pattern that explains the effect, in a sense of 'explain' that we understand as well as any. If reason and action illustrate a different pattern of explanation, that pattern must be identified" (692).

In response to Davidson's claim that the causal-pattern provides an illuminating answer to how desires explain action, one can note that the lack of agreement about how to understand the concept of causation at play here,[20] the many decades of (in my view) unsuccessful attempts to resolve the problem of "deviant causal chains,"[21] and the distinctive type of disposition that desires turn out to be together suggest that applying the causal pattern does not guarantee that "we now understand the sort of explanation involved" (1963: 692).

As for the challenge, I have introduced the idea of a manifestation-dependent disposition and suggested that desires are dispositions of that sort and that, therefore, we should understand how desires explain actions by reference to *that* notion of disposition. That idea captures a pattern of explanation we understand well for, as we have seen, that's the distinctive notion of disposition at play in conceiving of desires as dispositions. These two considerations suggest that the "context-placing" pattern of explanation I have identified as characteristic of desires is more illuminating than the causal pattern of explanation characteristic of physical dispositions that Davidson favored.

These brief remarks do not of course constitute a full account, let alone a defense, of how desires explain actions, but I hope I have provided grounds for thinking that understanding their relation to action in the way suggested is a promising way of going about that task.[22]

## Notes

1. Davidson adds that, although we are not always in a position to know what the triggering event was, we know that there must have been one. And this is true, he says, for explanations of inanimate events, which we take to be causal, as well as for action explanations.

2. C. B. Martin (2008: 184), for example, writes, "The fact that belief and desire states are dispositional is both familiar and obvious." This is a widespread view in the literature on dispositions; see e.g. McKitrick 2004: 2. In the philosophy of mind, different views highlight different concepts in order to characterize desires: behavior, pleasure/pain, the good, reward, etc. (see Schroeder 2004). But most, if not all, of those views implicitly involve or are compatible with the idea that desires are dispositional states.

3. The causal view of dispositions is widely but not universally held. It has been rejected by some who argue, for example, that it is a disposition's causal basis, rather than the disposition, that is causally relevant or causally efficacious. The rejection is implicit in David Lewis's (1986: 223–224) remark: "I take for granted that a disposition requires a certain causal basis: one has the disposition iff one has a property that occupies a certain causal role." (See also Prior, Pargeter, and Jackson 1982.). I put aside this objection because, if right, it applies to all dispositions and not just to desires, which is the topic at issue. For a critical discussion of this suggestion see McKitrick 2004, 2005.

4. Desires are also sometimes thought of as "propositional attitudes" (following Russell [1918] 2010: 60). This characterization, however, is not ideal, as it has been argued by various authors (see Schueler 1991; Zangwill 1998; Alvarez 2010: 66ff.). Briefly, it cannot accommodate the desires of creatures who lack the ability to entertain propositions, such as babies and (most?) non-human animals. (See also Döring and Eker, Friedrich, *this volume*.)

5. A disposition may also be manifested in preventing, sustaining, etc. changes or processes that would otherwise occur—but this sort of manifestation is also in principle

perceivable. For ease of exposition I shall talk of manifestations as occurrences but using the term to include all these things.

6. "Observable occurrences" is here to be contrasted with the internal manifestations I outline elsewhere. There are also neurophysiological changes inside the body correlated with desires, but I do not include these among the internal manifestations partly because they are in principle also observable—though not without the aid of a special apparatus. Internal physiological changes could also count as, in some sense, external "manifestations" of a state of desiring—at least in the sense that they are correlated with the presence of the desire. But it matters that the identification of such neurophysiological changes as manifestations of a particular desire depends on their correlation with the external and internal manifestations described elsewhere.

7. Schwitzgebel (2002) makes a similar point about the manifestation of beliefs. This view is also found in Quine (1990).

8. I use the term *purposive behavior* to include intentional behavior, which is typically what we do for reasons (though there may be things done intentionally but not for a reason), but also the behavior of animals that are not capable of reasoning. And the term *behavior* is intended to include linguistic behavior as well as refrainings, etc. (see Alvarez 2013).

9. So, for example, John Hyman (2014: 85) writes:

> A desire is manifested in two main ways: first, by purposive or goal-directed behaviour, specifically, behaviour aimed at satisfying the desire, in other words, at getting what it is a desire to have, or at doing what it is a desire to do; and second, by feeling glad, pleased or relieved if the desire is satisfied, and sorry, displeased or disappointed if it is frustrated.

And he adds that there are other things related to desires that may be signs or symptoms of desires, but these are not manifestations of the desire. But even if it's right that the mere physiological changes are not manifestations but only signs or symptoms of desire, Hyman's range of possible manifestations seems too narrow. For in addition to purposive acting and feelings, there is a range of (intentional and non-intentional) mental activity as well as expressive non-purposive behavior that seem legitimate candidates to be counted among possible manifestations of a desire. Unless we have a principled way of deciding what is a genuine manifestation of a desire, the claim that only goal-directed behavior and feelings of pleasure or displeasure concerning its satisfaction or frustration count as manifestations seems a stipulation.

10. The distinctive feature is also had by other psychological dispositional states, for instance, character traits and perhaps beliefs, although I shall not discuss those here.

11. "Typically" because it is claimed that there are physical dispositions that are unusual in that e.g. they "manifest spontaneously, without the need for stimulation" (Molnar 2003: 85), or others that do not have a categorial base. See McKitrick 2003; Molnar 2003; Mumford 2006. But see Armstrong 1968.

12. See, e.g., Martin 2008: ch. 2.

13. See Cross (2012) for a summary.

14. Being a smoker is a habit which is also normally dispositional, i.e. disposes the subject to certain manifestations, while being generous is a character trait. I have argued for this view of character traits in Alvarez 2015.

15. Thus, some philosophers have privileged one of these concepts (action, pleasure, conscious thoughts, etc.) over others in characterizing desires, or have even claimed

that the preferred concept is what desires reduce to. Recently, Tim Schroeder (2004) has criticized many traditional positions and proposed an alternative, based on the idea that desire is "a natural kind" essentially linked to the concept of reward (though the somewhat technical concept of reward is deployed in the empirical literature he discusses.). It is not possible to do justice to Schroeder's arguments here, but it is worth noting that his criticisms of the rival theories he examines are not effective against the sort of pluralist conception of desires suggested above.

16. I'm putting aside the possibility of life after death because if there is such a thing, one would be able to manifest one's desires then, if only mentally.

17. It seems, moreover, that desires have no necessary triggers for their manifestation. The presence of the object of desire may sometimes act as a trigger for the desire to be manifested, but one may manifest a desire in the absence of the object of desire or anything connected to it; indeed, the manifestation may consist precisely in spontaneously imagining, thinking about, or seeking the object of desire (say, water, or a new house) in spite of its total absence in the agent's environment, indeed in spite of its non-existence. I do not mean that nothing will have triggered these thoughts, images, etc. but rather that there is no specific kind of occurrence that is necessary to trigger the manifestation of a desire.

18. Of course if the desire is satisfied, it will not be manifested further, but then it is a desire that the agent no longer has. Note that to have what one wants need not be to have one's desire satisfied if one's desire is, e.g. to keep what one has.

19. My suggestion is in the same spirit as the views defended in Schroeder (2001) and Tanney (2009). I do not take myself to be arguing against the claim that reason/desire explanations are in *some* sense also causal, for reasons given in the following paragraphs above.

20. For instance, in Davidson's neo-Humean terms? In terms of counterfactuals? As Anscombe ([1971] 1993: 91) suggests, simply in terms of "the derivativeness of an effect from its causes"? In some other way?

21. Applied to our topic: an action may be caused by a desire and yet not be a manifestation of that desire if it is not caused "in the right way."

22. I would like to thank Edgar Phillips, Lucy Campbell, and audiences at several seminars where I presented this paper, as well as the editors and referee for this collection for helpful comments on previous versions of this paper. This paper was completed during my tenure of a Leverhulme Trust Major Research Fellowship, and I thank the Trust for the award of the fellowship.

## References

Alvarez, M. (2010). *Kinds of Reasons*. Oxford: Oxford University Press.

———. (2013). 'Agency and Two-way Powers', *Proceedings of the Aristotelian Society*, 113 (1), 101–121.

———. (2015). 'Ryle on Motives and Dispositions', in D. Dolby (ed.), *Ryle on Mind and Language*. London: Palgrave.

Anscombe, G. E. M. (1971) 'Causality and Determination', in E. Sosa and M. Tooley (eds.), *Causation* (1993). Oxford: Oxford University Press.

Armstrong, D. (1968). *A Materialist Theory of the Mind*. London: Routledge.
Bird, A. (1998). 'Dispositions and Antidotes', *Philosophical Quarterly*, 48, 227–234.
Choi, S., and Fara, M. (2016). 'Dispositions', in Edward N. Zalta (ed.), *The Stanford Encyclopedia of Philosophy* (spring 2016 edition), URL = <http://plato.stanford.edu/archives/spr2016/entries/dispositions/>.
Cross, T. (2012). 'Recent Work on Dispositions', *Analysis*, 72 (1), 115–124.
Davidson, D. (1963). 'Actions, Reasons, and Causes', *Journal of Philosophy*, 60 (23), 685–700.
Hyman, J. (2014). 'Desires, Dispositions and Deviant Causal Chains', *Philosophy*, 89, 83–112.
Lewis, D. (1986). 'Causal Explanation', *Philosophical Papers*, vol. 2. Oxford: Oxford University Press.
Martin, C. B. (1994). 'Dispositions and Conditionals', *Philosophical Quarterly*, 44, 1–8.
———. (2008). *The Mind in Nature*. Oxford: Oxford University Press.
McKitrick, J. (2003). 'The Bare Metaphysical Possibility of Bare Dispositions', *Philosophy and Phenomenological Research*, 66, 349–369.
———. (2004). 'A Defence of the Causal Efficacy of Dispositions', *Sats: Nordic Journal of Philosophy*, 5, 110–130.
———. (2005). 'Are Dispositions Causally Relevant?', *Synthese*, 144: 357–371.
Molnar, G. (2003). *Powers: A Study in Metaphysics*. Oxford: Oxford University Press.
Mumford, S. (1998). *Dispositions*. Oxford: Oxford University Press.
———. (2006). 'The Ungrounded Argument', *Synthese*, 149, 471–489.
Prior, E. W., Pargeter, R., and Jackson, F. (1982). 'Three Theses about Dispositions', *American Philosophical Quarterly*, 19 (3), 251–257.
Quine, W. V. O. (1990). *Quiddities*. London: Penguin.
Russell, B. (1918). 'The Philosophy of Logical Atomism', *Monist*, 28 (4), 495–527. Reprinted in Russell, B. (2010). *The Philosophy of Logical Atomism*. London: Routledge.
Ryle, G. (1949). *The Concept of Mind*. London: Hutchinson.
Schwitzgebel, E. (2002). 'A Phenomenal, Dispositional Account of Belief', *Noûs*, 36 (2), 249–275.
Schroeder, S. (2001). 'Are Reasons Causes? A Wittgensteinian Response to Davidson', in S. Schroeder (ed.). *Wittgenstein and Contemporary Philosophy of Mind*. London: Palgrave.
Schroeder, T. (2004). *Three Faces of Desire*. Oxford: Oxford University Press.
Schueler, G. F. (1991). 'Pro-Attitudes and Direction of Fit', *Mind*, 100, 277–282.
———. (1995). *Desire: Its Role in Practical Reason and the Explanation of Action*. Cambridge, Mass.: MIT Press.
Strawson, G. (1994). *Mental Reality*, Cambridge, Mass.: MIT Press.
Tanney, J. (2009). 'Reasons as Non-Causal, Context-Placing Explanations', in C. Sandis (ed.), *New Essays on the Explanation of Action*. London: Palgrave Macmillan.
Zangwill, N. (1998). 'Direction of Fit and Normative Functionalism', *Philosophical Studies*, 91 (2), 173–203.

# *The Deontic Alternative: Desires, Norms, and Reasons*

# CHAPTER 5 | The "Guise of the Ought-to-Be"

## *A Deontic View of the Intentionality of Desire*

FEDERICO LAURIA

IF WE LOOK inside ourselves, as the traditional metaphor goes, we see myriad doubts, memories, fears, regrets, loves, and desires. Some people desire to see the ocean; others aspire to become great musicians; Romeo pines for Juliet. Despite the pivotal role of desire in our lives, the nature of desire has rarely been addressed in detail in the philosophical literature.[1] What are desires? How do desires represent the world, and how are we to understand their intentionality? The aim of this inquiry is to investigate these questions. Given that the liver was thought to be the seat of desire in a tradition that started with Plato and remained influential in the Middle Ages, we may echo Blaise Pascal's famous "Logic of the Heart" by describing this as an attempt at discovering the "Logic of the Liver."[2]

Allow me to start with a thought experiment in order to approach the issue with a more intuitive touch. Imagine a world inhabited by creatures that are exactly like us in all respects but one. They have doubts, memories, and maybe even emotions and sentiments similar to ours. But unlike us, they have no desires whatsoever. The relevant question is the following: How exactly would this *desireless* world differ from the actual world, where desire is ubiquitous?

In the history of philosophy as well as in the contemporary literature, two prevailing answers to this question have been put forward, which correspond to two classical views of desire.

On the first conception, which is Aristotelian in spirit, desires are essentially positive evaluations.[3] Roughly, desiring a state of affairs is representing it as being good. In desiring to see the ocean, say, one positively evaluates this state of affairs. On this view, a *desireless* world would be a world of creatures that do not evaluate anything in a positive light or, at least, that are deprived of the positive evaluation constituted by desire.

According to the second classical view, which is Humean in spirit, desires are essentially motivational states. Desiring that p, it is claimed, is being motivated to act in such a way that p obtains.[4] For instance, desiring to visit Los Angeles is to be moved to act so as to realize this state of affairs. *Desireless* creatures would be inert or would at least lack the motivational "oomph" characteristic of desire. This conception of desire is often taken for granted in the philosophical, psychological and neuroscientific literature.[5]

My purpose is to explore and question these two classical pictures so as to motivate an alternative approach: the deontic view of desire. On this conception, the key to understanding desire is neither goodness nor motivation but a deontic feature: norms of the "ought-to-be" type. Some states of affairs are such that they ought to obtain, and desire, I claim, bears an essential relation to what ought to be. More precisely, the proposal is that desires involve a specific way or manner of representing content: a deontic *mode*. To desire p is to represent p *as what ought to be* or, if one prefers, *as what should be*. Desiring to live in New York is representing this state of affairs *as what ought to be*. Desire thus involves the "guise of the ought-to-be," so to speak.

To proceed carefully, it is worth formulating three *desiderata* that an appealing view of desire's intentionality should meet. This will provide the guidelines for our exploration.

According to the "direction of fit" metaphor, beliefs are supposed to conform to the world, whereas the world is supposed to conform to our desires.[6] This contrast appears clearly in cases of mismatch. Suppose Sam believes that it is sunny in London, when it is, in fact, raining. What should be modified is his *belief*, not the *facts*. Beliefs thus have the *mind-to-world* direction of fit. Consider now that Sam desires that it is sunny, when it is raining. Much to his displeasure, his desire is frustrated. Yet this is not a sufficient reason for him to get rid of or modify his desire, since doing so may well amount to a form of cheating or resentment. As illustrated in La Fontaine's story of sour grapes, there is something wrong in discarding a desire solely on the grounds that it is doomed to frustration: the fox is wrong in believing the grapes are sour and in ceasing to desire them just because he could not get them. If anything, and as far as the satisfaction of desire is concerned, the *world* should change so as to fit the desire: desire thus has the *world-to-mind* direction of fit.[7] Much more could be said, since the interpretation of this metaphor has proven very controversial.

What is important in the present context, though, is that any promising view of desire's intentionality should be *compatible* with and *account* for the intuition that desire has the *world-to-mind* direction of fit.[8]

While the first *desideratum* concerns the relation between desire and the world, the next two *desiderata* concern the relation between a subject's desires and her other mental states. Sometimes desires are partly explained by other mental states, such as the subject's affective dispositions. In other cases, desires partly explain other mental states, such as intentions. Sam desires to go New York *because* he likes to go to New York, and this desire in turn explains why he intends to go there. Explanations of this type are crucial for understanding people's behavior. Any elegant theory of desire's intentionality should be *compatible* with the explanatory relations that desires bear with other mental states and should ideally *explain* these relations. Call this *desideratum* "consonance."

By contrast, some relations between desire and other representations are dissonant. One such dissonance is the combination of a desire with the belief that the desire is satisfied. Imagine that Sam desires to see Niagara Falls. Mary offers to take him there. There they are, enjoying the breathtaking panorama. At some point, Sam says, "I want to see Niagara Falls." "Sam, you *are* seeing Niagara Falls," replies a quite surprised Mary. We understand Mary's astonishment. It is strange to express a desire to see something while in the midst of seeing it. Sam might express a desire to *continue* seeing the Falls, but this is a different desire than a desire simply to see the Falls. How could he desire simply to *see* the Falls while he is seeing them and is aware of his doing so? It appears that desire is incompatible with the representation that its content obtains. Let us call this phenomenon the "death of desire" principle. According to this principle, a desire for p ceases to exist once the subject represents that p obtains, for instance once one starts believing that p.[9] In other words, desires are about states of affairs that are *not* represented as actual. This principle is often taken for granted in the literature and has a long pedigree—from Plato and Aquinas to Descartes, Locke, Hobbes, and Sartre.[10] To the extent that it is true, an attractive theory of desire's intentionality should be *compatible* with and ideally *illuminate* this principle.[11]

A theory of desire should thus strive to account for desire's direction of fit, as well as for the aforementioned consonant and dissonant combinations of desire with other mental phenomena. In what follows, I shall examine the extent to which the evaluative (§1) and motivational (§2) conceptions of desire meet this constraint. The upshot is that these classical views do not adequately satisfy those *desiderata*, which calls for a revisionary account of desire. In the last section (§3), I argue that adopting the deontic conception of desire is the best alternative.

## 1. Desire and the Good: The Evaluative Conception

Imagine that you desire to listen to Brahms's 4th Symphony. From a first-person perspective, listening to this symphony seems good to you in some way (e.g. it seems pleasant). The thesis that desire involves a positive evaluation is almost a dogma in philosophy, tracing back to Plato. It is nicely captured by the Scholastic formula of the "guise of the good": *Nihil appetimus, nisi sub ratione boni*" (There is nothing that is desired, except under the appearance of the good).[12] After all, how could one desire something without seeing any good in it? One way of accounting for this facet of desires is to think of them as positive evaluations.[13] There are different ways of understanding this idea, so let us present a variety of specific shapes the evaluative conception can take (§1.1) before raising three challenges to this view (§1.2).

### 1.1. Types of Evaluative Views

The most influential form of the evaluative approach to desire—the perceptual model—relies on an analogy between perceptual experience and desire. The relation between desire and the good is alleged to mirror that between, say, visual perception and colors and shapes.[14] As vision presents us with colors and shapes, desire presents us with the good. Since perceptual experiences can be understood as being sensory seemings or appearances, the analogy amounts to conceiving of desires as being *value* seemings or appearances of the good.[15] Defenders of this view emphasize similarities between desire and perceptual experiences. For instance, both are representations held from a particular perspective. Seeing the stars in the sky involves a determinate perspective, namely that of a particular human being who is located miles away from the stars. Similarly, moving from spatial to evaluative perspectives, going to the opera tonight may appear good to me, but not to Sally, depending on our respective cares and concerns.[16] Whatever the merit of the analogy, one needs not adopt it to defend the evaluative conception, since there exist at least two other versions of the latter.[17]

According to the doxastic model of the evaluative approach, desires are evaluative beliefs—to desire p is to believe that p is good.[18] On this view, as in the perceptual model, values are part of desire's *content*. Yet it is common to think that representations involve an intentional *mode* in addition to content—an idea that can be exploited to defend a third variant of the evaluative approach.

Consider belief. Intuitively, in believing something (say, that the cat is on the mat), one represents this thing *as being true* or *as actual*. By contrast, remembering something seems to involve a different manner of representing it, namely *as belonging to the past*. In both cases, there is a specific *way* in which content is represented: a way that seems essential to the psychological type under consideration. In this respect, intentional modes should not be confused with traditional modes of presentation, the latter not being essential to types of representations. For instance, seeing a cup from above and seeing one from the right involve distinct modes of presentation. Yet both representations belong to the same psychological type: visual perception. Intentional modes are thus more than a manner of representing—they are ways of representing that are good candidates for distinguishing between types of representations.

Just as belief might be understood as representing a state of affairs *as actual* and memory might be conceived as the representation of a state of affairs *as past*, where this is part of the *manner* of representing, desire can be thought as representing a state of affairs *as good*. On this proposal, the value is part of the mode in which the content is represented.[19]

## 1.2. The Evaluative Conception and the *Desiderata*

Whatever the variant of the evaluative view one favors, it appears that the conception faces major challenges corresponding to the aforementioned *desiderata*.[20]

### 1.2.1. Evaluation and the "Death of Desire" Principle

Does the axiological view meet the death of desire or the intuition that one cannot desire a state of affairs that is represented as actual? The answer depends, of course, on how appealing to a sort of *evaluation* fares in this respect. And there are reasons to think that evaluations do not fare very well.

First, evaluations *are* compatible with believing that their content obtains. Such beliefs are sometimes even required by evaluative states. For instance, how could one be happy that Mary is on one's side and thus positively evaluate this state of affairs, if one did not believe her to be on one's side? Since the "death of desire" principle consists in the claim that desires are *incompatible* with the representation that their content obtains, it appears that conceiving of desire along evaluative lines does not fit well with the principle.

The aficionado of the evaluative conception might reply that this does not prevent desire from constituting a type of evaluation that, unlike other ones, satisfies this *desideratum.*[21] Nothing in the axiological view should lead us to think that no sort of evaluation meets this constraint. Still, one important question arises: Why think that the evaluation at stake in desire satisfies this principle, while other types of evaluation do not? In the absence of a convincing answer to this question, the reply seems *ad hoc*.

Second, given that not all evaluations satisfy the "death of desire" principle, the axiological view has difficulty *explaining* this feature of desire, which is something a theory of desire should ideally do. Even if one assumes that some types of evaluation satisfy the relevant principle, this would still have to be conceived as a brute fact or, at least, as a facet that cannot be explained by desire's evaluative nature only. The question remains: Why is it odd for Sam to desire seeing Niagara Falls when he is aware of seeing them?

A friend of the evaluative view might go so far as to reject the "death of desire" principle, one's *modus tollens* being another's *modus ponens*. In fact, the evaluative view fares well with the denial of the "death of desire" principle.[22] However, even if one is convinced that the principle is not true for *all* desires, it remains to be shown why it is a paradigmatic feature of many desires—and appealing to their evaluative nature may prove insufficient in this regard.

I shall now emphasize that similar worries for the evaluative conception arise in connection with the direction of fit *desideratum*, mounting further evidence that the evaluative approach is unable to account for the intuitive features of desire.

### 1.2.2. Evaluation and Direction of Fit

Does the axiological view provide a plausible picture of desire's direction of fit, i.e. the intuition that the world should conform to our desires? The answer to this question depends on the direction of fit of the evaluations recruited by one's approach to desire. Unfortunately for the defender of the axiological view, evaluations generally seem to have the *mind-to-world* direction of fit, unlike that of desire.

Paying attention to the *satisfaction conditions* and the *correctness conditions* of a representation will reveal why. A belief is satisfied if, and only if, its content obtains, i.e. when it is true. Since true beliefs are nothing but correct beliefs, it follows that beliefs' satisfaction conditions are identical to their correctness conditions. By contrast, the satisfaction of desires does not amount to those desires being accurate: correct desires might be frustrated (unlucky, virtuous Juliet), and incorrect desires might be fulfilled (lucky, vicious Romeo). The algorithm is thus the following: When its conditions of satisfaction and correctness are identical, a representation has the *mind-to-world* direction of fit; otherwise it has the *world-to-mind* direction of fit.[23]

With this algorithm in mind, our question can be reformulated as follows: Are the satisfaction conditions of evaluations identical to their correctness conditions? On the face of it, the answer is positive—a positive evaluation of an object or a state of affairs is satisfied if, and only if, that object or state of affairs is good, which amounts to the evaluation being accurate. This is plausible for evaluative beliefs, but also for emotions, which can be understood as another type of evaluative state with the *mind-to-world* direction of fit.[24] This is exactly what is expected from evaluations insofar as they are meant to inform us about what is good or bad for us. After all, why should the world conform to our evaluations? So it appears that evaluations have the direction of fit opposite to that of desire.

As before, it might simply be assumed as primitive fact that desire is a type of evaluation that has the *world-to-mind* direction of fit. But this reply appears to be as suspiciously *ad hoc* as the one we considered in relation to the "death of desire" principle. And if the key to understanding desire is its being an evaluation, then desire's evaluative nature should help explain its direction of fit. However, the evaluative view seems to fail to deliver such an explanation, since evaluations typically instantiate the opposite direction of fit.[25] The intuition that the world should conform to our desires remains enigmatic.

### 1.2.3. Evaluative Consonance

One day, on a whim, I wanted a paper plane. You might wonder why. When confronted with an apparently awkward desire, pointing out the features of the desired object that one regards as desirable gives some intelligibility to the desire.[26] As soon as I tell you that I find paper planes to be beautiful, the mystery surrounding my desire may vanish a little. These explanations amount to specifying the manner in which something is positively evaluated. Furthermore, desires can be explained with reference to various types of evaluation. Sam may desire to swim in the river *because* doing so seems good to him (i.e. in virtue of an appearance of the good) or because he represents swimming in the river *as good* (i.e. in virtue of the evaluative manner of representing content), and so on for other types of positive evaluation.

Now, it is tempting to think that these sorts of explanations are at least partly causal explanations: the fact that one evaluates a state of affairs positively causes one to desire that state. This means that the axiological view faces an immediate challenge. Causal relations are irreflexive: they require distinct *relata*. For instance, the statement "p because p," understood as "the cause of p is p," does not constitute an explanation: when one wonders why it rains and is answered "Because it rains," one has not been provided with an explanation. If desires were positive evaluations, then explaining a desire for something by a positive evaluation of this thing would be similarly vacuous. As outlined, however, explaining desires by positive evaluation is far from being vacuous. This should lead us to conclude that the axiological picture cannot make sense of our intuitions regarding the sorts of explanations to which desires are subject.[27]

If this is correct, it appears that the evaluative conception does not satisfy our *desiderata* adequately. However, a positive moral emerges: evaluations can be *the grounds* of desire.[28] Desire can involve the "guise of the good" without *being* an evaluation but in virtue of *depending* on an evaluation. This nicely captures the intuition driving the axiological view while avoiding its difficulties. A world in which creatures do not evaluate anything would, indeed, be a *desireless* world. However, this is the case because evaluation is a necessary condition for desire—not because desire is a kind of evaluation. It is time now to turn our attention to the second classical conception of desire.

## 2. Desire and Action: The Motivational Conception

Juliet intensely desires to see Romeo. It is likely that this strong desire will give her the motivation to act in ways that will make this desire come true. She might not know how to do so. She might hesitate. She might be afraid of satisfying this desire. Still, she is disposed to realize it. According to the motivational conception of desire, this is the key to understanding desire. On this very popular view, desire is nothing but a motivational state.[29] Since motivation is considered to be desire's function, this picture corresponds to the standard functionalist approach to desire. In this section, I shall present the motivational conception (§2.1) before assessing it in light of our three *desiderata* (§2.2).

### 2.1. The Motivational Dogma

The standard way of defining desire in motivational terms is by conceiving it as a disposition to act in favor of the obtaining of its content.[30] In other words, in desiring p, a subject is disposed to act in favor of p or, at least, in ways she believes will bring about p. For instance, desiring to contemplate the stars is being disposed to act in such a way that is conducive (or so we believe it to be) to being absorbed by them. Since desires are understood as dispositions to act, this view is compatible with the existence of desires that do not manifest themselves in actions and, more controversially, with desiring subjects who are not *actually* motivated to act. In desiring to change the past, for instance, Romeo might not be *actually* motivated to act in such a way that what he desires comes about. In this case, it is reasonable to explain the absence of actual motivation by the idea that being *actually* motivated to act requires believing that one has the power to realize the desire—a belief that Romeo does not hold. Yet although Romeo is not *actually* motivated to act, he is still *disposed* to act so that the desired state of affairs obtains. Were he to believe that he could erase the past, he would try to do so, all things being equal.[31]

One might think that the standard motivational conception is at odds with a first-person approach to the intentionality of desire that aims at capturing how desires represent their content. After all, the dispositional picture is silent on this point; it seems to capture desire from the outside, so to speak. A more promising approach is to construe desires as involving a motivational mode. On this variant, desiring a state of affairs is representing it *as a goal* or *as what ought to be done*.[32] For instance, desiring to see Juliet is representing this state *as a goal* or *as what ought to be done*. Be that as it may, is a motivational approach to desire more promising than an evaluative one? I shall argue that this is not the case as motivational and evaluative accounts face the same problems.[33]

## 2.2. The Motivational Conception and the *Desiderata*

This last assertion may be surprising. At first glance, one might be inclined to think that the motivational conception has the resources to meet the three *desiderata*. First, the standard interpretation of the direction of fit is motivational in spirit: the fact that the world should conform to our desires—the *world-to-mind* direction of fit—is usually equated with the thought that desires dispose us to act. Second, the motivational view also seems to be in a position to satisfy the "death of desire" principle. After all, one is not disposed to act in favor of a state of affairs that one believes already obtains. How could Desdemona be disposed to marry Othello if she were aware that she had already married him? Finally, dispositions to act appear to lend themselves to being explained by evaluations in the same way as desires. Romeo's disposition to visit the MoMA can be explained by his positive evaluation of this state, just like his desire to visit the MoMA. On these grounds, it is tempting to adopt the motivational conception of desire. However, I think that this temptation should be resisted. Let us begin with what may well be the most surprising claim, namely the one concerning direction of fit.

### 2.2.1. Motivation and Direction of Fit

According to the standard interpretation, the *world-to-mind* direction of fit amounts to the following. In the case of a mismatch between desire and the world, i.e. when a desire is frustrated, one should not change the desire. Rather (and this is where the motivational view enters the picture), the subject should *act* in such a way that the desire will be satisfied.[34] For this is desire's function.

One general problem with the motivational conception and the aforementioned interpretation of the *world-to-mind* direction of fit hangs on the satisfaction conditions of dispositions to act and, more generally, of motivational states. Indeed, it is natural to think that the satisfaction conditions of motivational states consist in the subject intentionally *acting*. If Sam is disposed to go to London, his disposition is realized or satisfied when he intentionally goes there. This is explicit in the functionalist picture of desire, especially in its teleosemantic version.[35] In case this intuition is not shared, let me emphasize that desire's satisfaction conditions should bear a particular relation to action in order for the motivational view to secure an essential link between desire and action. The worry is that the satisfaction conditions of desire refer to the obtaining of its content, which can happen independently of the subject's action. The desire that it rains, say, is satisfied by the fact that it rains, period. If this is on the right track, then the conclusion is that the motivational approach does not deliver the right satisfaction conditions for desires.[36]

This in turn has an impact on the direction of fit *desideratum*, since the direction of fit of a representation is conditioned on its *satisfaction*.[37] Indeed, the world should conform to our desires only insofar as their *satisfaction* is concerned. For instance, all things considered, the world should not conform to our immoral desires, as this would lead to a world of evil. Yet as far as the satisfaction of those desires is concerned, it remains true that the world should conform to them, although this consideration is defeated by their immoral nature. Since it appears that the motivational view does not deliver the right satisfaction conditions for desires, it is difficult to see how it could account for their direction of fit in an appealing way.

In fact, it delivers counterintuitive verdicts in situations where the content of a desire obtains independently of the subject's action. If satisfaction consists in the subject's acting such that the desire's content obtains, the desire will not count as satisfied when the subject gets what she wants independently of her actions. Hence the world should still conform to the desire. This sounds far-fetched, to put it mildly. Even if it assumed that the desire is satisfied in such circumstances, the norm that the subject act so as to satisfy the desire has not been met. This is problematic, as the following case will illustrate.

Imagine that Romeo desires to see Juliet and can arrange a meeting by writing a letter to her. Before having the opportunity to do so, he meets her in Venice by pure chance. According to the motivational interpretation of desire's direction of fit, Romeo should have acted to bring about the satisfaction of his desire. But he did not comply with this norm. We should then conclude that something went wrong: Romeo's behavior was inappropriate or dysfunctional. But this is absurd: Romeo did nothing wrong, and such cases seem far from dysfunctional. Isn't it ideal to get what one wants without making any effort? One might reply that the inappropriate character of Romeo's behavior is defeated by other considerations: Romeo has been prevented from acting, and ultimately the right result happened, provided that this reunion is a good thing. Yet this reply should lead one to suspect that what matters for desire satisfaction is that the content of the desire obtains, whether in the presence of action or in its absence. After all, the satisfaction conditions of desire do not make any reference to action, so why put so much emphasis on action? A conception of desire that clearly implies that desires are satisfied when their content obtains is more elegant.

Consequently, it is not clear that desire's direction of fit should be equated with the norm that desiring subjects *act* so as to satisfy their desire. Rather, a more modest norm suggests itself: that the *world* should change for the desire to be satisfied. The motivational conception might well make sense of the direction of fit of intentions or dispositions to act, since the satisfaction conditions of those phenomena are constituted by actions. Still, as far as desire is concerned, the view seems to be slightly off target. And the reason is that it fails to capture the right conditions of desire gratification.

### 2.2.2. Motivation and the "Death of Desire" Principle

As emphasized earlier, it is tempting to think that the motivational approach has the resources to meet the "death of desire" *desideratum*. For subjects are not disposed to bringing about states of affairs they believe already obtain.[38] As intuitive as this may sound, I think this explanation is suspect.

First, according to the "death of desire" principle, a desire for a state of affairs ceases to exist when one represents that one's desire has been *satisfied*. The principle then appears to depend on the representation of desire's satisfaction. Now, if the motivational view delivers the wrong picture of desire's satisfaction conditions, as I argued, it cannot elegantly meet the *desideratum* on the death of desire either. This argument relies on the same considerations as the ones presented in section 2.2.1, so let us turn our attention to a further problem.

In order to make full sense of the "death of desire" principle, the motivational view should explain the apparent incompatibility between desiring p and representing p as obtaining. Why are we not disposed to act in favor of states of affairs that we believe already obtain? It is quite plausible to think that one is disposed to act in favor of a state of affairs only if one believes that there is something one could do, albeit maybe in an ideal world, to bring it about. Now, if the state of affairs already obtains, then there is nothing one can do to bring it about. So, presumably, if a subject believes that a state of affairs obtains, she will not believe that there is something she could do to bring it about.[39] The belief in a desire's satisfaction thereby prevents one from being motivated, since it is incompatible with the belief that one can bring about the desire's satisfaction. Believing that a desire is satisfied will thereby kill the desire.

Despite being intuitive, the story remains problematic. Imagine that Othello believes that a state of affairs obtains and also believes that he can change the past. He will very likely believe that he can act in favor of the obtaining of this state, despite his belief that the state already obtains. It is thus not clear why believing that a state obtains should require the absence of the belief that one could act in its favor. And since no alternative motivational story of the "death of desire" principle suggests itself, the lesson is that the motivational view fails to provide a satisfactory explanation of it.

This observation should lead us to worry whether the motivational conception is compatible with the "death of desire" principle in the first place. Imagine that Othello believes that he had a gin and tonic, while also believing that he can go back in time. He might still be disposed to act in favor of having this very same drink, despite believing that he has just had it. Indeed, were he to travel back in time and at this point have the desire for this cocktail again, he would act so as to have it again. It is important to remind the reader that, in order to account for desires that do not involve *actual* motivation, the motivational view should provide room for such *counterfactual* motivation, as outlined earlier.[40]

This case would be harmless if desires did not vanish when subjects believe both that they can bring about a state of affairs and that this same state of affairs obtains. However, restricting the principle in this way is not really an option. Even if Othello believes that he can travel back in time, he might cease to desire to drink this particular gin and tonic at the instant he believes that he just drank it. True, as soon as he believes that he has traveled back in time, he might again desire that cocktail. But this might be because he then believes that he did *not* have this very same gin and tonic. In this respect, dispositions to act differ from desires: even before he traveled back in time, and despite believing that he just had this gin and tonic, Othello *is* disposed to have this drink. According to the motivational view, one should conclude that he still desires so. Yet, as just emphasized, this conclusion is counterintuitive. As far-fetched as this scenario may seem, it reveals that the motivational conception does not account for the death of desire: when one represents that a desire is satisfied, the desire vanishes, yet the disposition to act may still remain alive.

### 2.2.3. Motivational Consonance

We commonly explain one's motivations with reference to one's evaluations in the same way as we do for desire. At first sight, the motivational view thus seems well placed to illuminate the explanation *of* desires. But does it capture explanations *by* desires?

Consider the following explanation. Mary *loves* the Metropolitan Opera. This is why she *desires* to go to the Metropolitan Opera. And she is *disposed* to go to the Metropolitan Opera *because* she desires to go to there. The more we know about Mary's mental states, the more we understand why she is disposed to act in this way. One explanation of the disposition is provided by her desire, which is in turn grounded in a positive evaluation (love). Although the mention of Mary's desire might be insufficient to justify her disposition to act, *prima facie* it provides a partial explanation of it. Moreover, the explanation seems to be partly causal: the desire causes and might also be the reason for her motivation.

Now, given the already mentioned irreflexivity of causal relations, such explanations turn out to be vacuous if desires are nothing but dispositions to act. Yet intuitively, these explanations appear to be informative. It thus seems that the motivational view fails to make sense of desire's explanatory power.

This argument of course relies on a conception of motivation that the defender of the motivational conception of desire is unlikely to share. On this approach, desiring just *is* being motivated, and the alleged explanatory relations are vacuous. By contrast, our argument invites us to think of motivation as being partly *dependent* on desire rather than as being identical to it.[41] In order to motivate this picture, it is fruitful to consult our modal intuitions about cases in which someone desires a state of affairs but is not disposed to act in its favor. If such inert desires are conceivable, then we have a reason to think of desire as *grounding* motivation rather than *being* a motivation.[42]

Imagine that Romeo is suffering from a particular type of depression. His depression is such that it has deprived him of having any dispositions to act. Still, it is conceivable that he desires certain states of affairs. He might desire that his beloved Juliet fares well, despite not being disposed to do anything to bring this about. This case should not be confused with others in which a person fails to be motivated to act so as to satisfy some desire because a second, stronger desire of hers outweighs the motivation of the first one. In the case under discussion, Romeo has no stronger desire, nor is he lacking the modal beliefs necessary for being disposed to act. He strongly wants that p, has no conflicting desire, and believes that he can act in favor of p, yet fails to be disposed to act. The depression has not only masked the manifestation of the disposition; it has damaged the motivational system. This, I contend, is conceivable. Empirical studies even suggest that patients suffering from Parkinson's disease or akinetic mutism manifest this kind of inertia, despite the fact that these people seem to have desires.[43] Moreover, the intuitive verdict of such cases is instructive: it is natural to diagnose Romeo as suffering from strong practical irrationality, or at least from an absence of practical rationality. This suggests that desires provide some reason to be disposed to act in favor of their satisfaction, although they might do so with the help of the evaluation on which they are based. This is one way that desires can ground motivations.

If this argument is on the right track, then it appears that motivation is at most a sufficient condition for desire but not a necessary one. A *desireless* world could thus be a world without motivation, possibly inhabited by totally passive creatures. But this is explained by desires *grounding* motivations rather than being *identical* with them. The motivational "oomph" of desire could then be captured by means of this grounding relation.

To sum up the dialectical situation, the classical conceptions of desire face inverted problems. On the one hand, axiological views focus on a necessary but insufficient condition for desire by outlining the evaluative ground of desire. On the other hand, motivational views focus on what is at most a sufficient but not necessary condition for desire, as they put emphasis on motivations based on desire. If this is correct, then the grain of truth in these approaches concerns the grounding relations instantiated by desire: what is grounded on desire (motivation) and what desire is grounded in (evaluation). This is why they seem to miss what they should capture: this thing called desire.

This conclusion has been motivated by means of philosophical exploration, but the neuroscientific evidence on desire points our inquiry in the same direction. It is almost a dogma in neuroscience that desires are involved in the reward system and are related to the neurotransmitter dopamine.[44] According to the neuroscientific picture, desire comes with an anticipation of reward that regulates motivation and is in turn regulated by the experience of the actual reward. One important challenge is to translate these findings in folk-psychological terms so as to shed light on the intentionality of desire. In this respect, Schroeder has done substantial work in claiming that the neuroscientific findings call for a picture of desire that differs from the classical ones. He argues that equating desire with an evaluative cognition fares poorly in the face of the empirical evidence.[45] Similarly, he claims that the neuroscientific picture does not favor the motivational conception of desire.[46] It goes far beyond the scope of this essay to discuss this issue in detail. However, as far as our dialectic is concerned, it seems that the conclusions drawn so far in this chapter are in line with Schroeder's interpretation of the neuroscientific evidence. Furthermore, studies reveal that motivation is strongly influenced by desire and, in turn, by positive anticipation. It thus appears that the neuroscientific picture of desire aligns itself with the moral that has emerged: positive evaluation might ground desire, and desire might ground motivation. In light of the empirical evidence, Schroeder has proposed to identify desires with representations of rewards.[47] I venture that the deontic view of desire is one way of understanding what representations of rewards are from a first-person perspective. In section 3, I argue that the deontic conception can fill the explanatory gap between evaluation and motivation that has appeared on *a priori* grounds and that our neuroscientific interlude has corroborated.

## 3. Desire and Ought-to-Be: The Deontic Conception

What if desires, like vows, prayers, and demands, were essentially deontic representations, i.e. representations concerning what *should be* the case? Desiring to live in New York would amount to being somehow struck by the fact that one's living there is *how things should be*. This is the intuition that drives the deontic conception of desire defended in this essay. This section presents this view (§3.1) and sketches three arguments in its favor (§3.2).

### 3.1. The Deontic View

The deontic conception I shall defend has it that desiring is representing a state of affairs *as what ought to be* or *as what should be*, where this captures the deontic *mode* of representing.

Given that this proposal refers to norms of the ought-to-be type, let me say a few words about them. There is a plethora of norms: one ought to keep one's promises, to avoid inflicting unnecessary suffering, and to eat properly, etc. In these examples, the word *ought* refers to the obligation for given subjects to act in certain ways. We use the same word *ought* with a closely related but distinct purpose when we say, for instance, that cancer ought not to exist, that Mary being happy is how things should be, or that things turned out the way they should have. *Prima facie*, no appeal to obligation to act in a certain way seems necessary to explain these uses of *ought*. I shall assume here that the latter are ought-to-*be* norms—they are about states of affairs—and should be contrasted with ought-to-*do* norms.[48] For the remainder of my discussion, it is important to keep in mind that the deontic view appeals exclusively to ought-to-*be* norms.[49]

It is another feature of the deontic conception that it rests on the distinction between mode and content.[50] Desiring p is representing p *as what ought to be* or, if one prefers, *as what should be*. The content of a desire is a state of affairs (typically a non-deontic one), while its deontic character is taken care of at the level of the mode of representing the content. Desires are thus distinct from deontic beliefs: while deontic beliefs take deontic states of affairs as their content, desires involve a deontic manner of representing. In order to clarify the contrast, let me formulate an analogous proposal for belief. In believing p (say, that it rains), one represents p *as obtaining* or *as actual*. Within this picture, the difference between desire and belief consists in the presence either of a deontic or of an "existential" feature in the respective modes.[51] Most philosophers acknowledge the existence of intentional modes but often assume that they are reducible to functional roles.[52] On my proposal, it is important to observe that the deontic mode is irreducible to the functional role of desire, namely motivation.[53] My approach takes modes seriously and uses them to unravel desire's semantics, which, I think, was the credo of early phenomenologists.[54]

To my knowledge, there are no advocates of the deontic view in the contemporary literature, but Velleman and Massin defend related accounts.[55] Meinong, however, if I interpret him correctly, has proposed this picture of desire.[56] Be that as it may, the conception has the resources to meet our three *desiderata*, or so I will argue.

## 3.2. The Deontic View and the *Desiderata*

The main idea is that ought-to-be norms are all we need to make sense of our *desiderata* because these norms instantiate the properties that were singled out in each *desideratum*. Let us address them in turn.

### 3.2.1. Direction of Fit and Ought-to-Be

Let us assume that there is a sense in which norms have a direction of fit. This sense might not be literal. Directions of fit are features of representations, and considering that norms may not be representations, the assumption may seem far-fetched. But there are reasons to think it is not. If the idea of a direction of fit is to be understood in terms of appropriate ways for fit or satisfaction to obtain, then norms may well have a direction of fit. Norms, like desires, can be satisfied in the sense that their content can obtain. More importantly, in cases of mismatch between a norm and the world, it is clear that what should be changed, all things being equal, is the world. Consider that Sam ought to keep his promise. It is an essential feature of this norm that what should be changed, if anything, is the world—not the norm. As in the case of desire, changing the norm rather than the world would amount to cheating. This facet of norms is what makes them crucial in regulating people's behavior and ideally making the world a better place. This observation, of course, emerges from considering the *satisfaction* of norms and is entirely compatible with some norms being inappropriate and thus in need of being changed. Still, if we focus exclusively on satisfaction, even inappropriate norms are such that the world should conform to them. In all these respects, then, norms behave exactly like desires. Note too that the differences between ought-to-do and the ought-to-be norms are irrelevant here as there is no reason to think that these norms differ in this regard. It is essential to the norm according to which, say, it ought not to be that people die in terrible pain that the world should conform to it rather than the other way around.

This feature of norms, I contend, is the key to understanding the direction of fit of desire. Indeed, if desires involve a deontic mode, then the world must conform to them in order for satisfaction to obtain. The reason is that the world should meet norms. The contrast in direction of fit is made manifest when we focus on representations not involving a deontic mode. Consider the similar proposal made for beliefs. In believing that it rains, say, one represents the state of affairs that it rains *as obtaining*. Unlike desire, which involves a deontic manner of representing content, beliefs can be described from a first-person perspective without reference to any norm. After all, facts (i.e. what obtains) are not deontic entities, unlike norms. Since facts are not such that the world should conform to them, representing a state of affairs *as obtaining* does not imply that the world should conform to the representation. Rather, if anything, the *representation* of content as actual should conform to the facts, given that it represents its content *as a fact*. Beliefs thus come with the norm of conforming to reality, i.e. the *mind-to-world* direction of fit.

The deontic view, then, is not only compatible with the direction of fit of desire; it also provides an appealing elucidation of this vexed metaphor. Desires have the *world-to-mind* direction of fit *because* they involve a deontic mode. In contrast to the evaluative conception, the proposal under discussion, grounded as it is in an essential feature of norms, is not *ad hoc*. Similarly, given its emphasis on ought-to-*be* rather than ought-to-*do* norms, the deontic view delivers the right satisfaction conditions for desire, unlike the motivational picture. The world should thus conform to our desires because the world is supposed to fit norms.

### 3.2.2. The "Death of Desire" Principle and Ought-to-Be

How does the deontic conception fare with the death of desire? Again, norms seem to satisfy a principle close to that of the death of desire.

Consider this sentence: "Sam ought to answer this question now, and Sam has answered this question now." *Prima facie*, this sentence sounds odd. Intuitively, if Sam has answered the question, then it is not the case that he ought to answer it, for he just did. Likewise, if Sam ought to answer the question, then it is not the case that he did, precisely because answering it is what he ought to do. Within this sentence, then, the deontic operator does not coexist happily with the existential operator.

Now, there is *prima facie* no reason to think that the ought-to-be operator differs from the ought-to-do operator in this respect. It then follows that deontic operators are incompatible with the existential operator governing the very same content. In other words, norms are incompatible with the obtaining of their content. The norm is in place as long as its content does not obtain. As soon as its content is realized, it disappears. Norms do not survive their satisfaction. Or so it is intuitive to think.[57]

If there is indeed an incompatibility between a norm being in place and its being satisfied, then the following claim suggests itself: desires die when one believes that they are satisfied. For desire involves a deontic mode, while belief involves an existential one. As norms are incompatible with the facts that constitute their satisfaction, so are desires incompatible with beliefs about their actual satisfaction. Again, the symmetry between norms and desires is the key to explaining the "death of desire" principle.[58]

This being said, the deontic view is compatible with a more modest attitude vis-à-vis the "death of desire" principle. There are apparent counterexamples to the principle. For instance, my desire to treat other people with respect seems compatible with my belief that I treat them with respect. The same is true of any desire about general or non-dated states of affairs.[59]

It is important to recognize that any apparent counterexamples in the case of desires also have analogous counterparts in the case of norms.[60] Indeed, if we focus our attention on general norms, e.g. the norm that one should respect other people, then one might start questioning the alleged incompatibility of norms with their satisfaction. After all, at least *prima facie*, some people do respect others while still being supposed to do so. Sometimes things are exactly as they should be.[61] Since the deontic view is committed to an analogy between desires and norms, it is not committed to the truth of the "death of desire" principle but merely to the mirroring of desire and norms in relevant respects. It can accommodate counterexamples to the "death of desire" principle where there are symmetrical counterexamples to the claim that norms are incompatible with their satisfaction. Depending on one's intuitions, one may endorse a stronger or weaker claim about the principle without impacting on the force of its deontic explanation.

The deontic conception can thus illuminate the "death of desire" principle whether or not the principle is true of all desire. Unlike the evaluative view, and provided that norms satisfy a similar principle to some extent, it does so without being *ad hoc*. In contrast with the motivational picture, it delivers the right satisfaction conditions while avoiding the problem that comes with an appeal to dispositions. Scheler already pointed out that norms are incompatible with facts and that representations of norms are in the same way incompatible with representations of facts.[62] The originality of my proposal lies in equating the relevant representations of norms with desires, which shares the spirit of Meinong's suggestion.[63]

### 3.2.3. Consonance and Ought-to-Be

In light of our discussion of the classical conceptions of desire, the deontic proposal should provide room and account for the following explanatory relations: desires are partly explained by positive evaluations and can partly explain motivations. The deontic view appears to meet this requirement. It is intuitive to explain why Sam represents being in New York as what ought to be with reference to his positive evaluation of this state of affairs. Similarly, it makes sense to explain why Mary is motivated to go to Los Angeles with reference to her representing this state of affairs as what ought to be. Can we substantiate these intuitions further? The answer will depend on whether values, ought-to-be norms, and ought-to-do norms instantiate similar relations.

At first approximation, this seems to be the case. It is natural to think that p ought to be *because* p is valuable.[64] Consider the norm that it ought to be that people heed traffic lights. This norm seems to be grounded in the goodness of heeding traffic lights, which, in turn, is inherited from the value of life. Likewise, obligations to act in given ways seem to be explainable by what ought to be, i.e. the state of affairs resulting from the action required. Mary ought to go to Los Angeles because it ought to *be* that she lives there. This might constitute only part of the explanation of the ought-to-do norm. Appealing to the evaluative property grounding the norm will provide a (more) complete explanation. Still, since explanatory relations are (at least to some extent) transitive, this is compatible with the idea that ought-to-be norms partly explain ought-to-do norms.

Of course, much more can be said about the relations ought-to-be norms bear to values and ought-to-do norms.[65] In particular, it should be shown that they are irreducible to these other entities, since reduction here would make the corresponding explanations vacuous.[66] Yet on the face of it, the suggested articulation of the relations between values, ought-to-be norms, and ought to-do norms seems to be informative or, more to the point, as consonant as the explanatory relations holding between desires, evaluations, and motivations. Desires can explain motivations and be explained by evaluations because ought-to-be norms ground ought-to-do norms and are built on goodness.

## Conclusion

In this chapter, I argued that the deontic conception of desire constitutes a promising approach to the intentionality of desire. Desiring is representing a state of affairs *as what ought to be*. Indeed, classical views face the challenge of explaining desire's direction of fit, accommodating the "death of desire" principle, and articulating satisfactorily the explanatory relations instantiated by desire. I claimed that the deontic view can meet the three crucial *desiderata*, since norms of the ought-to-be type share the relevant properties. In a nutshell, the deontic mode elegantly espouses the contours of desire: desires and ought-to-be fit like hand and glove. This is not to say that the classical views of desire fail to capture anything about desire. Quite the contrary, in fact: if the deontic conception is correct, then the classical views of desire emphasize what appear to be the grounding relations instantiated by desire. In this respect, the deontic conception can secure the grain of truth of the classical views without suffering from their pitfalls.

In addition to offering an alternative picture of desire, the proposal is a first step in reinstalling intentional modes at the heart of our philosophical preoccupations. It is not clear that functional roles capture all there is about intentionality. There is room for a first-person approach to the mind that takes seriously the idea that mental representations are different points of view about the world. Specifying this idea in terms of intentional modes could then disclose the "logic" of mental representations, as I tried to do with the case of desire.

A *desireless* world would thus be a world in which creatures do not represent anything as what ought to be, do not require anything of the world, and do not care whether or not some states of affairs obtain. It would be a dull world deprived of any aspirations—and of much of its charm—because desire is the "eye" of what *should* be.[67]

## Notes

1. Notable exceptions are, among others, Schroeder 2004; Oddie 2005; Tenenbaum 2007; Arpaly and Schroeder 2013.

2. See in particular, Plato 1953: *Timaeus*, 70c–72b; Galen 2005: 6.8.6–6.8.77. I owe this metaphor and the following thought experiment to Kevin Mulligan.

3. See Stampe 1986; Oddie 2005; Tenenbaum 2007; section 1 of this essay. In this volume, see Oddie, Friedrich.

4. See Smith 1994; Dancy 2000; section 2 of this essay. In this volume, see Döring and Eker, Alvarez. I use "p" to refer to the content of desire without implying that the content is necessarily propositional.

5. See Schroeder 2004: 3; introduction to this volume.

6. See, among others, Anscombe 1963; Platts 1979; Searle 1983; Humberstone 1992. In this volume, see Railton's, Gregory's, and Wall's contributions as well as the introduction.

7. The contrast in directions of fit extends more generally to cognitive and conative representations as well as to speech acts.

8. For the thought that the idea of a direction of fit is dubious, see Sobel and Copp 2001; Milliken 2008; Frost 2014.

9. The representation that p obtains might be a belief or whatever state that represents content as actual (e.g. perceiving that p, seeming to one that p).

10. Plato 1953: *Symposium*; Aquinas 1920–1942: Ia IIae, 30, 2 ad1; Descartes 1989: [57]; Locke 1975: II, 20, 6: 174; Hobbes 1994: [6]; Sartre 1984. For contemporary discussions, see Kenny 1963: 81–84, 115–116; Armstrong 1968: 155; Boghossian 2003: 42–43; Oddie 2005: 72. In this volume, see Oddie, Massin, Döring and Eker, and the introduction.

11. One might want to deny this principle. But this comes at a cost, as similar principles intuitively hold for all types of conations. For instance, intending to do something and simultaneously believing that one has executed one's intention is odd. This suggests that the principle captures something essential to conations.

12. My translation. Kant 1997: AA 05-59, 12–14. On the guise of the good, see Tenenbaum 2013, and, in this volume, Oddie, Massin. For doubts, see Velleman 1992, Döring and Eker *this volume*.

13. Another way of accounting for this feature consists in thinking of positive evaluation as a necessary feature of desire without being identical to it (see end of section 1).

14. For the sake of the argument, I assume that the perceptual analogy consists in the claim that desire is analogous rather than identical to perceptual experience.

15. Stampe 1986; Oddie 2005, *this volume*; Tenenbaum 2007.

16. Oddie 2005: 60–63.

17. For skepticism on the perceptual model, see Friedrich, Döring and Eker, Gregory, Ashwell *this volume*.

18. Davidson 2001. See Friedrich, Döring and Eker, Ashwell *this volume* for objections.

19. Friedrich 2012, *this volume*.

20. For further criticism of the evaluative conception, see Döring and Eker, Massin, Ashwell *this volume*.

21. See Oddie *this volume*.

22. See Oddie 2005: 70–72, *this volume*.

23. See De Sousa 2011: 56–57.

24. See, for instance, De Sousa 1987; Tappolet 2000; Deonna and Teroni 2012.

25. One might reply that desire has both directions of fit (see Railton, Gregory *this volume*). For reasons I do not have the space to present here, I think this move is not helpful (Lauria 2014: 56–59).

26. See Anscombe 1963: 70–78.

27. One might reply that some reflexive explanations are informative. I have argued that this reply does not stand, given the disanalogies between reflexive, informative explanation and the explanation of desire by evaluations (Lauria 2014: 61–63).

28. See Massin (*this volume*) and Meinong (1917) for a similar view; see, however, Döring and Eker *this volume*.

29. See, for instance, Armstrong 1968; Stampe 1986; Stalnaker 1984; Smith 1994; Dancy 2000; in this volume, Döring and Eker, Alvarez, Railton, Ashwell.

30. See, for instance, Stalnaker 1984: 15.

31. Some have argued that those cases are counterexamples to the motivational view (Mele 2003) or mark the distinction between wishes and desires (Döring and Eker *this volume*). However, see Armstrong (1968: 155), Schroeder (2004: 17), and Dancy (2000: 87–88) for a reply.

32. See e.g. Schafer 2013.

33. For further criticism of the motivational view, see Döring and Eker, Alvarez, Gregory, Railton *this volume*.

34. See, for instance, Searle 1983; Smith 1994. In this volume, this interpretation is assumed in Railton's and Gregory's contributions.

35. See e.g. Millikan 2005; Papineau 1984.

36. See Friedrich (2008: 5–6) for a similar objection.

37. This is motivated further by the thought that the fitting relation *is* satisfaction (Lauria 2014: 142–146).

38. Stampe 1987: 336–337. See also Armstrong (1968: 155), Dretske (1988: 114), and Goldman (2009: 96), although the last two do not appeal to *representations* of facts but merely to facts. See also Russell's analysis of desire in Kenny 1963: 72.

39. See Döring and Eker *this volume*.

40. The worry presented focuses on the dispositional variant of the motivational view, but extends as well to the variant appealing to a motivational mode.

41. See Marks 1986: 139–141; Schroeder 2004: 139; Friedrich 2008: 6–7.

42. See Strawson's (2009) Weather Watchers for a candidate of inert desire.

43. See Schroeder 2004: 173–174.

44. See Schroeder, Railton *this volume*.

45. See Schroeder *this volume*.

46. Schroeder 2004: 107–130.

47. Schroeder 2004.

48. On the distinction between ought-to-do and ought-to-be norms, see Harman 1973; Geach 1982; Jackson 1985; Von Wright 1998; Wedgwood 2006, 2007; Schroeder 2011.

49. In this respect, the view I favor differs from the other deontic accounts in this volume, which appeal to reasons to act (Gregory) or norms in general (Massin). It is also different from accounts relying on the imperative mode or force, at least if the latter is constituted by an ought-to-do norm (see Schafer 2013; Archer 2015).

50. See Friedrich *this volume*. On modes, see Lauria 2014: 122–128.

51. Given the presence of the deontic feature in the mode, one might say that desiring p is *oughting* p. If it is assumed that oughts are requirements, it follows that desiring is, in a sense, requiring a state to obtain. I take it that those are equivalent formulations of the deontic view (Lauria 2014: 131).

52. This is explicit in the teleosemantic approach (e.g. Millikan 2005).

53. See Lauria 2016.

54. For other approaches to desire appealing to modes or force, see Friedrich 2012, *this volume*. Schafer (2013) and Archer (2015) use force to unravel justificatory or inferential relations, respectively.

55. Velleman (2000: 105) explicitly writes that desiring is representing some content *as to be made true*, while believing is representing content *as a fact*. However, it appears that Velleman equates the mode of desire with goodness (106, 115) and is thus

a proponent of an evaluative conception of desire. In this volume, Massin argues that desire's formal object is the ought-to-be or ought-to-do, whereas the present proposal focuses on ought-to-be norms. Moreover, Massin does not equate desires with deontic representations, unlike what I argue here. See also Mulligan (2007) for the idea that the formal objects of desires and wishes are, respectively, ought-to-do and ought-to-be.

56. See Meinong (1917: 91, 96) for the essential relation desires bear to the ought-to-be and Meinong (1917: 37) for the view that the ought-to-be is part of desire's mode, at least as I understand him.

57. See Castañeda 1970.

58. See Meinong 1917: 143–145.

59. See Oddie *this volume* for another counterexample.

60. See, however, Lauria (2014: 243–250) for a defense of the principle against those cases.

61. See Massin *this volume.*

62. Scheler 1973: 207–208.

63. As Massin *this volume* underlines, Meinong understood the "death of desire" principle in terms of the idea that we desire future and contingent states of affairs. My understanding is different (Lauria 2014). Yet the explanation of the principle is the same: the appeal to norms.

64. See Meinong 1917: 99; Scheler 1973: 184; Mulligan 1998; Ogien and Tappolet 2009; Tappolet *forthcoming*.

65. For a more detailed discussion, see Lauria 2014: 177–185.

66. On the distinction between values and norms, see Massin *this volume.*

67. This essay is a summary of my PhD dissertation. I wish to express my gratitude to the following people for their insights and support: Julien Deonna, Gianfranco Soldati, Fabrice Teroni, Kevin Mulligan, Graham Oddie, Peter Railton, Martine Nida-Rümelin, Richard Dub, Otto Brun, Alexander Bown, Clare Mac Cumhaill, Alexander Skiles, David Sander, Timothy Bayne, Olivier Massin, Amanda Garcia, Ghislain Guigon, Anne Meylan, Julien Dutant, and the contributors to this volume.

## References

Anscombe, G. E. M. (1963). *Intention*. Oxford: Blackwell.

Aquinas, T. (1920–1942). *Summa Theologica*. London: Burns, Oates & Washburne.

Archer, A. (2015). 'Reconceiving Direction of Fit', *Thought*, 4 (3), 171–180.

Armstrong, D. M. (1968). *A Materialist Theory of the Mind*. London: Routledge.

Arpaly, N., and Schroeder, T. (2013). *In Praise of Desire*. Oxford: Oxford University Press.

Boghossian, P. (2003). 'The Normativity of Content', *Philosophical Issues*, 13, 32–45.

Castañeda, H.-N. (1970). 'On the Semantics of the Ought-to-do', *Synthese*, 21 (3–4), 449–468.

Dancy, J. (2000). *Practical Reality*. Oxford: Oxford University Press.

Davidson, D. (2001). *Essays on Actions and Events*. Oxford: Oxford University Press.

Deonna, J., and Teroni, F. (2012). *The Emotions: A Philosophical Introduction*. London: Routledge.

Descartes, R. (1989). *The Passions of the Soul*, tr. S. H. Voss. Indianapolis: Hackett.

De Sousa, R. (1987). *The Rationality of Emotion*. Cambridge, Mass.: MIT Press.

———. (2011). *Emotional Truth*. Oxford: Oxford University Press.

Dretske, F. (1988). *Explaining Behavior: Reasons in a World of Causes*. Cambridge, UK: MIT Press.

Friedrich, D. G. (2008). 'An Affective Theory of Desire', PhD dissertation, Australian National University.

———. (2012). 'The Alluringness of Desire', *Philosophical Explorations: An International Journal for the Philosophy of Mind and Action*, 15 (3), 291–302.

Frost, K. (2014). 'On the Very Idea of Direction of Fit', *Philosophical Review*,123 (4), 429–484.

Galen. (2005) *On the Doctrines of Plato and Hippocrates*, ed. P. De Lacy. Berlin: Akademie Verlag.

Geach, P. T. (1982). 'Whatever Happened to Deontic Logic?', *Philosophia*, 11, 1–12.

Goldman, A. H. (2009). *Reasons from Within: Desires and Values*. Oxford: Oxford University Press.

Harman, G. (1973). 'Review of *The Significance of Sense: Meaning Modality, and Morality*', *Philosophical Review*, 82, 235–239.

Hobbes T. (1994). *Leviathan*, ed. E. Curley. Indianapolis: Hackett.

Humberstone, I. L. (1992). 'Direction of Fit', *Mind*, 101 (401), 59–83.

Jackson, F. (1985). 'On the Semantics and Logic of Obligation', *Mind*, 94 (374), 177–195.

Kant, I. (1997). *Critique of Practical Reason*, ed. M. Gregor. Cambridge, UK: Cambridge University Press.

Kenny, A. (1963). *Action, Emotion and Will*. London: Routledge.

Lauria, F. (2014). '"The Logic of the Liver": A Deontic View of the Intentionality of Desire', PhD dissertation, University of Geneva.

———. (2016). 'L'œil du devoir-être : La conception déontique de l'intentionnalité du désir et les modes intentionnels', in G. Fréchette, J. Friedrich, and A. Hügli (eds.), 'Intentionnalité et subjectivité,' special issue of *Studia Philosophica*, 75, 67-80.

Locke, J. (1975). *An Essay Concerning Human Understanding*, ed. P. H. Nidditch. Oxford: Clarendon Press.

Marks, J. (1986). 'The Difference between Motivation and Desire', in J. Marks (ed.), *The Ways of Desire: New Essays in Philosophical Psychology on the Concept of Wanting*. Chicago: Precedent.

Meinong, A. (1917). *On Emotional Presentation*. Translation (1972). Evanston, Ill.: Northwestern University Press.

Mele, A. (2003). *Motivation and Agency*. Oxford: Oxford University Press.

Millikan, R. G. (2005). *Language: A Biological Model*. Oxford: Oxford University Press.

Milliken, J. (2008). 'In a Fitter Direction: Moving beyond the Direction of Fit Picture of Belief and Desire', *Ethical Theory and Moral Practice*, 11, 563–571.

Mulligan, K. (1998). 'The Spectre of Inverted Emotions and the Space of Emotions', *Acta Analytica*, 12, 89–105.

———. (2007). 'Intentionality, Knowledge and Formal Objects', *Disputatio*, 2, 205–228

Oddie, G. (2005). *Value, Reality, and Desire*. Oxford: Oxford University Press.

Ogien, R., and Tappolet, C. (2009). *Les concepts de l'éthique : Faut-il être conséquentialiste?* Paris: Hermann Editeurs.

Papineau, D. (1984). 'Representation and Explanation', *Philosophy of Science*, 51, 550–572.

Plato. (1953). *The Dialogues of Plato*, tr. B. Jowett, 4th ed. Oxford: Clarendon Press.
Platts, M. (1979). *Ways of Meaning: An Introduction to a Philosophy of Language*. London: Routledge & Kegan Paul.
Sartre, J.-P. (1984). *Being and Nothingness*, tr. H. E. Barnes. New York: Washington Square Press.
Schafer, K. (2013). 'Perception and the Rational Force of Desire', *Journal of Philosophy*, 110 (5), 258–281.
Scheler, M. (1973). *Formalism in Ethics and Non-Formal Ethics of Values: A New Attempt toward the Foundation of an Ethical Personalism*. Evanston, Ill.: Northwestern University Press.
Schroeder, M. (2011). '*Ought*, Agents, and Actions', *Philosophical Review*, 120, 1–41.
Schroeder T. (2004). *Three Faces of Desire*. Oxford: Oxford University Press.
Searle, J. R. (1983). *Intentionality. An Essay in the Philosophy of Mind*. Cambridge, UK: Cambridge University Press.
Smith, M. (1994). *The Moral Problem*. Oxford: Blackwell.
Sobel, D., and Copp, D. (2001). 'Against Direction of Fit Accounts of Belief and Desire', *Analysis*, 61 (1), 44–53.
Stalnaker, R. (1984). *Inquiry*. Cambridge, Mass.: MIT Press.
Stampe, D. W. (1986). 'Defining Desire', in J. Marks (ed.), *The Ways of Desire: New Essays in Philosophical Psychology on the Concept of Wanting*. Chicago: Precedent.
———. (1987). 'The Authority of Desire', *Philosophical Review*, 96 (3), 335–381.
Strawson, G. (2009). *Mental Reality*. Cambridge, Mass.: MIT Press.
Tappolet, C. (2000). *Emotions et valeurs*. Paris: Presses Universitaires de France.
———. (*forthcoming*) 'Evaluative vs. Deontic Concepts', in H. Lafollette (ed.), *International Encyclopedia of Ethics*. Oxford: Wiley-Blackwell.
Tenenbaum, S. (2007). *Appearances of the Good: An Essay on the Nature of Practical Reason*. Cambridge, UK: Cambridge University Press.
———. (2013). 'The Guise of the Good', in H. Lafollette (ed.), *International Encyclopedia of Ethics*. Oxford: Wiley-Blackwell.
Velleman, J. D. (1992). 'The Guise of the Good', *Noûs*, 26 (1), 3–26.
———, (2000). *The Possibility of Practical Reason*. Oxford: Clarendon Press.
Von Wright, G. H. (1998). 'Ought to Be—Ought to Do', in G. Meggle (ed.), *Actions, Norms, Values*. Berlin: De Gruyter.
Wedgwood, R. (2006). 'The Meaning of "Ought"', *Oxford Studies in Metaethics*, 1, 127–160.
———. (2007). *The Nature of Normativity*. Oxford: Oxford University Press.

# CHAPTER 6 | Desires, Values and Norms

OLIVIER MASSIN

The language of desire, and aversion, is imperative; *as, Do this, forbear that.*

—HOBBES, *Leviathan*

WHEN ONE DESIRES something, philosophers used to agree, one desires it under the guise of the good. In Scholastic terminology, the *formal objects* of desires are values. One issue raised by this traditional view is that values are also widely claimed to be formal objects of emotions. When one entertains a positive emotion toward something, it necessarily appears good to us. For those who put hope in the project of individuating kinds of attitudes—such as beliefs, emotions, and desires—through their formal objects and want to keep emotions and desires distinct, this is bad news. Both emotions and desires end up having the same sort of formal objects and, relatedly, the same kind of correctness conditions.

Meinong (1972) proposed a neat way out: emotions require presentations of values, but desires require presentations of norms. In a nutshell, one cannot have a positive emotion toward something without it appearing good in some way, and one cannot desire something without it appearing as something that ought to be. Values are the formal objects of emotions; norms are the formal objects of desires. This paper focuses on the desire side of Meinong's proposal: on the view that *desires, by nature, require presentations of norms*. Taking up Lauria's (*this volume*) apt expression, I shall call this the "guise of the ought" in contrast to the traditional "guise of the good" thesis, which claims that desires require by nature presentations of values. My claim is that *the "guise of the ought" thesis fares better than the "guise of the good" thesis.*

Although Meinong's view about *emotions*—according to which emotions are essentially connected with presentations of values—has become widely influential within contemporary philosophy (see in particular Tappolet 2000 for pioneering work), his correlative views about *desires* have remained widely unnoticed outside circles of Meinong scholars. Yet one of the first systems of deontic logic—the one developed by Ernst Mally (1926: 241) in his tellingly entitled book *The Basic Laws of Ought: Elements of the Logic of Willing*—crucially relies on Meinong's view that the formal object of willing is the *Seinsollen* of states of affairs. More recently, Mulligan (1998: §2) and Konrad (2000) mention Meinong's view of desire favorably, and Lauria (2014, *this volume*) deserves full credit for having reintroduced Meinong's theory to the contemporary philosophy of desire. One possible reason for this neglect is that although Meinong's views are conceptually limpid, they are not always easy to get at due to his idiosyncratic terminology.[1]

A more substantial reason for this neglect, worth dismissing from the start, is that *prima facie* it sounds preposterous to claim that we cannot desire but what appears to us as something that ought to be or that we ought to do. The guise of the ought seems to capture only these self-righteous desires, arising from some Kantian sense of moral duty. It apparently leaves most mundane desires out of the picture. If I desire to drink a glass of Burgundy, I am clearly not under the impression that it is my *duty* to do so. This objection relies on a misunderstanding about the sense of *ought* in Meinong's proposal. Though *ought* often has moral connotations, Meinong's *ought* is not restricted to the moral domain. Any kind of obligation (rational, aesthetic, legal, etc.) is relevant, including instrumental obligation (Meinong, 1972: 98ff.). The *ought* under consideration in the "guise of the ought" thesis is the normative, unqualified ought: *ought morally, ought rationally, ought aesthetically*, etc. are only species of *ought simpliciter*.

The arguments I shall advance in favor of the guise of the ought, as against the guise of the good, rely on the view that the opposition between desire and aversion is of the same kind as the opposition between obligation and interdiction, but of a different kind from the opposition between goodness and badness. Section 1 introduces the guise of the ought by locating it within Meinong's full deontic account of desire and by contrasting it with the guise of the good thesis. Section 2 argues that one neglected difference between values and norms is that obligations and interdiction of contradictory contents are equivalent, which is not the case with *good that* and *bad that*. Section 3 argues that the very same difference holds between desires and emotions: wanting *p* is equivalent to diswanting *non-p*, which is not true of positive and negative emotions. Section 4 relies on this analogy between desires and norms and disanalogies between desires and values to defend two arguments in favor of the guise of the ought as against the guise of the good. Section 5 addresses some objections to the guise of the ought.

## 1 The Guise of the Ought

### 1.1 Meinong's Deontic Conception of Desires

The idea that norms are to desires what values are to emotions was defended by the late Meinong (1972: 28, 37–38). According to Meinong, emotions (*das Fühlen*) are presentations of values, while desires (*das Begehren*) are presentations of norms.[2] Contrary to evaluative conceptions of desires, which equate desires with presentations of values,[3] Meinong (and Lauria, *this volume*, following him) equates desires with presentation of norms, namely, *oughts-to-be*:

> **Meinong's deontic conception of desires:** To desire something is to be presented with it as something that ought to be.[4]

To desire to eat a florentine is to be under the impression that it ought to be the case that one eats a florentine. Are values deprived of any motivational oomph in such an account? And does Meinong's view entail that desire is a faculty that allows us to grasp the ought-to-be-ness of a state of affairs independently of any of its other natural features? No, because Meinong's deontic conception of desires leans against two further claims:

1. Necessarily, if one has some presentation of norms, one has some presentation of values.[5]
2. Necessarily, if one has some presentation of values, one has some presentation of natural properties.[6]

These two claims are the psychological counterparts of the claims that norms are grounded in values and of the claim that values are grounded in natural properties (two claims also endorsed by Meinong 1972: 99). Since

Meinong equates emotions with presentations of values, the first claim boils down to the claim that desires are grounded in emotions.

Although in this chapter I take my lead from Meinong's approach to desires, I have two main objections to his deontic conception of desires—one questioning its sufficiency, the other its necessity.

My worry concerning necessity stems from the fact that the deontic conceptions of desires mentions only oughts-to-be, at the expense of oughts-to-do. This distinction, however, would help the deontic conception of desires to account for the difference between propositional desires, or *desires-that*, and *desires-to* (Kenny 1966: 86 ff.). Desiring that *p* would be equated with the impression that *p* ought to be, while desiring to ϕ would be equated with the impression that one ought to ϕ. Meinong does not take this distinction seriously: he thinks that *oughts-to-do* reduce to *oughts-to-be* (the so-called Meinong-Chishom reduction). Indeed, the corresponding view with respect to desires is quite standard: *desires-to* are taken to be reducible to *desires-that* (Schueler 1995: 12). Now, neither of these two reductions, even if widespread, is uncontroversial. So it would be better for the deontic conception of desires not to be committed to either of them.

My objection concerning the sufficiency of Meinong's analysis of desires is that since (i) one can be under the impression that things are as they ought to be and (ii) one cannot desire what one thinks is already the case, then some deontic presentations are not desires. Meinong agrees with (ii). He even provides one of the most precise specifications advanced so far of what one can desire (Meinong 1972: 85, 143ff.). In essence, Meinong's view is that our desires are directed at states of affairs (*objectives*) that the desirer takes to be *future and contingent*. We cannot desire what we take to be already the case. And among the states of affairs that, we think, do not obtain, we can desire only those that, we think, will neither necessarily obtain nor impossibly obtain.

But Meinong rejects (i). Oughts-to-be, he claims, necessarily apply to non-actual states of affairs.[7] This is precisely why, in his account, desires essentially bear on apparently non-actual states of affairs. The view that desires are directed toward what is presented as contingent futures derives, then, from the view that oughts-to-be apply to contingent futures (Meinong 1972: 143–145). This is where I disagree with Meinong. There is no conceptual inconsistency, *pace* Meinong, in saying that *things are as they should be* or that *some things have been, are, and necessarily will be as they ought to be*.[8] When Meinong insists that such things "cannot be said," he presumably conflates pragmatics with semantics. (A similar conflation, if I am right, is to be found in Lauria, 2014:

237 ff.; *this volume.*) One common reason one *mentions* norms, admittedly, is to improve their fulfillment. But in other contexts, mentioning fulfilled norms is relevant: for instance when, in a more contemplative or conservative mood, we wish to argue that certain things should not be changed. Even if mentioning things that are as they ought to be is often pragmatically irrelevant, it remains perfectly meaningful semantically. Hence the view that desire essentially involves presentations of oughts-to-be does not entail the strong restrictions that Meinong thinks it does with respect to the kinds of states of affairs we can desire. If desires are indeed future-directed—as I tend to think, following Meinong and many others—this is not a consequence of their being norm-directed. Hence the nature of desires is not exhausted by their being directed at states of affairs that (seemingly) ought to be. Presentations of norms are necessary but not sufficient to desires.

Meinong's deontic view, *minus* the reduction of oughts-to-be to oughts-to-do, and *minus* the view that presentations of norms are sufficient to explain desires, leaves us with the view that *desires entail presentations of oughts-to-be or presentations of oughts-to-do.* This view, the guise of the ought, is, I believe, the essential grain of truth in Meinong's deontic conception of desires.

### 1.2 The Guise of the Good versus the Guise of the Ought

The guise of the ought (henceforth, GO) is entailed by Meinong's deontic view but is weaker than that view. It is best introduced in contrast to its famous cousin, the guise of the good (GG), which I define as follows:

> **"Guise of the Good" Thesis:** In virtue of the immediate nature of desire:
> 1. If *S* desires that *p*, it seems to *S* that *p* is good.
> 2. If *S* desires to $\phi$, it seems to *S* that $\phi$*-ing* is good.

In order to remain non-committal with respect to the reduction of *desires-to* to *desires-that*, in accordance with the above, this definition of the GO mentions two sorts of desires. The definition departs in two other ways from more standard formulations of GG. First, it claims that evaluative presentations are not only necessary but also essential to desire. The reason the necessity at stake is claimed to be grounded in the nature of desire is that GG purports to shed light on what desires are and that not everything that is necessary to desire is essential to it (Fine 1994). Besides, the nature of desire is claimed to be *immediate* rather than mediate. (The distinction between immediate and mediate nature is taken from Fine 1995: §5.) This pertains to Meinong's view, mentioned earlier, that all desires require some presentations of values because they require presentations of norms. This does not make Meinong an upholder of GG: the presentation of values, under Meinong's approach, belongs only to the *mediate* nature of desire. GG, by contrast, claims that evaluative presentations belong to their immediate essence.

Second, the definition of GG appeals to evaluative *seemings* instead of the more usual evaluative *beliefs* or *thoughts*. The reason for this is to allow GG to deal with counterexamples, such as the squash player desiring to slam her racket against her opponent: although the player might well *believe* upon reflection that this is a bad thing to do, this action might still *appear* to her in that very moment as a good one.[9] I shall speak indifferently of value *seemings* or value *presentations* (which is Meinong's terminology) and assume that presentations or seemings are neither factive (in order to include incorrect desires) nor anti-factive (in order to include correct ones).[10] Furthermore, I shall be interested in GG only insofar as it purports to shed light on the following sort of desires, which are my *explananda*:

1. The desires and emotions at stake are those directed toward states of affairs or actions, whose contents can be expressed by propositions (loving/desiring that *p*) or infinitive complements (loving/desiring to $\phi$).[11] The contrast I shall emphasize between desires and emotions relies on the way desiring and "emoting" behave when their content is negated. To the extent that referring expressions—names—cannot be negated (Geach 1980: §31), no such contrast holds for objectual desires, if there are such things.[12]
2. I shall assume that GG is restricted to *occurrent* desires, in contrast to standing and dispositional ones. Döring and Eker (*this volume*) point out, against GG, that dispositional desires do not entail occurrent seemings of values. Insofar as GG is restricted to occurrent desires, it is immune to that objection.
3. I shall be interested here only in *thin* desires, in the sense of desires taken apart from any of their affective accompaniments. Schueler (1995: 11ff.) points out that there are cold desires, deprived of strong phenomenological character, such as desiring to arrive on time or desiring to buy some milk, and that there are also desires accompanied with strong feelings, which, like hunger and other cravings,

urges, or appetites, can be felt. What I call *thin* desires are desires taken apart from their affective clothes. Thick desires, by contrast, are complex states, involving affects (bodily sensations, feelings, emotions, moods, etc.) somehow related to thin desires. Hunger, for instance, might refer to a complex state involving the feeling of hunger together with the thin desire to eat (see Hamilton 1882: vol. 2, 433; Gregory *this volume*). Perhaps there are only thick desires; perhaps thin desires are only abstractions that, in reality, always come clothed with affects (even if of low intensity). But this does not threaten the conceptual distinction between thin and thick desires. Even if desires are necessarily thick, one can grasp thin desires, in abstract thought, by peeling off their affective skin.

In sum, the focus is on *thin propositional occurrent desires*. Speaking of *desirings* might help make clear that the desires at stake are occurrent. But *desiring* is often used to express desires connected to strong feelings: *desirings* are occurrent, but they are still too thick. *Wantings* is perhaps the best candidate for expressing what we are after here. *Wantings* are at once more occurrent and less affectively loaded than *desires*. As it happens, *wanting* is often used instead of *desiring* in the literature on desire (see e.g. Kenny 1966: ch. 5; Audi 1986).

With this in hand, the "guise of the ought" thesis might be introduced as follows:

**"Guise of the Ought" Thesis:** In virtue of the immediate nature of desire:

1. If *S* desires that *p*, it seems to *S* that *p* ought to be.
2. If *S* desires to $\phi$, it seems to *S* that he ought to $\phi$.

GG claims that because occurrent desires are what they are, it is immediately impossible to desire something without being under the impression that it is good in some way. GO claims that because occurrent desires are what they are, it is immediately impossible to desire something without being under the impression that it ought to be. GO therefore is only a small, albeit crucial modification of GG (just replace *good* with *ought*). GG and GO are close cousins: both claim that desires essentially entail *normative presentations*, by which I mean presentations that are *either evaluative or deontic*.

It is worth stressing that neither GG nor GO entails that normative presentations are *constituents or parts* of desires. Compare this to emotions.

It has been maintained that presentations of values are essential to emotions without being for all that constituents of emotions: emotions could be *reactions* to presentations of values.[13] Although less often noticed (but see Tenenbaum 2007: 23), the same possibility holds as far as desires are concerned: the claim that desires require normative presentations—GG or GO—is compatible with the view that presentations of values or norms are essential to but not constitutive of desires. One interesting thing about that view is that normative presentations can then be said to provide *internalist justification* to desires, to constitute *subjective reasons* for desires. The reason Julie desires to laugh is that laughing seems good to her (GG) or that it seems to her that she ought to laugh (GO). To the extent that justification is irreflexive, such a move is not open to the evaluative nor to the deontic conceptions of desire.[14]

## 1.3 Guises and Formal Objects

GG and GO might be usefully rephrased in the "formal object" jargon: GG amounts to the view that *values are the formal objects of desires*, while GO amounts to the claim that *norms are the formal object of desires.* This connection with the concept of "formal objects" presents two interesting points.[15]

First, it helps make clear what the correctness conditions of desires are under GG and GO. There are two mains conceptions of *formal objects* in the literature:

- The first, in line with Kenny (1966: ch. 9), relies on the idea that kinds of intentional episodes put some restriction on the kinds of objects that these episodes *can* bear upon. The kind of object that episodes of some kind necessarily bear upon constitute their formal object. Accordingly, the formal objects of desires have to be internalized: for GG the formal objects of desires are *presented* values; for GO they are *presented* norms.
- The second approach to formal objects relies on the idea that kinds of intentional episodes put some restriction on the kinds of objects that these episodes *should* bear upon. Formal objects are here equated with the kinds of objects that attitudes of a kind ought to bear upon. Formal objects are then external "*correct-makers*."

GG and GO allow for a straightforward explanation of the connection between the internal and external formal object of desires. A desire is correct if and only if the axiological or deontic presentation it involves is veridical. Hence GG will say a desire is correct if and only if its object is good, while GO will have it that a desire is correct if and only if its object ought to be (or if the desirer ought to do it).[16]

Second, the "formal object" jargon allows us to rephrase GG and GO in yet another, third way. Kenny distinguishes *trivial* formal objects, which are obtained by "modalising the relevant verb," from *non-trivial* ones. The trivial formal object of desire, admittedly, is *the desirable* (i.e. what we desire is presented as desirable to us, and our desire is correct if and only if what we desire is desirable). GG and GO are views about the *non-trivial* formal objects of desires. *According to GG, the desirable is what is good. According to GO, the desirable is what ought to be, or what the desirer ought to do.*

The thesis to be defended now is conditional: *If we have to choose between GG and GO, we should endorse GO.* Since I focus on the relative advantage of GO over GG, I shall assume that the arguments and replies advanced by upholders of GG are available, *mutadis mutandis*, to the upholders of GO. For instance, the annoyed squash player might believe that it would be wrong to smash her racket against her opponent, but the action might still non-epistemically appear to her as right, as an action she ought to do.

But why should we even choose between GG and GO? Since GO (contrary to the deontic view of desires) does not give sufficient conditions for desires, and since GG (contrary to evaluative view of desires) does not give sufficient conditions either, both are in principle compatible. Since each purports to provide only a partial insight into the nature of desires, one could accept both. But that wouldn't be a very comfortable position to be in. What we can gain from having two independent normative presentations essentially tied to desires is unclear, but what is to be lost is much clearer. First, the conjunction of GG and GO is open to two sets of objections: those raised against GG and those raised against GO. Second, the conjunction of GG and GO over-complexifies the nature of desire: every desire would go, in virtue of its immediate essence, with both deontic and evaluative presentations. Third, insofar as goodness and oughtness are not co-extensive, as I shall argue, the conjunction of GG and GO entails that a desire can be partly correct and partly incorrect. It is no accident that the conjunction of GG and GO has found no proponents yet. Hence I shall assume that *GG and GO are rival views.*

One reason to favor GO over GG is that GG, together with the view that emotions have values as formal objects, leads to the view that emotions and desires share their formal objects. If desires and emotions are distinct kinds of mental episodes, and if formal objects individuate kinds of attitudes, then GO is preferable to GG (Mulligan 2010). Likewise, if emotions and desires with the same content can have different correctness conditions, then GO is preferable to GG. Although I sympathize with this line of thought, I shall press for another kind of argument here. Its key premise is that *desires, like norms—and contrary to values and emotions—forbid indifference to the negation of their content*. To establish this, let us first contrast values and norms in that respect.

## 2 Norms versus Values

Although the Humean fact/value dichotomy tends to conflate them, there is a distinction between *values* (good, bad, elegant, etc.) and *norms* (obligatory, impermissible, ought, etc.). Where exactly the distinction lies, however, is a tricky and somewhat neglected issue.[17] Several criteria have been advanced. At the risk of adding confusion, I shall introduce another one, seemingly overlooked.

That values essentially have a *polarity* is one of the few fairly uncontroversial claims in value theory.[18] Such a claim is more rarely made with respect to norms, but one might think that in the same way that good is positive and bad negative, obligation is positive and interdiction negative. What I want to bring out is that the way positive and negative values are opposed to each other essentially differs from the way that positive and negative norms are opposed to each other. Although superficially similar, the positive/negative opposition found in the axiological sphere is distinct from that found in the deontic realm. (The difference I am going to introduce holds only for values and norms that have a negatable content: propositions, states of affairs, or actions; see Schroeder 2007.)

### 2.1 Formal Analogies between Values and Norms

In the same way that there are the good, the neutral, and the bad, there are the obligatory, the optional, and the forbidden. Both the axiological and the deontic spaces are carved out in a trichotomic way, giving rise to the analogous axiological and deontic squares of opposition (see Figure 6.1, building on McNamara 2006):

Correspondingly, many tautologies about norms and values closely match each other (see Goble 1990). Good, neutral, and bad are contraries,

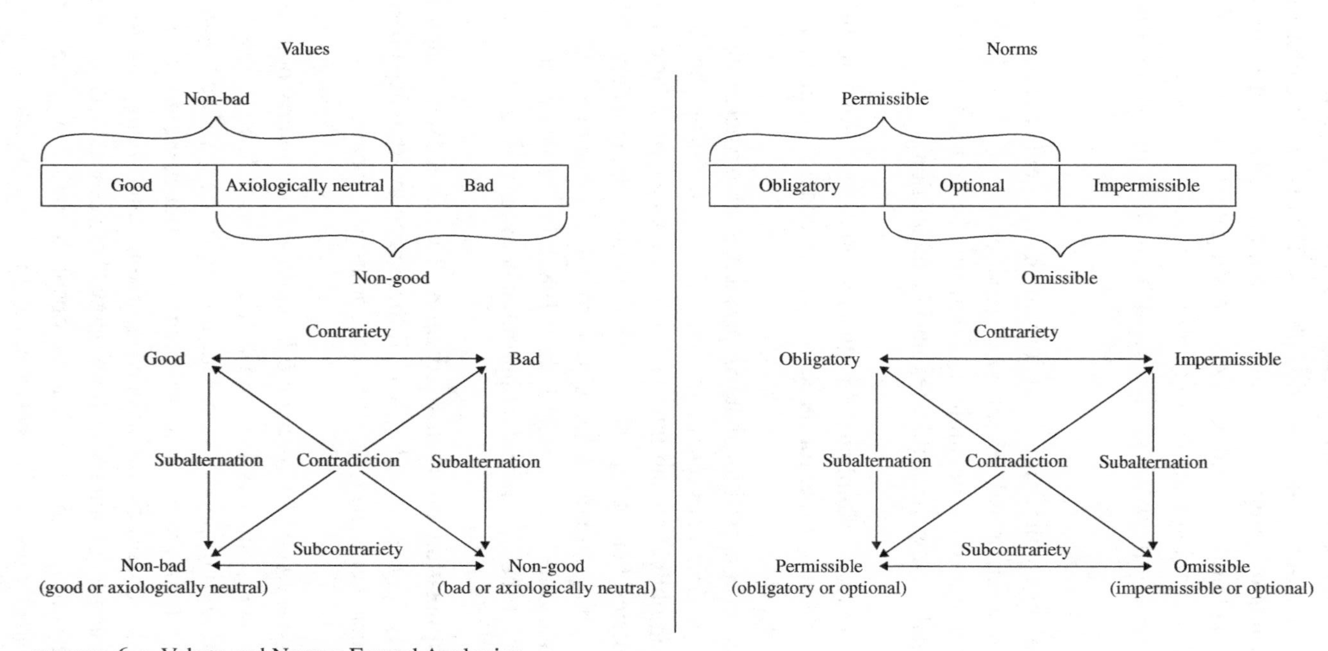


FIGURE 6.1 Values and Norms: Formal Analogies

and the disjunction of any two of them is the contradictory of the third. The same holds for obligatory, optional, and forbidden.

What we are trichotomizing here is not the whole world but, respectively, the axiological and deontic spheres. That is, we are considering only the kinds or categories of objects that *could* be said to be good, neutral, or bad or that could be said to be obligatory, optional, or forbidden.[19] Not everything that is neither obligatory nor forbidden is optional (the number 2, for instance): it has to be deontically assessable. We then have:

- If *p* belongs to the axiological domain, then *p* is either good, axiologically neutral, or bad. (exclusive disjunction)
- If *p* belongs to the deontological domain, then *p* is either obligatory, optional, or impermissible. (exclusive disjunction)

(I am assuming for simplicity that the relevant conditions are fulfilled, such as: at the same time, for the same person, under the same respect, in the same way, etc.)

The relation of opposition that will play a central role here is the relation of *polar opposition* between, on the one hand, goodness and badness, and on the other, obligation and interdiction. The concept of polar opposition that is of interest here is one sub-species of contrariety: polar opposites are contraries falling on both sides of a "zero point" (Meinong 1996: 145[20]), "indifference zone" (Lehrer and Lehrer 1982), or "pivotal region" (Cruse 1995: 205).[21] I shall define polar opposition between predicates as follows:

**Polar opposition between predicates:** Two predicates *P* and *Q* are polarly opposed if and only if (i) there is an indifference predicate *I* between them; (ii) *P*, *Q*, and *I* are contrary predicates.

Thus *being very good* and *being mildly good* are not polarly opposed, for no indifference point lies between them. Likewise *being good* and *not being good* are not polarly opposed, for *not being good* and *being axiologically neutral* are not contrary predicates. But *being good* and *being bad* are polar opposites, for in between them stands *being axiologically neutral*, which is a contrary of both. How "betweenness" is to be understood here is a question I shall leave open: the intuitive sense in which the axiologically neutral lies between the good and the bad is enough for our present purpose. Likewise, *being obligatory* and *being impermissible* are polar opposites, for in between them stands *being optional*. So are *it is obligatory that* and *it is impermissible that,* provided the contrariety relations between properties also hold, *mutatis mutandis*, between unary connectives. We shall say that two unary connectives are contraries if and only if, for any sentence, the two sentences formed from them cannot both be true. We can then define polar opposition between connectives as we defined polar opposition between predicates:

> **Polar opposition between connectives:** Two connnectives *C* and *C"* stand in a relation of polar opposition if and only if (i) there is a neutral connective *C'* between *C* and *C"*; and (ii) *C, C'*, and C" are contrary connectives.

Thus *it is necessary that* and *it is impossible that* are polarly opposed, for in between them stands *it is contingent that,* and these three connectives are contrary to each other.

*Being good* and *being bad*, like *being obligatory* and *being forbidden*, are polarly opposed predicates; *it is good that* and *it is bad that*, like *it is obligatory that* and *it is impermissible that*, are polarly opposed connectives. Both the axiological realm and the deontic realms are trichotomized and polarly structured.

## 2.2 Formal Disanalogies between Values and Norms

Appearances notwithstanding, however, the polar opposition between *goodness* and *badness* is crucially different from the polar opposition between *obligation* and *interdiction.*[22] While all norms (of the same type) can be defined in terms of obligation and standard logical connectives alone, there is no way to define values (of the same type) in terms of goodness and such connectives alone. Let us review four deontic tautologies that, on intuitive grounds, have no axiological counterpart. (*G* stands for "good that," *N* for "axiologically neutral that," and *B* for "bad that"; *OB* stands for "obligatory that," *OP* for "optional that," and *IM* for "impermissible that.")

First:

(1) $(p)(IMp \leftrightarrow OB\neg p)$

It is impermissible to smoke if and only if it is obligatory not to smoke. Obligation and interdiction are *interdefinable through negation* (as are necessity and impossibility). But the corresponding formula does not hold true of values: "It is bad that *p*" is not equivalent to "It is good that $\neg p$":

$$(1') \quad \neg(p)(Bp \leftrightarrow G\neg p)$$

That it is bad to bully for fun does not entail that it is good not to bully for fun. That might be axiologically neutral. Conversely, that it is good to laugh does not entail that it is bad not to laugh. For while its being good to laugh perhaps entails that it is not good not to laugh,[23] its being good to laugh is compatible with its being axiologically neutral not to laugh. A famous example is given by Chisholm and Sosa (1966): assume that only happiness is intrinsically good, and unhappiness intrinsically bad. Then, that there are unhappy egrets is bad. But there being no unhappy egrets does not add any positive value to the universe. This is a neutral state of affairs, even if its negation is good. *While the obligatoriness of a state of affairs is equivalent to the impermissibility of its negation, the goodness of a state of affairs is not equivalent to the badness of its negation* (nor is its badness equivalent to the goodness of its negation).

Consequently, for norms, we also have:

$$(2) \quad (p)(OBp \rightarrow \neg OP\neg p)$$

$$(3) \quad (p)(IMp \rightarrow \neg OP\neg p)$$

If it is obligatory to drive on the right, it cannot be optional not to drive on the right: this has to be forbidden. And it cannot be impermissible to smoke and optional not to smoke. This has to be obligatory. On the other hand, "It is good that *p*" is compatible with "It is neutral that $\neg p$."

$$(2') \quad \neg(p)(Gp \rightarrow \neg N\neg p)$$

$$(3') \quad \neg(p)(Bp \rightarrow \neg N\neg p)$$

It might be elegant to wear a hat without it being inelegant not to wear a hat: not wearing a hat might be axiologically neutral. It might be bad to steal and neutral not to steal. States of affairs might be good or bad while their absence is axiologically neutral. *That a state of affairs is obligatory entails that its negation is not optional, but that a state of affairs is good is compatible with its negation being neutral.* In Chisholm's (1968: 24) words: "Good states of affairs and bad states of affairs, then, have this feature in common: they have neutral negations, negations that are neither good nor bad." Obligatory states of affairs, on the contrary, have no neutral negations, that is, no negations that are neither obligatory nor impermissible.

Relatedly, the following equivalence holds tautologically for norms:

$$(4) \quad (p)\left[OPp \leftrightarrow (\neg OBp \wedge \neg OB\neg p)\right]$$

Smiling is optional if and only if it is neither obligatory to smile nor obligatory not to smile. But axiological neutrality, contrary to deontic indifference, cannot be defined in terms of goodness and logical connectives alone:

$$(4') \quad \neg(p)\left[Np \leftrightarrow (\neg Gp \wedge \neg G\neg p)\right]$$

A state of affairs might be neutral while its negation is good or bad. Not experiencing pleasure is neutral. But experiencing pleasure is good.

Interestingly, the negated equivalence here might still be used to define other concepts, distinct from axiological neutrality. One might call—somewhat paradoxically—*positively indifferent* a state of affairs of which neither it nor its negation are good. A state of affairs will then be *negatively indifferent* iff neither it nor its negation are bad. Finally a state of affairs will be indifferent, *tout court*, if it is both positively and negatively indifferent. Consequently, all states of affairs indifferent *tout court* are neutral (and so are their negation). But not all neutral states of affairs are indifferent *tout court*, because some neutral states of affairs might be such that their negation is good or bad.[24]

These contrasts between values and norms are not confined to values and norms viewed as propositional connectives. They also hold for axiological and deontological predications:

- $\phi$-*ing* is obligatory$\leftrightarrow$ $\neg\phi$-*ing* is forbidden.

Again, the corresponding axiological equivalence does not hold:

- $\neg$($\phi$-*ing* is good$\leftrightarrow$ $\neg\phi$-*ing* is bad)

If smiling is obligatory, then not smiling is forbidden. But that smiling is good does not entail that not smiling is bad. Not smiling might be axiologically neutral.

Neither is this asymmetry restricted to thin values and norms. It also holds for thicker or specified ones:

- $(p)$ (it is morally obligatory that $p \leftrightarrow$ It is morally forbidden that $\neg p$)

The corresponding equivalences do not hold for adverbially specified values:

- $\neg(p)$ (it is morally good that $p \leftrightarrow$ It is morally bad that $\neg p$)

Nor do they hold for thick values:

- $\neg(p)$ (it is admirable that $p \leftrightarrow$ It is despicable that $\neg p$)

Whether connectives or predicables, indeterminate or adverbially specified, operating on propositions, actions, or state of affairs, obligation and interdiction are interdefinable only with the help of negation. Goodness and badness are not. The goodness of something is not equivalent to the badness of its negation. One would strive in vain to get goodness out of badness and negation alone.

The polar opposition between goodness and badness is therefore importantly distinct from the polar opposition between obligation and interdiction. The polar opposition between obligation and interdiction might be called *formal* in the sense that one can get from one to the other by applying standard logical connectives. The polar opposition between goodness and badness, on the other hand, is *material*, in the sense that no matter how one plays with standard logical connectives, one cannot get from the one to the other.

**Formal polar opposition between connectives:** Two unary sentential connectives $C$ and $C$" stand in relation of *formal* polar opposition if and only if (i) they are polarly opposed; and (ii) for any proposition $p$, $Cp \leftrightarrow C"\neg p$ .

**Material polar opposition between connectives:** Two unary sentential connectives $C$ and $C$" stand in relation of *material* polar opposition if and only if (i) they are polarly opposed; and (ii) they are not formally polarly opposed.

While material polar opposition is ubiquitous among axiological concepts, it is nowhere to be found among deontic ones. That deontic concepts are formally related is what allows standard deontic logic to rely on a formal language that contains only *one* primitive deontic concept (*permission*, as in Von Wright 1951, or more standardly *obligations or oughts*). Although the other deontic concepts do not figure in the basic language, they are easily introduced by adding some definitional patch that *defines* each of the missing deontic modalities in terms of the fundamental one ("the traditional definitional scheme," as McNamara 2006 calls it). By contrast, no definitional scheme of the sort could be added to a logic of goodness, say, so as to get a logic of neutrality and badness. A logic of values requires at least two axiological primitives (which might be one reason logics of values are less developed than deontic ones).

## 3 Desires versus Emotions

This section argues that the above analogies and disanalogies between values and norms closely match the analogies and disanologies between emotions and desires.

### 3.1 Formal Analogies between Desires and Emotions

Like the axiological and deontic realms, the affective and conative are spheres displaying a tripartite distinction. There are positive and negative emotions, and there are states of affective indifference. There are positive and negative conations, and there are states of conative indifference. Following the Brentanian use, let us use "love" to subsume all the positive emotions and "hate" to subsume all the negative ones. And following standard philosophical use, let us call "desire" the positive conation and "aversion" the negative conation. None of these terminological choices is unproblematic. In particular, "aversion," perhaps even more than "desire," suggests a thick conative attitude instead of the thin one we are after. Suffice it to say that the term "aversion" is here used in a theoretical sense, to label the opposite of *thin occurrent propositional desire* (see 1.2). If "wanting" is the best way to express such desire, then "diswanting" could be perhaps a better way to express the polar opposite of thin desires.

Figure 6. 2 represents two squares of oppositions that might be built from the affective and conative trichotomies.[25] As with values and norms, these two trichotomies are understood as dividing not all entities but,

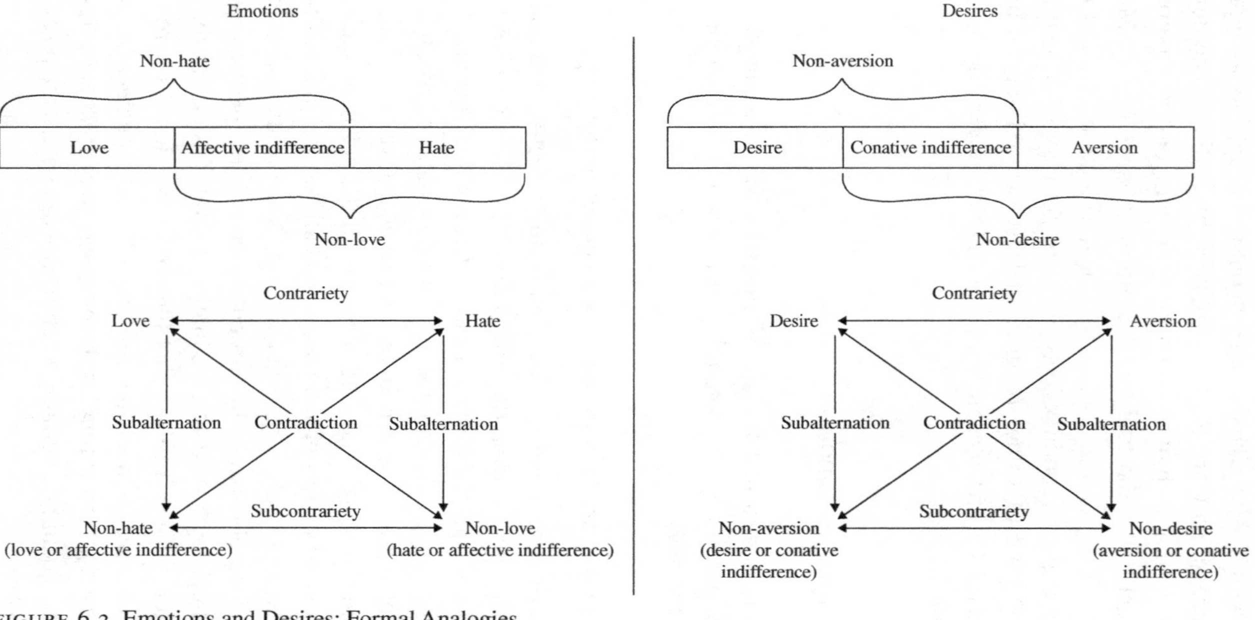


FIGURE 6.2 Emotions and Desires: Formal Analogies

respectively, the affective and conative domains. Accordingly, they can be rephrased as follows:

- If *p* is an affective content, then *p* is either loved, affectively indifferent, or hated. (exclusive disjunction)
- If *p* is a conative content, then *p* is either wanted (desire), conatively indifferent, or diswanted (aversion). (exclusive disjunction)

(I am assuming for simplicity that the relevant conditions are fulfilled, such as: at the same time, by the same person, under the same respect, in the same way, etc.)

Desire and aversion, like love and hate, are polar opposites. Desires, like emotions, have a polarity: aversion is negative; desire is positive. In Davidsonian terminology, desire is a "*pro*-attitude," aversion a "*con*-attitude." In between desire and aversion lies the *conatively indifferent* in the same way that in between love and hate stands the *affectively indifferent.*

### 3.2 Formal Disanalogies between Desires and Emotions

As it first appears, the formal relations between desire and its opposites seem to match closely those between love and its opposites. However, these superficial analogies conceal a deeper disanalogy. Desire and aversion are interdefinable through negation, as are obligation and interdiction (see e.g. Heathwood 2007). If *D* stands for "*S* desires that," *A* for "*S* is averse to," and *CI* for "*S* is conatively indifferent to," we have:

(5) $(p)(Dp \leftrightarrow A\neg p)$

For instance, being averse to being in pain is equivalent to desiring not being in pain. This equivalence might be challenged on terminological grounds, for, as noted earlier, aversion seems to involve more than mere "desiring not" (Schroeder 2004: 26). But recall that aversion is here used as a term of art to denote the polar opposite of thin occurrent desire. Terminological issues aside, the substantial point is that one cannot think of a polar opposite to desire that would not be co-extensional with desiring not. The fundamental reason for this is *that one cannot desire something and be conatively indifferent to its negation. If we want the presence of something, we cannot but diswant its absence.* If Julie desires to smoke, she cannot be indifferent to not smoking. She has to be averse to it. Nor can we be averse to something and be indifferent to its negation: if Julie is averse to being in pain, she cannot be indifferent to not being in pain. She has to desire it. Hence we also have:

(6) $(p)(Dp \rightarrow \neg CI\neg p)$

(7) $(p)(Ap \rightarrow \neg CI\neg p)$

By contrast, the polar opposite of love (of positive emotions) is not co-extensional with loving-not. Loving to do something is not tautologically equivalent to hating not doing it (*L* stands for "*S* loves that," *H* for "*S* hates that," and *AI* for "*S* is affectively indifferent to"):

(5') $\neg(p)(Lp \leftrightarrow H\neg p)$

While "Suzy wants to swim" is equivalent to "Suzy diswants not to swim," "Suzy likes swimming" is not equivalent to "Suzy dislikes not-swimming." This is true, it seems, of all polarly opposed emotions that have a propositional content. Thus, that Paul would be proud if Julie was his wife does not entail that Paul would be ashamed if Julie was not his wife. Or: that one enjoys reading Stendhal does not entail that one suffers not reading him.

This is due to the fact that it is possible to love something and to be indifferent to its negation: Julie might love smoking without hating not smoking. Or Julie might hate being in pain without loving not to be in pain.

(6') $\neg(p)(Lp \rightarrow \neg AI\neg p)$

(7') $\neg(p)(Hp \rightarrow \neg AI\neg p)$

Finally, being conatively indifferent to something is equivalent to being neither desirous of it nor desirous of its negation. Paul is conatively indifferent to walking if and only if he neither desires to walk nor desires not to walk.

(8) $(p)\left[CIp \leftrightarrow (\neg Dp \wedge \neg D\neg p)\right]$

But emotional indifference is not like this. One can be affectively indifferent to being healthy while strongly disliking not being healthy. One can be affectively indifferent to the absence of bears but still afraid of their presence. The lack of perfume from a rose leaves us cold, while we would be delighted by its presence.[26]

$$(8') \quad \neg(p)\left[AIp \leftrightarrow (\neg Lp \wedge \neg L\neg p)\right]$$

In sum, while conative indifference and aversion can be defined only with the help of desire and the standard logical connectives, affective indifference and hate cannot be defined in the same way from love and standard propositional connectives. *Desires and aversion are formal polar opposites; love and hate are material polar opposites.*

This disanalogy between emotions and desires, I surmise, stems from the fact that positive and negative emotions have—while positive and negative conations lack—*opposite hedonic valences.* The polar opposition between pleasantness and unpleasantness is of the very same kind as the polar opposition between positive and negative values (Klocksiem 2010): in the same way that *bad that p* is not equivalent to *good that not p, pleasant that p* is not equivalent to *unpleasant that not p*. Desire and aversion, on the other hand, do not differ with respect to their hedonic valence, thus licensing their interdefinability through negation.[27]

## 4 In Favor of the Guise of the Ought

The analogies between norms and desires, on the one hand, and values and emotions, on the other, are quite strong: the four necessary truths (1–4) about norms have the same logical form as the four necessary truths about desire (5–8); the four necessary truths about values (1'–4') have the same logical form as the four necessary truths about emotions (5'–8'); and the conative-deontic truths, on the one hand, and affective-axiological truths, on the other, have distinct logical forms. Although these formal analogies between norms and desires do not *per se* constitute an argument in favor of GO, they certainly do raise suspicion in favor of GO as against GG: it would come as a surprise that desires connect more closely to values than to norms. I shall propose two arguments to that effect, both relying on these formal analogies.

### 4.1 The Formal Objects of Aversion and Conative Indifference

To do so, I need first to make clear what the formal objects of conative indifference and aversion are under GG and GO. Under GO, necessarily, the object of aversion will be presented under the "guise of the forbidden"; whatever is "diswanted" will be presented as something that ought not to be.

**GO**$_{\textbf{(aversion)}}$**:** In virtue of the immediate nature of aversion (desiring not):

1. If $S$ desires that $\neg p$, it seems to $S$ that $\neg p$ ought to be.
2. If $S$ desires to $\neg\phi$, t seems to $S$ that he ought to $\neg\phi$.

While under GG we will have, in virtue of the above:

**GG**$_{\textbf{(aversion)}}$**:** In virtue of the immediate nature of aversion (desiring not):

1. If $S$ desires that $\neg p$, it seems to $S$ that $\neg p$ is good.
2. If $S$ desires to $\neg\phi$, it seems to $S$ that his $\neg\phi$-*ing* is good.

As for conative indifference, which is equivalent to "neither desiring nor desiring-not," one might think at first that it requires only the absence of any normative presentation. But recall that conative indifference toward $p$, which is here understood as an *occurrent* episode, is not *only* the absence of desire and aversion toward $p$. Conative indifference must, on top of that, *belong to the conative domain.* (Sets or spatial regions, for instance, are not conatively indifferent.) Under these assumptions, in order to be conatively indifferent to some action or state of affairs, one has to *be presented with its normative status.* Under GG and GO, one cannot be in a state of occurrent conative indifference toward something without considering its axiological or deontic status. Accordingly, in the case of GO what we are conatively indifferent to must be presented to us *as optional*, while, for GG, what we are conatively indifferent to must be presented to us *as axiologically neutral*:

**GO**$_{\textbf{(indifference)}}$**:** In virtue of the immediate nature of conative indifference:

1. If $S$ is conatively indifferent to $p$, it seems to $S$ that (neither $p$ nor $\neg p$ ought to be).
2. If $S$ is conatively indifferent to $\phi$-*ing*, it seems to $S$ that ($S$ neither ought to $\phi$ nor ought to to $\neg\phi$).

**GG**$_{\textbf{(indifference)}}$**:** In virtue of the immediate nature of conative indifference:

1. If $S$ is conatively indifferent to $p$, it seems to $S$ that (neither $p$ nor $\neg p$ are good).
2. If $S$ is conatively indifferent to $\phi$-*ing*, it seems to $S$ that (it is neither good that $S$ $\phi$-*s* nor good that $S$ does not $\phi$-*s*).

One this basis, two arguments in favor of GO as against GG might be advanced.

## 4.2 First Argument: The Explanatory Advantage of GO over GG

Values and emotions license indifference to the negation of their content; norms and desires forbid such an indifference. If one desires something, one cannot be indifferent to its negation. The first argument in favor of GO as against GG is that *GO, contrary to GG, provides a natural explanation of this impossibility.*

How is it that Julie cannot desire to laugh while being indifferent to not laughing? According to GO, if Julie desires to laugh, she is under the impression that *she ought to* laugh. Now suppose Julie were also conatively indifferent to not laughing. GO entails that she would be under the impression that *it is not the case that she ought to laugh*. But then she would have two simultaneous presentations with contradictory contents: she would feel that she was both under the obligation to laugh and not under that obligation. Hence, by reductio, Julie cannot be indifferent to not laughing.

Besides, if the upholder of GO endorses, following Meinong, the view that *values* are the formal objects of *emotions*, he will be in a position to explain why Julie *can* love to laugh and to be affectively indifferent to not laughing. Since it is *possible* that laughing is good and that not laughing is indifferent, Julie can, without contradiction, be presented with its being good to laugh *and* with its being axiologically indifferent not to laugh. So the reason emotions license indifference to the negation of their content is that their formal object—values—do the same. And the reason desires forbid indifference to the negation of their content is that their formal object—norms—do the same.

Under GG, by contrast, no such explanation is at hand. Julie's desire to laugh entails that laughing seems good to her. This presentation is *compatible* with not laughing seeming neutral to her, so no explanation of why she cannot be conatively indifferent to not laughing is available here. Furthermore, if values are also the formal objects of emotions, then obviously GG cannot provide an explanation of the formal contrast between conations and emotions by relying on their formal objects.

One could object that the explanation advanced on behalf of GO shows only that it would be *irrational* for Julie to desire to sleep while being indifferent to it: it does not show that this is *impossible*. But even if we grant this, GO's comparative advantage remains. For upholders of the view that contradictory deontic presentations are not impossible but irrational will also be led to say that all the psychological necessities we have been putting forward are in fact just necessities of rational psychology. Suppose it is not impossible but only irrational to desire something while being aversive to its negation. GO's explanatory advantage remains, *mutatis mutandis*: the reason one cannot rationally desire to laugh while being indifferent to not-laughing becomes that one cannot rationally be presented with laughing as something that ought to be and be presented with not-laughing as something optional.

Another possible objection is that the explanation advanced goes backward. A subjectivist or a buck-passer about norms could think that, if anything, the formal relations between norms derives from the formal relations between desires: "obligatory that *p*" forbids "optional that non-*p*" because "desire that *p*" forbids "conative indifference to non-*p*." Here again, even if this is granted, the explanatory advantage of GO over GG remains. For a GO buck-passer, for instance, will be in a position to say that the reason the obligation to $\phi$ entails the interdiction to not $\phi$ is that *being obligatory* amounts to *being the object of an appropriate desire*, while *being forbidden* amounts to *being the object of some appropriate aversion.* He will then appeal to the more fundamental fact, according to him, that desiring to $\phi$ entails being avert to $\neg\phi$ to explain the corresponding deontic truth. A GG buck-passer could not do that.

In sum, under GO, deontological necessary truths might be used to explain conative necessary ones (or the reverse), which cannot be done under GG. Besides, the upholder of GO can straightforwardly explain the contrast between emotions and desires by appealing to the analogous contrast between values and norms. For upholders of GG these startling analogies are purely coincidental—which is implausible and renders the explanatory agenda quite heavy.

## 4.3 Second Argument: The Motivational Inertness of the Bad

Second, the fact that one cannot be conatively indifferent to the negation of what one desires is not only something that GG, contrary to GO, fails to explain; it is also an important troublemaker for it. For it leads to the consequence that badness is not the formal object of any conation. Only goodness is motivationally relevant: badness is deprived of any immediate motivational oomph. This directly follows from the way that formal objects of desire, conative indifference, and aversion are understood under GG. To recall:

1. The formal object of desire is the good (it is good that $p$).
2. The formal object of conative indifference is *not* the axiologically neutral (but: neither $p$ nor $\neg p$ is good, which is not equivalent to $p$'s being axiologically neutral).
3. The formal object of aversion is *not* the bad (but: $\neg p$ is good, which is not equivalent to $p$ is bad).

That goodness is our only motive and that badness is motivationally inert under GG is clearly seen by looking at conative indifference. Since conative indifference requires only *finding "neither p nor ¬p good,"* and that *neither p nor ¬p are good* is compatible with *p is bad*, it is possible to be conatively indifferent to $p$ while finding $p$ bad. Conative indifference is not essentially connected to axiological neutrality (but only to "positive indifference"; see §2.2 and note 26). GG captures the attractiveness of the good at the price of giving up the repulsiveness of the bad.

GO, on the other hand, has no problem handling the motivational role of impermissibility, for if something is obligatory, its negation has to be impermissible:

1. The formal object of *desire* is the *obligatory* (it ought to be that $p$).
2. The formal object of *conative* indifference is co-extensional with the *optional* (neither $p$ nor $\neg p$ ought to be).
3. The formal object of *aversion* is co-extensional with the *impermissible* (it ought to be that $\neg p$).

Under GO, the three elements of the deontic trichotomy are presented, respectively, by one element of the conative trichotomy. Under GG, only the first element of the axiological trichotomy, goodness, figures in the content of all three types of conation.

## 5 Objections Answered

### 5.1 *Ought* Has No Polar Opposite

In order to argue that the deontic domain is formally polarly structured, I have focused on obligation and interdiction. But, one might object, *ought*, contrary to obligation, has no polar opposite. If this is correct, formal polar opposition is not essential to deontic concepts, and it cannot be true that norms, contrary to values, are formally polarly opposed. Worse, if *ought* is the central deontic concept, this suggests that interdiction is just a notational variation for *ought to not* instead of a *sui generis* deontic concept, so that in the end polar opposition would be completely absent from the deontic realm.

As a first reply, I want to suggest that *ought* does have a polar opposite. True, *ought* has no *lexical* polar opposite in English, French, or German. But it is easy to construe such a polar opposite from negation: the polar opposite of *ought*, I submit, is *ought not*. *Ought not*, as Meinong (1972: 97, 103) rightly stresses, is emphatically *not* the contradictory—or external—negation of *ought*. This is due to the fact that *ought*, as linguists say, is a *neg-raising* verb (Horn 1989: 308–330; Gajewski 2007). A verb is neg-raising if its external negation typically entails its internal negation. Thus "It ought not to be that people starve" does not (only) mean "It is not the case that it ought to be that people starve," for it also entails "It ought to be that people do not starve."

But this does not show yet that *ought* has a polar opposite, for, granting that the negation in *ought not to* $\phi$ is not external, it then appears to be internal, that is, to modify *ought*'s content: *ought to not-*$\phi$. All we would have then are *ought*s with contradictory contents but not polarly opposed *ought*s. One plausible suggestion, however, is that the negation in *ought not* is *neither external nor internal*. "It ought not to be that *p*" is neither the same as "It is not the case that *p* ought to be" *nor the same as* "It ought to be that ¬p." The idea is that in *ought not* the negation modifies *ought* rather than its sentential complement. A first hint that it might be so is that English modals license the contraction of negation (oughtn't, shouldn't, etc.). Second, consider:

1.
   (a) Paul ne doit pas rire. [Paul ought not to laugh.]
   (b) Paul doit ne pas rire. [Paul ought to not laugh. (?)]
2.
   (a) It ought not to be that people starve.
   (b) It ought to be that people do not starve.
3.
   (a) What A ought not do is B.
   (b) What A ought to do is not B. (Horn 1989: 87)

Because ought is neg-raising, there are no external negations in any of these examples, in particular in sentences (a). Relatedly, sentences (a) and (b) have the same truth conditions. But intuitively they have different connotations or meanings. That negation is in one case constructed with the modal and in the other with its complement, suggesting that even if we lack modals for interdiction, we still have linguistic resources to mark them *qua* distinct for obligation with negative content. (See Horn 1989: 86–89 for further considerations to this effect.)

Although I sympathize with this reply, there is another reply to the present objection that is less committal. According to it, all that is required for the arguments above to go through is that *ought*, like *desiring* but contrary to *good, forbids indifference to its contradictory content*. Even if *ought* has no polar opposite, "It ought to be that *p*" is incompatible with "It is optional that ¬*p*," in particular with "It ought to be that ¬*p*." The same is true, *mutatis mutandis*, for *desire-that* but false for "It is good that."

## 5.2 *Right* and *Wrong* Are Not Formal Polar Opposites

Another objection, brought to my attention by Federico Lauria, has it that some deontic predicates—such as right and wrong—are not formally but materially opposed. If this is true, some deontic concepts display the same formal relations as axiological concepts and are consequently closer to emotions than to desires. The argument goes as follows:

P1 *Right* and *wrong* are deontic predicates.
P2 *Right* and *wrong* are polarly opposed predicates.
P3 Its being *right* to wear a hat does not entail its being *wrong* not to wear a hat.
C The polar opposition between some deontic predicate (right and wrong) is not formal (given the definition of formal polar opposition above) but material.

This objection, I submit, relies on an equivocation about the extension of *right*. *Right* has a broad and a narrow sense (Timmons 2002: 7–9). In the broad sense, *right* is co-extensional with *obligatory* or *optional*, that is, with *permissible*. In the narrow sense, *right* is co-extensional with *obligatory*. If *right* is used in the broad sense, P3 is true (for it can be optional to wear a hat) but P2 is false (for there is no indifference zone between right—permissible—and wrong). If right is read in the narrow sense, then P2 is true (optional lies in between right and wrong), but P3 is false (for if it is right—obligatory—to wear a hat, then it has to be wrong not be wear one).

## 5.3 *Desire* Has No Polar Opposite

In the same way as modals like *ought* and *should, desire* seems to lack any proper English opposite. As noted above, *aversion* is a rather poor term for the polar opposite of *thin* desires, for it is affectively loaded. One might indeed use *aversion* in a cold technical sense, but it then becomes unclear that aversion is anything other than desiring-not. McTaggart (1927: §449, p. 138) presses the point conspicuously:

> I think we must say that there are no such things as negative desires. The quality of being a desire is not a genus with two species, one of which has the quality of being positive, and the other the quality of being negative. In the cases which we distinguished ... as positive and negative, there is no difference in the desire itself. The difference is only in the object desired. One is a desire for A to be X, the other is a desire for A not to be X. The nature of that which is desired is different, but the nature of the desire is the same.

If desire has indeed no polar opposite, then the central claim above, according to which the polar opposition between desire and aversion is of a distinct kind from the polar opposition between positive and negative emotions, collapses.

A first reply is to reject McTaggart's proposal and maintain the existence of negative desires. A first hint that this might be true is that if, as suggested above, *wanting* is the best way to express thin occurrent desires, then other languages provide words corresponding to *diswanting*, such as *disvolere* in Italian (see Wierzbicka 1994: 476–477 for other examples). Second, since *wanting* is neg-raising—contrary to *desiring* (see Horn 1989: 321)—one could here again rely on the difference between "Julie does not want to laugh" and "Julie wants not to laugh" to argue that diswanting something is not merely wanting its negation (although the two are equivalent). So *wanting* might, after all, have a polar opposite.

A second reply is simply to accept McTaggart's proposal that the distinction between positive and negative desires boils down to a distinction in the objects of desires, but to reject that this threatens any of the arguments above. Even if the formal polar opposition between desire and aversion, wanting and diswanting, are just notational variations, as long as wanting or desiring forbid conative indifference to the negation of their content, contrary to emotions, we have all we need to carry through these arguments.

## 5.4 The Guise of the Better

Another objection has it that a close cousin of GG is immune to the objections raised above. According to this, the formal objects of desires are comparative values: whatever one desires is presented to us as better than its negation:

> **Guise of the Better (GB):** In virtue of the immediate nature of desire:
> 1. If $S$ desires that $p$, it seems to $S$ that $p$ is better than $\neg p$.
> 2. If $S$ desires to $\phi$, it seems to $S$ that $\phi$-*ing* is better than $\neg\phi$-*ing*.

Under GB, the formal object of conative indifference will be "having the *same value as* its negation," while the formal object of aversion will be "being worse than its negation." So construed, GB is immune to the two objections raised against GG, for *better than, same value as*, and *worse than* behave like *obligatory that, optional that*, and impermissible *that*—and unlike *good that, neutral that*, and *bad that. Better than* and *worse than* are *formal* polar opposites: "$p$ is better than $\neg p$" iff "$\neg p$ is worse than $p$."

Why, then, prefer GO to GB? The cautious answer is that the view defended here is only the preferability of GO over GG and that GB is not a version of GG. True, upholders of GG sometimes switch more or less surreptitiously from the guise of the good to the *guise of the better* (Davidson 2001; Tenenbaum 2013). But since *being good* is neither necessary nor sufficient for *being better*, this is a substantial step toward a distinct theory. Let me, however, hint at two reasons GO might still fare better than GB.

First, one main motivation in favor of GO is to preserve the one-to-one correspondence between kinds of attitudes and kinds of formal objects. But betterness is naturally construed as the formal object of *preferences* rather than of desires. In the same way that GG leads to the view that desires and emotions share their formal objects, GB leads to the view that desires and preferences share their formal objects.

Second, it is unclear that desiring that $p$ always entails taking $p$ to be better than $\neg p$, for the reason that some desires might not be grounded in values at all, even comparative ones. These are desires whose formal objects are *norms that are not grounded on the values of their bearers*. Such as:

1. Norms grounded on values other than those of their bearer. Such as (i) *conventional norms*: the obligation to drive on the right side of the road is arguably not grounded in its being good or better to drive on the right;[28] (ii) *instrumental norms*: Meinong (1972: 103–104) suggests that instrumental oughts ground instrumental values rather than the reverse. (iii) Relatedly, some *consequentialist norms* for actions, grounded on the value of their results or consequences.
2. Norms directly grounded in natural/non-normative properties:[29] Julie ought to do what she promised, arguably, simply because of the nature of promises.
3. Norms directly grounded on rights or freedoms (property rights, freedom of speech, etc.). Julie's obligation not to steal Paul's bike is arguably directly grounded in Paul's property rights to this bike.[30]
4. Norms not grounded, or self-grounded: categorical imperatives perhaps; or norms governing reactive attitudes: that one ought to have positive attitudes toward things of positive values is perhaps not grounded in its being good, or better, to have such attitudes.[31]

When such obligations are motivating, no presentation of monadic or comparative value is required.

## 5.5 The Motivational Force of Values

Finally, one might object that GO is an even worse position than GG with respect to the motivational role of values, for according to GO, *no value at all (not even goodness) is essentially presented with desires*. Presentations of values do not belong to the immediate nature of desires: conations are under the tyranny of norms.

One way to account for the motivational role of values in the context of GO is, following Meinong, to claim that our presentations of norms are grounded in our presentation of values. Typically (but not always, as we just saw), things seem to ought to be because they seem to have (or lack) some value. This claim is the psychological counterpart of the ontological claim that norms are grounded in values (Meinong 1972: 99). Values, in Meinong's terms, are *borrowed* objects of desire. Given the formal disanalogies between values and norms, it cannot, however, be claimed that "*p* ought to be" iff "*p* is good," and "*p* ought not to be" iff "*p* is bad." Norms grounded on values have to be grounded on *comparative* values, which, as we saw, stand in relations of formal polar opposition. More precisely, when norms are grounded on the values of their bearer, we will have:

- It is obligatory that $p$ (partly) because $p$ is *better than* $\neg p$.
- It is optional that $p$ (partly) because $p$ has *the same value as* $\neg p$.
- It is impermissible that $p$ (partly) because $p$ is *worse than* $\neg p$.

Hansson (2007: 144) and Tappolet (2014) recall that two main accounts of the relation between *oughts* and *values* have been advanced. One equates *ought* with *good*: it has to be rejected for the reasons advanced above. The other equates *ought* with *best* and is in tune with the present proposal, for norms that are grounded on values.

A natural objection to such a proposal is that it ends up giving a pretty complicated picture of the motivational force of values. To motivate, monadic values have to ground comparative values, which in turn have to ground norms. If monadic values are presented by emotions, if comparative values are presented by preferences, and if norms are presented by desires, then to act on the basis of a monadic value we need to go through emotions, preferences, and, at last, desires. This might sounds far-fetched. But this is not necessarily the only way to act on the basis of values. GO is not committed to the view that only desires motivate. Emotions might directly motivate. For instance, we might sometimes *act out of our emotions* without the help of any desires.

Finally, note that the present objection to GO, according to which it cannot account for the motivational role of value, has a counterpart objection directed against GG. For in the very same way that desires are value-blind under GO, *desires are norm-blind under GG*. Upholders of GG owe us an account for the motivational force of norms.

I conclude that if desires are grounded on some normative presentations, as agreed by both upholders of GG and of GO, these presentations are better construed as presentations of norms than as presentations of values.[32]

## Notes

1. On top of Findlay's foreword and Kalsi's introduction to Meinong (1972), other useful presentations of Meinong's late views about emotions, desires, values, and norms are to be found in Findlay 1935, 1963; Kalsi 1978; Chrudzimski 2009; Marek 2010. Raspa (2012) compares Meinong's view on these issues with the close view of his pupil France Veber.

2. Meinong also calls values "dignitatives" and norms "desideratives." To be more precise, on top of being presentations of values and norms, emotions and desires are also self-presentations, according to him.

3. See Oddie (2005, *this volume*), Tenenbaum (2007), and Friedrich (*this volume*) for some defenses of the evaluative conceptions of desires.

4. Other deontic conceptions of desire are possible. One of them would be to equate desires with presentations of ought-to-do (rather than ought-to-be). To the extent that normative reasons are deontic concepts, as he seems to admit, Gregory (2013, *this volume*) might be defending as such an ought-to-do version of the deontic conception of desires, according to which desires are beliefs about normative reasons for actions.

5. In Meinong's terms, presentations of *dignitatives* are the psychological presuppositions of presentations of *desideratives.*

6. In Meinong's terms, presentations of *objecta* or *objectives* are the psychological presuppositions of presentations of *dignitatives.*

7. Similar restrictions about the content of norms are commonplace among realist phenomenologists. That what ought to be cannot exist is also defended by Scheler (1973: 207); that obligation necessarily bears on future behaviors is defended by Reinach (1983: 11).

8. A point emphasized by Hartmann 1932: vol. 1, ch. 18(a).

9. The squash player example is from Watson (1975). This answer is defended, as far as GG in concerned, by Tenenbaum (2007: 41).

10. See Döring and Eker (*this volume*) and Oddie (*this volume*) for more on the distinction between doxastic and perceptual evaluativism about desires.

11. I'm here following Meinong and Merricks (2009) in assuming that propositional desires (and emotions) are not directed toward propositions (we do not, typically, desire or love propositions) but toward states of affairs (which are expressed by propositions in attitude ascriptions). This is arguably an important distinction between desires and beliefs: we believe propositions; we desire states of affairs.

12. It is standardly accepted that objectual desires are propositional desires in disguise, but see Brewer (2006) and Forbes (2006: ch. 4).

13. See Mulligan (2007) for a recent defense of that view and Teroni (2007) for a more Meinongian approach in reply.

14. See Deonna and Teroni (2012) for an analogous and more detailed objection to perceptualist accounts of emotions.

15. On formal objects, see Teroni 2007; Mulligan 2007.

16. That oughtness is the formal object of desire is accepted by Mulligan (2007, 2010).

17. See Mulligan (1989, 1998), Konrad (2000), Ogien and Tappolet (2009: ch. 2), Wedgwood (2009), Tappolet (2013, *forthcoming*), Fassio (2013) for some explicit attempts to tackle this problem.

18. Scheler 1955: 103; Hartmann 1932: vol. 2, ch. 36). See Tappolet (2000: 17) for further references.

19. Such restrictions on the range of contraries are defended by Woods (1969), Barnes (1969), and Lehrer and Lehrer (1982). As for values, a similar restriction to "axiological regions" is introduced by Husserl (2009: 165, 169). See Mulligan 2006.

20. Meinong, however, does not think that polar opposites have to be contraries.

21. See Massin (2014: §§1–2) for further details.

22. Some of the value/norm disanologies to be introduced may have been anticipated by Meinong (1996: ch. 15).

23. See Chisholm and Sosa (1966: 248, Theorem 22), Iwin (1975: 113ff.); Hansson (2007: 120).

24. Substantially the same point is made by Chisholm and Sosa (1966) in their seminal paper, where they introduce the distinction between axiological neutrality and indifference.

25. The conative square of opposition can be found in Kenny (1966: 88).

26. As with values (see §2.2), one can define others kinds of affective indifference. "Positive affective indifference" corresponds to the case where one neither loves a state of affairs nor loves its negation. "Negative affective indifference" corresponds to the case where one hates neither a state of affairs nor its negation. "Affective super-indifference" corresponds to the case where one neither loves nor hates a state of affairs *nor its negation*.

27. The two main views in the literature about the hedonic tone of desires apply to both desires and aversions indifferently. They are:

1. Desires and aversions are essentially unpleasant, and hence do not have opposite valences (see, e.g., Locke 2008: ch. 21, §§31–32; Bain 1859; Marshall 1891).
2. Desire and aversion do not have any hedonic tone essentially (Sidgwick 1892, 1981, cf. long note at the end of ch. 4; Allen 1930: 27ff., Hamilton 1882: vol. 2, 433; Schueler 1995: 11ff.).

One argument in favor of the first view is that since one cannot desire what one thinks is the case, desires are essentially unsatisfied, which is essentially unpleasant. (See Meinong 1972: 86; Lauria, Oddie, *this volume*, on the "death of desire" principle.) One possible reply is that conditional desires whose condition is not met (such as Paul's desire to buy Mary a diamond if he wins the lottery) are not frustrated but only canceled (McDaniel and Bradley 2008), so that canceled desires do not have to be unpleasant.

28. I thank Christine Tappolet for calling my attention to such cases.

29. Reinach 1983: §4.

30. Ibid., §5.

31. Tappolet *forthcoming*.

32. I wish to express my thanks to Davide Fassio, Federico Lauria, Christine Tappolet, and Fabrice Teroni for their detailed and very useful comments on earlier versions of this paper, as well as to Julien Deonna, Anne Meylan, and Kevin Mulligan for helpful discussions and suggestions. Thanks to Riccardo Braglia, CEO and managing director of Helsinn Holding SA and the Fondazione Reginaldus (Lugano) for financial support of the work published here.

## References

Allen, A. H. (1930). *Pleasure and Instinct: A Study in the Psychology of Human Action*. London: Kegan Paul.

Audi, R. (1986). 'Intending, Intentional Action and Desire', in J. Marks (ed.), *The Ways of Desire: New Essays in Philosophical Psychology on the Concept of Wanting*. Chicago: Transaction.

Bain, A. (1859). *The Emotions and the Will*. London: John W. Parker and Son.
Barnes, J. (1969). 'The Law of Contradiction', *Philosophical Quarterly*, 19, 302-309.
Brewer, T. (2006). 'Three Dogmas of Desire', in T. Chappell (ed.), *Values and Virtues*. New York: Oxford University Press.
Chisholm, R., and E. Sosa. (1966). 'On the Logic of "Intrinsically Better"', *American Philosophical Quarterly*, 3, 244–249.
Chisholm, R. M. (1968). 'The Defeat of Good and Evil', *Proceedings and Addresses of the American Philosophical Association*, 42, 21–38.
Chrudzimski, A. (2009). 'Brentano, Marty, and Meinong on Emotions and Values', in B. Centi and W. Huemer (eds.), *Values and Ontology: Problems and Perspectives*. Frankfurt: Ontos Verlag.
Cruse, D. (1995). *Lexical Semantics*. Cambridge, UK: Cambridge University Press.
Davidson, D. (2001). 'How Is Weakness of Will Possible?', in *Essays on Actions and Events*. New York: Oxford University Press.
Deonna, J. A., and F. Teroni. (2012). 'From Justified Emotions to Justified Evaluative Judgements', *Dialogue*, 51, 55–77.
Fassio, D. (2013). 'How to Distinguish Norms from Values', in F. Forlè and S. Songhorian (eds.), *The Place of Values in a World of Norms*. Pavia, Italy: IUSS Press.
Findlay, J. (1935). 'Emotional Presentation', *Australasian Journal of Psychology and Philosophy*, 13, 111–121.
———. (1963). *Meinong's Theory of Objects and Values*. New York: Oxford University Press.
Fine, K. 1994. 'Essence and Modality: The Second Philosophical Perspectives Lecture', *Philosophical Perspectives*, 8, 1–16.
———. (1995). 'Senses of Essence', in W. Sinnott-Armstrong, D. Raffman and N. Asher (eds.), *Modality, Morality, and Belief: Essays in Honor of Ruth Barcan Marcus*. Cambridge, UK: Cambridge University Press.
Forbes, G. (2006). *Attitude Problems*. Oxford: Oxford University Press.
Gajewski, J. R. (2007). 'Neg-Raising and Polarity', *Linguistics and Philosophy*, 30, 289–328.
Geach, P. T. (1980). *Reference and Generality: An Examination of Some Medieval and Modern Theories*. Ithaca, N.Y.: Cornell University Press.
Goble, L. (1990). 'A Logic of Good, Should, and Would', *Journal of Philosophical Logic*, 19, 169–199.
Gregory, A. (2013). 'The Guise of Reasons', *American Philosophical Quarterly*, 50, 63–72.
Hamilton, W. (1882). *Lectures on Metaphysics and Logic*, vol. 1-4, ed. H. L. Mansel and J. Veitch. Edinburgh: William Blackwood and Sons.
Hansson, S. O. (2007). *The Structure of Values and Norms*. Cambridge, UK: Cambridge University Press.
Hartmann, N. (1932). *Ethics*, 3 vols., tr. Stanton Coit. London: George Allen & Unwin.
Heathwood, C. (2007). 'The Reduction of Sensory Pleasure to Desire', *Philosophical Studies*, 133, 23–44.
Hobbes, T. (2010). *Leviathan*. New Haven, Ct.: Yale University Press.
Horn, L. (1989). *A Natural History of Negation*. Chicago: University of Chicago Press.

Husserl, E. (2009). *Leçons sur l'éthique et la théorie de la valeur (1908–1914)*. Paris: Presses Universitaires de France.

Iwin, A. (1975). *Grundlagen der Logik von Wertungen: Bearbeitet und herausgegeben von Horst Wessel*. Berlin: Akademie Verlag.

Kalsi, M. L. S. (1978). 'On Objects of Higher Order and Their Relationship to Internal Perception', in *Alexius Meinong*. The Hague, Netherlands: Springer.

Kenny, A. (1966). *Action, Emotion and Will*. London: Routledge & Kegan Paul.

Klocksiem, J. (2010). 'Pleasure, Desire and Oppositeness', *Journal of Ethics and Social Philosophy*, May, 1–6.

Konrad, M. (2000). *Werte versus Normen als Handlungsgründe*. Bern: Peter Lang.

Lauria, F. (2014). '"The Logic of the Liver": A Deontic View of the Intentionality of Desire', PhD dissertation, University of Geneva.

Lehrer, A., and K. Lehrer. (1982). 'Antonymy', *Linguistics and Philosophy*, 5, 483–501.

Locke, J. (2008). *An Essay Concerning Human Understanding*. Oxford World's Classics. Oxford: Oxford University Press.

Mally, E. (1926). *Grundgesetze des Sollens: Elemente der Logik des Willens*, in K. Wolff and P. Weingartner (eds.), *E. Mally, Logische Schriften: Großes Logikfragment, Grundgesetze des Sollens*. 1971. Dordrecht: Reidel,.

Marek, J. (2010). 'Alexius Meinong', *The Stanford Encyclopedia of Philosophy*, Edward N. Zalta (ed.), URL = <https://plato.stanford.edu/archives/fall2013/entries/meinong/>.

Marshall, H. R. (1891). 'The Physical Basis of Pleasure and Pain (II)', *Mind*, 16, 470–497.

Massin, O. (2014). 'Pleasure and Its Contraries', *Review of Philosophy and Psychology*, 5, 15–40.

McDaniel, K., and B. Bradley. (2008). 'Desires', *Mind*, 117, 267–302.

McNamara, P. (2006). 'Deontic Logic', in D. Gabbay and J. Woods (eds.), *Logic and the Modalities in the Twentieth Century*. Amsterdam: Elsevier Press.

McTaggart, J. (1927). *The Nature of Existence*. Vol. 2. Cambridge, UK: Cambridge University Press.

Meinong, A. (1972). *On Emotional Presentation*, tr. M.-L. Schubert Kalsi. Evanston, Ill.: Northwestern University Press.

———. (1996). *Elements of Ethics: With Translation of the Fragment Ethische Bausteine*, tr. Marie-Luise. Schubert Kalsi. Dordrecht: Kluwer Academic.

Merricks, T. (2009). 'Propositional Attitudes?', *Proceedings of the Aristotelian Society*, 109, 207–232.

Mulligan, K. (1989). 'Wie verhalten sich Normen und Werte zueinander?', unpublished manuscript.

———. (1998). 'From Appropriate Emotions to Values', *Monist*, 81, 161–188.

———. (2006). 'Husserl sur les "Logiques" de la valorisation, des valeurs et des normes', *Philosophia Scientiae* 10, I, 71–107.

———. (2007). 'Intentionality, Knowledge and Formal Objects', *Disputatio*, 2, 205–228.

———. (2010). 'Emotions and Values', in P. Goldie (ed.), *Oxford Companion to the Philosophy of Emotions*. Oxford: Oxford University Press.

Oddie, G. (2005). *Value, Desire and Reality*. Oxford: Oxford University Press.

Ogien, R., and C. Tappolet. (2009). *Les concepts de l'éthique: Faut-il être conséquentialiste?* Paris: Hermann.

Raspa, V. (2012). 'Is "Ought" an Object? Meinong's and Veber's Answers', in T. E. Pirc (ed.), *Object, Person, and Reality: An Introduction to France Veber*. Ljubljana, Slovenia: JSKD.
Reinach, A. (1983). 'The Apriori Foundations of the Civil Law', *Aletheia*, 3, 1–142.
Scheler, M. (1955). *Le formalisme en éthique et l'éhique matériale des valeurs: Essai nouveau pour fonder un personnalisme éthique*, tr. M. de Gandillac. Paris: Gallimard.
———. (1973). *Formalism in Ethics and Non-Formal Ethics of Value*, tr. M. Frings and R. L. Funk. Evanston, Ill.: Northwestern University Press.
Schroeder, M. (2007). 'Do Oughts Take Proposition?', unpublished manuscript.
Schroeder, T. (2004). *Three Faces of Desire*. New York: Oxford University Press.
Schueler, G. F. (1995). *Desire: Its Role in Practical Reason and the Explanation of Action*. Cambridge, Mass.: MIT Press.
Sidgwick, H. (1892). 'The Feeling-Tone of Desire and Aversion', *Mind*, 1, 94–101.
———. (1981). *Methods of Ethics*. Indianapolis: Hacket.
Tappolet, C. (2000). *Emotions et valeurs*. Paris: Presses Universitaires de France.
———. (2013). 'Evaluative vs. Deontic Concepts', in H. Lafollette (ed.), *International Encyclopedia of Ethics*. Oxford: Wiley-Blackwell. 1791–1799.
———. (2014). 'The Normativity of Evaluative Concepts', in A. Reboul (ed.), *Mind, Values and Metaphysics: Philosophical Papers Dedicated to Kevin Mulligan*, vol 2. Dordrecht: Springer, 39–54.
Tenenbaum, S. (2007). *Appearances of the Good: An Essay on the Nature of Practical Reason*. Cambridge, UK: Cambridge University Press.
———. (2013). 'The Guise of the Good', in H. Lafollette (ed.), *International Encyclopedia of Ethics*. Oxford: Wiley-Blackwell.
Teroni, F. (2007). 'Emotions and Formal Objects', *Dialectica*, 61, 395–415.
Timmons, M. (2002). *Moral Theory: An Introduction*. Lanham: Rowman & Littlefield.
Von Wright, G. H. (1951). 'Deontic Logic', *Mind*, 60, 1–15.
Watson, G. (1975). 'Free Agency', *Journal of Philosophy*, 172, 205–220.
Wedgwood, R. (2009). 'The "Good" and the "Right" Revisited', *Philosophical Perspectives*, 23, 499–519.
Wierzbicka, A. (1994). 'Semantic Primitives across Languages: A Critical Review', in C. Goddard and A. Wierzbicka (eds.), *Semantic and Lexical Universals: Theory and Empirical Findings*. Amsterdam, Philadephia: John Benjamins.
Woods, J. (1969). 'Predicate Ranges', *Philosophy and Phenomenological Research*, 30, 259–269.

# CHAPTER 7 | Might Desires Be Beliefs about Normative Reasons for Action?

ALEX GREGORY

IN THIS PAPER I shall defend the view that desires are beliefs about normative reasons for action. More precisely, I shall defend a view I call DAB, according to which to desire to φ just is to believe that you have normative reason to φ. (For other defenses of views similar to DAB, see Humberstone 1987; McNaughton 1988: 106–117; McDowell 1998; Massin, Lauria *this volume.*) Though I shall briefly sketch some attractions of DAB, my main task in this paper is defensive. It may seem as though DAB is obviously false because it is subject to decisive objections. But I shall show that the most obvious objections to it fail. I shall also compare DAB to views on which desires are mere appearances of normative properties rather than full-blown beliefs.

The paper is structured as follows. In section 1, I describe the view, and swiftly lay out three attractive features it has. Then, in section 2, I respond to five objections to the view: that it is inconsistent with the distinction between the direction of fit of belief and desire, that it is falsified by the existence of appetites, that beliefs about reasons are not sufficient for desire, that beliefs about reasons are not necessary for desire, and that animals have desires but no beliefs about normative reasons.[1] Finally, in section 3, I compare DAB to the view that desires are appearances of the good.

## 1. Desires as Beliefs about Normative Reasons for Action

To remind you, here is the view that I shall defend:

*DAB*: To desire to φ is to believe that you have normative reason to φ.[2]

Let me illustrate DAB with two examples. First, imagine that I desire to read Asimov's *Foundation*. According to DAB, this is just the same as my believing that I have a reason to read Asimov's *Foundation*. (Perhaps I think it will be fun.) Second, imagine that I believe I have a reason to buy a new scarf today. (I've lost the old one.) According to DAB, this is just the same as my desiring to buy a new scarf today.

DAB is an account of *desire*. I take desires to be the same as wants and as the constituents of preferences. DAB analyzes only desires to act, which I take to be the paradigm case of desire. I assume that DAB could be extended by treating other desires as desires to act so as to bring about some state of affairs, but I shall not make that case here. Desires come in varying strengths, and when I talk about what an agent desires to do, I am talking about what she has *some* desire to do, not what she most wants to do, all things considered.

DAB analyzes desires in terms of beliefs about *normative reasons for action*. A normative reason to perform an action is something that counts in favor of that action (see, e.g., Parfit 2011: 31; Scanlon 1998: 17). Hereafter, for brevity, I will often use the word *reason* to mean "normative reason for action." Note that not all such reasons are moral reasons: I am not offering a moralized account of desire. Further, note that reasons, like desires, come in varying strengths. When I talk about what an agent believes she has reason to do, I am talking about what she believes she has *some* reason to do, and not what she believes she has most reason to do, all things considered.

DAB has at least three attractive features. First, because DAB identifies desires and beliefs about reasons, we do not have to see these two as competitors in our motivational system. That allows us to solve a certain puzzle about moral motivation: DAB entitles us to agree that normative judgments are beliefs and to agree that such judgments have the power to motivate us to act, while also allowing us to accept the Humean claim that only desires have the power to motivate us to act (cf. McNaughton 1988: 23, 46).[3] It is only if we accept DAB that these three plausible claims are consistent.

Second, DAB explains why desires are sensitive to evidence about what we have reason to do (cf. Fernández 2007; Byrne 2011; Moran 2001: 119). If you want to vote Conservative, I might get you to rationally abandon this desire by presenting you with evidence that there are no good reasons to vote Conservative. Or, for another example, if I ask you whether you want my spare plane ticket to China, you will respond by considering the reasons for and against taking this choice: the sights, the food, the weather, etc. DAB explains why desires are sensitive to evidence about reasons: because they are beliefs about reasons.

Third, DAB resolves disagreement about whether what we ought to do depends on our desires (see, e.g., Joyce 2001; Schroeder 2007; Williams 1981, 1995). If DAB is true, this amounts to the claim that what we ought to do depends on our beliefs about what we have reason to do. It is very plausible that this claim is ambiguous between something true and something false. It is false in the sense that one's beliefs might be false. But it is true in the sense that what we *rationally* ought to do does depend on our beliefs about what we have reason to do (see, e.g., Scanlon 1998: 25). So DAB resolves the controversy regarding whether what we ought to do depends on our desires.

These three points are helpful for contrasting DAB with motivational theories of desire (e.g. Smith 1994: 113). DAB coincides with motivational theories insofar as both claim that desires have the power to motivate. DAB says that desires have motivational potential because they are beliefs about reasons to act, and such beliefs have motivational potential. But DAB goes beyond motivational theories of desire because it also makes other claims about desire. In particular, it explains how they are under rational control and explains the broader role they play in determining how we ought to act.

In summary, I hope it is clear that DAB has some appeal. To provide conclusive support for DAB I would need to defend these arguments at much greater length, and I do not have space to do that here. But in light of the remarks above, we should at least be curious about whether DAB can withstand criticism. So now I can turn to the real focus of this paper: Are there any convincing objections to DAB? We should remember throughout that my goal is purely defensive. My goal is the modest one of showing that if there is good independent reason to accept DAB, the issues below provide no evidence to the contrary.

## 2. Objections

### 2.1. DAB Is Inconsistent with the Distinction between Directions of Fit

An initial worry is that DAB is inconsistent with the distinction between the direction of fit of belief and desire. According to that distinction, beliefs aim to fit the world, whereas desires aim to have the world fit them. Roughly, where there is a discrepancy between what you believe and what is true, you should change your beliefs. But where there is a discrepancy between what you desire and what is true, you should change what's true. There are many questions about how to formulate this contrast more precisely (see Gregory 2012; Humberstone 1992; Smith 1987, 1994: 111–116; Railton, Lauria *this volume*). But regardless of how we do this, the underlying issue for DAB is the same: if beliefs and desires contrast with one another in this way, how could desires be beliefs, as DAB says?

The answer is that the direction of fit metaphor should not be understood, at its most fundamental, as describing a contrast between beliefs and desires. The easiest way to see this is to note that other states of mind—such as intentions and memories—also have a direction of fit. So the direction of fit metaphor is best understood not as a contrast between beliefs and desires, as such, but rather as a contrast between two functional roles a mental state might play. On the one hand, a state of mind might be sensitive to evidence in a certain manner: being such that it ought to fit certain facts about the world. On the other hand, a state of mind might have motivational power: being such that facts about the world ought to fit the state.

One can allow that there is this contrast between these functional roles and nonetheless maintain DAB. We merely need to say that some mental states play both of these functional roles: that some mental states have both directions of fit. This is exactly what DAB says. It says that there is a state of mind that represents one proposition as fitting the world, namely that one has reason to φ, and simultaneously represents another proposition as something that the world should fit, namely that one φ-s. That is, DAB says that there is a state of mind that is sensitive to evidence and that also has motivational power. There is nothing problematic about this. In short, the direction of fit metaphor is consistent with DAB. The direction of fit metaphor is best understood as stating a contrast between two functional roles, and that is consistent with DAB, which says that some states of mind play both functional roles.

Note further that DAB implies that we have two different names for a single state of mind. We might explain this by appeal to the claim that those names highlight different features it has (cf. the different names you might use to refer to one and the same multi-purpose penknife). So the truth of DAB is consistent with the fact that when you describe a state of mind as a "desire," you draw attention to its motivational power, and when you describe a state of mind as a "belief about a reason," you draw attention to its sensitivity to evidence. In turn, DAB is consistent with the fact that one direction of fit is more associated with desire, and the other with belief. But this is a matter of what we draw attention to when we describe this state in these ways, and not a difference between which features it in fact has.

There is a worry with what I have said in response to this objection. It might seem problematic if DAB entails that desires bear both functional roles to one and the same proposition. That would be deeply problematic (Smith 1994: 118). But this is not what DAB says. DAB says that desires represent one thing as to be made true (that I φ) and something else (that I have reason to φ) as true (Little 1997: 64; Price 1989: 120–121). So desires bear these functional roles toward different propositions.

In summary, the direction of fit metaphor is consistent with DAB. The direction of fit metaphor is best understood as drawing a contrast between two different functional roles, and defenders of DAB just need to say that desires—beliefs about reasons—play both.

### 2.2. Appetites Are Desires but Are Not Beliefs about Reasons

One obvious complaint about DAB is that while some desires may somehow involve beliefs about reasons, others do not. And appetites like hunger and thirst seem to fall into the latter category (see Nagel 1970: 29; Parfit 2011: 52–53; Schueler 1995: 9–10; Railton *this volume*). In what follows, I shall focus on hunger, but it should be clear that my remarks will generalize to other states, such as thirst.

The problem is that hunger seems to be a desire to eat, and yet there seem to be numerous reasons for thinking that hunger is not a belief about a reason to eat. For example, it seems that hunger is outside of rational control: it just assails us. Or, for another example, hunger seems to have a distinctive phenomenology that no belief could have.

But in cases of this kind we should distinguish two things. First, there is the feeling of hunger (predominantly located in one's abdomen), and second, there is the desire to eat. It is easy to confuse these two because the former normally leads to the latter. But they are nonetheless distinct. We can desire food even when we are not hungry. For example, you might want to eat some food in order to be polite or for the taste. (How often do you want dessert because you're hungry?) Vice versa, it would be unusual, but seems possible, that you might be hungry and yet not have any desire for food. For example, you might be on a religious fast or be a particular kind of anorexic.

With this distinction between the feeling of hunger and the desire to eat in hand, it's easy to see that DAB can overcome the objection. Defenders of DAB can grant that the feeling of hunger is not a belief about a reason to eat. But this leaves open the possibility that the desire to eat *is* a belief that one has a reason to eat. This claim seems plausible. Normally, we want to eat because we are hungry. According to DAB, this comes out as the plausible claim that we often take our hunger to be a reason to eat. In other circumstances we might want to eat even when we aren't hungry, as when we want to eat something for the taste. According to DAB this comes out as the plausible claim that we might believe that other things, such as the taste of the food, are reasons for eating. In still other (rare) circumstances someone might be hungry and yet not want to eat, as when on a religious fast. According to DAB this comes out as the plausible claim that in other (rare) circumstances someone might be hungry and yet believe that this gives him no reason to eat.

In summary, once we distinguish the feeling of hunger from the desire for food, it is clear that hunger is no threat at all to DAB. The feeling of hunger is isolated from belief, but the desire for food is not, and so DAB is quite consistent with the existence of appetites. Though the feeling of hunger just assails us and is not a rational response to anything, the desire for food is under rational control and is a rational response to the reasons as we see them—often responsive to the reasons we see for quelling our hunger.

One final worry is that if my defense of DAB requires that I deny that hunger is a desire, then it is revisionary to an implausible degree. Hunger, we might think, is the paradigmatic desire, and if a theory of desires excludes hunger from its purview, then it is no longer a theory of *desire* at all.[4] However, it would be misleading to say that I deny that hunger is a desire. Rather, my claim is that 'hunger' is ambiguous between a desire, a feeling, and the combination of both of these. The fact that the word has this loose meaning should not be surprising, since normally feelings of hunger and the desire for food go together. But if we want our theorizing to carve nature at the joints, we should anticipate that these different things will need different analyses. Certainly, if we try to give a theory of "desire" that makes sense of all of these things at once, as well as common desires such as to catch the train, to finish a paper, or to tie your shoelaces, we are going to end up with a disjointed theory, since such desires do not have any associated feelings (see, however, Friedrich *this volume*). There is a more general lesson here, which is that the word 'desire' may carry certain connotations—such as the presence of physical sensations—that are not really part of our subject matter when we investigate desires. After all, we are supposed to think of desires as the same as wants and as systematically related to preferences, but 'want' and 'prefer' do not necessarily carry these same bodily connotations.

## 2.3. Beliefs about Reasons Are Not Sufficient for Desire

In this section, I address counterexamples that aim to show that beliefs about reasons are not sufficient for desire. One might think that we are sometimes weak-willed in that we don't want to do things that we believe we have reason to do (e.g. Smith 1994: 117–125; Stocker 1979: esp. 741–746). I shall address two representative examples. First:

> *Smoking Sally*: Sally is a smoker. She knows full well that she has very good reasons to quit: smoking is costly and unhealthy. But she is weak-willed and continues to smoke.

Such a case might seem to threaten DAB. Isn't Sally's problem that while she knows she should quit, she doesn't want to?

To understand the issue, we should first distinguish desiring to φ from being motivated to φ (*pace* Dancy 2000: 85–88). We should distinguish these for various reasons, of which I shall mention two. First, though we desire very many things—a list of all your desires would be enormous—motivation is a more limited resource that we have to spend frugally. Second, when Humeans claim that only desires motivate, they are not making the trivial claim that only motivations motivate. Considerations like these make clear that desiring to ϕ is distinct from being motivated to ϕ.

It is worth briefly revisiting a claim I made earlier: that desires have the potential to motivate. It should be clear that this claim is consistent with the above distinction between desire and motivation. My claim is that desires and motivation are distinct, though the former have the power to generate the latter. An analogy may help: on my view, desires stand to motivation as beer stands to inebriation. Beer has the power to inebriate, but it does not always exercise this power. Equally, desires have the power to motivate, but they do not always exercise this power.

With this distinction in mind, it seems plausible to suppose that, assuming Sally really does think she has very good reasons for quitting, she has some desire to quit smoking. Imagine asking Sally, "Would you prefer to stop smoking or continue doing so?" It would be incredible if she responded that she preferred to smoke. She clearly wants to stop: this is precisely why finding yourself in a situation like Sally's can be frustrating. But this does nothing to show that Sally must be motivated to quit smoking. Precisely her problem is that although she wants to quit, she cannot motivate herself sufficiently to achieve this goal. (Her desire is failing to exercise its motivational power.) This seems to be a much more natural way to describe her problem, as well as the similar problem faced by those who think they should eat less, exercise more, and other such cases. In cases like Sally's, the problem is that we lack the motivation to achieve our goals. If weakness of will is a lack of motivation to achieve one's goals, it is consistent with DAB.

Once we make this distinction between desiring to do something and being motivated to do it, DAB can also handle numerous other apparent counterexamples, such as people with depression (Stocker 1979: 744–746; see also Smith 1994: 119–121; cf. Garrard and McNaughton 1998: 49). Clearly, we might believe that we have reason to do something and not be in the least motivated to do it. But this is irrelevant to the truth of DAB (*pace* Oddie 2005: 37; Tenenbaum 2007: 227–298). DAB entails only that beliefs about reasons are sufficient for desire, not that beliefs about reasons are sufficient for motivation, and as such is perfectly consistent with weakness of will.[5]

I now turn to a second example that aims to show that beliefs about reasons are not sufficient for desire (cf. Scanlon 1998: 39):

> *Teething Tabatha*: Tabatha knows that she has good reason to go to the dentist: her teeth are in an awful state. But she will quite keenly insist that she doesn't want to go to the dentist—who does?

This kind of case seems to be as much a problem for the Humean theory of motivation as for DAB, since it is natural to suppose that Tabatha might go to the dentist even though she has no desire to do so. Just as Humeans should try to find some interpretation of Tabatha that does justice to what she says but that also attributes to her a desire to go to the dentist's, so too should defenders of DAB.[6]

One way to see that something puzzling is going on here is to imagine that Tabatha is indeed going to go to the dentist (as she knows she should) but hasn't made her appointment yet. She picks up the phone, gets through to the secretary, and might quite normally say, "Hi, I want to see the dentist today, please." Or imagine that she's made the appointment and intends to take a taxi there. She might quite normally ask the taxi driver, "I want to go to the dentist, please." One possibility here is that Tabatha is just contradicting herself when she insists in one breath that she doesn't want to visit the dentist, and then asserts in the next breath that she does want to see the dentist. But a more plausible interpretation is that her initial claim was implicitly restricted in scope. When she insists that she doesn't want to go to the dentist, she really means only that she doesn't want the pain that she'll experience there. But this is of course consistent with wanting, all things considered, to go.

Because of this, DAB is vindicated. Clearly, Tabatha doesn't think she has good reason to seek out the pain at the dentist. This is the sense in which she doesn't want to go. But all the same, Tabatha does think she has good reason to visit the dentist, all things considered. And all things considered, she does want to go. Once we acknowledge this restriction of scope in her initial claim, it is clear that DAB is not undermined by the example.

In summary, so long as we attend to the fact that DAB identifies beliefs about reasons with desire and not motivation, and so long as we make sure to attend to possible implicit restrictions of scope in claims about what someone does or doesn't want to do, DAB is unobjectionable for implying that beliefs about reasons are sufficient for desire.

## 2.4. Beliefs about Reasons Are Not Necessary for Desire

In this section I address counterexamples that aim to show that beliefs about reasons are not necessary for desire. One might think that we sometimes want to do things that we don't believe we have reason to do (e.g. Stocker 1979: 746–749; Velleman 1992).

In this respect, DAB commits us to something like *the guise of the good* (see, e.g., Anscombe 1963: 75; Aquinas ST I-II.1.1, DV 24.2; Davidson 2001: 22–23; Raz 2010; Döring and Eker, Massin, Oddie *this volume*). It entails that we can want to do something only if we think there is some merit in it. There are various putative counterexamples to the guise of the good, such as Satan, who desires to do things precisely because they are bad (Velleman 1992: 18), and the person who, in a fit of guilt, desires to make his own life worse (Stocker 1979: 748). But we must take care to remember that DAB analyzes desires as beliefs about *reasons* rather than as beliefs about *goodness* (cf. Massin *this volume*). As such DAB is perfectly consistent with such possibilities: we merely have to endorse the plausible claim that Satan believes he has normative reasons to do bad things, and the plausible claim that those with self-destructive desires believe that there are normative reasons for them to make their lives worse. (I discuss these issues in greater detail in Gregory 2013.)

However, there is one other counterexample of this kind that is sometimes thought to threaten DAB specifically, and which I shall therefore address directly:

*Addict Amy*: Amy has been a heroin addict for many years. She believes that she has very little reason to take the drug. But she strongly craves it nonetheless. (cf. Frankfurt 1982: 87–88; see also Smith 1994: 134)

Cases like this may appear to threaten DAB. But again, this is not true. There are at least three ways in which we might understand this case consistently with DAB. First, earlier I described some cases of weakness of will as involving a mismatch between desire and motivation, where one is not motivated, or undermotivated, to pursue something that one wants. If we allow for that possibility, it seems as though we should also allow for the reverse possibility, where one is overmotivated by one's desires. Sometimes, one's desires may generate more motivation than they ought to. Perhaps this is the situation Amy is in. Perhaps Amy's problem is that though she has only a weak desire to take heroin—she thinks she has only a very weak reason to take the drug—this desire is very strongly motivating her to take it.

Second, we might say that to the extent Amy is motivated to take heroin by a state of mind that is completely irrational and insensitive to facts about what she has reason to do, we might think that she is being motivated not by a desire but instead by some more primitive compulsion or drive (cf. Railton *this volume*).[7] This way of describing addiction fits well with the natural thought that addicts don't really want to do what they do but are instead compelled to by their condition.

A third (best?) possibility is a hybrid view. Real-life addicts might be partly motivated by a genuine desire to avoid withdrawal symptoms, partly overmotivated by a very weak desire to take the drug, and partly compelled to take the drug by some drive. These things together might generate a strong motivation to take the drug in someone who believes he has only weak reason to take it. This possibility is entirely consistent with DAB.

## 2.5. Animals Have Desires but No Beliefs about Reasons

In section 2.4, I defended the claim that beliefs about reasons are necessary for desire. Another putative counterexample to that claim needs separate treatment, and that is the desires of animals[8] (see, e.g., Döring and

Eker, Friedrich *this volume*). Animals may seem to have many desires but no beliefs about reasons at all. For example, you might think that cats can want milk but are incapable of having any beliefs about what they have reason to do. Clearly there is a great deal to be said here about the appropriateness of attributing various mental states to animals, but let me just note two broad possibilities left open by DAB.

First, one might be generous in attributing states of mind to animals. One might insist that animals have both desires and beliefs about reasons. Just as we might think that cats can desire milk even though they have only an extremely minimal grasp of the concept of milk—Do cats know that milk must come from a mammal?—we might think that cats can believe that they have reason to do things, even though they have only an extremely minimal grasp of the concept of a reason. Of course animals can't understand reasons at the level of sophistication that we can, but we might nevertheless think they can see an action as being favored in some respect ("Good dog!"), and to acknowledge this is just to think that they believe there is a reason to perform that action (cf., e.g., Korsgaard 2009: 110–112).

Second, one might be stingy in attributing states of mind to animals. One might insist that animals have neither desires nor beliefs about reasons. Just as one might think that animals have no beliefs but instead only representations, one might think that animals have no desires but instead only drives. Certainly, our desires are very different from animal "desires" in various respects, such as that they are under a greater degree of rational guidance and can be expressed in language. We might think that differences like these justify the claim that there is a difference in kind between our desires and animal "desires" (cf. e.g., McDowell 1994: 114–124). It certainly seems that the defender of DAB should distinguish desires from drives (see section 2.4), and once this distinction is made, it is not that implausible to suppose that the motives of animals are more similar to our drives than to our desires.

This second view may seem unduly revisionary, since we do often *say* that animals want things. But this is not at all decisive, since we also often say that flies, plants, computers, and cars want things (e.g. "The car doesn't want to start today"). Unless we adopt some extremely broad theory of desire that aims to capture all of these claims (e.g. Dennett 1987), a better option is to claim that some uses of the word *desire* are looser than others and to aim for a theory that captures only the more precise uses of the term. If we take this second approach, we might claim that attributions of desires to animals are only of this looser kind.

The defender of DAB can of course also appeal to a combination of these two strategies. The former response may be more plausible for higher animals (e.g. chimps), and the latter response may be more plausible for lower animals (e.g. salmon). And they might also say that between these extremes there is some indeterminacy as to which is the correct account. It is far from clear that there is anything objectionable about such a theory.

## 3. Desires as Appearances

In summary, DAB can overcome the five objections above. That is, the most obvious objections to DAB all fail. I now turn to explain how DAB is superior to one popular nearby view, which is the view that desires are appearances of the good (see Oddie 2005: 28–46, *this volume*; Stampe 1987; Tenenbaum 2007). One difference between this view and DAB is that DAB analyzes desires as representations of *reasons* rather than as representations of *goodness*. I discussed this briefly in section 2.4 and discuss it in more detail elsewhere (Gregory 2013; again, see also Massin *this volume*). In this section I shall instead focus on the other difference between DAB and this rival, which is that this rival analyzes desires as mere appearances rather than full-blown beliefs. This view states that desires involve actions *seeming* to be good, and this is neither necessary nor sufficient for *believing* that some act is good, just as it seeming that a stick in water is bent is neither necessary nor sufficient for believing that it is.

Scanlon's (1998: 37–49) view is also of this kind. One might think that he endorses something like DAB, but this is not true (one might be encouraged by his remarks on 7–8, but see the unambiguous remarks on 43–44). He claims that to desire to φ is for certain facts to be highly salient in consciousness and to *seem* like reasons to φ (39–40). That is, to desire to φ is for φ-ing to often be present in consciousness in a positive light. But Scanlon insists that some act might appear in consciousness in this way even when you don't actually believe you have any reason to perform it (43–44) and that you might believe you have reason to perform some action without it often appearing in consciousness in a positive light (38–39). By implication, on Scanlon's view beliefs about reasons are neither necessary nor sufficient for desire (see, however, Schroeder *this volume* for another sense of *desire* in Scanlon).

I will call the Oddie-Scanlon-Stampe-Tenenbaum view *the appearance theory*. The appearance theory may appear to promise similar payoffs to DAB without being so bold. But there is little reason to endorse the appearance theory. It is generally preferred to DAB on the grounds of the kinds of example that I addressed in sections 2.3 and 2.4 (see, e.g., Oddie 2005: 36–38, 40–43; Tenenbaum 2007: 227–298). But DAB is consistent with those examples, so it is doubtful that they really support the appearance theory over DAB. To confirm the point, I shall address an example that Scanlon employs to argue that the appearance theory is superior to DAB. I will then offer two examples of my own that show DAB to be superior to the appearance theory.

Here is Scanlon's (1998: 43) example:

> *Scanlon's computer*: Suppose that . . . I am beset by a desire to have a new computer. . . . I find myself looking eagerly at the computer advertisements in each Tuesday's *New York Times*. I keep thinking about various new models and taking their features to count in favour of having them. . . . Such a state can occur . . . even when my considered judgement is that I in fact have no reason to buy a new machine.

In this case, two things are contributing to the impression that Scanlon wants a new computer but believes he has no reason to buy one. First, Scanlon is understating the degree to which he believes he has reason to buy a new computer. He clearly thinks there is some reason to buy a new machine: they are more fun than his present machine, more efficient than his present machine, some of their features might come in handy someday, and so on. I take it that Scanlon would agree that he should upgrade if he could do so for free and with absolutely no hassle.

The second thing contributing to the impression that Scanlon wants a new computer but believes he has no reason to buy one is that he is overstating the degree to which he wants to buy a new computer. This desire might keep popping into his mind, but we should not think that phenomenology provides an infallible guide to the strengths of our desires (Smith 1994: 104–111). For example, I want to avoid torturing people much more than I want bacon sandwiches, though the former desire almost never occurs to me, and the latter desire often does. Once we distinguish the strength of a desire from its phenomenological salience, it seems plausible to think that Scanlon's desire for a new computer is actually relatively weak: that's precisely why he's unlikely to buy one.[9]

These two facts combine to give us the correct description of the case: Scanlon believes he has weak reason to buy a fancy new computer, and he weakly desires to buy one, though this desire, it so happens, is highly phenomenologically salient. This is all consistent with DAB.

In short, Scanlon's example fails to show that the appearance theory is an improvement over DAB. I now look at two examples that I believe demonstrate DAB to be superior to the appearance theory. I take them together:

*Conan the Barbarian*: I visit the cinema and see a trailer for the remake of *Conan the Barbarian*. The film looks absolutely thrilling, engaging, and just plain awesome. But wait: I've seen the reviews and heard from friends that the film is terrible. It looks good, but I know better.

*The King's Speech*: I visit the cinema and see a trailer for *The King's Speech*. The film looks excruciatingly dull. I have no interest in the monarchy, and still less interest in their speech impediments. But wait: I've seen the reviews and heard from friends that the film is just fantastic. It looks terrible, but I know better.

In these examples, it seems clear that my desires will track my beliefs rather than the appearances. In the first case, I might well not much want to see *Conan the Barbarian* (I didn't), and in the second case, I might well strongly want to see *The King's Speech*, and even make various sacrifices to do so (I did). So DAB is superior to the appearance theory.[10]

These examples highlight a broader problem with the appearance theory. This is that it cannot account for the effect testimony, and also deliberation, can have on desires (see also Setiya 2010: 106, n16). We can receive advice that influences what we want, but it is abnormal, at best, for testimony to affect how things appear to us. And we very often deliberate about what to desire, but again, it is abnormal, at best, for mere deliberation to affect how things appear to us. Indeed, the very point of appearances is that they remain despite deliberation and testimony: they involve an external imposition on us over which we have no rational control. But desires are not like this: they are responsive to evidence, including evidence gained via testimony and deliberation. So it is doubtful that desires can be understood as appearances of any kind.

In summary, the appearance theory is not well motivated, faces clear counterexamples, and more broadly cannot explain how testimony and deliberation can influence our desires.

## 4. Conclusion

In this paper I have outlined and defended DAB, according to which to desire to perform some action just is to believe that one has some normative reason to perform that action. After describing the view and setting out three appealing features it has, I defended it from five objections: that it is inconsistent with the distinction between the direction of fit of belief and desire, that it cannot account for appetites, that beliefs about reasons are not sufficient for desire, that beliefs about reasons are not necessary for desire, and that animals have desires but no beliefs about reasons. I then argued that DAB is superior to the view that desires are appearances of the good. In summary, DAB has some *prima facie* appeal, is defensible, and is superior to rivals. It therefore merits further investigation.[11]

## Notes

1. In this paper I shall not address David Lewis's (1988, 1996) decision-theoretic objection to DAB. I hope to explore this elsewhere.

2. Alternatively: To desire to ϕ in respect R is to believe that R is a normative reason for one to ϕ. I shall not adjudicate between these two formulations here.

3. For this general problem, see Smith 1994; Brink 1989: 43–44, 52; Darwall 1983: 28. My formulation of the problem above is slightly nonstandard, in that it appeals to the motivational *powers* of the relevant states of mind. Crucially, the existence of such powers is consistent with the possibility that those powers are not always exercised. This will be important later.

4. I thank Julien Deonna for raising this worry.

5. Of course, it is also consistent with the kind of weakness of will that Richard Holton (1999) discusses, according to which one can be weak-willed by being overready to modify one's intentions.

6. In what follows I say nothing more about the Humean theory of motivation, but it should be clear that my remarks stand to benefit that view as well as DAB.

7. This possibility seems to also explain Ayer's (1982: 20) case of the kleptomaniac: such a person is not acting on his desires at all and so is not a counterexample to DAB (*pace* Smith 1994: 133).

8. Here I use *animal* to mean "non-human animal," though everything I say in this section could plausibly also be said about very young humans.

9. Earlier I argued that the strength of a desire does not necessarily correlate with the degree of motivation (sections 2.3 and 2.4). But this does not undermine the thought that in some circumstances a lack of motivation can be defeasible evidence that an agent lacks desire, as is the case here.

10. A defender of the appearance theory might claim that my informants change how good the films seem to me, and thereby claim that the examples do not demonstrate that DAB is superior to her theory. But testimony cannot change how things perceptually appear to us, so it is unclear why things would be different here. At any rate, once she allows that this kind of information changes how things appear, it becomes far less clear how appearances are distinct from beliefs, and in turn how the appearance theory is supposed to be distinct from DAB. I thank Graham Oddie for raising this issue.

11. For help with the ideas in this paper, I thank the editors of this volume and the audience at the conference on which this volume is based, as well as Jonathan Dancy, Bart Streumer, and too many others to list.

## References


Aquinas, T. (1920–1942). *Summa Theologica*. London: Burns, Oates & Washburne.

Anscombe, G. E. M. (1963). *Intention*, 2nd ed. Cambridge, Mass.: Harvard University Press.

Ayer, A. J. (1982). 'Freedom and Necessity', in G. Watson (ed.), *Free Will*. Oxford: Oxford University Press.

Brink, D. (1989). *Moral Realism and the Foundations of Ethics*. Cambridge, UK: Cambridge University Press.

Byrne, A. (2011). 'Knowing What I Want', in J. Liu and J. Perry (eds.), *Consciousness and the Self: New Essays*. Cambridge, UK: Cambridge University Press.

Dancy, J. (2000). *Practical Reality*. Oxford: Oxford University Press.

Darwall, S. (1983). *Impartial Reason*. Ithaca, N.Y.: Cornell University Press.

Davidson, D. (2001). 'How Is Weakness of the Will Possible?', in *Essays on Actions and Events*. Oxford: Oxford University Press.

Dennett, D. (1987) *The Intentional Stance*. Cambridge, Mass.: Bradford Books.

Fernández, J. (2007). 'Desire and Self-Knowledge', *Australasian Journal of Philosophy*, 84 (4), 517–536.

Frankfurt, H. (1982). 'Freedom of the Will and the Concept of a Person', in G. Watson (ed.), *Free Will*. Oxford: Oxford University Press.

Garrard, E., and McNaughton, D. (1998). 'Mapping Moral Motivation', *Ethical Theory and Moral Practice*, 1, 45–89.

Gregory, A. (2012). 'Changing Direction on Direction of Fit', *Ethical Theory and Moral Practice*, 15 (5), 603–614.

———. (2013). 'The Guise of Reasons', *American Philosophical Quarterly*, 50 (1), 63–72.

Holton, R. (1999). 'Intention and Weakness of Will', *Journal of Philosophy*, 96 (5), 241–262.

Humberstone, L. (1987). 'Wanting as Believing', *Canadian Journal of Philosophy*, 17 49–62.

———. (1992). 'Directions of Fit', *Mind*, 101 (401), 59–83.

Joyce, R. (2001). *The Myth of Morality*. Cambridge, UK: Cambridge University Press.

Korsgaard, C. (2009). *Self-Constitution*. Oxford: Oxford University Press.

Lewis, D. (1988). 'Desire as Belief', *Mind*, 97 (387), 323–332.

———. (1996). 'Desire as Belief II', *Mind*, 105 (418), 303–313.

Little, M. (1997). 'Virtue as Knowledge: Objections from the Philosophy of Mind', *Nous*, 311 (1), 59–79.

McDowell, J. (1994). *Mind and World*. Cambridge, Mass.: Harvard University Press.

———. (1998). 'Are Moral Requirements Hypothetical Imperatives?', in *Mind, Value, and Reality*. Cambridge, Mass.: Harvard University Press.

McNaughton, D. (1988). *Moral Vision: An Introduction to Ethics*. Oxford: Blackwell.

Moran, R. (2001). *Authority and Estrangement*. Princeton, N.J.: Princeton University Press.

Nagel, T. (1970). *The Possibility of Altruism*. Princeton, N.J.: Princeton University Press.

Oddie, G. (2005). *Value, Reality, and Desire*. Oxford: Oxford University Press.
Parfit, D. (2011). *On What Matters*, vol. 1. Oxford: Oxford University Press.
Price, H. (1989). 'Defending Desire as Belief', *Mind*, 98 (389), 119–127.
Raz, J. (2010). 'On the Guise of the Good', in S. Tenenbaum (ed.), *Desire, Practical Reason, and the Good*. Oxford: Oxford University Press.
Scanlon, T. (1998). *What We Owe to Each Other*. Cambridge, Mass.: Harvard University Press.
Schroeder, M. (2007). *Slaves of the Passions*. Oxford: Oxford University Press.
Schueler, G. (1995). *Desire*. Cambridge, Mass.: MIT Press.
Setiya, K. (2010). 'Sympathy for the Devil', in S. Tenenbaum (ed.), *Desire, Practical Reason, and the Good*. Oxford: Oxford University Press.
Smith, M. (1987). 'The Humean Theory of Motivation', *Mind*, 96 (381), 36–61.
———. (1994). *The Moral Problem*. Oxford: Blackwell.
Stampe, D. (1987). 'The Authority of Desire', *Philosophical Review*, 96, 335–381.
Stocker, M. (1979). 'Desiring the Bad: An Essay in Moral Psychology', *Journal of Philosophy*, 76 (12), 738–753.
Tenenbaum, S. (2007). *Appearances of the Good*. Cambridge, UK: Cambridge University Press.
Velleman, D. (1992). 'The Guise of the Good', *Nous*, 26, 3–26.
Williams, B. (1981). 'Internal and External Reasons', in *Moral Luck*. Cambridge, UK: Cambridge University Press.
———. (1995). 'Internal Reasons and the Obscurity of Blame', in *Making Sense of Humanity, and Other Philosophical Papers*. Cambridge, UK: Cambridge University Press.

# *Empirical Perspectives: Desire, the Reward System, and Learning*

CHAPTER 8

# Empirical Evidence against a Cognitivist Theory of Desire and Action

TIMOTHY SCHROEDER

IF ONE HAD a map of the flow of cause and effect through the brain on the way to bodily movement, it would allow philosophers to dismiss certain theories of action as inconsistent with this "causal map" while supporting others as being at least consistent with it.[1] So, at least, one might think. For instance, if the causal map revealed two distinct types of routes to bodily movements, that would suggest a philosophy of action with two distinct types of motivating mental states (Reason and Appetite, perhaps) and tell against theories of action with just one type of motivating mental state (pure Reason, perhaps) or theories with three types of motivating mental states (Reason, Spirit, and Appetite, perhaps).

In this paper, I describe one familiar theory of action, nestled within a family of related theories, and criticize that theory (and, less forcefully, the family of related theories) on the basis of what is known at present about the causal map, i.e., on the basis of what is known from low-level neuroscience about the pathways taken by causal influences through the brain on the way to movement production. In doing this, I hope to make a moderately compelling argument against the theory on which I focus, of course. But I also hope to suggest the shape of a much larger project: the project of describing the causal map and using it to answer philosophical questions. This larger project, if undertaken fully, would either vindicate or undermine the arguments that I will make in this paper, so the arguments here are for the most part advanced somewhat tentatively. But everything has to start somewhere, and I propose to start here.

## 1. Scanlonian Cognitivism

In *What We Owe to Each Other*, T. M. Scanlon holds that there are two senses of the term *desire*: a broad one and a narrow one. In the broad sense, "anything that moves us (at least to intentional action) is likely to count as such a desire" (Scanlon 1998: 37). Scanlon's own preferred theory of what moves us is that judgments about our reasons to act play this role (33ff.). Thus, such judgments are desires in the broad sense. In this sense, a desire to be truthful is a judgment that one has reason to be truthful; a desire for more institutional power is a judgment that one has reason to have more institutional power; and so on. (Notice that a mere impulse to, say, turn on radios is not a judgment that one has a reason to turn on radios and so is not a desire to do so. In this way, Scanlon's theory can distinguish true desires from mere behavioral impulses.) In the narrow sense, desires are non-cognitive attitudes that play a central role in explaining why it is that, sometimes, we find it hard to do what we judge we have most reason to do (see Gregory *this volume*). But desires in this narrow sense are not a countervailing motivational force. On the contrary, "insofar as 'having a desire' is understood as a state that is distinct from 'seeing something as a reason,' it plays almost no role in the justification and explanation of action" (18). Instead, desires in this narrow sense are a matter of our dispositions to attend. "A person has a desire in the [narrow] directed-attention sense that P if the thought of P keeps occurring to him or her in a favorable light, that is to say, if the person's attention is directed insistently toward considerations that present themselves as counting in favor of P" (39). In this sense, a desire for cake (for example) is a pattern of having one's attention repeatedly directed toward the sweetness and chocolate-frostedness of the cake. But in this sense, having a desire for cake is powerless to move one to eat cake until one judges that the sweetness or chocolate frosting are reasons for one to eat the cake, that is, until one comes to have a desire in the first sense.

Thus, on Scanlon's view, the sole springs of action (intentional action, anyway) are judgments about reasons.

Scanlon is far from the only philosopher to hold that select cognitive attitudes are the only springs of action (see also, e.g., McDowell 1998: ch.4; Oddie 2005, *this volume*; Stampe 1987 Tenenbaum 2007), but his view is recent, popular, and very clearly articulated, so I will focus on it in this paper. I will call the family of related views, holding that (1) there is only one fundamental source of motivation, and (2) this source of motivation is a belief, judgment, perception, or other cognitive state, "cognitivism," and Scanlon's version of it "Scanlonian cognitivism."

To see just where Scanlon's theory stands, it might be helpful to see that diametrically opposed to cognitivism is what is commonly called "neo-Humeanism" (found, for example, in Blackburn 1998; Schroeder 2004; Smith 1994; Friedrich *this volume*). According to neo-Humeanism (1) there is only one fundamental source of motivation, but (2) this source of motivation is a non-cognitive attitude known as a desire. The difference between, say, McDowell's cognitivism and neo-Humeanism is obvious: McDowell denies that desires are unique motivators, while neo-Humeans assert that they are. But the difference between Scanlonian cognitivism and neo-Humeanism is a little more subtle. Scanlonian cognitivism and neo-Humeanism agree that desires motivate all actions (along with means-end beliefs) but disagree about the nature of desires. Scanlon holds that desires are identical to certain cognitive states (see also Gregory *this volume*), while the neo-Humean holds that they are a different sort of attitude altogether, a non-cognitive one.

An important feature of Scanlonian cognitivism is that it has certain empirical (specifically, neuroscientific) commitments. These commitments are modest, and they do not come without any further philosophical reflection, but they exist nonetheless. Unfortunately for Scanlonian cognitivism, they appear not to be met. The empirical facts do not support Scanlonian cognitivism, or any other form of cognitivism. Motivation centrally involves something non-cognitive. This is not decisive good news for the neo-Humean, but it is certainly news that warrants hopeful optimism from that camp.

## 2. Empirical Commitments

Most actions involve movements of the body, and for these actions it is a difficult but straightforward scientific challenge to trace the cause of the body's movement back to the spinal cord, the primary motor cortex, and then deeper into the brain. According to Scanlon, insofar as bodily movements are intentional actions, they are the product of judgments about reasons. Thus, Scanlon holds that, as the neuroscientist traces the chain of cause and effect backward, she will find that her ultimate stopping point (ultimate just with respect to the immediate explanation of the particular bodily movement) is an event in the brain that can reasonably be interpreted as (or as the realizer of, or as the subvenience base of, etc.) a judgment about reasons.

There are philosophers who reject the idea that judgments can be identified with, realized by, supervene on, or otherwise be closely related to states of the brain. Robert Brandom (1994), for instance, holds that what a person judges is to be identified with (roughly) that person's current state of play in the larger social game of giving and asking for reasons, and thus the judgment is identical to a complexly distributed social fact, not localized within a particular brain. But Scanlon is not one of these philosophers. In fact, in an endnote Scanlon (1998: 21n2) appeals to Davidson for help in defense of the claim that "it is the connection with judgment-sensitive attitudes that makes events actions." Here "connection" can only be "causal connection," if Davidson is to be of help.

Now, even if Scanlon is committed to the claim that judgments of reasons cause movements of the body, it might be thought that he does not have *substantive* empirical commitments of a sort that might cause problems for his theory. One might think this for a number of reasons; I will consider two. The first stems from the methodology of philosophy and the second stems from the methodology of the psychological sciences.

The philosophical reason to think that Scanlon does not have substantive empirical commitments is that he has open to him (as every cognitivist does) a variety of undemanding theories of mind. Davidsonian interpretationism and causal role functionalism, for instance, might be thought to give endless flexibility in interpreting the brain. So long as the brain contains some mechanism that produces bodily movements of the right sorts, the Davidsonian interpretationist can interpret the event of that mechanism's activity as a judgment about reasons given the interpretive principle that we understand such movements (the ones we see as intentional actions) as stemming from such judgments. Likewise, the causal role functionalist can interpret it as a judgment about reasons given the functionalist principle that what it is to be such a judgment is, in part, to play such a role in causing such bodily movements. Scanlon could embrace either theory of mind, or some similarly flexible theory, or simply be agnostic but accept that one such theory within a range must be correct, and thereby—it would seem—escape any putatively problematic empirical commitments.

However, this sanguine attitude comes under pressure once the philosopher interpreting the brain acknowledges more than one causal commitment. If a bodily movement is produced, it obviously has some cause. But that cause is not guaranteed to have every other causal property one might expect it to have.

For example, a philosopher who claims that every episode of akrasia is caused by pleasure can come under empirical pressure if also committed to claims such as: pleasure is almost always a conscious state, it is almost always poised to be remembered, it is normally caused by the prospect of wanted things occurring, and so on. Although a philosopher can always interpret a particular event in the brain as an episode of pleasure, given that it has played a distinctive role in causing a paradigmatic instance of akrasia, it is not guaranteed that the same event in the brain will play all of these other causal roles, either in general (as a causal role functionalist might require) or in a particular token instance (as a Davidsonian interpretationist might require).

Likewise, Scanlon can claim that judgments about reasons cause all intentional actions, but his view can come under empirical pressure if he is also committed to claims such as: such judgments are occurrent events; when one is consciously and (paradigmatically) wholeheartedly judging that one has most reason to take action A one is not simultaneously unconsciously judging that one has most reason to take conflicting actions B, C, D, E, etc.; judging that one has good reason to A is not normally a cause of being pleased; judgments of what one has most reason to do are not normally drivers of operant conditioning; judgments about reasons for action are not found in cats, rats, or most other mammals; and so on.

More could be said here, but I hope the reader will accept the principle, at least tentatively, for now. Later in the paper, I will address the specific causal commitments I take it Scanlon and other cognitivist theorists of action will want to hold and the specific problems that such causal commitments generate; if there are deep problems for the approach I am advocating, they should be evident at that point.

The scientific reason to be skeptical that there are substantive empirical commitments behind cognitivism is the straightforward thought that we do not know very much about causal relationships in the brain. The brain is just too complex an organ to draw any conclusions about philosophical theories at this point. This sort of skepticism is thus practical rather than principled: perhaps one day the psychological sciences will be able to put pressure on philosophical claims about action, but not—it might be thought—today. For today, the philosopher can safely ignore the scientific findings.

I am sympathetic to a weaker version of this view. If one looks only to the findings of conventional cognitive psychology or to neuroimaging studies, one will be hard-pressed to discover facts that put substantive pressure on cognitivism, or indeed on almost any philosophical theory of the mind (so to this extent I am sympathetic to the arguments of Berker (2009)). But fortunately there is more to the science of the mind than these branches of it. In this paper, my starting point will be what is sometimes called "functional neuroanatomy." This is the study of how the neural shin bone is connected to the neural knee bone, and how it in turn is connected to the neural thigh bone: the study of each step in the causal pathway through the brain toward a given outcome. Although the brain is indeed a very complicated place, it is not so complicated that nothing can be known about the step-by-step causal production of movement. On the contrary, an enormous amount is known about the causal production of the bodily movements found in paradigmatic actions. Understanding this causal process at the level of individual neurons or clusters of neurons provides a solid foundation for testing causal claims.

## 3. The Causal Map of Movement Production

In order to beg as few questions as possible, I begin with a description of action production in terms close to those preferred by neuroscience. I apologize if this tour through the neuroscience tries the philosophical reader's patience. The reward for the hard work will be an understanding of the basic causal map involved in action production: the basic framework required for any scientifically acceptable theory of action. In spite of the level of detail in this section, the sketch of the causal map will still be partial and crude; perhaps, though, it will be enough. (The reader will probably find it helpful to refer to Figure 8.1 throughout this section.)

Begin with the last neural structure to be involved in any action: the spinal cord. The spinal cord is obviously crucial for most voluntary behavior,[2] but it is equally obviously not the place to look for beliefs, desires, or the like (even their realizers or subvenience bases), and I will not linger over it.

Above the spinal cord lies the motor cortex, then the pre-motor cortex, and finally motor regions of prefrontal cortex, organized more or less hierarchically. For convenience, I will sometimes discuss these regions together as "the motor hierarchy." The label is not a standard neuroscientific label, but it will keep things as simple as possible.

The motor cortex is the last structure to be activated in the brain before the body is caused to move, and it is absolutely essential to movement: loss of the motor cortex (from both hemispheres of the brain[3]) causes complete paralysis.[4] Essential as it is, however, the motor cortex is also relatively simple in its operations. Each region of the motor cortex is dedicated to moving one part of the body, and the movements that one of these regions can cause to be made are very, very basic: the balling of a fist, the swinging of a leg, the protrusion of the tongue, and so on.[5] One such dedicated region

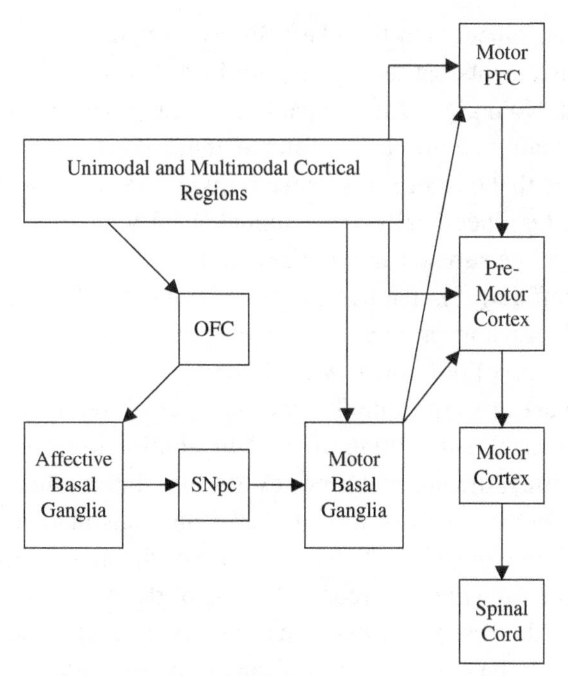


FIGURE 8.1 Action Production in the Human Brain

of motor cortex cannot cause, say, crossing the arms over the chest: such a movement would require the involvement of multiple sub-regions of the motor cortex and would require not just a single activation of these sub-regions but a sequence of activations over time. All this suggests an interpretation of the movements commanded by the motor cortex as Arthur Danto's "basic actions" or Donald Davidson's "primitive actions." That is, movements commanded by the motor cortex appear to be the things we do without doing them by doing anything else.[6] But arguing for such an interpretation would take us far afield.

Above the motor cortex is the pre-motor cortex, made up of the supplementary motor area, the motor region of the anterior cingulate cortex, the lateral ventral pre-motor area, and the lateral dorsal pre-motor area.[7] These regions are like the motor cortex in that they are divided into sub-regions specializing in giving commands to particular parts of the body. Unlike the motor cortex, however, they are capable of organizing more complex, integrated patterns of movement. Whereas the activity of a single region of motor cortex can be expected to produce only a simple effect such as the extension or retraction of a limb, activity of a single region of pre-motor cortex can produce effects such as the utterance of a syllable, a strumming-type movement, a grasping movement directed at a particular object, and the like.[8] But as these examples suggest, the scope of movements caused by activity in the pre-motor cortex is still very limited. No region of it is capable of causing one to get to the nearest phone to call for a pizza, for example, much less take the steps necessary to ensure that one's car insurance is up to date. Widespread injury to these structures, specifically to the supplementary motor area and motor anterior cingulate cortex, can produce a profound sort of paralysis. Those who have suffered this paralysis only temporarily (the injury being in the form of bruising or swelling, which pressed on the structures but resolved over time) report that while immobile they had no spontaneous impulses to act or even to think. One such person reported she had not spoken because "I had nothing to say."[9] In addition to its influence upon the motor cortex, the pre-motor cortex also has direct influence over the spinal cord, but in terms of the number of neurons involved this influence is small in comparison to the influence of the motor cortex, and the pre-motor cortex cannot overcome the loss of the motor cortex to cause movement in the absence of that structure.[10] As a result, it seems reasonable to diagram the relationship between pre-motor cortex, motor cortex, and the spinal cord as a linear hierarchy, at least to a first approximation (as in Figure 8.1).

At the top of the motor hierarchy lie the motor regions of the prefrontal cortex (specifically those located in Brodmann's area 46). One of the most important functions of the motor PFC is to direct the performance of the pre-motor cortex *in the near future*. Damage to motor PFC does not seem to impair the performance of any movement as such. Rather, it seems to impair the ability of an individual to keep a movement in mind until the time is ripe for that movement.[11] Imagine that one is standing over a pot, watching for the hot chocolate to show the first signs of boiling, and one's plan is to remove the pot at the first sign. This is the sort of task that damage to the motor PFC impairs: one can still stand over the pot and watch it, yet when the hot chocolate starts boiling, a person with an injured motor PFC will not automatically reach out and take the pot off the stove—that decision would have to be made again, from scratch. Damage to the motor PFC does not seem to affect episodic memory. It simply turns out that actively waiting to make a movement on some appropriate cue requires more than merely storing the belief that one was going to make the behavior plus having the relevant goals and abilities. One also, it turns out, needs the motor PFC to be intact. All this strongly suggests some role for the motor PFC in a full theory of intention,[12] but as with basic actions, this is again a matter for another day.

With the motor hierarchy in view, it is time to examine the two major inputs to the hierarchy.[13] The first is from an enormous sweep of cortex: from the brain's unimodal sensory regions (though not primary sensory cortex) and its multimodal association regions. These contain the structures that respond to single senses (unimodal sensory regions) and that respond to multiple senses (multimodal association regions).[14] Unimodal sensory regions can be quite primitive in their response dispositions (e.g., being triggered by pressure to the middle of the pad of the first finger on the left hand), or intermediate in complexity (e.g., being triggered by hearing particular phonemes), or quite impressive in complexity (e.g., being triggered by seeing faces of particular people, regardless of the orientation of the face).

Multimodal association regions are even more complex in their response dispositions, and also more complexly organized. At least two regions of multimodal association cortex are worth mentioning in any story of behavior production. One, in the temporal lobe, is found where high-level visual processing meets high-level auditory processing. Though it is not yet well understood how this structure operates, it is thought to be a key locus of "semantic knowledge," also known as our general beliefs about the world, no doubt in association with other, related regions of cortex.[15] The other region of multimodal association cortex that should be singled out is found in the parietal lobe and plays a crucial role in visually guided behavior production, especially for reaching and grasping movements.[16] However, it seems that injury to this region does not deprive the sufferer of the ability to reach or grasp as such so much as deprive the sufferer of accuracy and ease in making such movements. Thus, important as this region is to life, it is less important when the concern is with anything like acting for reasons as such, and I will not make anything more of this region.

An interesting feature of both unimodal and multimodal regions is the way they causally affect other parts of the brain. Both are made up of neurons which, by and large, are naturally quiescent.[17] It takes an energetic event, in a sensory receptor or elsewhere in the brain, to activate these neurons, and so to make them have causal effects on the motor system: neurons are not, in general, capable of endless high rates of activity. So only those structures currently being used in the cortex have any causal influence on the motor hierarchy or any other part of the brain. This is no surprise in the case of the unimodal sensory cortex, but it is more informative and important when considering the multimodal association cortex. In particular, the structures encoding our general beliefs about the world are not constantly active, and so, in all likelihood, our general beliefs about the world are not all constantly affecting the motor and pre-motor cortex. Rather, regions of the multimodal association cortex are activated at any given time, with the region activated being influenced by current sensory activation, activation of episodic memory, of attentional systems, and no doubt activation of still other regions of the brain.

Finally there are the motor regions of the basal ganglia (BG), the second of the two major sources of input to the motor hierarchy.[18] The motor BG takes two sorts of input and produces one sort of output. Its inputs are from the unimodal sensory and multimodal association regions of the cortex (i.e., from the neural bases of perception and cognition) and also from the substantia nigra (pars compacta), or SNpc, a very small deep-brain structure, signals from which are carried in the form of a distinctive compound, dopamine.[19] Input to the motor BG from the unimodal and multimodal cortex creates activation patterns within the motor BG, which input in the form of dopamine then alters, driving down some patterns of activation (those weak at the moment) and enhancing other patterns of activation (those strong at the moment).[20] The output of the motor BG affects both levels of the motor hierarchy above the motor cortex: the pre-motor cortex and the motor PFC.[21] Because the motor cortex is dependent upon the higher levels of the motor hierarchy for its activation (recall that damage to the pre-motor cortex causes paralysis even when the motor cortex is intact), this effectively means that the motor BG has direct influence over the entire motor hierarchy.

The motor hierarchy is not a quiet place.[22] Above the motor cortex, the motor hierarchy is constantly bubbling with activity, produced by input from unimodal and multimodal regions. That is, sensory and higher-level cognitive responses to the world are constantly, directly, activating motor hierarchy responses. However, there is little coherence to these directly activated motor responses. Seeing a friend might prompt activity in the motor hierarchy of the sort that would cause one's arms to spread wide, as for a hug, while also prompting activity of the sort that would cause one's right hand to extend forward, fingers straight out, as for a warm handshake. Of course, one cannot make both movements at once, and if both activation patterns were allowed to go forward, one's muscles would seize up at the conflicting signals. Preventing this from happening is, in part, the motor BG. The motor BG's default state is one in which it suppresses every form of activity found in the motor hierarchy. So, while seeing a friend is likely to prompt all sorts of varied and potentially conflicting motor responses to be somewhat activated, all of this activation will be damped down by the motor BG as a routine matter. However, the motor BG's output is not restricted to this chronic suppression of the motor hierarchy. It can also selectively release its suppression, allowing selected regions of the motor hierarchy to become activated after all. This selective release of suppression is exactly what is produced as a result of input to the motor BG by the sensory and multimodal cortex, on the one hand, and by dopamine from the SNpc, on the other.

The normal manner in which the body gets moved, then, is this: one perceives whatever one does, and perhaps also recalls memories and has occurrent thoughts. The activated cortex then sends causal influences forward to the motor hierarchy in a way that would—left unchecked—result in numerous motor commands being formed for numerous (possibly incompatible) movements. These causal influences are checked, however, by the chronic suppressant influence of the motor BG. But the motor BG too is receiving causal influences from perception and thought and from the dopamine-releasing cells of the SNpc. Under these influences, it can selectively release its inhibition from regions of the motor hierarchy. Assuming these regions are independently being activated by the cortex, this will result in motor commands being passed down the motor hierarchy to the motor cortex itself, and then out to the spine, causing the body to perform the commanded movement.

This whole process, though slow to describe, operates with impressive speed and is constantly engaged in ever renewed cycles of behavior production as one goes through life, building one's small behaviors into larger, coherent sequences.

Only one crucial stage remains to be described, and that is the production of the dopamine signal out of the SNpc and into the motor BG. It turns out that this is a very complex affair. This signal is one half of the output of what scientists call the brain's reward system, the other half coming from the immediately adjacent ventral tegmental area.[23,24] The brain's reward system computes the difference between actual reward and expected reward and produces a positive "spike" if the difference is positive (more reward than expected), a constant baseline if the difference is zero, and a negative "dip" if the difference is negative (less reward than expected).[25] Calculation of expected reward appears to be performed in the ventral, affective region of the basal ganglia, or affective BG,[26] and so to be distinct from conscious expectations (these being thought to rely on multimodal association regions for their existence, since they are, after all, general beliefs). Because they are distinct from what one consciously calculates, they may helpfully be thought of as one's gut-level expectations, what one takes for granted, what one is hardened to or jaded about. Actual reward appears to be calculated in part of the orbitofrontal cortex, or OFC.[27] And the OFC, in turn, makes this calculation based on activation of unimodal sensory and multimodal association regions of the cortex.[28]

Since the label "reward" is interpretatively loaded, it is better for the moment to understand the system in less loaded terms. What happens is that sensory events, memories, conscious thoughts, and the like get realized by activations of the unimodal and multimodal cortex. This activation sends signals forward to the OFC. The OFC has fairly stable, though not immutable, long-term dispositions to discriminate between these input signals. In response to some, nothing happens. In response to others, a signal is sent along to the affective BG. There a comparison is made: was the signal expected or not? The result of such processing (not yet fully understood) is reflected in the brain's dopamine signal, some of which is directed specifically at the motor BG. Spikes in the signal contribute specially to behavior release but are not necessary. However, it is essential that some level of dopamine input from the SNpc reach the motor BG. Loss of normal input causes Parkinson's disease, and total loss of dopamine input to the motor BG causes Parkinson's disease so severe that the sufferer is completely paralyzed.[29]

In addition to a reward system, the brain almost certainly also contains a distinct punishment system. Its existence may be inferred from such facts as that intuitively rewarding stimuli and intuitively punishing stimuli cause distinct but similarly located responses in OFC and distinct but similarly located responses in the affective BG, and from the fact that there are special brain chemicals particularly released in animals like us under punishing conditions and causing, e.g., freezing behavior in rats.[30] Unfortunately, the effects of the punishment system on behavior can only be inferred by analogy to the effects of the reward system, as there is as yet no clear identification of the punishment system's output structure. Without fuller information, this part of behavior production will have to be left to speculation. It is quite likely that a box for punishment should be included in Figure 8.1, but without the necessary information, this box cannot yet be drawn in.

After all of this, quick mention should be made of the cerebellum: no claim to comprehensively survey pathways to behavior production would be complete without it. This very large structure is important to the production of normal behavior, but in spite of its size a human being can survive its loss with only moderate ill effects and without any loss in the basic ability to act in response to perceived reasons. It seems that the role of the cerebellum is to contribute to the smooth sequencing of behaviors rather than behavior selection itself.[31] But since behavior selection rather than behavior smoothness is what is of interest for action theory, no further mention of the cerebellum will be made here.

There are other parts of the brain than those mentioned here, and of course all are important in one respect or another. But the parts that have been covered are those central to what is generally regarded as voluntary behavior. Any contribution to voluntary behavior must at some point affect the system already described, and so here the survey will stop.

## 4. Interpreting the Causal Map

One reasonable interpretation of the neuroscientific account might go as follows: one senses the world and makes judgments about it. These sense experiences and judgments are realized in the unimodal sensory and multimodal association cortex. They cause possible basic or primitive actions to be primed, with the priming of more complex possible actions (say, strumming a guitar) causing the priming of the less complex possible actions that are required (say, shaping one's hand in a certain way, moving one's arm, etc.). These primed actions can be commanded by clusters of neurons found in the motor hierarchy, naturally. Primed possible actions existing at a given time are typically more numerous than the actions one actually performs or would wish to perform. Thus, primed possible actions are all chronically suppressed, this being the role of the motor BG. At the same time as possible actions become primed, one's experiences and judgments cause a response in one's reward system. This response combines, in the motor BG, with one's experiences and judgments. And this combination of experiences, thoughts, and reward signals in the motor BG causes a release of some of the primed possible actions. Those primed actions that are released then get performed. Figure 8.2 illustrates this interpretation.

An example might help. Suppose a new book is waiting for you when you walk into your office. Your eyes fall on the book, and then you behave: you reach out and grab the book. How does this happen?

First, of course, you see the book (itself a very complex process) and have the thought that you have received a new book. The thought primes possible behaviors: saying the word *book*, perhaps, and reaching out to grasp the book. These primed behaviors are suppressed for the moment. But mere milliseconds after perceiving and thinking about the book, activity reaches your reward system. Since (suppose) getting a new book is a reward for you, your reward system sends a signal to your motor BG that

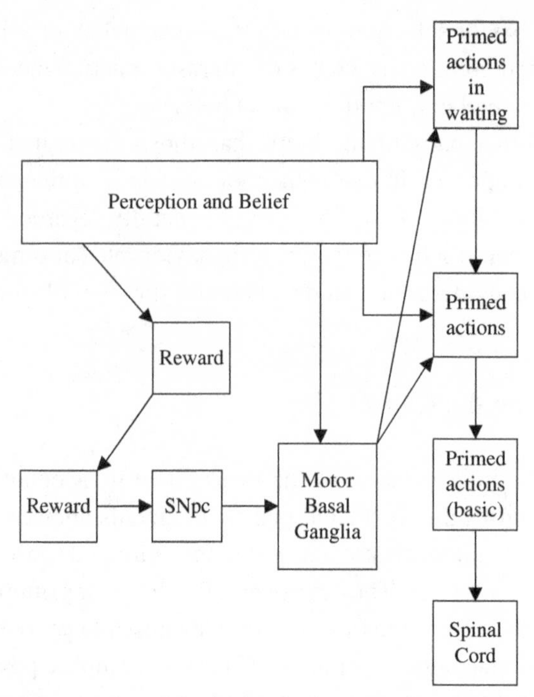


FIGURE 8.2 Partially Interpreted Action Production in the Human Brain

combines with your perceptions of and thoughts of the book. This combination causes the motor BG to selectively release its inhibition over one of the primed behaviors. In this particular case, perhaps, it releases the inhibition against reaching out and grasping the book. Thus, you reach out and grasp the book.

Though this picture of behavior makes it seem complex, it is the sort of thing that happens without subjective effort all the time, for all of our movements.

## 5. A Problem for the Cognitivist

The textbook neuroscience of action production presents an immediate and obvious problem for the cognitivist. The neuroscience of action suggests a two-factor account of the production of actions. One is the cognitive factor: perception, memory, knowledge, and so on. The other is the reward (and, presumably, punishment) factor, a factor not yet interpreted in cognitive or non-cognitive terms, but a second factor nonetheless.

According to the cognitivist, behavior begins with perception or thought alone: with only a cognitive state. According to the Scanlonian cognitivist, it begins with a judgment regarding reasons. These perceptions or judgments would seem to be found in the unimodal perceptual cortex or in multimodal association cortex, that is, to be found in the regions of the brain that neuroscientists take to realize our perceptions, memories, knowledge, and other cognitive states. But these neural structures are not the only ones involved in producing actions. The reward (and punishment) system is also poised to be causally involved.

The cognitivist needs to resist any interpretation of the neuroscience that gives a central role to a non-cognitive factor. I see three promising strategies for doing so. The first is to deny that the reward (and punishment) factor is important in causing paradigmatic intentional actions. The second is to hold that the contribution of the reward (and punishment) factor is identical to (or is the realization of, or subvenience base of, etc.) judgments about reasons. And the third is to hold that the contribution of the reward (and punishment) factor is a necessary condition for selected cognitive states counting as states with the correct contents.

I'll consider each strategy in turn.

### 5.1. Is the Reward (and Punishment) System a Needed Contributor to Paradigmatic Action?

A glance at Figure 8.1 or Figure 8.2 reveals that there are two possible ways for perception or thought to cause action in the absence of influence from the reward (and punishment) system. The first causal pathway runs from the unimodal and multimodal cortex (from perception and belief) directly to the motor hierarchy (to the priming of possible behaviors). The second causal pathway runs from the unimodal and multimodal cortex down to the motor BG, and from there to the motor hierarchy. So far as contemporary neuroscience is aware, these are the only significant causal pathways by which complex, coherent behavior might be produced in the absence of influence from the reward (and punishment) system.[32] But in fact, neither pathway supports the production of paradigmatic actions.

Consider the first pathway. It looks like an especially promising candidate pathway for the cognitivist. If it were efficacious, one would simply see, or think about, one's reasons to act, and thereby become moved to act. Seeing that one has hurt the feelings of a niece, and thinking that this counts in favor of saying something kind, one would be moved to say something kind.

As it happens, however, this first pathway is not as innocuous as it looks. The causal connection between perception and thought, on the one hand, and action preparation, on the other, is indeed real. But recall that all of the potential actions primed through this causal pathway are suppressed, by default, by a signal coming from the motor BG. This signal coming from the motor BG is crucially influenced by reward information. Thus, for the first pathway to lead to behavior independently of a reward signal, the potential behavior that is primed by perception or thought must override this inhibitory signal. And such overriding is not innocuous. The only natural model we have for it is found in Tourette syndrome.

People with Tourette syndrome are prone to verbal and gestural tics, often taking the form of eye blinks, twitches, barks, grunts, the uttering of vulgarities and profanities, imitative movements, and so on.[33] The best current theory of Tourette syndrome has it that the disorder is exactly a failure of the inhibitory system based in the motor BG.[34] In Tourettic people, possible behaviors are primed just as in the rest of us. But in Tourettic people, not all of these primed possible behaviors are fully inhibited. Instead, they are often partly but not fully activated, giving rise to felt urges to act. And they sometimes spontaneously cross the borderline into full activation, independently of the normal mechanisms of behavior release, giving rise to what people with Tourette syndrome describe as involuntary tics.[35]

If paradigmatic action generally relies upon the first pathway, overriding the inhibition controlled by reward (and punishment) information, then paradigmatic action is analogous to Tourettic ticcing. But of course it is not.

There is also a phenomenological reason to deny that the first pathway is the pathway of paradigmatic action. The sense Tourettic people have that their urges to tic are not their own—are alien, non-self, external—is tied closely to the means by which the tics are produced. When a Tourettic urge overwhelms a person and forces an involuntary tic, the motor hierarchy is activated quite independently of its release by the normal mechanisms of the motor BG.[36] This same sort of overriding activation, when induced by direct electrical stimulation of the brain, likewise induces movements from which experimental subjects feel alienated.[37] But action does not typically have this sense of alienation tied to it. Thus, it seems that a precondition of acting without feelings of alienation is the normal involvement of one's motor BG in releasing one's action. If paradigmatic actions proceeded via the first pathway, then one would expect agents to typically experience alienation from their actions, and of course this is not the case.

Turn now to the second pathway under consideration for action independent of the influence of the reward system. This is the pathway leading from perception and thought, down to the motor BG, and then to the motor hierarchy. Once again, we seem to have a pathway that respects a cognitivist theory of action: one sees what is reasonable and is thereby moved to act. But once again, there are serious complications.

Normally, the motor BG is significantly influenced by the input of the reward system, so of course we must imagine something different, a mechanism by which the input of the reward system makes no difference to the behavior. Only the perceptions or thoughts acting as input are to make any difference to what behavior gets produced.

A simple objection to the second pathway is that the complete absence of reward input to the motor BG causes complete paralysis: this is Parkinson's disease taken to its absolute limit, beyond its most familiar symptoms (tremor and hesitation before initiating or changing courses of action). Hence in any scenario in which reward has no influence whatsoever upon the motor BG, no behavior whatsoever can be produced, no matter how strong a reason the agent judges herself to have to act.

The simple objection is too simple. All that is required for the second pathway to be said to operate without influence from the reward system is that the causal contribution to behavior caused by perception and thought be *largely* independent of the causal contribution of the reward system. Suppose that a judgment about reasons caused a powerful positive contribution toward releasing inhibition from relevant primed possible actions in the motor hierarchy, whether the current reward signal were above baseline, at it, or below it, so long as the current reward signal were above the levels found in severe Parkinson's disease. If this were the case, then we would seem to have a good case of action driven by judgments about reasons operating independently of the influence of the reward system.[38]

As it happens, this possibility is actual. Judgments about reasons probably do causally influence the motor BG in a way that promotes relevant behavior, whether or not a reward signal significantly contributes to this process—in some people, on some occasions, at least. However, this can be asserted with confidence only because every sort of perception or thought can, in principle, causally influence the motor BG in a way that promotes relevant behaviors, whether or not a reward signal does its part. This is simply the realization of behavioral habits in the brain.

For the second pathway to behavior to be efficacious, the pre-existing internal structure of the motor BG must strongly dispose the motor BG to respond to, e.g., ideas of what one has reason to do with appropriate output, regardless of input from the reward system. So how such a pre-existing internal structure might be created is vitally important. This is where the second pathway is revealed to be the pathway of habit. Extensive experiments have been done on human and non-human subjects dissociating two sorts of learning: straightforward learning by remembering what happened to one, and unconscious learning through the acquisition of behavioral habits. The former is realized in a structure known as the hippocampus (and its connections to the cortex), while the latter is realized in the internal structure of the motor BG.[39] The prime, and perhaps sole, mechanism by which the internal structure of the motor BG is shaped is through the input of dopamine from the brain's reward system.[40] This effect of dopamine is a slow-to-form, slow-to-disappear effect that is different from its other effect in the motor BG, that of directly influencing which primed possible behaviors in the motor hierarchy get released. A standard view in contemporary neuroscience is that the release of dopamine by the reward system into the dorsal striatum is what mediates operant conditioning, and behaviors that have been subject to strong operant conditioning are habits.[41] Thus, being moved by a combination of strong internal connections in the motor BG and perceptual or cognitive input is being moved by habit.

A particularly interesting dissociation experiment reveals the way habits of *thought* depend upon the motor BG just as behavioral habits do. In this study, people were asked to learn, by trial and error, whether an arbitrary visual stimulus predicted "rain" or "shine." After guessing, subjects got feedback on how they did. Anterograde amnesiacs (who retain old memories but cannot form new memories) were found to improve steadily over time, almost as quickly as normal control subjects, while people with Parkinson's disease (lacking a normal reward signal to the motor BG) performed throughout with nearly random success. Yet the Parkinsonian subjects had normal memory for what had happened, while anterograde amnesics could consciously recall nothing. The only deficit of the people with Parkinson's disease was their difficulty in "the gradual, incremental learning characteristic of habit learning."[42] This study shows both how influential the intrinsic connections of the motor BG can be and how pervasive habit and habit-like phenomena are in the control of action.

That said, paradigmatic action is no more habitual than it is Tourettic. Thus, the second pathway to reward-indifferent action is no more reasonable a candidate for the cognitivist to appeal to than the first.

Indeed, this whole approach was never particularly promising. The reward (and punishment) system is a biologically ancient system with a central role in not only action production but in many other mental processes besides. It is no surprise that none of our paradigmatic actions is produced in a manner that is indifferent to it, given its central position as one of two key biological inputs to the dorsal basal ganglia. If cognitivism is to be tenable, it must find a way to embrace the activity of the reward (and punishment) system rather than to ignore it.

## 5.2 Does the Reward System Realize Judgments about Reasons?

Much more promising than ignoring the reward (and punishment) system is interpreting it as the realization (or subvenience base, etc.) of judgments about reasons for action. Indeed, Gideon Yaffe has already proposed a similar interpretation of the reward system (in terms of representations of value) as part of a theory of addiction.[43] After all, upon reflection it seems clear enough that even the cognitivist needs a two-factor account of action. On the one hand, there is the judgment that one has reason to vote for the amendment (as it might be), and on the other hand there is the belief that now raising one's hand would be voting for the amendment. Both seem needed to explain how one gets to the point of now raising one's hand. The most naïve interpretation of the neuroscience might have suggested that both the judgment about reasons and the means-end belief would be realized in the perceptual or multimodal association cortex, but there is no need to stick to the most naïve interpretation.

This second cognitivist strategy also faces severe problems. I will focus on three.

First, this strategy has a problem with interpreting damage to the reward (and punishment) system. As Parkinson's disease becomes severe, people suffering from it find it increasingly difficult to initiate actions and increasingly difficult to change from one course of action to another when they find that a new course of action is desirable. These same people do not change what they say about what they have reason to do, however. An obvious interpretation of them is that, while their judgments about reasons are unaffected, their capacities to act on these judgments is impaired. However, given that Parkinson's disease is caused by the death of cells in the SNpc, that is, by the death of cells at the output end of the reward system, this obvious interpretation is not clearly open to the cognitivist. The cognitivist who holds that the judgments about reasons for action are identical to (realized by, subvened by, etc.) reward system events is under pressure to say that, when cell death prevents these events from transpiring, then it also prevents these judgments from being formed. The reason a person with Parkinson's disease has trouble initiating or switching courses of action thus turns out to be that, in spite of her protests to the contrary, she has difficulty judging what she has most overall reason to do. And a person with such severe Parkinson's disease that she is paralyzed is a person who has lost the capacity to judge what she has most overall reason to do. This is a fairly extraordinary interpretation of this disease.

Second, the putative judgments about reasons posited by this second approach are problematic in that they are causally isolated from memory and consciousness. Activity in the unimodal and multimodal cortex has potentially enormous reach, with output going to many different areas of the brain. As a result, many scientists have no hesitation in localizing sensory consciousness to the unimodal sensory cortex (when appropriately functionally engaged with the rest of the brain, of course). And if there are non-sensory conscious thoughts, then it would be natural to localize such thoughts in regions of the multimodal cortex that seem strongly related to our general capacities to conceptualize the world, or perhaps in regions of the multimodal cortex that seem strongly related to our general capacities to comprehend speech, if these are ultimately distinct. However, once one begins to look specifically at the reward system, one sees an absence of projections from this system to regions of the brain that seem involved either in consciousness or in episodic memory, at least, organized in a manner that would support being conscious of or remembering specific judgments of what one has most reason to do, all things considered.

Scanlon can allow for the existence of unconscious judgments about reasons for action, so the problem is not that such unconscious and unremembered judgments are required to exist. Rather, the problem is that on the present interpretation of the brain, there are no conscious or remembered judgments about reasons. Everything that seems to be such a judgment is not; there is an unbridgeable gulf between what is conscious or remembered and what is actually judged.

Third, a normal causal consequence of increased activity in the reward system is pleasure. This has been confirmed in a variety of ways, from direct electrical stimulation in non-human animals to drug studies in human beings to neuroimaging studies in human beings (reviewed in Schroeder 2004: ch. 3). But a normal causal consequence of judging that one has a reason to act is not pleasure. According to Scanlonian cognitivism, there are psychologically brute facts about what pleases us, and these facts provide us with some—though certainly not all—of our reasons to act. But this requires pleasure to be causally upstream of judgments about reasons, not causally downstream from them.

## 5.3 Is the Reward System a Component of Judgments about Reasons?

Of the three strategies being considered for the cognitivist, the most promising for interpreting the role of the reward system in action is also the strategy with the weakest commitments: perhaps the reward system is just a necessary part of any state that is a judgment about reasons for action.

This approach helps, at least, to deal with the problems about consciousness and memory raised earlier. The starting point for a reward signal is a representation in perceptual or conceptual regions of cortex. And activity in this same starting point is activity that can be expected to sometimes contribute to (or be a part of) consciousness and to be remembered as an episode in one's mental life. If only the activity in the brain that is specific to reward counts as the judgment (or as realizing it, or subvening on it, etc.), then activity in perceptual or conceptual systems cannot be judgments about reasons. But if the connection to reward signaling is only one necessary component of the system, then the activity at the very start of the process can also be a necessary component of the system. Thus, judgments about reasons can be found, partly, in these cortical regions that play roles in consciousness and memory, and also found, partly, in the reward system, where they play a vital role in the production of action.

On this view, one might have the thought "I have most reason to tell my mother the truth," but it would not be a sincere (or all-in, or likewise fully committed) belief about one's practical reasons, and so would not be an action-governing desire, if the neural basis of the thought were not appropriately causally connected to the reward system. This appropriate causal connection is, on this approach, what constitutes such thoughts (and thoughts about practical reasons in general) as genuine, committed, sincere, or the like.

Although helpful, this approach nonetheless suffers from severe problems as well. It does not do anything to answer the objection from Parkinson's disease or the objection from the causation of pleasure. It does not seem that Parkinson's disease diminishes the sincerity of judgments about what one has reasons to do, though it decreases the efficacy of such judgments in initiating new courses of action (and, at the limit of the disease, it does not seem that one stops making such judgments sincerely even while one is paralyzed through lack of activity in the reward system). And it does not seem that truly sincere thoughts about what practical reasons one has are particularly tied to feelings of pleasure. But perhaps these objections can be overcome.

Even if they can, there is a further and potentially deeper concern. The problem is that an enormously broad swath of the perceptual and conceptual cortex sends projections forward to the region of the OFC that in turn constitutes states of affairs as rewards (and punishments). Parts of the brain that are not, in any way, credible candidates to be the neural bases of judgments about practical reasons can have just as much power to generate dopamine signals in the reward system as parts of the brain that might credibly be the neural bases of practical judgments. Single modality (visual, auditory, gustatory, etc.) perceptual regions of the cortex can also generate dopamine responses, and some do: this is (at least part of) the neural basis of taking pleasure in the appearance of one abstract artwork more than another, for instance, or taking pleasure in the taste of one fruit more than another.[44] Such neural connections are likewise at least part of the neural basis of impulses to linger over certain artworks, to prefer certain fruits over others when selecting what to eat, and so on.

The problem created by these other regions of the brain is that, according to Scanlonian cognitivism (and cognitivism generally), there is just one source of motivation: a cognitive representation of reasons for action, value, or something similarly normative or evaluative. But on the present approach to interpreting the causal map, there are diverse sources of motivation that are not cognitive representations of reasons for action or anything else of a normative or evaluative nature, because they are mere perceptual representations of colors and shapes, of tastes and smells, and so on. The Scanlonian cognitivist has in her toolkit desires in the directed attention sense: inner states that direct one's attention to what seems positive (in some sense) about looking at an artwork or choosing a yellow mango. But, crucially, desires in the directed attention sense are not springs of action; it is only if one judges, on the basis of the facts to which one attends, that one has a reason to look at an artwork or eat a yellow mango that one will so act.

Given the role of perceptual representations in generating dopamine signals and so in prompting action, there seem to be two options for the Scanlonian cognitivist. One is to deny what appears to be the case and hold that, somehow, in the absence of a dopamine signal prompted by a judgment of reasons, dopamine signals prompted by the visual qualities of a painting or by the taste qualities of a piece of fruit will not actually lead to bodily movement. This cannot quite be ruled out given the current state of empirical knowledge, but it seems quite unlikely to be the case, as there is no special neural structure yet discovered that would mediate such an extraordinary level of control over dopamine release. The other option is not much more palatable: the Scanlonian cognitivist can hold that our bodies move in complex and seemingly goal-directed ways all the time, but only occasionally are these movements genuine actions. On many other occasions, seeming actions such as lingering over an abstract painting or reaching out for a slice of yellow mango turn out to be not actions but mere movements. Though this cannot be refuted on the basis of empirical considerations, it seems a high price to pay to save the theoretical claim that there is just one source of action, and it is a judgment about practical reasons.

As a result of these difficulties, it seems that this third strategy for interpreting the causal map in a manner consistent with Scanlonian cognitivism is not particularly promising. And at this point, I am out of suggestions.

Of course, that I am out of suggestions for the Scanlonian cognitivist is not to say that there is no way of interpreting the causal map such that it could satisfy the Scanlonian cognitivist, or perhaps a cognitivist of a different stripe. But at present, I would suggest, the path forward does not look promising.

## 6. A Neo-Humean Interpretation

It seems that the causal map strongly favors the thesis that there is a plurality of fundamental grounds of motivation to act and that what constitutes such grounds is something non-cognitive. To me, this is most naturally read as a story, not about representations of normative or evaluative properties but a story about what is intrinsically desired.

On the simplest approach to being a neo-Humean, one holds that there are many ends that can be desired for themselves (that is, intrinsically). Some of these ends might be perceptual in nature: being surrounded by bright primary colors or by muted earth tones, tasting peaches or savoring bitter dark chocolate. Others of these ends might be more conceptual in nature: not telling lies, having the Montreal Canadiens win the Stanley Cup, or discovering new philosophical truths.

On this simplest approach, one holds that desires characteristically dispose us to perform actions that seem likely to bring about (or make progress toward) the ends we intrinsically desire, and one holds that apparently getting some state of affairs disposes us to pleasure insofar as it is a state of affairs that is, or realizes, or makes progress toward some intrinsically desired state of affairs. One might add other characteristic effects of intrinsic desires (they generate motivated irrationality, they direct attention, and more), but on the simplest approach one focuses on just these two effects of having intrinsic desires.

This simple neo-Humeanism fits snugly within the contours of the causal map. Where cognitivism failed to find a home, neo-Humeanism does much better.

According to the causal map, motivation crucially involves certain representations of perceivable or conceivable contents, though not all such representations. The representations that matter to motivation are those that are connected in the right way to the reward system. By being connected in the right way, they generate dispositions to act so as to bring about the represented ends, and they generate dispositions to take pleasure in states of affairs that are identical to, realize, or make progress toward their contents.

Thus, if intrinsic desires are, or are realized by, or subvene on, perceptual and conceptual representations that are connected in the right way to the reward system (such that their contents are constituted as rewards), then intrinsic desires will turn out to have the properties and play the roles attributed to them by the simplest form of neo-Humeanism.

This is not to say that the interpretation of the causal map in neo-Humean terms is without controversy. But the basic outlines of the neo-Humean approach can be seen to fit tidily within the causal map. And that is a fact that should guide future inquiry.[45]

## 7. Conclusion

There is a tentative character to some of what has been argued for above, for there remain questions about what future neuroscience will learn, i.e., about the true shape of the causal map, and questions about how philosophers should interpret those findings. But already neuroscience has a large body of stable, textbook results, results that will be refined over time but not radically overthrown, and within that large body is a substantial literature on behavior. It is time that philosophers began to import this scientific knowledge into their own attempts to explain how actions are performed in general and how moral actions are performed in particular. This paper has been an early contribution to that process. As time goes on, I hope that other contributions will better it, refining our understanding of behavior in the bright light cast when the armchair reading lamp and the laboratory bench lamp are directed upon the same target.

## Notes

1. This paper has spent a long time gestating, and is perhaps still premature. Nonetheless, in writing it I have benefited greatly from many philosophers. The editors of

this volume I particularly thank, for their patient encouragement and a stimulating conference where Peter Railton and Graham Oddie, especially, provided helpful thoughts. I also owe thanks to the philosophers at the University of Texas at Austin, the University of Winnipeg, Washington University, and the members of the Moral Psychology Research Group, who heard talks based on ancestors of the present paper. Ancestral talks were also presented at meetings of the Western Canadian Philosophical Association and the Central Division of the American Philosophical Association; thanks to my commentators and my audiences on those occasions as well.

2. Although voluntary head movements involve the cranial nerves, which are a different tract that I will lump together with the nerves of the spinal cord for convenience of exposition.

3. Almost every structure in the brain comes in a pair, with one in the left hemisphere and one in the right hemisphere. For our purposes, this is a complexity that can be ignored, however, and so talk of hemispheres will by and large be suppressed for convenience of expression.

4. Kandel, Schwartz, and Jessell (2000: ch. 38). From here on, I will abbreviate citations to this canonical textbook as citations of KSJ.

5. Ibid. There is exciting work disputing just how to characterize the motor commands: as commanding postures, gestures, final poses, muscular activation patterns, etc. But this goes to a level of detail not required for present purposes.

6. Danto 1963, 1965; Davidson 1980: ch. 3.

7. KSJ ch. 38.

8. Ibid.; Fried et al. 1991; Devinsky, Morell, and Vogt 1995.

9. Damasio 1994: 73.

10. KSJ ch. 38.

11. Ibid.

12. Bratman 1987.

13. Goldman-Rakic 1987, 1998; KSJ chs. 19, 38.

14. KSJ ch. 19.

15. Ibid., chs. 19, 62.

16. Ibid., ch. 38; Jeannerod 1997.

17. More carefully: some are quiescent, some fire at a rate low enough to have no systematic or interesting downstream causal consequences, and some are continuously active but have their main effects by changes in this continuous activity. See KSJ ch. 2.

18. The motor BG operates via structures in the thalamus that seem to contribute little computationally, and are thus neglected here. See ibid., ch. 43.

19. Ibid.; Mink 1996.

20. Mink 1996.

21. KSJ ch. 43; Mink 1996.

22. For this paragraph, see KSJ ch. 43.

23. Ibid., ch. 51; Schultz, Tremblay, and Hollerman 2000; compare Berridge and Robinson 1998. Stellar and Stellar 1985 is an older classic. For philosophical treatments of the subject, compare Morillo 1990 to Schroeder 2004; see also Prinz 2004 ch. 7.

24. There may also be direct input from the amygdala (KSJ ch. 50; Price and Amaral 1981), a structure best known for its role in the classical conditioning of emotional responses, especially fear responses (KSJ ch. 50; LeDoux 1996). But this is certainly not the primary source of input, and, as it is clear that normal moral behavior is not generally

produced by anything resembling a classically conditioned fear or anger response, this connection will not be discussed further.

25. KSJ ch. 51; Schultz and Romo 1990; Schultz, Tremblay, and Hollerman 2000.

26. Knutson et al. 2001; Pagnoni et al. 2002; Schultz, Dayan, and Read Montague 1997.

27. And for very basic biological rewards such as calories, sexual opportunities, and hydration, in the hypothalamus. See KSJ ch. 49.

28. Rolls 2000; Schultz, Tremblay, and Hollerman 2000.

29. Langston and Palfreman 1995.

30. Deakin 1983; Rolls 2000; Soubrié 1986.

31. KSJ ch. 42.

32. And, it should be added, contemporary neuroscience has a very good understanding of the neural pathways that exist in the brain. Neuroanatomy is far more secure than many scientific disciplines.

33. American Psychiatric Association 1994.

34. Mink 1996, 2001.

35. Though see Cohen and Leckman 1992 and Leckman et al. 1993 for some complicating facts.

36. Ibid. See Schroeder (2005) for more on this.

37. Kremer et al. 2001; Talairach et al. 1973.

38. Compare this to the very different discussion of acting solely from the motive of duty in Herman 1993: ch. 1.

39. Packard and White 1991; White 1997.

40. See ibid. And perhaps there is room for a counterpart punishment mechanism here.

41. In addition to White 1997, see Houk, Adams, and Barto 1995.

42. Knowlton, Mangles, and Squire 1996: 1401.

43. Yaffe 2013.

44. For an extended argument on this topic, see Schroeder (2004: ch. 3).

45. For much more on this interpretation of the causal map, see ibid., esp. chs. 5 and 6.

## References


American Psychiatric Association. (1994). *Diagnostic and Statistical Manual of Mental Disorders: 4th ed.* Washington, DC: American Psychiatric Association.

Berker, S. (2009). 'The Normative Insignificance of Neuroscience', *Philosophy and Public Affairs*, 37, 293-329.

Berridge, K., and Robinson, T. (1998). 'What Is the Role of Dopamine in Reward: Hedonic Impact, Reward Learning, or Incentive Salience?', *Brain Research Reviews*, 28, 309–369.

Blackburn, S. (1998). *Ruling Passions: A Theory of Practical Reasoning*. New York: Oxford University Press.

Brandom, R. (1994). *Making It Explicit*. Cambridge, Mass.: Harvard University Press.

Bratman, Michael E. (1987). *Intention, Plans, and Practical Reason*. Cambridge, Mass.: Harvard University Press.

Cohen, A., and Leckman, J. (1992). 'Sensory Phenomena Associated with Gilles de la Tourette's Syndrome', *Journal of Clinical Psychiatry*, 53, 319–323.

Damasio, A. (1994). *Descartes' Error: Emotion, Reason, and the Human Brain*. New York: Putnam's.

Danto, A. (1963). 'What We Can Do', *Journal of Philosophy*, 60, 435–445.

———. (1965). 'Basic Behaviors', *American Philosophical Quarterly*, 2, 141–148.

Davidson, D. (1980). *Essays on Behaviors and Events*. Oxford: Oxford University Press.

Deakin, J. (1983). 'Role of Serotonergic Systems in Escape, Avoidance, and Other Behaviours', in S. Cooper (ed.), *Theory in Psychopharmacology*, vol. 2. New York: Academic.

Devinsky, O., Morell, M., and Vogt, B. (1995). 'Contributions of the Anterior Cingulate Cortex to Behavior', *Brain*, 118, 279–306.

Fried, I., Katz, A., McCarthy, G., Sass, K., Williamson, P., Spencer, S., and Spencer, D. (1991). 'Functional Organization of Human Supplementary Motor Cortex Studied by Electrical Stimulation', *Journal of Neuroscience*, 11, 3656–3666.

Goldman-Rakic, P. (1987). 'Circuitry of Primate Prefrontal Cortex and Regulation of Behavior by Representational Memory', in F. Plum (ed.), *Handbook of Physiology: The Nervous System, Higher Functions of the Brain*, sec. 1 vol. 5. Bethesda, Md.: American Physiological Society.

———. (1998). 'The Prefrontal Landscape: Implications of Functional Architecture for Understanding Human Mentation and the Central Executive', in A. Roberts, T. Robbins, and L. Weiskrantz (eds.), *The Prefrontal Cortex: Executive and Cognitive Functions*. New York: Oxford University Press.

Herman, B. (1993). *The Practice of Moral Judgment*. Cambridge, Mass.: Harvard University Press.

Houk, J., Adams, J., and Barto, A. (1995). 'A Model of How the Basal Ganglia Generate and Use Neural Signals That Predict Reinforcement', in J. Houk, J. Davis, and D. Beiser (eds.), *Models of Information Processing in the Basal Ganglia*. Cambridge, Mass.: MIT Press.

Jeannerod, M. (1997). *The Cognitive Neuroscience of Action*. Oxford: Blackwell.

Kandel, E., Schwartz, J., and Jessell, T. (2000). *Principles of Neural Science*, 4th ed. New York: McGraw-Hill.

Knowlton, B., Mangles, J., and Squire, L. (1996). 'A Neostriatal Habit Learning System in Humans', *Science*, 273, 1399–1402.

Knutson, B., Adams, C., Fong, G., and Hommer, D. (2001). 'Anticipation of Increasing Monetary Reward Selectively Recruits Nucleus Accumbens', *Journal of Neuroscience*, 21, 1–5.

Kremer, S., Chassagnon, S., Hoffmann, D., Benabid, A., and Kahane, P. (2001). 'The Cingulate Hidden Hand', *Journal of Neurology, Neurosurgery, and Psychiatry*, 70, 264–265.

Langston, J., and Palfreman, J. (1995). *The Case of the Frozen Addicts*. New York: Pantheon.

Leckman, J., Walker, D., Cohen, D. (1993). 'Premonitory Urges in Tourette's Syndrome', *American Journal of Psychiatry*, 150, 98–102.

LeDoux, J. (1996). *The Emotional Brain: The Mysterious Underpinnings of Emotional Life*. New York: Touchstone.

McDowell, J. (1998). *Mind, Value, and Reality*. Cambridge, Mass.: Harvard University Press.

Mink, J. (1996). 'The Basal Ganglia: Focussed Selection and Inhibition of Competing Motor Programs', *Progress in Neurobiology*, 50, 381–425.

———. (2001). 'Neurobiology of Basal Ganglia Circuits in Tourette Syndrome: Faulty Inhibition of Unwanted Motor Patterns?', in D. Cohen, C. Goetz, and J. Jankovic (eds.), *Tourette Syndrome*. Philadelphia: Lippincott, Williams, and Wilkins.

Morillo, C. (1990). 'The Reward Event and Motivation', *Journal of Philosophy*, 87, 169–186.

Oddie, G. (2005). *Value, Reality, and Desire*. Oxford: Oxford University Press.

Packard, M. and White, N. 'Dissociation of hippocampus and caudate nucleus memory systems by posttraining intracerebral injection of dopamine agonists', *Behavioral Neuroscience* 105, 295-306.

Pagnoni, G., Zink, C., Montague, P., and Berns, G. (2002). 'Activity in Human Ventral Striatum Locked to Errors of Reward Prediction', *Nature Neuroscience*, 5, 97–98.

Price, J., and Amaral, D. (1981). 'An Autoradiographic Study of the Projections of the Central Nucleus of the Monkey Amygdala', *Journal of Neuroscience*, 1, 1242–1259.

Prinz, J. (2004). *Gut Reactions: A Perceptual Theory of Emotion*. New York: Oxford University Press.

Rolls, E. (2000). 'Orbitofrontal Cortex and Reward', *Cerebral Cortex*, 10, 284–294.

Scanlon, T. (1998). *What We Owe to Each Other*. Cambridge, Mass.: Harvard University Press.

Schroeder, T. (2004). *Three Faces of Desire*. New York: Oxford University Press.

———. (2005). 'Moral Responsibility and Tourette Syndrome', *Philosophy and Phenomenological Research*, 71, 106-123.

Schultz, W., Dayan, P., and Read Montague, P. (1997). 'Neural Substrate of Prediction and Reward', *Science*, 275, 1593–1599.

Schultz, W., and Romo, R. (1990). 'Dopamine Neurons of the Monkey Midbrain: Contingencies of Response to Stimuli Eliciting Immediate Behavioral Reactions', *Journal of Neurophysiology*, 63, 607–624.

Schultz, W., Tremblay, L., and Hollerman, J. (2000). 'Reward Processing in Primate Orbitofrontal Cortex and Basal Ganglia', *Cerebral Cortex*, 10, 272–283.

Smith, M. (1994). *The Moral Problem*. Oxford: Blackwell.

Soubrié, P. (1986). 'Reconciling the Role of Central Serotonin Neurons in Human and Animal Behavior', *Behavioral and Brain Sciences*, 9, 319–364.

Stampe, D. (1987). 'The Authority of Desire', *Philosophical Review*, 96, 335–381.

Stellar, J., and Stellar, E. (1985). *The Neurobiology of Motivation and Reward*. New York: Springer-Verlag.

Talairach, J., Bancaud, J., Geier, S., Bordas-Ferrer, M., Bonis, A., Szikla, G., and Rusu, M. (1973). 'The Cingulate Gyrus and Human Behaviour', *Electronencephalography and Clinical Neurophysiology*, 34, 45–52.

Tenenbaum, S. (2007). *Appearances of the Good*. Cambridge, UK: Cambridge University Press.

Velleman, D. (1992). 'What Happens When Someone Acts?', *Mind*, 101, 461–481.

White, N. (1997). 'Mnemonic functions of the basal ganglia', *Current Opinion in Neurobiology*, 7, 164-169.

Yaffe, G. (2013). 'Are Addicts Akratic?', in N. Levy (ed.) *Addiction and Self-Control*. New York: Oxford University Press. 190-213.

# CHAPTER 9 | Learning as an Inherent Dynamic of Belief and Desire

PETER RAILTON

## Introduction: Beliefs, Desires, and Learning

Informally, at least, we speak of learning what we do or don't want, what's worth wanting, and what matters. Such learning, we think, takes place throughout life—through our own experience and from the experience or example of others. We can learn these lessons of life more or less well, and at greater or lesser cost to ourselves and others. Moreover, it seems clear that failure to learn such things is a way in which our lives as wholes can fail to go well. But these ways of talking also pose quandaries.

For a start, the term *learning* is a factive expression—you can't be said to *learn* that I'm back in town from a text I send you saying, "I'm back in town" unless I am in fact back in town when I send it. Even my sincerity and your epistemic conscientiousness don't suffice for learning to take place; if for some reason I am mistaken about being back in town, so that my text is non-deceptive, and I am usually reliable enough that you are warranted in believing on the basis of my message that I am back in town, still, you cannot learn what my text purports to tell you unless it's a fact.

Does this mean everything we learn has to be a fact? That seems too strong. You can learn to propel yourself forward on a skateboard without touching the ground with your feet, and learn to use the subjunctive in French, but these aren't facts in the usual sense. Even so, we might think that knowledge of facts is central to the explanation of these competencies. For example, recent years have seen a striking growth of research in cognitive science, psychology, and neuroscience that emphasizes the extent to which such acquired skills and competencies depend at base upon complex informational structures or "internal models," which can indeed be more or less accurate or faithful to the facts (Yarrow, Brown, and Krakauer 2009; Stanley and Krakauer 2013). Of course, other capacities are involved in the *expression* of these competencies or skills in action; for example, they involve controlled movements of the body and voice. But it appears that such movements themselves are controlled in these skilled or competent ways via the operation of internal models. Learning in such cases appears to have a factive core after all.

And that makes sense. Skills and competencies are ways of interacting successfully with the physical, social, and cultural worlds, and these cannot help but be information-intensive tasks. Skills and competencies moreover are generative; they enable us to contend with novel situations in novel ways. So their successful operation depends upon how well one *represents* these worlds and *anticipates* their possibilities and the potential effects of one's actions in them. Beliefs and internal models are, in effect, mental stand-ins for reality itself; by *re*-presenting facts within the mental economy, they permit these facts to enter into the processes of perception, thought, and the guidance of action.

As representational structures, beliefs and internal models are said to have a "mind-to-world" direction of fit: a representation that *p* is true just in case *p*. Moreover, the direction of "fit" relation is asymmetric—it is a matter of the mind fitting *to* the facts: a representation that *p* is true *because p*. This is a structural rather than a causal "because." For example, while it might matter for epistemic warrant whether the fact that my basement is leaking played a role in my belief that it is, if *in fact* my basement is leaking, then this belief would "fit" reality even if it came about from sheer guesswork.

But what, then, about learning what we really want, or learning what *to* want? Suppose I desire that *p*, but *p* is not the case: I'm thirsty and want water to drink but have none. Though the desire's representational content (*that PR be drinking water*) doesn't "fit" reality, we don't say that my desire is therefore *false*. Neither does this failure of "fit" make the desire seem to be defective. On the contrary, it would appear that wanting water when one is parched from lack of it is, other things equal, a paradigm case of desire doing what it is built to do: desire that *p* doesn't tell you that *p is* the case; rather, it motivates you to *make p* the case. Grant that. Now suppose that the desire has done its job, and I have brought it about that I am drinking the water I sought. Is the desire therefore now *true*? That's not how we speak, certainly. Yet if desires cannot be spoken of as true or false, then they would seem to lack the wherewithal to participate in learning—there appears to be no relevant *fact* to acquire.

On the orthodox view, desire contrasts with belief in just this way. Desire is said to have a "world-to-mind" direction of fit: to desire that *p* is not to represent *p* as true but as *to be made true.* That would explain why desires are not said to be true or false: desire that *p* might be said to have *p* as its target, but it is a conative rather than cognitive attitude toward that target. If I believe that I will succeed in threading this needle, and this belief encourages me to stick to the task until I do in fact succeed, then my belief will be revealed as true, but its motivational role is thought to be inessential to the belief. In desire things are reversed: the motivational role is essential rather than incidental, but successful motivation does not reveal the desire to be true. Instead, we say that the desire has been *satisfied*—the target is achieved, and the state of the world now fits the representational content of the desire. Far from being cemented in place as a lasting bit of learning, like my belief that I have threaded the needle, my desire is more likely simply to fade away, having completed its mission.

Perhaps, however, this is the wrong way to look at what learning in desire might consist in. Consider a law graduate who had secured her dream job of working for a leading private law firm in New York. Smart and unstinting in her commitment to success, she manages to reach the rank of partner well ahead of schedule. Her long-standing desire satisfied, she finds that *she* nonetheless isn't: "I finally made partner, but I've learned that this isn't the life I want after all."

Defenders of orthodoxy can, however, respond to such cases by saying that all the learning involved actually takes place in the individual's beliefs, not her desires. At the beginning of her career in law, she had certain beliefs about what the life of a partner in a top-flight law firm would be like, but her experience gradually changed these beliefs, so that now she no longer sees having such a career as a way of attaining her goal of leading a satisfying life. She isn't wrong in thinking that she's had a learning experience or that she has in some sense learned what to want, but the desire in question is an instrumental rather than intrinsic one—and it depended upon a false belief about what being a partner would be like. So her learning is factual or representational after all—cognitive, not conative.

Hume is seen as the inspiration for this way of translating such cases of apparent learning in desire into cases of real learning in belief. In the *Treatise* (1888),[1] for example, he places desire among the "passions" and writes, "A passion is an original existence, or, if you will, modification of existence, and contains not any representative quality." Desires, fears, hopes, joys, and the like are states of "affection" and bodily arousal, not "copies" of some matter of fact. They thus are not in a "strict and philosophic" sense capable of truth or falsity (II.ii.3).

> When I am angry, I am actually possest with the passion, and in that emotion have no more a reference to any other object, than when I am thirsty, or sick, or more than five foot high. It is impossible, therefore, that this passion can be opposed by, or be contradictory to truth ... since this contradiction consists in the disagreement of ideas, considered as copies, with those objects, which they represent. (II.iii.3)

Hume then, famously, draws an immediate lesson with respect to the power of "reason." "Reason," he argues, "is the discovery of truth and falshood" (III.i.1), and while we sometimes speak of a passion as irrational or unreasonable, still, "nothing can be contrary to truth or reason, except what has a reference to it, and as the judgments of our understanding only have this reference, it must follow, that passions can be contrary to reason only so far as they are *accompany'd* with some judgment or opinion" (II.iii.3). He explains:

> According to this principle, which is so obvious and natural, 'tis only in two senses, that any affection can be call'd unreasonable. First, When a passion, such as hope or fear, grief or joy, despair or security, is founded on the supposition of the existence of objects, which really do not exist. Secondly, When in exerting any passion in action, we chuse means insufficient for the design'd end, and deceive ourselves in our judgment of causes and effects. (II.iii.3)

Our lawyer, it would seem, has chosen "means insufficient for [her] design'd end" of living a satisfying life. Strictly speaking, the fault lies with her "judgment of causes and effects" rather than her desires or aims as such.

This contrast between belief and desire has powerful intuitive force. Moreover, it seems to fit well with contemporary rational decision theory, which divides the basic components of intentional action into two fundamental categories, *credences* and *preferences*, taken to be fundamentally different in kind (cf. Lewis 1988, 1996). Credences (belief-like degrees of confidence) are thought to be subject to principles of rationality in acquisition and revision (learning), while basic or intrinsic preferences (desire-like dispositions to choose) are treated as exogenously given and subject only to weak constraints of coherence (not learning). As a result, an individual's credences or changes in credence in response to experience can be deemed more or less rational, while his intrinsic preferences and changes in intrinsic preference, so long as the resulting set of preferences is coherent, escape all rational assessment. Indeed, according to some influential views, intrinsic preferences—e.g., for various rewarding qualities of experience or for the satisfaction of needs for enjoyment, security, affiliation, accomplishment, and self-esteem—are non-rational elements of our native human endowment and remain essentially the same throughout life (see Bradley 2007). On this view, what changes with experience and maturation are merely situational or instrumental preferences, as mediated by revised credences. Such instrumental preferences can be evaluated for a kind of means-end or hypothetical rationality but not for categorical rationality or rationality *tout court*.[2]

In what follows, I will be raising questions about both sides of this orthodox view of the belief-desire, or credence-preference, contrast. In place of that contrast I will argue for a more unified account of these two broad classes of mental states—an account that, I believe, fits better with contemporary psychology and neuroscience. This unified account enables us to see how *bona fide* learning can take place in desire and belief alike, and indeed to see how both states have an *inherent* tendency to learn from experience, based upon similar underlying dynamics. And I will be defending this unified account with the help of a surprising ally: David Hume.

## Hume on Belief

So let's begin with Hume and consider the key passages of the *Treatise* that are the basis for what has come to be known as the "Humean" distinction between cognitive, representational, truth-evaluable belief and conative, non-representational, non-truth-evaluable desire. The passages that inspired this distinction, which is not confined to card-carrying Humeans, are well-known. Recall that Hume writes:

> When I am angry, I am actually possest with the passion, and in that emotion have no more a reference to any other object, than when I am thirsty, or sick, or more than five foot high. It is impossible, therefore, that this passion can be opposed by, or be contradictory to truth . . . since this contradiction

consists in the disagreement of ideas, considered as copies, with those objects, which they represent.

> ... As nothing can be contrary to truth or reason, except what has a reference to it, and as the judgments of our understanding only have this reference, it must follow, that passions can be contrary to reason only so far as they are *accompany'd* with some judgment or opinion. (II.iii.3)

Reading these lines, one would naturally conclude that Hume is contrasting *passions*, a class of mental states in which he includes desire, anger, and approval, with *beliefs*—cognitions or "judgments or opinions." What could be more obvious?

And yet Hume has earlier formulated an important conclusion in Book I: "Belief is more properly an act of the sensitive, than of the cogitative part of our natures" (I.iv.1). And in the Appendix, where Hume attempts to explain some of the doctrines he expects to be most difficult for the reader to grasp, he gives pride of place to his view that "belief is nothing but a peculiar feeling, different from the simple conception." He formulates his final argument for this claim, which he expects readers to find surprising, by posing a dilemma: "What the nature is of ... belief ... few have had the curiosity to ask themselves. In my opinion, this dilemma is inevitable[:] Either the belief is some new idea, such as that of *reality* or *existence*, which we join to the simple conception of an object, or it is merely a peculiar *feeling* or *sentiment*" (Appendix). He dispatches the first horn in two moves: "*First*, We have no abstract idea of existence, distinguishable and separable from the idea of particular objects" (Appendix). As a modern might put it, to believe that *p* and to believe that *p* is true, or real, or extant, come to the same thing—there is no new idea which belief that *p* needs to *add* to *p*. Failure to understand this is failure to understand what it is to believe that *p*. He continues: "*Secondly*, The mind has the command over all its ideas, and can separate, unite, mix, and vary them as it pleases; so that if belief consisted merely in a new idea, annex'd to the conception, it wou'd be in a man's power to believe what he pleased" (Appendix). But we know that we cannot believe at will. While we are prone to many forms of wishful thinking and self-deception, these do not constitute a power to summon a belief into existence from scratch or in the face of the evidence. Contrast such mental states as imagining that *p* or supposing that *p*, in which we are free to "separate, unite, mix, and vary" ideas *ad libitum*, even in the face of overwhelming evidence against *p*.

What, then, *distinguishes* belief that *p* from idly thinking that *p*, or imagining that *p*, or merely supposing that *p*? It cannot be that belief has a mind-to-world direction of fit or is truth-evaluable, since idle thoughts, imaginings, and suppositions share both these features. The *object* or *content* of a belief may be a "copy," but that is true of these other states as well. Instead, it is the "peculiar manner of conceiving" its content that makes belief different from these other mental states, and gives it such a different role in our mental economy.[3]

As Hume argues in Book I:

> The idea of an object is an essential part of the belief of it, but not the whole. We conceive many things, which we do not believe. In order then to discover more fully the nature of belief . . . [I] maintain, that the belief of the existence joins no new ideas to those, which compose the idea of the object. When I think of God, when I think of him as existent, and when I believe him to be existent, my idea of him neither encreases nor diminishes. But as 'tis certain there is a great difference betwixt the simple conception of the existence of an object, and the belief of it, and as this difference lies not in the parts or composition of the idea, which we conceive; it follows, that it must lie in the *manner*, in which we conceive it. (I.iii.7)

But what could this "manner of conception" be, such that a belief that God exists could have such a different role from merely entertaining the thought of God as existent? The answer is that the belief must involve some *active* principle, some mental state that by its nature tends to influence how we think and act—to shape our will, even though we cannot shape *it* at will. For Hume, the answer is clear: such a state must be a "passion" or "sentiment" and not a mere "cogitation." He writes:

> [Belief] is something *felt* by the mind, which distinguishes the ideas of the judgment from the fictions of the imagination. It gives them more force and influence; makes them appear of greater importance; infixes them in the mind; and renders them the governing principles of all our actions. (Appendix)
>
> We may, therefore, conclude, that belief consists merely in a certain feeling or sentiment; in something, that depends not on the will, but must arise from certain determinate causes and principles, of which we are not masters. (Appendix)

In general, Hume uses "determinate causes and principles" to differentiate among mental states. For belief, e.g., an invariant perceptual experience of heavy objects falling when released gives rise to an expectation or belief that they will continue to do so (hence to surprise if a seemingly unsupported heavy object fails to fall). Similarly, an impression of contrariety among ideas *A* and *B* gives rise immediately to a mental resistance in response to a purported inference from *A* to *B*. By contrast, other mental states sharing belief's "mind-to-world" direction of fit, such as imagining or supposing, have different "determinate causes and principles"—e.g., we are free to *imagine* an unsupported heavy object that does not fall, and a dialectician can freely *suppose* for the sake of a *reductio* that *B* follows from *A*, despite her vivid sense of their contrariety.

Hume admits that it is difficult to explain in other terms the nature of the "peculiar sentiment" of belief, but he thinks we can characterize its distinctive functional role. For example, belief that *p* is *projective*: it involves, or yields, an *expectation* that *p* will continue to be the case. This projection, while caused by patterns in experience, is no mere logical consequence of them, so pure "cogitation" cannot produce it. Moreover, belief induces *reliance* in thought and action: when we believe that *p*, we think and plan and act as if *p*. As Robert Stalnaker (1984: 15) puts it, "To believe that *p* is to be disposed to act in ways that would tend to satisfy one's desires, whatever they are, in a world in which *p* (together with one's other beliefs) were true." Though belief that *p* yields expectation that *p* and reliance upon *p*, these are not *ideas* added to the content that *p*—which remains, simply, that *p*. And while belief that *p* is a *feeling*, it is unlike aroused, episodic emotional states such as fear, anger, or surprise that *p*, which signal something awry. Belief is rather an unaroused state of assurance that persists unobtrusively in the background (Pettit and Smith 1990), with little by way of distinctive phenomenology. Hume therefore speaks of belief that *p* as a "firm," "steady," or "strong" conception of *p* that places *p* itself in the foreground, akin to the way a perceptual impression that *p* places *p* in the foreground:

> The act of the mind [in belief] exceeds not a simple conception; and the only remarkable difference, which occurs on this occasion, is, when we join belief to the conception, and are perswaded of the truth of what we conceive. This act of the mind has never yet been explain'd by any philosopher; and therefore I am at liberty to propose my hypothesis concerning it; which is, that 'tis only a strong and steady conception of any idea, and such as approaches in some measure to an immediate impression. (I, n20)

Just as a strong and lively "immediate impression" carries with it a "sense" of the truth of what we perceive, so does belief that *p* carry with it a "sense" of *p*'s reality. And this "perswasion" then imparts to *p* a role in the guidance of thought and action like the role of a perception that *p*.

This way of talking, moreover, draws our attention to another important feature of belief and the way in which, in belief, "the idea of an object is an essential part of the belief of it, but not the whole" (I.iii.7). For just as impressions can be *more or less* strong and lively, with concomitant variation in how much "perswasion" they yield, so can beliefs be *more or less* strong, lively, firm, or steady, with concomitant variation in the manner in which they shape thought and action. A weak sensory impression on a foggy night as of a moving, roughly skunk-like animal on the sidewalk ahead will make me cautious and walk to the other side of the street, but I won't be much surprised if the animal, passing under a light, is revealed to be an opossum. Similarly, occasional irregularities in the behavior of my watch when I'm in a tropical country will undermine the strong, immediate reliance upon its readings I exhibit in more temperate climes, and so I will tend, as I would not elsewhere, to seek some confirmation of my watch's readings when I must make an important rendezvous.

How, then, does belief differ from sensation, since Hume admits that not all strong and lively impressions are believed (I.iii.13)? It should be clear that, while an uncertain sensory impression as of a skunk has a vague and shadowy *content*, an uncertain belief that it is twelve o'clock, after consulting my somewhat unreliable watch, has a perfectly definite *content*, namely, "It is twelve o'clock." My "weak" or "unsteady" manner of conception of this content does not translate into the content itself, which does not admit of degrees in this way and is, simply, either true or false, not "weakly" or "unsteadily" true. A lack of firm evidence yields a lack of firm belief, and this shows itself in the "active principle" of the belief, so I will proceed more cautiously. By way of contrast, my lack of firm evidence that my watch is reliable is no barrier to my *imagining* that I have instead a perfectly accurate watch.

Here, then, is an interesting fact about belief that distinguishes it from imagining or supposing: it will tend by its nature to wax or wane in strength in proportion to the waxing or waning of my evidence. In the present context, we might put this by saying that belief has an *inherent learning dynamic*.

What might be a psychological model of belief that would fit Hume's sentimentalist account and exhibit this form of spontaneous learning from experience? Here is a proposal:

**(Bel *p*)** A belief that *p* is a compound state consisting in (1) a degree of confidence or trust in a representation, *p*, that (2) gives rise to and regulates a degree of expectation that things are or will be as *p* portrays them, and (3) this degree of confidence or trust is disposed to strengthen or weaken in response to the extent to which this expectation that *p* is met or violated in subsequent experience.

Do we have any reason to take seriously such a model of the psychology of belief? We will return to that question, but first we must look more closely at what becomes of Hume's alleged contrast between belief and desire once we recognize belief as a passion or sentiment.

## Hume on Desire

Here is how Hume describes the acquisition of desires or desire-like states:

> An impression first strikes upon the senses, and makes us perceive heat or cold, thirst or hunger, pleasure or pain of some kind or other. Of this impression there is a copy taken by the mind, which remains after the impression ceases; and this we call an idea. This idea of pleasure or pain, when it returns upon the soul, produces the new impressions of desire and aversion, hope and fear, which may properly be called impressions of reflexion, because derived from it. (I.i.2)

The distinctive "manner of conception" of *p* that constitutes desire that *p*, in contrast to belief that *p*, *does* add something to "simple conception" that *p*. Not additional *content* as such—for desire that *p* and aversion to *p* share the same content. Rather, desire that *p* is an "impression" of *p* of a special kind—a *favorable* impression, arising from the prospect of potential pleasure, satisfaction, relief of pain, or other benefit from the realization of *p*. Desire, to that extent, presents *p* in a positive light. Aversion, by contrast, is an *unfavorable* impression of what it would be to bring about or sustain *p*, arising from the prospect of displeasure, pain, or other loss from the realization of *p*; it presents *p* in a negative light.

As in belief, the distinctive "feeling to the mind" or "manner of conception" of desire or aversion is more than a passive registration of *p*; instead it is a psychically "active principle" that has a direct influence on how we are disposed to act with respect to *p*: "It is obvious, that when we have the prospect of pain or pleasure from any object, we feel a consequent emotion of aversion or propensity, and are carried to avoid or embrace what will give us this uneasiness or satisfaction" (II.iii.3). And there is more to this active principle than mere attraction or repulsion: it shapes how we are disposed to think, priming practical reasoning to identify and initiate actions that would bring about or avoid *p*. Continuing the passage just quoted: "It is also obvious that this emotion rests not here, but making us cast our view on every side, comprehends whatever objects are connected with its original one by the relation of cause and effect. Here then reasoning takes place to discover this relation; and accordingly as our reasoning varies, our actions receive a subsequent variation" (II.iii.3). Desire and aversion, then, spontaneously tend to motivate not only pursuit or avoidance of their objects but also of what we can see to be the means toward these objects: "these emotions extend themselves to the causes and effects of that object, as they are pointed out to us by reason and experience" (II.iii.3). Metaphorically, we might say that these means to realizing or preventing *p* are themselves brought under the favorable light of desire or unfavorable light of aversion. More functionally, as Stalnaker (1984: 15) puts it, "To desire that *p* is to be disposed to act in ways that would tend to bring it about that *p* in a world in which one's beliefs, whatever they are, were true." Although desire that *p* adds something to the "simple conception" that *p*, we should be clear, as we were in the case of belief, that this is not the *conjoining* of the idea that *p* with some other idea, say, *goodness* or *desirability*. Hume's argument regarding belief can be redeployed. "The imagination has the command over all its ideas, and can join, and mix, and vary them in all ways possible" (Appendix). In supposition or imagination, we are entirely free to conjoin to the idea of goodness or desirability the idea that *p*, but we can no more desire at will than we can believe at will. Mere "cogitation" can produce the conjunction of the idea of *p* and the idea of goodness, but such a bare supposition does not yield a genuine *expectation* of benefit from *p*, and thus has no inherent tendency to prime thought or action aimed at realizing *p*.

Someone who desires that *p* has a favorable *prospect* for *p*, and this is reflected in the amount of time or effort she'll invest in trying to bring about or sustain *p*. She will be to some extent surprised and disappointed if *p* turns out to be worse than expected, failing to yield the pleasure or other benefits it promised. This, in turn, will tend to weaken her desire that *p* going forward. In this way, even powerful, long-standing desires, such as our lawyer's desire to make partner, tend to be undermined by persistent disappointment and dissatisfaction with what it is actually like to bring about their objects (although of course it can be difficult for individuals to identify the source of their disappointment or dissatisfaction). By contrast, someone averse to *p* has a negative expectation from *p* and will try to avoid or prevent it, and will be surprised but *not* disappointed if *p* turns out to be better than expected. Such an experience of favorable incongruity between expectation and experience will tend over time to lessen the aversion and perhaps even turn aversion into desire.

In supporting *feed-forward* action-guidance through expectation and reliance, and in supporting thereby a process of *feedback* from experience by assessing discrepancy with expectation, desire exhibits an *inherent learning dynamic*. The structure of this dynamic is essentially similar to belief: a sentiment toward *p* underwrites an expectation with respect to *p* that is compared with actual outcomes, and, when discrepancy is detected, the sentiment strengthens or weakens to reduce this discrepancy.

But if this is learning, what are the facts learned? Certainly one fact is that discussed earlier: one will tend to change one's beliefs about certain *means-end* relationships. Is that the whole of it? Hume wrote:

> Since a passion can never, in any sense, be call'd unreasonable, but when founded on a false supposition, or when it chuses means insufficient for the design'd end, 'tis impossible, that reason and passion can ever oppose each other, or dispute for the government of the will and actions. The moment we perceive the falshood of any supposition, or the insufficiency of any means our passions yield to our reason without any opposition. I may desire any fruit as of an excellent relish; but whenever you convince me of my mistake, my longing ceases. I may will the performance of certain actions as means of obtaining any desir'd good; but as my willing of these actions is only secondary, and founded on the supposition, that they are causes of the propos'd effect; as soon as I discover the falshood of that supposition, they must become indifferent to me. (II.iii.3)

This passage is often cited to justify the claim that Hume was an *instrumentalist* about value and thought that the only sort of learning possible in desire and valuation is means-end learning that takes place entirely within the realm of belief. But it is crucial to note that his emphasis here is on changes in the *will* and that his reference to "means" is to the *actions*, not to means-end beliefs about these actions. The focus of his discussion is the "government of the will and actions," not simply the regulation of belief.

We can see that Hume distinguished between changing beliefs and changing desires by looking at his discussions of ways in which desire can go astray. Astray from what? Astray from the actual *values*—and not merely their *instrumental* values. Thus he writes, "There is no quality in human nature, which causes more fatal errors in our conduct, than that which leads us to prefer whatever is present to the distant and remote, and makes us desire objects more according to their situation than their intrinsic value" (III.iii.7). Notice that here he is talking of what we *prefer* or *desire*, not what we *believe* to be preferable or desirable, and of "fatal errors in our conduct," not simply of mistaken beliefs. Indeed, he recognizes that it is one thing to come to believe that something is good or worthy, and another thing to desire or value it in accord with its goodness or worthiness. Proper "government of the will and actions"—proper *regulation* of our conduct in accord with intrinsic value—requires that our various "passions" or "affections," and not only those sentiments that constitute our beliefs, be proportional to the values at stake. Thus *mistakes* in governance are possible through disproportionate affection:

> It has been observ'd, in treating of the passions, that men are mightily govern'd by the imagination, and proportion their affections more to the light, under which any object appears to them, than to its real and intrinsic value. What strikes upon them with a strong and lively idea commonly prevails above what lies in a more obscure light; and it must be a great superiority of value, that is able to compensate this advantage. (III.ii.7)

Hume analyzes ways in which one's "affections" can fail to correspond to actual values, distinguishing these affective states and their "errors" from one's beliefs about value. For example, in the case of *proximity*:

> Now as every thing, that is contiguous to us, either in space or time, strikes upon us with such an idea, it has a proportional effect on the will and passions, and commonly operates with more force than any object, that lies in a more distant and obscure light. *Tho' we may be fully convinc'd, that the latter object excels the former,* we are not able to regulate our actions by this judgment; but yield to the sollicitations of our passions, which always plead in favour of whatever is near and contiguous. (III.ii.7, emphasis added)

A second source of disproportion between our "affections" and actual values is the effect of *adaptation*:

> 'Tis a quality observable in human nature, and which we shall endeavour to explain afterwards, that every thing, which is often presented, and to which we have been long accustom'd, loses its value in our eyes, and is in a little time despis'd and neglected. We likewise judge of objects more from comparison than from their real and intrinsic merit; and where we cannot by some contrast enhance their value, we are apt to overlook even what is

> essentially good in them . . . [even] tho' [they are] perhaps of a more excellent kind, than those on which, for their singularity, we set a much higher value. (II.i.6)

If Hume is to be believed, then, there is a space for learning and correction in desire and valuation that is not exhaustively explained by learning and correction in belief. Indeed, he seems especially concerned to point out that mistakes in desire and valuation are often the most serious sources of misfortune in human life, yielding preferences that are not corrected merely by knowledge of one's instrumental interests. Immediately after his remarks about the greater imaginative force of proximity, quoted above, he writes:

> This is the reason why men so often act in contradiction to their *known* interest; and in particular why they *prefer* any trivial advantage, that is present, to the maintenance of order in society, which so much depends on the observance of justice. The consequences of every breach of equity seem to lie very remote, and are not able to counter-ballance any immediate advantage, that may be reap'd from it. They are, however, never the less real for being remote. (III.ii.7, emphasis added)

Still, it is possible to learn from experience concerning such less salient values via the operation of *sympathy* for others (or for future selves): "We partake of their uneasiness by *sympathy*," and this in turn makes us uneasy with proceeding, and increases resistance to the allure of the immediate (III.ii.2). Hume writes that "sympathy is a very powerful principle in human nature" (III.iii.6), and not just in morality. It plays a central role in the processes by which, through experience, our preferences receive feedback that can bring them into accord with real, rather than apparent, value, a process that makes it appropriate to speak of *learning* in desire in a way that is not reducible to learning in belief.

What, then, might be a plausible psychological model of desire that would fit Hume's sentimentalist account and exhibit these forms of spontaneous learning from experience? Here is a proposal:

**(Des *p*)** A desire that *p* is a compound state consisting in (1) a degree of positive affect or favoring toward a representation, *p*, that (2) gives rise to and regulates a degree of expectation that *p* will be satisfying or beneficial and a corresponding degree of motivation to bring about or sustain *p*, and (3) this degree of positive affect or favoring is in turn disposed to strengthen or weaken in response to the extent to which this expectation that *p* is met, exceeded, or disappointed in subsequent experience.

Both belief and desire, on the *sentimentalist* account, thus are compound states that are instances of the form:

**(Sent *p*)** A compound mental state in which (1) a degree of sentiment toward a representation, *p*, that (2) gives rise to and regulates a degree of action-guiding and potentially motivating expectation with respect to *p*, and (3) this degree of sentiment is in turn disposed to be modulated by whether, and to what extent or in what direction, this expectation with respect to *p* is met or violated.

(Sent *p*) is a generic model of sentiments that take a propositional object. A given proposition, *p*, can be common to many sentiments at once. One can be confident of, attracted to, and intrinsically value the same state of affairs. Or one can be attracted to, but fearful and prospectively guilty about, taking an action that appears to be in violation of established norms. Sentiments respond to different dimensions of appraisal and enter collectively into the determination of action. Indeed, it is an important advantage of the sentimentalist account of belief and desire that it permits these states *as well as other sentiments operating at the same time* (such as fear, hope, valuing, prospective guilt, etc.) to function in an integrated way, contributing via a common affective system to directing or redirecting, strengthening or weakening, dispositions to think and act.

(Sent *p*) is also meant to capture the way *learning* takes place across the wide spectrum of sentiments; one might be born with various dispositions to trust, fear, like, take interest in, feel sad, etc., but it is only through the course of experience that one becomes skilled at discerning whom to trust, what to fear, what to like, what to regret, what's worth time or energy, and so on. It thus is vital to the effective operation of the sentiments as sources of appraisal, expectation, and action guidance, from the very outset of life on through the most complex circumstances of adulthood, that they have an *inherent* tendency to learn from experience by *priming* us with expectations which then turn action into *experimentation.*

Among sentiments, belief and desire have a distinctive, central role. (Bel *p*) and (Des *p*) are *paired* or *complementary* sentimental states—each contributes an indispensable element to action guidance, and each can operate in its characteristic way only thanks to the contribution of the other. Taken together, they furnish the *minimal* requisites for the guidance of thought and action—the degrees of credence and strengths of preference of classical decision theory. And, working together, they provide a system for feed-forward/feedback control of action, updated by discrepancy-based learning—a combination that now figures pervasively in the design of intelligent systems, since it can be shown formally that systems with this design will tend with increasing experience to *attune* themselves adaptively to meet their goals in a complex environment.[4]

## Affect

This is all fine, and even suggests a "how possibly" story about why intelligent creatures with states like (Bel *p*) and (Des *p*) might have evolved and been successful. But do we have any evidence that (Bel *p*) and (Des *p*) do in fact correspond to the actual psychological states we call beliefs and desires? The answer to this question lies in an understanding of the nature and function of the *affective system.*

Affect is the closest correlate in contemporary psychology to Hume's generic category of "passions and sentiments." Like Hume's category, affect includes transient and persistent states (e.g., episodic emotions and long-term moods), states of arousal and states of calm (e.g., anger and confidence), and on-line as well as off-line responses (conscious feelings and implicit or simulated affect). The affective *system* incorporates regions of the brain previously called the *limbic* and *reward systems* (the amygdala, hippocampus, nucleus accumbens, striatum, insula, hypothalamus, etc.), as well as several areas of the *prefrontal cortex*. This system is highly interconnected and has extensive projections to other areas of the brain. It functions continuously in perception, attention, memory, cognition, decision making, motivation, and action-control and -monitoring. Elements of the affective system enter early into perceptual processing and appear to help sort incoming information for relevance and urgency and to encode that information with positive and negative valence and weight.

The emerging explanation for the coordinated operation of the affective system, and its pivotal role in perception, thought, and action, is that affect is the brain's principal currency for *value*. The affective system is thus an *appraisal* system (Ellsworth and Scherer 2003), keeping track not only of patterns of reward and punishment and relevance to physiological and social needs or goal attainment, but also of degrees of confidence or uncertainty (Preuschoff, Bossaerts, and Quartz 2006; Singer,

Critchley, and Preuschoff 2009). That is why, although it might at first seem strange, Hume's view that belief is a sentiment makes good psychological sense: belief is a non-voluntary, conscious or unconscious attitude, not a judgment, which varies in degree of confidence, with corresponding variation in the effects it has on the guidance of perception, thought, and action. This is precisely the profile and role of affective states (for further discussion, see Railton 2014). Indeed, it has come to be thought that the chief function of the affective system is to *inform* and *regulate* in ways relevant to the well-being or success of the individual organism or group (Schwarz and Clore 1983, 2003; Nesse and Ellsworth 2009). From the perspective of cognitive and affective neuroscience, the traditional distinction between cognition and emotion has increasingly come to seem untenable (Pessoa 2008). For example, a critical dimension of epistemic appraisal is learning what or whom to trust and rely upon and to what degree. And it is via a dynamic interaction between perception and the appraisals sustained in the affective system, and then between the affective system and cortical regions, that the brain appears to keep track of past experience of successful or unsuccessful expectation and reliance and to project expectations that guide reliance in the future (Vuilleumier 2005; Bhatt et al. 2012).

The place of the affective system in the architecture of the mind reflects this dual function. The affective system is situated very early in the perceptual stream, coming online prior to conscious experience and interactively shaping subsequent mental processing. It appears from neuroscientific and behavioral studies to afford the primary substrate for error- or discrepancy-based learning (Schultz 2010), to play an essential role in the formation of episodic memories (Gilboa et al. 2004), and to play a wide role in the regulation of cognition and action—orienting attention and focus, priming memory and inference, supporting simulation of possible actions and outcomes, and shifting dispositions to act (Storbeck and Clore 2007, Quartz 2007). This makes affect the natural locus for an attitude with the functional "job description" of belief and fits it for the purpose of feed-forward/feedback guidance of thought and action.

Our impression that belief involves no affect, and that the affective system has only an accidental and often disruptive role in cognition, is due largely to the difference in salience between aroused episodic emotions, like anger, as opposed to calm, persistent affective states like assurance or trust (for example, the default confidence we have in our own senses or memories). It often is only with the *loss* of assurance or trust that the affective character of belief becomes visible. In the closing pages of Book I of the *Treatise*, Hume describes just such loss of assurance and trust in his faculties and situation, brought on by solitary, single-minded focus on the arguments of the skeptic:

> The *intense* view of these manifold contradictions and imperfections in human reason has so wrought upon me, and heated my brain, that I am ready to reject all belief and reasoning, and can look upon no opinion even as more probable or likely than another. Where am I, or what? From what causes do I derive my existence, and to what condition shall I return? Whose favour shall I court, and whose anger must I dread? What beings surround me? and on whom have I any influence, or who have any influence on me? (I.iv.7)

As someone prone to depression, Hume knew only too well how, if the usual support of assurance or trust in one's faculties, abilities, and relationships fails, one falls prey to such self-defeating thoughts: "I am confounded with all these questions, and begin to fancy myself in the most deplorable condition imaginable, inviron'd with the deepest darkness, and utterly depriv'd of the use of every member and faculty" (I.iv.7).

At this point, one can expect no help from reason—for how could one restore confidence in one's reasoning *by* reasoning in which one has no confidence? Hume instead turns to the capacity of the affective system to restore belief, once one quits the philosophical "closet" and its obsessions and brings ordinary experience back into play by engaging with the natural and social world: "Most fortunately it happens, that since reason is incapable of dispelling these clouds, nature herself suffices to that purpose, and cures me of this philosophical melancholy and delirium either by relaxing this bent of mind, or by some avocation, and lively impression of my senses, which obliterate all these chimeras" (I.iv.7). In responding this way to experience, affect does more than soothe the over-heated mind; it re-anchors the mind in reality, enabling it to be responsive once again to the *evidence* of the senses and memory, to return to "reasonableness" in its response to skeptical arguments:

> . . . must [I] torture my brain with subtilities and sophistries, at the very time that I cannot satisfy myself concerning the reasonableness of so painful an application, nor have any tolerable prospect of arriving by its means at truth and certainty. Under what obligation do I lie of making such an abuse of time? . . . Where I strive against my inclination, I shall have a good reason for my resistance; and will no more be led a wandering into such dreary solitudes, and rough passages, as I have hitherto met with. (I.iv.7)

## Desire and Direction of Fit

Let us return to the question of learning in desire and, in particular, how the sentimentalist account, (Des *p*), enables us to make sense of this idea. (Des *p*) is patterned on Hume's remarks about the nature of desire. It involves two primary elements: a *positive affective attitude* toward the content of the desire, *p*, and a *motivating expectation* directed toward actions that would tend to bring about or sustain the state of affairs, *p*. Following Hume, this affective attitude is not understood as a new idea, such as the idea of goodness, annexed to the idea that *p*. Rather, the attitude *presents p* "in a certain light," a positive light in which *p* is associated with a favorable *prospect* of some kind. It is this favorable prospect that gives rise to and regulates the strength of the motivating expectation directed toward bringing about or sustaining *p*. And it is this favorable light that is subject to *learning* depending upon whether the favorable prospect of *p* is borne out.

It might be objected that this picture of desire contravenes the widely accepted view that desire has world-to-mind direction of fit. Direction of fit is thought to be univocal—a state of mind with world-to-mind direction of fit cannot also have mind-to-world direction of fit. But in the sentimentalist account, the "favorable light" in which desire that *p* presents *p* seems to have mind-to-world direction of fit; as we have seen, it can be out of proportion to the actual value of *p*, as Hume emphasized, and as a result lead to "fatal errors in conduct."

But does the actual operation of desire involve genuine mind-to-world direction of fit? Consider for example hunger, as it is typically conceived.[5] After a period without food, it is thought, an animal enters a deficit state, signaled by various physiological markers, including a form of discomfort we call hunger. When these markers are present, the animal's dispositions are re-oriented in a coordinated way: foodstuffs attract more attention, mobilize active approach, and, when proximate, trigger consumption behavior. Hunger typically involves a distinctive phenomenology, part of which is a physical discomfort and part of which is an alteration in how the world appears to us; the sight and smell of food, for example, become more salient. One could call this distinctive phenomenology a "favorable light," but note that it is a *consequence* of hunger, not hunger itself—for hunger is a motivating bodily state that need have no propositional object. One isn't hungry *that* one needs food, or even hungry *that* one consume food—and if one's hunger is for whatever reason disproportionate to one's need of food, we do not say that it is *incorrect*. For, while hunger is a more or less reliable *indicator* of the need for food, it is an appetitive state, a *conation*, not a more or less reliable representation of any state of affairs. Call this the *drive model* of hunger.

If the drive model were the right model for all of desire, it would be difficult indeed to make a case for learning in desire that is parallel with learning in belief. However, philosophers and psychologists have long distinguished two kinds of motivational states. In Aristotle, for example, motivation (*orexis*) can be either appetitive drive (*epithumia*) or telic goal-pursuit (*boulesis*). In appetition, no intentional object need be present, and thus *epithumia* can be found even in animals who lack any ideational capacity (Aristotle 2000: 1113a20).[6] But in *boulesis* the representation of an action or goal is central, since it is this representation that affords the basis for means-end inference and practical deliberation. (A *boule*, for example, is a deliberative assembly of citizens.) Desire of this kind essentially requires an imagination (*phantasia*), since it must be capable of presenting to the mind a representation of an action or state of affairs that has never been perceived (since it occurs in the future[7]) and perhaps has never yet, and will never, exist.[8]

A defender of the univocality of the world-to-mind direction of fit of desire would be ill advised, however, to look to drives as a model. To apply the metaphor of world-to-mind direction of fit, something in the desiderative state must furnish a *mental template* or *goal* that can be compared with the state of the world and assessed for fit. But while we do speak of satisfying a hunger, this refers to a change of bodily state—drive reduction or satiety—not a way in which the world has come to fit a mental or representational state. As the behaviorists emphasized, the drive model permitted experimentalists to talk of motivation *without* what they saw as the "pernicious mentalism" of positing intentional content or goals (Lashley 1929).

Perhaps, if hunger makes available no representation of eating as a state-to-be-realized, we could call the reduction of the bodily deficit, and thus of the drive itself, the goal of the appetitive state? Even supposing that we could set aside the conceptual difficulties of this position, it encounters serious empirical problems—problems that have led motivation theory over the past half-century away from the drive-reduction approach to reward, even in the case of appetitive states such as hunger. The neuroscientist Kent Berridge (2004: 191) writes:

> Many drive theories of motivation between 1930 and 1970 posited that drive reduction is the chief mechanism of reward. If motivation is due to drive, then, the reduction of deficit signals should satisfy this drive and essentially

> could be [the] goal of the entire motivation. Thus, food could be a reward because it reduces hunger drive, water is a reward when thirsty because it reduces thirst drive, and so on. The drive reduction concept of reward is so intuitive that it was thought to be self-evident for decades. The power of this idea is so great that some behavioral neuroscientists today still talk and write as though they believe it. All the more pity, perhaps, that the idea turns out not to be true. Drive reduction is not really a chief mechanism of reward.

For example, dogs whose stomachs were kept full by a feeding tube nonetheless retained a strong desire to eat when food was presented. What was the goal of this eating if there was no food deficit and hence no deficit-reduction drive? The answer given by contemporary affective neuroscience is that the dog has a favorable representation of eating; its affective system encodes a positive value for eating, and this then elicits a motivation to eat.

In Berridge's account, for example, two fundamental components of motivation are distinguished: *liking* and *wanting*. *Liking* is an affective state, a *positive hedonic gloss* for a represented action or state, while *wanting* is a motive state, an *incentive salience* directed toward performing an action or bringing about an outcome. In normal motivation, these two states are coupled—the dog *likes* eating, and this induces it to *want* to eat, even in the absence of food deficit (Berridge 2009).

But are these two elements of desire, the favorable affective representation and the motivated striving, genuinely distinct? Since they are normally coupled in the manner just suggested, we must look to cases of *dysfunction* in desire to see how they can come apart. In addiction, for example, individuals can continue to experience powerful craving for a drug even when they no longer experience any euphoria from it and thus lack a positive affective representation of drug taking (Robinson and Berridge 2000). And in "weakness of will," even a powerful positive representation of an action or goal can fail to elicit motivated striving of comparable force.

Thus we arrive at an empirical basis for a compound picture of desire in which an affective, evaluative component regulates a conative, action-guiding component—essentially, the structure of the Humean view as formulated by (Des *p*). Moreover, because the affective component of (Des *p*) *is* evaluative, it can be subject to the Humean mechanisms described above for learning proportionality to actual value; that is, it can have mind-to-world direction of fit. At the same time, because this evaluative component has a representational content (e.g., a favorable representation *of eating*) and regulates motivational effort toward realizing that content (e.g., toward *eating*), the state also has a world-to-mind direction of fit.

The worry that no mental state could have both directions of fit is dispelled by seeing that desire, like belief (Bel *p*), and like sentiment generally (Sent *p*), is a *compound* state.[9] Desire thus has two ways of going awry. We have already seen one, the wresting of motivation away from regulation by evaluation, as found in addiction and weakness of will. What is the second? We have seen that, too: in Hume's accounts of the ways in which strength of preference can fail to be proportional to actual value.

## Novel Belief and Novel Desire

It is a feature of this compound picture that we can acquire new motivations by making new appraisals, whether this is the favorable appraisal of desire or affection, or the unfavorable appraisal of aversion or fear. Creatures are not bound to a set of basic drives or goals (plus instrumental motives directed at fulfilling these) but are capable of adapting their motivation to whatever they can see in a sufficiently favorable light. The mechanism here is essentially parallel to belief. Creatures are not bound to a set of basic beliefs either, but rather can acquire new beliefs whenever circumstances or persons present compelling evidence for something not currently believed.

This is a good thing, since we know that adults have desires, including intrinsic desires, that they did not have as tiny infants. This process can qualify as a form of learning when, as in the parallel case of belief, the change is the result of responsiveness to relevant evidence, and the new valuations thus acquired correspond to genuine values.

However, this same capacity for novelty is also a vulnerability of our beliefs and desires, since there are many ways in which a convincing but deceptive *appearance* can be created of facts and values. This is not lost on advertisers or propagandists, who typically attempt to manipulate belief and desire together in order to change behavior in ways that serve their purposes (Railton 2012). Doing this successfully often requires planting in the target audience's mind a sufficiently convincing and favorable (or disfavorable) image, even in the absence of actual experience or need. Think of the ubiquitous ads featuring lovingly photographed watches in the presence of attractive, confident people, with a text exuding the authority and status of a *grande marque*. Such images are calculated to make readily available in the mind of the viewer a confident, favorable "manner of conceiving" the idea of owning and wearing such a watch, regardless of the viewer's actual need state or sense of how the world actually works. Or think of the way that ugly, hate-inducing propagandistic imagery can incite one social, religious, or ethnic group to turn upon another with horrible violence, even though the groups had lived together for years in peace and have ample evidence of the falsity of the stereotypes presented.

The *generative* character of belief and desire are fundamental to humankind's capacity to adapt to the most varied environments or undertake the most dramatic individual or social changes in knowledge, culture, or ways of living. The results are not always happy. Fortunately, however, the learning dynamic inherent in (Bel *p*) and (Des *p*) makes it clear why producing a mere appearance of trustworthiness or desirability does not always suffice to sustain belief and desire in the long run. If, by acting on a compelling but false image, or a seductive but misleading evaluative appearance, we experience outcomes that violate the expectations created by this "affective forecast" (Wilson and Gilbert 2005), we have a chance to rescue ourselves from our own folly.

## The "Aim" of Desire?

If desire, like belief, supports an appearance/reality distinction and functions dynamically to reduce the gap between the two, should we say that desire "aims at the good"?

Desire indeed involves evaluative appraisal, but there are many kinds of value besides "the good"—not all the ways something might attract us, engage us, excite us, entice us, or hold promise for us are ways that it seems appropriate to describe as belonging to the "the good" or seeming to do so. Still less is it plausible to say that desire that *p* involves a *judgment* that *p* is good. Desire is a pervasive fact of life, consciously and unconsciously varying in response to experience and influencing not only what we do but what we attend to, perceive, think, and remember at all levels. It does all this in ways that do not depend upon the formation of judgments and that can be quite independent of what we judge to be the case, as Hume observed (III.ii.7).

Should we swing the other way, and say that desire does not attend to "the good," or even to goods—having as its essence simply to motivate the individual to make the world fit her preferred picture of things, whatever this might happen to be? (Des *p*) makes it clear why that is only half of it. A creature with mental states capable of motivating action, but that does not at the same time use feedback from the outcome of motivated action to inform subsequent motivation, would be a danger to itself and others. The more we recognize the pervasive, often unconscious role of desire in regulating our mental economy, the greater this danger can be seen to be.

Better to affirm both aspects of desire and say that desire is "built" for the conjoint task of *guiding action in light of values* and *learning values in light of outcomes*. These are "aims" in the evolutionary sense: the advantages of a functional integration of action-guidance with learning from action helps explain *why* desire is built the way it is, in much the same way that the advantages of a functional integration of action-guidance with learning from action helps explain why belief is built the way *it* is. Strikingly, neural activity in the affective and reward systems exhibit the characteristics of classical value functions—e.g., transitivity, cardinality, diminishing marginal returns, and risk sensitivity—and shape decision and motivation in ways characteristic of rational decision theory (Quartz 2007; Grabenhorst and Rolls 2011; Lak, Stauffer, and Schultz 2014; Stauffer, Lak, and Schultz 2014).

Of course, we have been considering here mostly simple cases, where desire that *p* has a content to which experience of "what *p* is really like" is directly relevant. This has made it easier to present a picture of how discrepancy-based learning is possible, since it is easy to see how actual experience could fail to live up to experiential expectations, even for intrinsic desires, such as those of the young lawyer considered earlier. Yet it is possible for learning to occur in the case of more abstract or impersonal desires—so long as the individual is capable of detecting, even indirectly, a discrepancy between an imagined possibility and the actual reality of bringing that possibility into existence (for discussion, see Railton 1986).

Recent research on the affective system has emphasized the diversity of the evaluative expectations the affective system appears to generate and spontaneously revise in the face of experience, representing not only parameters of immediate need but also prospective goal relevance and social value, including calibration to levels of risk and assessment of fairness or cooperativeness in second- and third-party transactions (Reynolds and Berridge 2008; Behrens, Hunt, and Rushworth 2009). It appears that the affective system supports the development of models of the social as well as physical environment and that these models serve to guide both physical movement and choice behavior (Bhatt et al. 2012; Lin, Adolphs, and Rangel 2012; Xiang, Lohrenz, and Montague 2013).

## Conclusion

We have not tried to make a case for the possibility of learning across the full range of desire; rather, our aim has been the more modest goal of establishing the possibility of such learning in core cases of desire and to relate this to larger questions about the intelligent guidance of thought and action.

Belief and desire, we have argued, are complementary states, each with a similar, compound architecture involving an affective component that tracks value, whether epistemic or practical, and an action-guiding component regulated by this valuation, such as the allocation of expectation by degree of confidence or allocation of effort by strength of preference. Together these states make possible spontaneous action that is regulated by *expected value* in a way that is evidence-sensitive and effective, that is, intelligent. Belief and desire moreover each has a *representational* component that gives shape to their forward function (action-guiding expectation and effort) and provides a standard for their inverse function (discrepancy-based feedback).

The worry, expressed at the outset, that learning is possible only in mental states with truth conditions, can now be seen as misplaced—even in the case of belief. For degrees of confidence are no more capable of truth or falsity than degrees of prospective liking, yet both can be more or less responsive to the evidence or fitting to the situation, and thus capable of *learning* in a way that tends, with increasing quantity and diversity of experience, to lessen the gap between appearance and reality. It is no offense to common sense (or, for that matter, to contemporary empirical psychology) to speak of learning "the hard way," that is, through painful experience, what or whom to trust, or what or whom to seek or avoid, and to what degree.

The Hume-inspired models we developed of belief and desire, (Bel *p*) and (Des *p*), give an essential role to sentiment, which may seem jarring if we are trying to make a case for so cognitive a phenomenon as learning. But we can note that sentiment generally is susceptible to the full range of epistemic assessments: confidence in a person can be warranted, fears about a situation can be confirmed, admiration of a person can be out of proportion to the evidence, anger at a situation can be irrational, wanting a result can turn out to be mistaken, and attraction to an idea can be ill-grounded or misplaced. Thinking about epistemic rationality has undergone a revolution in recent years toward more dynamic models: rather than demand that we find a privileged starting point secure from doubt, rationality is seen as requiring that we be appropriately responsive to new experience *given* where we start. Thinking about rationality in desire should follow suit—there might be no answer to the question of which desires are *a priori* required, but surely there are better or worse answers to the question of how our desires should respond to the outcomes we experience as we act upon them. And it would seem to be part of the business of rationality to help us find these answers.[10]

## Notes

1. Unless otherwise noted, all references to Hume are to the Selby-Bigge edition of the *Treatise* (1888). References to specific locations in the *Treatise* will be given as (Book.Part.Section).

2. Interestingly, a literature in cognitive science has recently appeared that challenges this decision-theoretic orthodoxy and develops a model of the decision makers in which their preferences evolve over time via a mechanism quite similar to the process of desire revision described in this paper. For a summary of this development, see Busenmeyer 2015.

3. For further discussion of the distinction between the "mental force" or "mode" of belief and its content, see the essays by Friedrich, Lauria *this volume*.

4. See Franklin et al. 2008; Lebreton et al. 2009. Nothing, of course, is guaranteed; for example, any finite body of evidence can fail to be representative, so the tendency of discrepancy-based learning to converge upon actual expectation values is only a probabilistic tendency. Moreover, while the influence of initial expectations tends to decrease with increasing evidence, the very possibility of discrepancy-based learning depends upon which categories the learner can recognize, and these might or might not be adequate to the task of representing relevant features of the environment.

5. For discussion of hunger and the phenomenology of desire, see Gregory, Massin *this volume*.

6. For a discussion of the distinction between drives and desires, see Gregory *this volume*.

7. For Aristotle, all practical thought concerns what is, or appears to be, feasible. And whatever we are *now* in a position to do lies ahead of us, not behind. Even a desire for the *status quo* is a desire for its continuation into the future. For discussion of nonactuality in desire, see also Oddie, Döring and Eker, Lauria, Massin *this volume*.

8. It is easiest to think of this in terms of visual imagery, but all that is needed are appropriate representational vehicles, whether visual, propositional, or something else.

9. Gregory, in his essay for this volume, also argues that desires have both directions of fit. Lauria, in his contribution, argues against this.

10. This paper has benefited from discussions with many colleagues and students and from the Workshop on Desire at the Center for the Affective Sciences in Geneva (June 2014). I would particularly like to thank Kent Berridge and Phoebe Ellsworth for their helpful guidance through the psychological literature, and Federico Lauria for detailed and helpful comments on an earlier draft of this paper. For further discussion of the conception of desire presented here, see Railton 2012.

## References


Aristotle (2000). *Nicomachean Ethics*, tr. and ed. Roger Crisp. Cambridge, UK: Cambridge University Press.

Behrens, T. J., Hunt, L. T., and Rushworth, M. F. S. (2009). 'The Computation of Social Behavior', *Science*, 324, 1160–1164.

Berridge, K. C. (2004). 'Motivation Concepts in Behavioral Neuroscience', *Physiology and Behavior*, 81, 179–209.

———. (2009). 'Wanting and Liking: Observations from the Neuroscience and Psychology Laboratory', *Inquiry*, 52, 378–398.

Bhatt, M. A., Lohrenz, T., Camerer, C. F., and Montague, P. R. (2012). 'Distinct Contributions of the Amygdala and Parahippocampal Gyrus to Suspicion in a Repeated Bargaining Game', *Proceedings of the National Academy of Science*, 109, 8728–8733.

Bradley, R. (2007). 'Becker's Thesis and Three Models of Preference Change', CPNSS Working Paper 4.1. London School of Economics.

Busemeyer, J. R. (2015). 'Cognitive Science Contributions to Decision Science', *Cognition*, 135, 43–46.

Ellsworth, P. C., and Scherer, K. R. (2003). 'Appraisal Processes in Emotion', in R. J. Davidson, K. R. Scherer, and H. H. Goldsmith (eds.), *Handbook of Affective Sciences*. Series in Affective Science. New York: Oxford University Press.

Franklin, D. W., Burdet, E., Tee, K. P., Osu, R., Chew, C.-M., Milner, T. E., and Kawato, M. (2008). 'CNS Learns Stable, Accurate, and Efficient Movements Using a Simple Algorithm', *Journal of Neuroscience*, 28, 11165–11173.

Gilboa, A., Winocur, G., Grady, C. L., Hevenor, S. J., and Moscovitch, M. (2004). 'Remembering Our Past: Functional Neuroanatomy of Recollection of Recent and Very Remote Personal Events', *Cerebral Cortex*, 14, 1214–1225.

Grabenhorst, F., and Rolls, E. T. (2011). 'Value, Pleasure, and Choice in the Ventral Prefrontal Cortex', *Trends in Cognitive Sciences*, 15, 56–67.

Hume, D. (1888). *Treatise of Human Nature*, ed. L. A. Selby-Bigge. Oxford: Clarendon Press.

Lak, A., Stauffer, W. R., and Schultz, W. (2014). 'Dopamine Prediction Error Responses Integrate Subjective Value from Different Reward Dimensions', *PNAS*, 111, 2343–2348.

Lashley, K. (1929). *Brain Mechanisms and Intelligence*. Chicago: University of Chicago Press.

Lebreton, M., Soledad, J., Michel, V., Thirion, B., and Pessiglione, M. (2009). 'An Automatic Valuation System in the Human Brain: Evidence from Functional Neuroimaging', *Neuron*, 64, 431–439.

Lewis, D. K. (1988). 'Desire as Belief', *Mind*, 97, 323–332.

———. (1996). 'Desire as Belief, II', *Mind*, 105, 303–313.

Lin, A., Adolphs, R. and Rangel, A. (2012). 'Social and Monetary Reward Learning Engage Overlapping Neural Substrates, *Scan*, 7, 274–281.

Nesse, R. M., and Ellsworth, P. C. (2009). 'Evolution, Emotions, and Emotional Disorders', *American Psychologist*, 64, 129–139.

Pessoa, L. (2008). 'On the Relationship between Emotion and Cognition', *Nature Reviews Neuroscience*, 9, 148–158.

Pettit, P., and M. Smith (1990). 'Backgrounding Desire', *Philosophical Review*, 99, 565–592.

Preuschoff, K., Bossaerts, P., and Quartz, S. R. (2006). 'Neural Differentiation of Expected Reward and Risk in Human Subcortical Structures', *Neuron*, 51, 381–390.

Quartz, S. R. (2007). 'Reason, Emotion, and Decision-Making: Risk and Reward Computation with Feeling', *Trends in Cognitive Sciences*, 13, 209–215.

Railton, P. (1986). 'Facts and Values', *Philosophical Topics*, 14, 5–31.

———. (2012). 'That Obscure Object: Desire', *Proceedings and Addresses of the American Philosophical Association*, 86(2): 22–46.

———. (2014). 'Reliance, Trust, and Belief', *Inquiry*, 57, 122–150.

Reynolds, S. M., and Berridge K. C. (2008). 'Emotional Environments Retune the Valence of Appetitive versus Fearful Functions in Nucleus Accumbens', *Nature Neuroscience*, 8, 423–425.

Robinson, T., and Berridge, K. C. (2000). 'The Psychology and Neurobiology of Addiction: The Incentive-Sensitization View', *Addiction*, 95 (supplement 2), S91–S117.

Schultz, W. (2010). 'Dopamine Signals for Reward Value and Risk: Basic and Recent Data', *Behavioral and Brain Functions*, 6, 1–9.

Schwarz, N., and Clore, G. L. (1983). 'Mood, Misattribution, and Judgments of Well-being: Informative and Directive Functions of Affective States', *Journal of Personality and Social Research*, 45, 513–523.

Schwarz, N., and Clore, G. L. (2003). 'Mood as Information: 20 Years Later', *Psychological Inquiry*, 14, 296–303.

Singer, T., Critchley, H. D., and Preuschoff, K. (2009). 'A Common Role of Insula in Feelings, Empathy and Uncertainty', *Trends in Cognitive Sciences*, 13, 333–340.

Stalnaker, R. (1984). *Inquiry*. Cambridge, Mass.: MIT Press.

Stanley, J., and Krakauer, J. W. (2013). 'Motor Skill Depends on Knowledge of Facts', *Frontiers in Human Neuroscience*, 7, article 503.1–11.

Stauffer, W. R., Lak, A., and Schultz, W. (2014). 'Dopamine Reward Prediction Error Responses Reflect Marginal Utility', *Current Biology*, 24, 2491–2500.

Storbeck, J., and Clore, G. L. (2007). 'On the Interdependence of Cognition and Emotion', *Cognition and Emotion*, 21, 1212–1237.

Vuilleumier, P. (2005). 'How Brains Beware: Neural Mechanisms of Emotional Attention', *Trends in Cognitive Sciences*, 9, 585–594.

Wilson, T. D., and Gilbert, D. G. (2005). 'Affective Forecasting: Knowing What to Want', *Current Directions in Psychological Science*, 14, 131–134.

Yarrow, K., Brown, P., and Krakauer, J. W. (2009). 'Inside the Brain of the Elite Athlete: The Neural Processes That Support High Achievement in Sports', *Nature Reviews Neuroscience*, 19, 181–189.

Xiang, T., Lohrenz, T., and Montague, P. R. (2013). 'Computational Substrates of Norms and Their Violations during Social Exchange', *Journal of Neuroscience*, 33, 1099–1108.

# PART II | Desiderative Puzzles

# CHAPTER 10 | Desiderative Inconsistency, Moore's Paradox, and Norms of Desire

DAVID WALL

INTUITIVELY THERE SEEMS to be something wrong with having desires that conflict, such as wanting to eat cake and wanting to stay healthy. Furthermore, there seems something worse about having desires that essentially conflict (or being desideratively inconsistent), such as wanting to be monogamous and wanting to have open relationships, compared to what is bad about having desires that conflict merely contingently. Consider some examples to illustrate: Suppose that Jean-Paul desires that he goes to fight with the Resistance, and at the same time desires that he takes care of his sick mother. Unfortunately for Jean-Paul, given the way the world is both his desires cannot be satisfied; they are in conflict. However, this conflict is merely contingent: there is a possible world in which both desires can be satisfied at the same time, perhaps a world in which the Resistance has good health care insurance for its members, allowing Jean-Paul to afford a live-in carer for his mother while he is defending his country against the occupying forces. Of course, this might be of no help in the actual world, and depending on how strongly he holds each of these desires, whether he is able to prioritize one desire over the other, whether he is able to work toward changing current conditions in the actual world so that it is like a possible world in which they no longer conflict, and so on, there might be various negative effects for Jean-Paul. For example, he might experience disappointment that he cannot get everything he wants; he might become indecisive and unable to act to try to satisfy either of his conflicting desires; he might experience dissatisfaction with himself, come to question his values, etc. However, none of these negative effects is inevitable merely because he has such a conflict of desires. We can imagine that

Jean-Paul experiences no such effects.[1] Although we typically think there is something wrong with having conflicting desires, any problems seem relative to the agent and what is desired.

Now consider Don, who desires that he stays faithful to his wife, and also desires that he sleeps with his mistress. Like Jean-Paul, Don has conflicting desires, but in his case the conflict is not merely contingent: there is no possible world in which he can both be faithful to his wife and sleep with his mistress. Don has essentially conflicting desires, or is desideratively inconsistent.[2] It is typically thought that having essentially conflicting desires is bad for someone in a way that having merely contingently conflicting desires is not; that is, that desiderative inconsistency is intrinsically bad or criticizable. Note that Don might be able to prioritize one desire over the other, just as someone might be able to if the conflict between her desires is merely contingent. The kind of desire I am concerned with in these cases are pro tanto, or prima facie, desires and not all-things-considered desires. Nonetheless, while Don holds both of his essentially conflicting prima facie desires there seems to be something wrong with him that is not wrong with Jean-Paul while he holds both of his contingently conflicting desires (see for discussion Blackburn 1988: 509–510, contra Schueler 1988).

But what exactly is wrong with such desiderative inconsistency as experienced by Don? And what explains the special problem with having essentially conflicting desires, like Don, over and above whatever, if anything, might be wrong with having merely contingently conflicting desires, like Jean-Paul? These questions, while distinct, are related. Scholars such as Harry Frankfurt, Gabriele Taylor, and David Velleman have often focused on the first question, suggesting variously that desiderative inconsistency leads an agent to become alienated from and unable to identify with her actions, become indecisive and inauthentic, be unable to accept at least one of the elements of her psychology, and typically being troubled as a consequence.[3] However, I will focus on the second question, at least initially: What explains the problem thought to be involved in having essentially conflicting desires over and above what might be wrong with having merely contingently conflicting desires? Many prominent suggestions claim that having essentially conflicting desires involves a failure of rationality in some way (e.g. Blackburn 1988, Brink 1994, and Smith 2004 offer differing explanations of this kind), something that is not involved in having merely contingently conflicting desires.[4] However, Patricia Marino (2009, 2010, 2011) has recently argued that these explanations are unsuccessful and that, in fact, there is nothing especially wrong with having essentially conflicting desires over and above whatever might be wrong with having merely contingently conflicting desires. Marino discusses a number of responses to this second question and argues that all of them either fail to identify something about being desideratively inconsistent that is problematic at all or fail to identify something about it that is not also a feature of having contingently conflicting desires. Inferring that those proposals are the only alternatives, she therefore argues by elimination that there is no special problem with desiderative inconsistency. The only complaint we might have about having desires that conflict is that they result in frustration of at least one of our desires, with the various practical consequences that might follow from that. Given that frustration of desires does not only occur when we have conflicting desires, we might infer from this that there is nothing wrong here at all, as well as there being nothing specially wrong with having essentially conflicting desires. Any problems arising from having conflicting desires will be agent-relative and over-ridable: that is, whether having conflicting desires creates any problems for the agent will depend on what it is she desires, whether those things are trivial and how they fit in with her broader situation and aims, her character and temperament, such as whether she is regimented or easy-going, and so on.

However, while I agree that the problem with having conflicting desires is a matter of frustration of desires, I think this is more than merely a pragmatic issue. By appealing to what is a plausible counterpart of Moore's Paradox for desire we can see that there are norms of desire that impose standards of correctness on how we should go about forming desires. Avoiding having frustrated desires is one such norm. What is especially wrong with desiderative inconsistency is then that it involves violating a norm of desire necessarily and not merely contingently. Of course, this is not to exaggerate the sense in which an agent is at fault for doing this, but it does identify a fault particular to desiderative inconsistency, and this is what was in need of explanation.

In the next sections I will present Marino's argument by elimination, that there is nothing especially wrong with having essentially conflicting desires, followed by her diagnosis of why we typically think there is a special problem, appealing to frustration of desires. But this appeal is instructive and suggests that there is actually something more problematic about these conflicts, that they involve violating a norm of desire and doing so necessarily. In the subsequent sections I will try to motivate and explain this, first by drawing an analogy with the norms of belief and using Moore's Paradox to illustrate how violating such norms is problematic.

I then appeal to a counterpart of Moore's Paradox for desire to show that analogous norms apply to desires and that violating those norms is similarly problematic. Finally I use this to explain why having essentially conflicting desires is particularly bad and discuss briefly what implications this might have for how we understand the nature of desire.

Some caveats for what follows: Marino discusses inconsistency in various kinds of attitude, including desires; other pro-attitudes such as intentions; evaluations; affective attitudes such as emotions; and so on. For the sake of this paper I am concerned only with desires, the kind of mental state that we attribute to someone when we say things like "Adam desires that his numbers come up in the lottery"; "Brenda wants to go to the beach"; and "Carl desires an ice-cream." Also, despite these different ways we have of ascribing desires to people, in terms of wanting objects or to perform actions, I will follow standard practice in taking desires as propositional attitudes such that these attributions are most accurately expressed in the form "S desires that p," and other expressions are merely paraphrases of that.

## An Argument by Elimination

Marino argues by elimination that there is nothing especially wrong with desiderative inconsistency, but the strength of such an argument depends on the alternatives considered and ruled out. So which alternative explanations does Marino consider?

First, Marino argues that we cannot distinguish between essentially conflicting and merely contingently conflicting desires in terms of some practical or pragmatic problems that the former but not the latter create. For instance, there is no reason to think that someone who has essentially conflicting desires will be unable to act, or will be "paralyzed with indecision," and that this is bad for her from a practical point of view (see, e.g., Blackburn 1988 for this suggestion). This might be true if the kind of conflict of attitudes we were interested in was between all-things-considered desires or intentions, but here we are concerned with conflicts between overridable prima facie, or pro tanto, desires. Someone who has essentially conflicting prima facie desires must prioritize between them if she is to act on one or other, but this need not be something that will be especially problematic (Marino 2009: 282). There is no reason to think that Don will be unable to prioritize his desire that he is faithful to his wife over his desire that he sleeps with his mistress (or vice versa) and can then form a corresponding intention to act. Moreover, this is something that someone who has merely contingently conflicting desires must do as well if she is to act on one of those desires. Given the way the world actually is, Jean-Paul must prioritize one of his conflicting desires in just the same way as Don is required to do if he is to act on one of his contingently conflicting desires. So this cannot be what distinguishes essentially conflicting desires as being *especially* problematic, and it is not clear that it shows that they are problematic at all.

Relatedly, cases of essential and contingent conflicts cannot be distinguished in terms of the possibility of bringing about a world in which the desires do not conflict (Marino 2009: 283). It is true that in some cases of contingently conflicting desires this is possible. For instance, someone who wants to eat cookies and wants to be healthy might work to make the actual world one in which both her desires can be satisfied by developing a healthy cookie. But this may not always be the case; whether it is possible will depend on the content of the contingently conflicting desires and whether the agent has the information and resources needed to bring about the relevant changes so that they no longer conflict. Jean-Paul might be ignorant about how to change the world so that he can both fight with the Resistance and look after his sick mother, or if he did know how to do this he might not have the resources or time to bring about those changes. So he would be unable to resolve the conflict between his desires. In this respect he is no different from Don, who cannot do this because there is no possible world in which the conflict between his desires is resolved. Again, this fails to distinguish between the kinds of conflict of desires.

A different suggestion is that "what is bad about essentially conflicting desires is that one is bound to be dissatisfied" (Marino 2009: 282–283). Again, however, Marino points out that this does not distinguish between essential and contingent conflicts of desires. Whether or not Jean-Paul will experience dissatisfaction or will be troubled by the fact that he cannot get everything he wants will depend on how strongly he desires those different things.[5] But this is also the case with Don, whose desires conflict essentially. So causing dissatisfaction cannot be what makes having essentially conflicting desires especially problematic.[6]

Can a distinction be found between essentially conflicting desires and contingently conflicting desires in terms of a failure of rationality in the former but not the latter cases? Again Marino dismisses such suggestions. First she argues that neither case entails that an agent has straightforwardly inconsistent beliefs (see, e.g., Brink 1994). Someone might desire that *p* and desire that *not-p* without forming any corresponding evaluative beliefs that *p is good* and that *p is not good.* Or even if she did form such evaluative beliefs they might be more detailed in how they represent the object of the corresponding desires. For instance, she might believe that *p is good in virtue of having x* and believe that *p is not good in virtue of having y.* Such beliefs are not inconsistent. And contra Brink, if her desiderative attitudes are based on such evaluative beliefs, this need not entail that those desires are similarly fine-grained in how their objects are represented. Admittedly some cases that are prima facie cases of conflict in fact turn out not to be because what is desired are different aspects of a particular object. For example, someone initially described as wanting to eat cookies and wanting not to eat cookies might be more accurately represented as wanting to eat tasty food and wanting not to eat unhealthy food. But such fine-grained representation of what is wanted cannot be assumed in all cases.[7] It is possible that someone is attracted to different features of a particular object but that she is not explicitly aware of what these different features are.[8] Her actual psychology is then most accurately represented on a straightforward coarse-grained level, as desiring that *p* and desiring that *not-p.* Moreover, it is even less justified to assume this in cases of essentially conflicting desires that are not full-blown instances of ambivalence. Someone such as Don who desires that he stays faithful to his wife and also desires that he sleeps with his mistress might be ignorant of the fact that being faithful entails not sleeping with his mistress. Or even if he is aware he might simply have the corresponding evaluative beliefs that being faithful to his wife is good and that sleeping with his mistress is good; this need not entail that he also believes that being faithful to his wife is not good or that sleeping with his mistress is not good. So having conflicting desires, even in the extreme case of genuine ambivalence, need not involve any logical inconsistency in one's beliefs at all, and is no more likely to do so in cases of essentially conflicting desires than in cases of contingently conflicting desires (Marino 2009: 280–281; 2010: 241–242).

If desiderative inconsistency is not bad in virtue of entailing having logically inconsistent beliefs, does it involve some other kind of mistake of rationality? According to Smith (2004), you have normative reason to do what your fully rational self would want you to do, that is, what your fully informed counterpart who has a maximally coherent, unified set of desires would want you to do. As Marino puts it, to find out what we have normative reason to do we deliberate about what such a counterpart would want us to do, and part of this includes trying to reach a reflective equilibrium between our desires such that they are integrated into a "coherent" and "unified" outlook. So we should try to identify general desires that explain and justify our more specific desires and add those general desires to our overall desire set, thereby making it more unified. For instance, someone finding herself desiring to listen to Led Zeppelin and desiring to listen to Black Sabbath might adopt a general desire to listen to heavy metal music that would explain these more particular desires. And if this implied adopting other specific desires, such as a desire to listen to Deep Purple, she might adopt those too. Conversely if it implied something that conflicted with desires she already had, such as a desire not to listen to glam metal such as Motley Crue, she might reject that general desire and instead try to find some other general desire that would fit and better unify her overall desire set. As Smith (2004) acknowledges, it will not do to adopt any general desire; you have to generalize in the right way. And he recognizes that sometimes normative reasons conflict and one or other is overridden, such that your fully rational counterpart can have conflicting prima facie desires about what she wants you to do. However, she will weigh up these conflicting desires, and one will override the other, leading to an all-things-considered desire about what she wants you to do. It is this that you have normative reason to (perhaps prima facie) desire: you should not share the conflict in prima facie desires that your fully rational counterpart has. So, for Smith, rationality requires you to have a "tendency towards coherence" where this means "something like systematic unification among prima facie overridable desires, in a way that maximises generality" (Marino 2010: 234). Given that essentially conflicting desires cannot be part of such a coherent set, someone with such desires will be less than fully rational in that respect. This failure of rationality is then what is wrong with having essentially conflicting desires.

Marino is prepared to concede this to Smith when it comes to what we have moral reason to do and what morally significant desires we should have. However, when it comes to non-moral matters she denies that having conflicting desires, either essentially conflicting or contingently conflicting, and thereby lacking coherence, would mean that someone was irrational. As described earlier, having conflicting desires need not entail having logically inconsistent beliefs, so it cannot be irrational in virtue of that. But further, coherence is understood in terms of generality and unity, but neither feature within someone's set of desires seems a specifically rational requirement. Consider first generality: Marino argues that having the appropriate general desire is not what makes particular desires seem non-arbitrary and therefore not liable to rational criticism (which is the connection with rationality claimed by Smith 2004: 268–270). Rather, what makes an instrumental desire non-arbitrary is its being understood as a means to the agent's ends, and what typically makes an intrinsic desire non-arbitrary is that it is for something that we think will make us happy, along with our intuitions that it makes sense to want what will make us happy. But this is independent of whether or not the desires can be generalized. Indeed, general desires can be as vulnerable to a charge of being arbitrary as particular desires. Just as someone might reasonably be asked to justify and explain her desire to play Tetris, if the explanation is in terms of her general desire that she wants to play all video games, then she might just as reasonably be asked to justify and explain this general desire too. So the rational requirement toward coherence in desires and not having essentially conflicting desires cannot be explained in terms of generality. Similarly, there seems nothing especially rational about unity in someone's desires, that is, those desires being ones that everyone would share or converge on because they would also see that such desires are justified. (So perhaps *universalizability* would be a better term here; see Smith 2004: 263–264.) It might make good pragmatic sense to share the general desires of one's community such that you have common aims and can get along more easily, be able to resolve disputes in a way that others accept, and so on. And we might be able to give justifications for our desires along those lines so that others would recognize such justification and adopt the same desires. But this need not make their desires non-arbitrary and therefore immune from rational criticism. Suppose someone justified her desire to support Tottenham Hotspur to others in North London on grounds that everyone in that region should support the same football club to avoid the risk of violence between fans of rival clubs, and suppose that all the other North Londoners recognized that justification and converged in the desire to support Tottenham. Although this desire is supported by a justification that others would accept, it is still arbitrary to some degree, as an equivalent justification could presumably be given for everyone to share the desire to support Arsenal. So despite being unified, that desire to support Tottenham is nonetheless arbitrary and so, according to Smith, vulnerable to rational criticism. So even if considerations of generality or unity require someone to have a more coherent set of desires, and not to have essentially conflicting desires, these are not considerations of rationality. So, contra Smith, rationality (at least when understood in terms of generality and unity) cannot distinguish between cases of essentially conflicting and contingently conflicting desires and cannot explain what is wrong with having essentially conflicting desires at all.[9]

According to Marino, these are the only alternative explanations, and she believes she has successfully argued that none of them identifies something about having essentially conflicting desires that is both always a feature of it and is problematic, or that is distinctive of it and not shared by cases of having contingently conflicting desires. Hence she concludes that there is nothing especially wrong with having essentially conflicting desires.

## Frustrated Desires

For the sake of this paper, grant Marino her dismissal of the alternatives she considers in her argument by elimination. How does she explain the (according to her, mistaken) intuition many have that there is something wrong with having conflicting desires? According to Marino, this is due to the fact that during the period when an agent has conflicting desires, either essentially conflicting or contingently conflicting, she must have at least one desire that is going to be frustrated (Marino 2009: 285; 2011: 66–67). This is obviously the case where someone has essentially conflicting desires but must also be the case where the conflict between her desires is merely contingent: even if she is able to do something to change the actual world such that her desires no longer conflict, until she achieves this she is still in a world in which her desires cannot be jointly satisfied. And we typically think that there is something bad about having our desires frustrated. For instance, a common way of understanding people's well-being is in terms of desire satisfaction: someone is doing better to the extent that more of her strongest desires are satisfied and, conversely, doing worse to the extent that more of her strongest desires are frustrated.[10] So if having conflicting desires means that someone has at least one desire that is frustrated, then her well-being will inevitably be lower than it would be if she was not conflicted, other things being equal, and this is bad. Furthermore, this diagnosis in terms of frustration provides a point of difference between essential conflicts and contingent conflicts: the person with essentially conflicting desires is necessarily frustrated, whereas the person with contingently conflicting desires is only contingently frustrated. Hence our intuition that there is something especially bad about having essentially conflicting desires: it means you will necessarily have at least one frustrated desire, so will necessarily be worse off than you would be without the conflict.

However, according to Marino, there is nothing necessarily bad about having frustrated desires (Marino 2011: 66–69). Whether or not it is bad will depend on the content of the desire and the agent's other attitudes.

Consider someone who desires that the apartheid regime remains in power in South Africa. Intuitively apartheid is bad, so it is better that this particular desire is frustrated, whatever the implications for the supporter of apartheid and his attitudes. And it can even be good by an agent's own lights that one of her desires is frustrated. Consider a conflicted and unwilling addict who has both the conflicting first-order desires that she takes drugs and that she stays clean, and the higher-order desire that she does not have the first-order desire that she takes drugs. If she could not rid herself of the first-order desire that she takes drugs, then she would consider it better that that desire remains frustrated. So according to Marino, it is because having desires frustrated is typically but mistakenly assumed to be bad that we think there is something wrong with desire conflicts, and it is because having essentially conflicting desires means that necessarily an agent has a frustrated desire that we mistakenly think this is worse than having merely contingently conflicting desires where the frustration is also merely contingent. But if she is correct, whether there is anything bad with having desires that conflict either contingently or essentially depends on the particular agent, what the conflicting desires are for, and how they fit with her broader interests and concerns.

Again, for the sake of this paper I will grant much of what Marino says about this. However, where I disagree is with her understanding of desire frustration. Marino seems to assume that the only way having a desire frustrated could be bad is if what is desired is good, or improves one's well-being, or is beneficial, and so on. That is, she explains the badness of frustration in terms of the content of particular desires that are frustrated. In that sense she might be correct that having a desire frustrated can be good if the content of the desire is for something bad, as with the supporter of apartheid, or can be good by an agent's own lights, as with the conflicted, unwilling addict. Nonetheless there would still be something wrong with having a frustrated desire. What is wrong with it is that it violates a norm of desire.[11] So the agent with a frustrated desire is doing something wrong considered from the point of view of how she should regulate her desires, and the agent with essentially conflicting desires is necessarily going wrong in this way. And this is *independent* of the content of those desires that are frustrated. Of course this is not to over-exaggerate the seriousness of the mistake the desideratively inconsistent agent is committing: in everyday contexts it might seem trivial whether or not we meet certain norms that apply to us in virtue of our being agents that form desires. But she is going wrong nonetheless. And she is doing so as a result of her having essentially conflicting desires, and that is more serious than the way someone with merely contingently conflicting desires is going wrong. But why think that there are any norms of desire, and if there are, why think that having a frustrated desire violates such a norm?

## Moore's Paradox and Norms of Belief

Consider an analogous question asked about belief: Why think there are any norms of belief, and what particular norms might there be if there are any at all? Moore's Paradox is instructive in this respect. Moore's Paradox is a paradox involving beliefs and assertions of propositions like the following:

1. It is raining and I believe it is not raining.
2. It is raining and I do not believe it is raining.

Focus just on those cases involving belief rather than assertion, and further focus on belief of propositions like (1), sometimes called commissive Moorean beliefs. Propositions like (1) can be and often are true of an agent: any time someone has a false belief, then a proposition like (1) is true of her. So believing such a proposition does not involve believing something that is inconsistent in the way that believing that it is raining and it is not raining would do. Further, the problem is not merely that having such a belief is uncommon. We can imagine contexts, perhaps jerry-rigged and artificial, in which someone brought herself in some roundabout way to have a commissive Moorean belief.[12] Nonetheless there would seem something wrong or odd with having that belief. And it seems wrong regardless of whether an agent asserts that belief, so it cannot be explained in terms of pragmatic norms about what can be properly asserted. What is wrong with having a commissive Moorean belief? I will not attempt here to provide a solution to Moore's Paradox (for detailed discussion see, e.g., Sorenson (1988), Shoemaker (1997), Moran (2001)) but will merely highlight some noteworthy features that suggest an implication about what norms are relevant here, sometimes called doxastic norms. First, note that belief is mentioned as part of the content of a commissive Moorean belief such that for someone to be able to have that belief she must possess the concept of belief. Without engaging in a detailed debate about what is involved in grasping a concept, it seems plausible that someone must have a grasp of the norms and constraints for using the concept correctly. So, if someone can employ the concept of belief, then she knows when she can ascribe particular beliefs to others, how to distinguish belief from other kinds of mental state, when someone is doing something wrong in the way she is attempting to form his beliefs and is criticizable for that, and so on. This knowledge may only be approximate and implicit, but it is the kind of thing that someone must know and be sensitive to if she is to be able to employ the concept correctly, as is required to possess that concept.

Second, note that having a commissive Moorean belief involves self-ascription of a belief: if it is sincere, then she has judged that she herself can be correctly assigned the particular belief mentioned within the Moorean belief (in (1) the belief that it is not raining). So she judges that she has satisfied the norms and constraints on forming that particular belief. If she judged that she did not satisfy those norms and constraints, and so was wrong in holding that belief, then we would expect her either to withhold ascription of that particular belief or try to rid herself of the belief.

It is the tension between these features in the particular case of having a commissive Moorean belief that seems to explain the intuitive oddness. Because she is using the concept of belief we think that she must be able to recognize when someone is not forming beliefs correctly in line with the norms and constraints on forming beliefs. And because she ascribes a particular belief, for example in (1) that it is not raining, then she has judged that she has satisfied the appropriate doxastic norms. Yet it seems odd that she can ascribe that particular belief while also recognizing that it is in conflict with other particular beliefs that she has, such that at least one of those particular beliefs must be false. It suggests either she does not have adequate grasp of the concept of belief to be able to employ it correctly after all, as she has not recognized that she has not satisfied the doxastic norms on having those particular beliefs, or it suggests that the mental state she is ascribing is not genuinely a belief at all, so its correct ascription does not depend on meeting doxastic norms. And in the commissive Moorean case it is the continued self-ascription of a particular belief recognized as false that is problematic. It commits her to knowingly maintaining a particular false belief; if the commissive Moorean belief is true, then the belief it is partly about is false, or if that belief is true, then the commissive Moorean belief itself is false. This suggests that it is a norm of belief to not have false beliefs, such that someone is going wrong with respect to that doxastic norm if she forms or maintains a false belief. Of course, this is not surprising and is something that has long been recognized about belief. For example, William James famously wrote that we should "believe the true and not believe the false" (James 1897).[13] [14] More recently Shah and Velleman have attempted to describe how this norm of truth is part of the concept of belief:

> To conceive of an attitude as a belief is to conceive of it as a cognition regulated for truth, at least in some sense and to some extent. . . . Also part of the concept is a standard of correctness. Classifying an attitude as a belief entails applying to it the standard of being correct if and only if it is true. (Shah and Velleman 2005: 498)

By "correct" they mean something that one is entitled to believe and that involves no error in believing. Conversely, someone would be making a mistake by believing something that was not true. Of course, the fact that someone is making such an error does not mean that she will always be criticizable in an everyday sense. It is plausible that there are a number of doxastic norms, that in certain real-world belief-forming contexts it might not be possible to satisfy them all, and that satisfying one might have to be traded off against satisfying others. For example, in real-world situations in which there are limits on time and investigative resources someone might have to merely form those beliefs best supported by her incomplete evidence, even if this results in her having a number of false beliefs. Strictly speaking she would be criticizable from a purely doxastic standpoint in virtue of having failed to meet that norm of belief, not to have false beliefs, but it is unlikely that she would actually be criticized if she has done her best with the resources available to try to meet it. Yet that merely shows that we do not assess people solely from a doxastic standpoint. It does not show that avoiding having false beliefs is not one of the doxastic norms or that these norms are not genuine standards that we are required to meet. Note also that this norm does not determine how someone should respond if it turns out that she has formed a false belief. It would be equally in line with that norm to respond by changing the world so as to make the belief in question true as it would be in line with that norm to stop holding that belief. Of course, the second way of responding is a more typical response, but this might be because of other considerations, such as our limited ability to change the world: the norm itself is neutral about how to respond to violating it. And as Moore's Paradox helps to show, it is plausible that avoiding having false beliefs is a genuine doxastic norm, something that should constrain how we form beliefs. If the norms that apply to a state and regulate its correct occurrence, when there is something wrong with it, and so on, partly determine (or more strongly, partly constitute) what kind of state it is, then by helping clarify one of the norms of belief Moore's Paradox provides some insight into the nature of belief.

Notice that if this is correct, then it both complements and conflicts with a different, common way of trying to articulate the nature of belief, that is in terms of its *direction of fit* (see, e.g., Anscombe 1957; Smith 1994; Lauria, Gregory, Railton *this collection* for more extensive discussion of this notion). Belief is often said to have a "mind-to-world" direction of fit, which is sometimes fleshed out by saying that a belief "should," or "aims at," or is going wrong in some way unless it "fits with" how the world actually is. But what do these phrases mean? A natural way of understanding a belief "fitting" with how the world is is in terms of it accurately representing the world, but the idea of a belief "aiming at" fitting how the world is is more difficult to articulate substantially: What is the sense in which a belief "should" fit the world? It is here that this norm of avoiding falsity can help elaborate this notion of direction of fit. The idea of a belief aiming at fitting with how the world is can be understood in terms of an agent violating a doxastic norm if she has a belief that does not accurately represent the world, i.e. having a belief that is false. So in helping to elaborate on this notion of direction of fit in terms of doxastic norms, the norm of avoiding falsity complements that way of describing the nature of belief.[15]

However, there is also a conflict between the norm of avoiding false beliefs I have argued for and the idea that belief has a mind-to-world direction of fit. As mentioned, whereas the norm of avoiding falsity is neutral with respect to how someone satisfies that norm, belief's direction of fit is not. According to the latter, correspondence between how the world is and how one's belief represents the world as being should not be achieved by altering the world; if someone's belief does not accurately represent the world, then she would not be in line with the direction of fit of belief if she maintained that belief but altered the world so that her belief did accurately represent it. Assuming that what I have argued about avoiding falsity being a norm of belief is correct, there are at least two ways we could respond here. A more confrontational approach might say that in fact there is nothing more than mere regularity to this second aspect of the direction of fit of belief: we typically meet the norm of avoiding having false beliefs by adjusting our beliefs rather than the world, perhaps because it is easier to satisfy the norm in this way given our physical limitations and other conditions in the world. But while this might make us think that this is the right way to satisfy that norm, in fact there is no error in satisfying it in the opposite way. So the notion of direction of fit tells us nothing about the nature of belief over and above what is revealed by showing that avoiding falsity is a norm of belief.[16] On the other hand we could adopt a more conciliatory approach and try to reconcile this norm of belief with belief having a mind-to-world direction of fit. One way of doing this would be to appeal to the norm of avoiding having false beliefs as what explains the sense in which a belief *should* accurately represent how the world is: this is in terms of someone satisfying the requirement on her as a doxastic agent. We could then appeal to some other doxastic norm, whatever that might be, to explain the other side of the mind-to-world direction of fit.[17] In that way the direction of fit of belief would tell us something about the nature of belief, but it would do so by articulating, or being short-hand for, two of the norms of belief. Exploring this further is beyond the scope of this paper, but either way of responding would be informative about the nature of belief.

## A Counterpart of Moore's Paradox for Desire

If Moore's Paradox shows that certain constraints are doxastic norms, is there a counterpart of Moore's Paradox for desire that might help identify what, if any, constraints there are on how we form desires, or *orectic* norms?[18,19] Note that I am concerned here only with identifying a counterpart of Moore's Paradox for and norms that apply to desire. I am not concerned with other kinds of pro-attitude, such as intentions, wishes, and hopes. Perhaps there are also norms constraining the formation of those kinds of mental state, but they are likely to be different from those applying to desire. Note also that I am interested only in whether there is something analogous to Moore's Paradox in the case of desire, that is, whether there are propositions that would be odd to desire in a way that is analogous to how propositions like (1) and (2) are odd to believe. Given that belief and desire are different kinds of mental state it is unlikely that the same things would be problematic objects of desire as are problematic objects of belief, or that the same norms would apply to desire as apply to belief. But there might be analogous problems and norms nonetheless. So, is there a counterpart of Moore's Paradox for desire?

Consider propositions like the following:

3. I have cheesecake and desire that I do not have cheesecake.
4. I have cheesecake and do not desire that I have cheesecake.

Now suppose that someone had an intrinsic desire for a proposition like (3) or (4) (that is, desired it for its own sake and did not merely desire it instrumentally as a means toward some other desired end).[20,21] Note that in each case this would be a single desire for a complex state of affairs, a desire that she both has some cheesecake and has a desire to not have any cheesecake, or a desire that she both has some cheesecake and lacks a desire for cheesecake, respectively. These single desires are both first-order and higher-order. But the cases are not ones in which someone has a first-order desire and a distinct, higher-order desire. Note also that the attitude taken toward these propositions is one of desire, so she might express the desire for (3) by saying something like "Give me some cheesecake but make me averse to it" or "I want to have some cheesecake and to not want any," and that the attitude mentioned within the propositions is one of desire as well.[22] There would be something odd if someone were to have such an intrinsic desire for a proposition like (3) or (4).[23] But what explains this oddness? It is not that what is desired is something impossible, such that the desire could not be satisfied. Propositions like (3) and (4) can be true of someone, and it is likely that they frequently are: a proposition like (3) will be true of someone whenever she has a frustrated desire, while a proposition like (4) will be true of someone whenever she is indifferent about something that actually is the case. And we can un-problematically imagine wanting someone else to have a frustrated desire, say, motivated by envy of her success, or wanting someone else to be indifferent to something, perhaps motivated by annoyance at his general over-excitement. While we might disapprove of having such mean-spirited attitudes, it would not be especially puzzling to have them. But there is something odd about desiring for yourself that you have a particular desire that is frustrated or desiring for yourself that a particular state of affairs obtains about which you will be indifferent. And as I will argue, this oddness is analogous to the oddness of having a belief in a proposition like (1) or (2). It indicates that such a desire would violate certain norms of desire, just as the oddness of Moorean beliefs indicates that such beliefs would violate certain norms of belief.

Focus on a desire for a proposition like (3), a desire that *I have cheesecake and desire that I do not have cheesecake*. This will be most relevant in the context of this paper. It is a desire that you have a particular desire that is frustrated. This is analogous to having a commissive Moorean belief, a belief in a proposition like (1): in each case the content of the attitude mentioned within the content of the broader belief or desire does not obtain. Frustration for a desire is formally analogous to falsity for a belief in that respect; the proposition the mental state is directed toward does not obtain. So what explains the oddness of having a desire for a proposition like (3), a desire that you have a particular desire that is frustrated? This is a desire in part about having a desire, so someone must possess the concept of desire if she is to have this desire for a proposition like (3). As before, whatever else is necessary for possessing a concept it is plausible that it involves knowing and being sensitive to the norms and constraints that determine when the concept can be correctly applied, even if this is known only implicitly and approximately. In the case of someone possessing the concept of desire, this would require her to know and be sensitive to the orectic norms such that she is able to decide whether someone has met those norms and constraints and can be attributed a particular desire, when she has done something wrong in the way she is forming desires, how to distinguish desires from other kinds of mental state, and so on.

In addition, if someone were to have a desire for a proposition like (3), then she would be desiring that she has or comes to have a particular desire herself. In having that desire she is treating having a particular desire that is frustrated as a suitable object of desire: she considers both wanting to have that frustrated desire and having that frustrated desire as in line with the relevant orectic norms that she is committed to being constrained by. If this were not the case, then we would expect her to try to give up the desire for a proposition like (3).

In an analogy with the commissive Moorean belief, it is the tension between these features that explains the oddness of having a desire for a proposition like (3). For someone to have that desire she must be aware of and sensitive to the norms and constraints of desire formation that determine what are appropriate objects of desire. But in forming the desire for a proposition like (3) she seems not to be following those orectic norms herself. It suggests either that she is not sensitive to those norms after all, so could not in fact be having this desire about a desire (because she does not possess that concept, so cannot have a desire that employs it), or that the mental state she wants to have is not genuinely a desire, that it is some other kind of mental state that has been mis-described, so her wanting it and obtaining it does not violate any norms of desire. And in this case it is the continued wanting to have a particular desire that is frustrated that is problematic. It commits her to knowingly desiring to have at least one frustrated desire: if the desire for a proposition like (3) is satisfied, then she will have the frustrated desire that is part of its content, or if that desire is not frustrated, then the desire for the proposition like (3) itself will remain frustrated. Because this is odd it suggests that it is a norm of desire to not have frustrated desires and that someone is going wrong by having and maintaining frustrated desires. This kind of desire, for a proposition like

(3), is a good candidate for being a counterpart of a Moorean belief: it is a commissive Moorean desire.

Perhaps it is more surprising that avoiding having frustrated desires is an orectic norm than that avoiding having false beliefs is a doxastic norm. But consider how we typically respond to wanting something: other things equal, we typically try to get what we want. And if successful this means no longer having a frustrated desire.[24] Indeed someone would be considered instrumentally irrational if she did not act to satisfy a desire if doing so was not overly costly and did not conflict with her satisfying other, stronger desires.

Of course, this orectic norm itself does not determine how someone should respond to having a frustrated desire. She could do so by bringing about what is desired so it is no longer frustrated, or by ridding herself of that desire. The former kind of response is more common, perhaps due to the difficulty of bringing about a change in our desires compared to bringing about a change in the world, but they are on a par in terms of what is required to conform to that norm. But we would certainly expect her to respond in some way or would suspect something was amiss. For example, suppose someone appeared to be expressing a current desire by saying "I want a doughnut" while standing next to a bakery, having plenty of money in her pocket, denying that she had any stronger conflicting desires, such as a desire to get the bus about to pull away from the stop across the road, or had other reason to want to rid herself of that desire, such as having a desire to eat fewer pastries, and so on. Other things equal, if she did not go on to buy a doughnut and satisfy her desire when she could so easily do so, then we would tend to question whether she properly possessed the concept of desire that she was attributing to herself, or question whether there was something wrong with her to explain this appearance of practical irrationality.[25]

Admittedly most of us do actually have a number of frustrated desires most of the time yet are not criticized for this or considered to be going wrong in doing so. But this merely reflects that avoiding having frustrated desires is not the only orectic norm and that in real-world situations it may be in tension with other norms that it is more important, in that situation, to conform to. For instance, in the real world we are limited by time and resources in our abilities to satisfy our desires, so often have to prioritize satisfying certain desires and leaving others frustrated. This can often be a reasonable use of resources even if it results in having some desires that are frustrated. And given that the world is not always cooperative there may be situations in which something we want is unachievable despite there being good reasons for desiring it. Further, we rarely assess people purely from an orectic standpoint, whether they are forming desires in a way that meets the norms and constraints of desire formation. But this does not show that there are no orectic norms. And as the commissive Moorean desire suggests, avoiding having frustrated desires is among these orectic norms. Analogously with the case of belief described earlier, by identifying one of the norms that constrain what desires it is appropriate for someone to have, and if we think that the norms that apply to a state partly determine what kind of state it is, then this provides insight into the nature of desire.

Consider a number of implications that the norm of avoiding having frustrated desires has for our understanding of desire. Again analogously with the earlier belief case, it helps to elucidate a common way of trying to capture the nature of desire, in terms of its *direction of fit*. Whereas belief is said to have a mind-to-world direction of fit, as mentioned, desire is said to have a world-to-mind direction of fit. Desire is said to "aim at" having the world "fit" with it such that someone who desires that *p* should try to make the world the way it is represented by her desire. We can understand this in terms of a requirement on an agent to meet orectic norms similarly to the way we can understand belief's mind-to-world direction of fit in terms of an agent meeting doxastic norms. So it is partly because desires are constrained by an orectic norm of avoiding having frustrated desires that someone who has a desire should try to make the world the way it is represented by her desire, as this will satisfy that desire and thereby meet that norm. So this orectic norm complements the understanding of desire in terms of it having a world-to-mind direction of fit.

But just as with the case of belief, there is also a conflict here. If what I have argued is correct, then this particular orectic norm does not specify how an agent should avoid having frustrated desires to comply with that norm. One way is to act to try to satisfy that desire. But it is also in line with that norm to cease having that particular desire. In both cases the agent will no longer have a frustrated desire. But the second way conflicts with the idea that desire has a world-to-mind direction of fit as it involves someone changing her mind, what desires she has, rather than changing the world to bring about the *fit* between them. Again there are at least two ways to respond to this. On one hand we could insist that the fact that we expect people to bring about correspondence between how the world is and how their desires represent it to be by acting to try to change the world rather than by giving up their frustrated desires is merely because people typically do this. That is, we dismiss this part of the world-to-mind direction of fit as mere regularity and telling us nothing about the nature of desire over and above what is revealed by it being an orectic norm that people should avoid having frustrated desires.[26] On the other hand we could be more concessive and postulate that the fact that we expect people to act on the world rather than alter their desires when they have a frustrated desire is explained by a different orectic norm from the norm of avoiding having frustrated desires. So the idea of desire having a world-to-mind direction of fit would capture more than one orectic norm and thereby would be informative about the nature of desire. Which of these responses is best is a matter beyond the scope of this paper.

## Moorean Desires and Desiderative Inconsistency

Typically we think there is something wrong with having conflicting desires, and in particular with having desires that conflict essentially and not merely contingently. But what is it that is wrong with such cases, and why is it worse for someone's desires to be for things that necessarily cannot be satisfied at the same time? In recent papers Marino has attempted to dismiss these intuitions and questions, arguing that any problems that arise in such cases will depend on the particular things that are desired and the agent's broader aims, concerns, and so on; she denies that there is anything fundamentally wrong with having conflicting desires at all, and a fortiori nothing especially wrong with having desires that conflict essentially. However, we can now see that this is mistaken and there *is* a problem that needs addressing. By considering a counterpart of Moore's Paradox for desire I have argued that having frustrated desires is always bad, and not merely for any practical, psychological, or other contingent reasons that might be overridden or depend on the particular agent, as Marino claims. Rather having a frustrated desire violates an orectic norm, or norm of desire, that constrains what desires it is appropriate for an agent to have. Such orectic norms apply to agents that are capable of having desires, similar to the way doxastic norms apply to agents that are capable of having belief: they constrain how someone should regulate that part of her psychology simply in virtue of her being that kind of agent, one who can form desires. When someone has desires that conflict and cannot be satisfied at the same time it is inevitable that she will have at least one frustrated desire. So while she has those desires she will be violating a norm of desire: she will be falling short of what is required of her as a good orectic agent, one who is capable of having desires. And where her desires conflict essentially, she is violating such an orectic norm necessarily and not merely contingently. So there is always something wrong with having conflicting desires, and there is something especially wrong with having desires that essentially conflict and not merely contingently conflict. It does not matter that the kind of mistake being made here is a mistake specifically as someone considered in respect of her management of a particular portion of psychology. And it does not matter that this kind of mistake is something that might not be pressing in many everyday situations. It is a mistake nonetheless. Nor does it matter that the additional seriousness of the error in cases of essential conflicts between desires is merely a modal one. Again it is a difference that arguably makes the mistake worse. So our original intuitions were correct.

Furthermore, the answers to these questions are informative about the nature of desire itself and not merely this particular problem. If we think that the norms that constrain what mental states it is appropriate for someone to have partly determine, or more strongly partly constitute, a particular mental state, then by identifying one of the orectic norms I have shown that it is part of what it is for a mental state to be a desire that it should not be frustrated. Interestingly this helps explain one aspect of the familiar idea that desire has a world-to-mind direction of fit (and raises further questions about how to understand that idea). That is, it explains the normative pressure for there to be correspondence between how the world is and how it is represented by someone's desire, even if it does not explain why we think that this correspondence should be brought about in a particular way. Perhaps surprisingly it also suggests that desire and belief are similar in nature in an important respect. In both cases there is normative pressure for such correspondence between how the world is and how the state represents it to be. This is due to the analogous norms of avoiding having frustrated desires and avoiding having false beliefs that create this orectic and doxastic pressure, respectively. So there is a genuine, essential similarity between these types of mental state. Whether they are also genuinely different, and in what ways, will depend on what other norms there are that apply to each. And this may inform whether we should think of desires as a particular kind of belief, or as a representation of a particular kind of content, or as states that have a particular motivating role, or as states with a particular affective character, and so on, as claimed by various theories of desire, and as discussed in other papers in this volume.[27]

## Notes

1. This is especially clear when we consider examples where someone's contingently conflicting desires are relatively trivial, in contrast with those of Jean-Paul here. Someone who wants both to have the steak for dinner and the fish for dinner, but cannot have both, is unlikely to experience any of these effects such as dissatisfaction with herself, questioning values, being unable to act, and so on.

2. For this terminology and way of distinguishing between types of conflict of desires see Marino (2009: 277–278), following a distinction between types of rules in Marcus (1980). See also Blackburn 1988: 509.

3. See, for example, Frankfurt 1992: 5–16; 1987 (as well as Taylor 1985 and Calhoun 1995 for discussion), Velleman 2006: 284–311 (who attributes a similar view to Korsgaard 1996), and Williams 1979 (as well as Calhoun 1995 for discussion).

4. They argue for this in different ways, but there is a common concern to reconcile moral realism with the idea that the (moral) reasons that someone has to act in a particular way are related to her desires in some way. However, I will set aside such moral issues for the sake of this discussion.

5. To illustrate, consider again a case where someone's contingently conflicting desires are for trivial things such as to have steak for dinner and to have fish for dinner, where she cannot have both (see n1). There is no reason to think she will be particularly disappointed to have either steak or fish even though in each case there would be something that she wanted that she did not get.

6. A related suggestion considered and dismissed by Marino (2009: 283–284) is that there would be a difference between what an agent was dissatisfied with between cases of essentially conflicting and contingently conflicting desires (assuming that she was dissatisfied). The suggestion is that in the case where an agent has essentially conflicting desires any dissatisfaction she feels will be with herself for having those desires, whereas if her desires merely contingently conflict then any dissatisfaction will be with the world for not being such that she can get all that she wants. But we cannot assume this would always be the case even if having such conflicting desires always led to dissatisfaction. Someone with essentially conflicting desires need not consider herself to be doing anything wrong, say, if she denies she has any substantial voluntary control over what desires she has, so need not feel any dissatisfaction with herself. On the other hand, someone with contingently conflicting desires might think she does have a high degree of voluntary control over her desires and think she should regulate them so as to avoid even such contingent conflicts, so be dissatisfied with herself for not doing so. So the target of any dissatisfaction on having conflicting desires cannot be what distinguishes essentially conflicting and contingently conflicting cases.

7. See Greenspan (1980: 228–234) for discussion of this in the case of ambivalence of emotions. Presumably something similar could be argued in the case of ambivalence of desires *mutatis mutandis*.

8. Suppose for example that someone liked the richness of cream while disliking its cloying mouth feel but was unable to consciously distinguish these features. She might then be most accurately described as simply desiring that she has cream with her pudding and desiring that she does not have cream with her pudding even though the explanation for each desire is a different feature of cream.

9. Perhaps there is some other sense of rationality that can explain what is wrong with conflicting desires and can distinguish between cases of essential and contingent conflicts, but these are the only kinds of rationality Marino considers and argues against. Indeed, it is just such a different sense of rationality that I will appeal to to try to explain this.

10. See, among others, for discussion, Brink 1989: esp. ch. 8; Hawkins 2010; Sumner 1996; Scanlon 1998; Heathwood 2006; Brandt 1966; Rawls 1971; Haybron 2008. Different versions of this approach appeal to satisfaction of actual desires or to satisfaction of those desires one would have if ideally rational, fully informed, etc.

11. One way to think of this is that there are certain intra-orectic pressures toward having consistent desires that can be satisfied at the same time. Marino (2010) discusses the case of mathematical beliefs and claims there are reasons specific to the subject matter of those beliefs for having consistent beliefs, or intra-mathematical pressures for logical consistency among those beliefs, related to what we do with those beliefs. Similarly she argues that in the specific case of moral desires there might be reasons specific to the subject matter of those desires for having consistent moral desires, or intra-moral pressures, related to the role that moral rules play in our lives. We can think of norms of desire, or one norm in particular, as providing intra-desire, or intra-orectic, pressure toward consistency in desires. There is a sense in which this is pragmatic, but that is merely because of the fact that desires are related to action. It is different from the way the other intra-subject pressures are pragmatic in that it is not dependent on how the specific content of the desire (or belief) plays a role in our lives. So this intra-orectic pressure, from the specific orectic norm to avoid frustration of desires that I will motivate in what follows, is not agent-relative or related to the subject matter of the desire. See also (Marino 2009: 285) where she explicitly denies this.

12. Consider for example someone at the moment she realizes that she is deceiving herself, yet before she rids herself of the false belief. In recognizing this about herself she might form a belief that "I believe that p, but not p," a commissive Moorean belief. Her recognition of this and formation of this belief might be what leads her to rid herself of the false belief. So it is possible for someone to have a Moorean belief. Nonetheless, given that self-deception is a condition in which someone is going wrong with respect to her beliefs, and the Moorean belief arises from that condition, it suggests something odd and deviant about that belief.

13. See also James's "Pragmatic Theory of Truth" (1917:12) where he writes when introducing and defending pragmatism, " 'What would be better for us to believe!' This sounds very much like a definition of truth. It comes very near to saying 'what we *ought* to believe,' and in *that* definition none of you would find any oddity."

14. See also, for example, Wedgewood (2002) for discussion.

15. Of course there might be different ways of explaining why that particular norm is a doxastic norm and applies to belief. For example, Railton (*this volume*) seems to explain it in terms of evolutionary usefulness, whereas I appeal to the notion of an idealized believer or doxastic agent (see Wall 2012). But it would take the paper too far from its main subject matter to discuss this in detail here.

16. Although it would still be informative about our ability to effect changes in the world by acting.

17. And recall I mentioned earlier that it is very plausible that there are further norms of belief in addition to the norm of avoiding falsity. Investigating what they are, however, is beyond the scope of this paper.

18. On this section see Wall (2012) for further discussion and argument.

19. I take the term *orectic* from Millgram (1997), although my use will differ from his. Whereas Millgram uses "orectic state" to "denote psychological states that seem to involve an attraction to their objects" (13), so might include states such as wishes, fantasies, whims, urges (13), I will use it exclusively to refer to desires, the kind of mental state we attribute when saying things like "Homer desires Marge," "Lisa wants to go to the museum," "Mr. Smithers desires that Mr. Burns returns his affections," and so on.

20. There is some terminological variation here, with intrinsic desires alternatively being called "final" desires, and instrumental desires sometimes called "means-end" desires. I use these terms interchangeably.

21. This distinction between intrinsic and instrumental desires is important here. It is not being claimed that it would not be possible for someone to have a desire for a proposition like (3) or (4) but merely that there would be something odd about having such a desire. Yet this is likely to be the case only if the desire is intrinsic. It may be relatively easy to imagine contexts in which it would be intelligible for someone to have this kind of desire, but this would set it in a broader context of the agent's other aims and desires, effectively making it an instrumental desire. And in that context it might not strike us as having any oddness that was in need of explanation. But if we were to focus on a desire for a proposition like (3) or (4) in isolation, desired for itself, it will seem to be in need of explanation. For example, it is plausible that the notion of some penalty counting as punishment requires that the person suffering the penalty is averse to suffering it. And we can make sense of someone wanting to be punished, say, if she believes it important for personal moral development or for maintaining social order and wants to achieve those things. This might then involve her having a desire such as a desire that *she is imprisoned and desires that she is not imprisoned*, which is a desire for a proposition like (3). But this is intelligible only considered as an instrumental desire, desired as a means toward achieving the desired end of being a better person or maintaining social order. Without this instrumental context it would seem odd for her to desire that *she is imprisoned and desires that she is not imprisoned*, and this is in need of explanation. We should expect intrinsic desires to be informative only about constraints specific to desire as opposed to constraints on practical reasoning. Thanks to Timothy Schroeder for this example and to him, Lauren Ashwell, and Alex Gregory for pressing me on this point to help clarify it.

22. These verbal expressions of the desires might be the kind of thing uttered in prayer, as a request, as a demand, and so on, analogous to assertions that are expressions of belief. Thanks to Federico Lauria for these suggestions.

23. This is not to deny that someone could actually have a desire like (3) or (4), merely that there would be something wrong or odd about her doing so. But in this respect these desires are analogous to Moorean beliefs (see n12).

24. Note that this need not be simply because getting what we want means no longer having a desire for that thing at all, and a fortiori no longer having a frustrated desire for it. It is possible to continue to desire something after it has been satisfied, and even when the agent is aware that her desire has been satisfied. Consider for example someone who desires to be a parent. In most cases she will not cease to desire to be a parent after having a child (sleepless nights excepted). Similarly, consider someone who gets her dream job and finds that it is as fulfilling as she imagined it to be. Before getting the position she desired to do that job and after getting it continues to desire to do that job. So being

successful in trying to get what we want means no longer having a frustrated desire, but does not necessarily mean no longer having a desire at all.

25. For instance, we might instead question whether she genuinely possesses the concept of the first person that she appears to be using in self-ascribing the desire. Compare what Matthew Boyle says about the different ways in which someone can use the first-person: "A subject who judges 'That plank is going to hit *A* in the head' and who has the normal aversion to being hit in the head, but whose so judging does not dispose him to take evasive action, is a subject whose use of '*A*' plainly does not express self-consciousness. By contrast, a subject whose use of '*A*' *is* connected in this sort of way with his decisions about what to do displays an awareness of the fact that the things he decides to do are the intentional actions of the thing he calls '*A*'" (Boyle 2009: 154).

26. Though again this might be informative about our psychological ability to alter our desires and our physical ability to alter the world nonetheless.

27. This paper was presented at the *Thumos* Nature of Desire conference at the University of Geneva in June 2012. Thanks to that audience for helpful discussion, and thanks to Julien Deonna and Federico Lauria for helpful comments on an earlier draft.

## References

Anscombe, G. E. M. (1957). *Intention*. Oxford: Basil Blackwell.

Blackburn, S. (1988). 'Attitudes and Contents', *Ethics*, 98, 501–517.

Boyle, M. (2009). 'Two Kinds of Self-Knowledge', *Philosophy and Phenomenological Research*, 78 (1), 133–164.

Brandt, R. (1996). 'The Concept of Welfare', in S. Krupp (ed.), *The Structure of Economic Science*. New York: Prentice Hall.

Brink, D. (1989). *Moral Realism and the Foundations of Ethics*. Cambridge, UK: Cambridge University Press.

———. (1994). 'Moral Conflict and Its Structure', *Philosophical Review*, 103, 215–247.

Calhoun, C. (1995). 'Standing for Something', *Journal of Philosophy*, 92 (5), 235–260.

Frankfurt, H. (1987). 'Identification and Wholeheartedness', in F. Schoeman (ed.), *Responsibility, Character, and the Emotions: New Essays in Moral Psychology*. Cambridge, UK: Cambridge University Press.

———. (1992). 'The Faintest Passion', *Proceedings and Addresses of the American Philosophical Association*, 66 (3), 5–16.

Greenspan, P. (1980). 'A Case of Mixed Feelings: Ambivalence and the Logic of Emotion', in A. Rorty (ed.), *Explaining Emotions*. Berkeley: University of California Press.

Hawkins, J. (2010). 'The Subjective Intuition', *Philosophical Studies*, 148, 61–68.

Haybron, D. (2008). 'Philosophy and the Science of Subjective Well-Being', in M. Eid and R. J. Larsen (eds.), *The Science of Subjective Well-Being*. New York: Guilford Press.

Heathwood, C. (2006). 'Desire Satisfaction and Hedonism', *Philosophical Studies*, 128, 539–563.

James, W. (1897). *The Will to Believe and Other Essays*. New York: Longmans, Green.

———. (1907). *Pragmatism: A New Name for Some Old Ways of Thinking*. New York: Longman Green and Co.

Korsgaard, C. (1996). 'Tanner Lectures', in O. O'Neill (ed.), *The Sources of Normativity*. Cambridge, UK: Cambridge University Press.
Marcus, R. (1980). 'Moral Dilemmas and Consistency', *Journal of Philosophy*, 77, 121–136.
Marino, P. (2009). 'On Essentially Conflicting Desires', *Philosophical Quarterly*, 59 (235), 274–291.
———. (2010). 'Moral Rationalism and the Normative Status of Desiderative Coherence', *Journal of Moral Philosophy*, 7, 227–252.
———. (2011). 'Ambivalence, Valuational Inconsistency, and the Divided Self', *Philosophy and Phenomenological Research*, 83 (1), 41–70.
Millgram, E. (1997). *Practical Induction*. Cambridge, Mass.: Harvard University Press.
Moran, R. (2001). *Authority and Estrangement: An Essay on Self-Knowledge*. Princeton: Princeton University Press.
Rawls, J. (1971). *A Theory of Justice*. Oxford: Oxford University Press.
Scanlon, T. M. (1998). *What We Owe to Each Other*. Cambridge, Mass.: Belknap Press.
Shoemaker, S. (1996). *The First-Person Perspective and Other Essays*. New York: Cambridge University Press.
Schueler, G. F. (1988). 'Modus Ponens and Moral Realism', *Ethics*, 98, 492–500.
Shah, N., and Velleman, D. (2005). 'Doxastic Deliberation', *Philosophical Review*, 114 (4), 497–534.
Smith, M. (1994). *The Moral Problem*. Oxford: Oxford University Press.
———. (2004). *Ethics and the A Priori*. Cambridge, UK: Cambridge University Press.
Sorenson, R. (1988). *Blindspots*. New York: Oxford University Press.
Sumner, L. W. (1996). *Welfare, Happiness, and Ethics*. Oxford: Clarendon Press.
Taylor, G. (1985). 'Integrity', in *Pride, Shame, and Guilt: Emotions of Self-Assessment*. Oxford: Oxford University Press.
Velleman, D. (2006). 'Willing the Law', in *Self to Self*. Cambridge, UK: Cambridge University Press.
Wall, D. (2012). 'A Moorean Paradox of Desire', *Philosophical Explorations*, 15 (1), 63–84.
Wedgewood, R. (2002). 'The Aim of Belief', *Philosophical Perspectives*, 16, 267–297.
Williams, B. (1979). 'Integrity', in *Utilitarianism: For and Against*. Cambridge, UK: Cambridge University Press.

# CHAPTER 11 | Deliberation and Desire

G. F. SCHUELER

The primitive sign of wanting is trying to get.

—ANSCOMBE 1963

Every day, do something you don't want to do.

—STUDENT COMMENCEMENT SPEAKER

## 1. Preliminaries

It is very plausible to think that desires motivate at least some intentional actions. At the same time it seems clear that at least some actions are done as a result of deliberation. That could not be true of all actions, since deliberation itself is an "action" in the sense of being something one can do intentionally and for a reason.[1] But it is plausible to think that deliberation must play a role, perhaps a conceptually central role, in the explanation of intentional action of rational agents.

In this paper, though, I will argue that there is a serious tension between deliberation and desire, as they are commonly understood, when they are both relevant to explaining the same action. The question this paper will address is how desires figure into the explanations of actions when the agent both has a desire that motivates the action and also deliberates and acts on the basis of her deliberation. How do the agent's desires figure into the explanations of such actions? I will argue that a common way of understanding this situation, contained in a standard version of the practical syllogism, is quite problematic. At the same time, sorting out the issues here will let us see what "motivation by what one wants" really is, at least when deliberation is involved. It will help to start by saying a little about how best to understand "desires" and what deliberation is.

The most straightforward procedure, which I will follow, is to take a desire to be present whenever a sentence of the form "X wants Y" is true (when X is an agent and Y is anything agents can intelligibly be said to want). This will allow us to remain neutral about "what desires really are," e.g. about whether they are really beliefs about whether their objects are good, or dispositions to be moved toward certain actions under certain conditions, or functionally describable parts of a complicated causal network. Similarly we can be neutral about whether their "contents" are or are not propositions and about whether they essentially involve feelings. For the same reason, as we will see, this allows us to avoid the question of whether intentions are "really" desires.[2]

Sentences of the form "X wants Y" cover two distinct phenomena: things the agent likes or is in favor of, and purposes, goals, or aims she has. The jargon term *pro-attitude* covers up the difference here, as indeed does the term *desire* itself often enough, but these are different things.[3] If I am watching my favorite team on television, I want them to win. I'll be glad if they do, unhappy if they don't. But the fact that I want them to win need not provide me with a goal that might lead me to do anything (such as email advice to the coach). I might believe that nothing I can do can influence this game. And so unless I am irrational I won't take their winning as the goal of anything I do. But I still want them to win. My desire that they win consists of the fact that I am in favor of this outcome.[4] Another example of this kind of desire is when I want my lottery number to have been drawn. I am in favor of that, but I don't have it as a goal since I don't believe I can change the past.[5]

The phenomenon involving goals and purposes is exemplified by intentional actions and may be at least part of what Anscombe meant when she said, "The primitive sign of wanting is trying to get."[6] One might hold that all intentional actions are done for reasons, but in any case some certainly are. And "the agent's reason" typically (or is it always?) refers to the goal or point of the action.[7] If I walk across campus to get some coffee my reason for doing this is the purpose of my action, i.e. to get some coffee. The natural way to describe this is by saying "I want to get some coffee." The purpose of the action, whatever it is, is one of the things typically referred to when we speak of an agent wanting something. In fact, I would say it follows from the fact that an agent did something for some reason that she wanted whatever it was that she was aiming at. From the fact that I walked across campus *in order to* get some coffee, it follows that I *wanted* to get some coffee.[8]

These two phenomena mostly overlap, which may be why we use the same term to refer to both. Our goals are usually things we like or have positive attitudes toward. And things we like we often try to achieve. But this is not always the case, as we can see from examples where the two conflict. Someone who has decided to try to lose weight might know that she would enjoy the pastry offered her and at the same time know that eating it would conflict with her goal. So does she want the pastry? She might have a strong positive attitude, even a craving, toward eating it. So in that sense she wants to eat it. At the same time, in the other sense, she doesn't want to eat it because it would conflict with her goal of losing weight. She is not lying when she tells the waiter she doesn't want a pastry. Whether or not she eats the pastry she will do something she wants to do and at the same time something she doesn't want to do. The two different senses (or kinds?) of "want" come apart here.[9]

So two different phenomena can be referred to by *want*. I will mark that by referring to the two "senses" or "uses" of this term. But there is one other thing to note about the "X wants Y" criterion for desires, namely that it obviously covers intentions. Someone who intends to stop at the grocery has this as a goal. So she wants to stop at the grocery. I can convey to someone my intention to stop at the grocery by saying "I want to stop at the grocery." Whether in the end we will want to hold that the mental states called "intentions" are or are not a variety of the ones we call "desires," either can be referred to when we speak of what some agent wants.

Turn now to deliberation. Deliberation is a conscious, psychological process, which should be sharply distinguished from the propositions that are the contents of the mental states that partly constitute it. It is held to come in two forms: theoretical reasoning, where the aim is to figure out whether some claim is true, and practical reasoning, where the aim is to figure out whether to do something.[10] We will focus on practical deliberation. There are lots of things about this sort of deliberation that have come in for philosophical debate, whether for instance the conclusion of such reasoning is a belief about what the agent should do or whether it is an intention to act, or even just an action. We can remain neutral on such issues for the moment. A start will be made on sorting out some of them below.

It is worth noticing here that not only is practical deliberation a goal-directed activity, but it is one governed by implicit norms. In order to be deliberating one must at a minimum think that there is, or may be, something more to be said for doing some things than others and that there is at least a chance of figuring out what that is. And like any reasoning, practical deliberation can go wrong. One might succeed in reasoning, even in reasoning as well as possible, but still fail at the implicit goal of reasoning. If one is engaged in theoretical reasoning the belief one arrives at might be false, or, in practical reasoning, the action one performs might not be the one that had the most to be said for it. Since practical deliberation is a form of reasoning, it can go wrong in any of the ways reasoning can go wrong.

## 2. Reasoning from One's Own Desires

So much for the preliminaries. As was mentioned earlier, the question this paper will address is how desires figure into the explanation of actions when the agent both has a desire that motivates the action and also deliberates and acts on the basis of her deliberation. How do the agent's desires figure into the explanations of such actions? One well-known answer is provided by Robert Audi, who represents one possible schema for deliberation as follows: "Major Premise—the motivational premise: I want phi; Minor Premise—the cognitive (instrumental) premise: My A-ing would contribute to realizing phi; Conclusion—the practical judgment: I should A."[11] This schema, a version of the practical syllogism, couldn't of course be the whole story about deliberation. There is no account here of cases where one has to weigh conflicting reasons, and there seem to be perfectly good examples of deliberation that start from a claim that something is worth doing or otherwise of some value or perhaps is in the interest of the agent, not from a reference to something the agent wants. But the central feature of this schema, the reference in the "motivational premise" to what the agent wants, gives a familiar answer to the question of how desires come into the explanation of actions when the agent deliberates. It seems plausible that if an agent has a desire on which she is to act, then in order for her to figure out how to satisfy that desire she must be aware of it. That is what the motivational premise encapsulates. So let's consider this answer.

There are several things to notice here. First, since we are considering Audi's proposal as a general account of how desires fit into deliberation, it seems implausible to take the wanting referred to in the motivational premise in this schema as being of the "liking" or "favoring" sort. I can want things in that sense without its being the case that I should try to get them, or even think that I should. As the TV football game example shows, there are plenty of things that I want to happen, i.e. that I am in favor of, but that I perfectly well know are outside my ability to achieve. And even when there is something I could do to promote what I favor, it seems false that the mere fact that I like or favor something, plus know of a way of promoting it, somehow automatically means I should try to get it. Though of course I can reason about how to achieve something I like, I can also like or favor some state of affairs without taking its realization as a goal.

This is clear if we think of whims or other trivial desires. For instance, I would like to return home some day to find my next-door neighbor's front lawn, which he always keeps trimmed to virtual golf course perfection, a riot of wildflowers and meadow grasses. It would look a lot better. But though I would like this to happen, I have no temptation to take making it happen as a goal or aim of mine even to the slightest degree. It is just a whim. So I would not deliberate about how to achieve this. I can perfectly well like the idea of this happening, and know of something I could do to "contribute to realizing it" (such as buying my neighbor a subscription to a natural gardening magazine) without actually having it as a goal or aim. And as the dieting example shows, I can have a goal or aim for which I feel no positive emotion at all. So aims and positive feelings are distinct things.

At the same time, when we explain actions in terms of what agents want it is the fact that we thereby pick out goals or aims the agent is trying to achieve that does the explanatory work.[12] One's goals and aims are just the sorts of things one does try to figure out how to accomplish. So this is really a conceptual point about how what we want explains our actions. Once we distinguish the in-favor-of sense from the purpose sense of "want," unless we take Audi's motivational premise as referring to a goal or purpose, there seems to be little plausibility in the thought that the agent ought to do what is required to achieve it. It may or may not be a mistake not to pursue what you want, i.e. favor having or achieving, depending on its value, or at least value to you. Notoriously, though, it is sometimes wiser not to pursue, perhaps even wiser to try to extinguish, some of your strongest desires. But other things being equal it is irrational not to try to achieve your goals in a way that it is not irrational not to try to achieve something you know you would like or are otherwise in favor of. Assuming I haven't dropped some goal or thought its pursuit precluded by some more important goal, failure to pursue one of my goals seems to call my agency into question. So for these reasons I will understand the motivational premise "I want phi" in Audi's schema as referring to some goal or purpose that I have. We will consider below the plausibility of taking this premise in the "liking" or "favoring" sense.

A second thing to notice about this schema is that as it stands there seems to be nothing essentially first-personal about it. Audi states it in the grammatical first person, but nothing in his schema requires this. If you know the relevant facts, you can reason just as well as I can about what I should do, though of course, since you are reasoning about me, you won't put things in the first person. It is obviously plausible to think that someone else can reason about what I should do as well as I can, as long as we are thinking of Audi's schema as a description of an argument, that is, as an abstract structure of propositions (or forms of propositions) which can be evaluated individually for their truth and, as an argument, for cogency.

But we are discussing deliberation, which is not an abstract structure of propositions but a psychological process that takes place in an agent. That is required by the question on which we are focusing, which involves the agent acting on the basis of her deliberation. As it stands Audi's schema, whatever else is true of it, doesn't seem equipped to make any distinction between the theoretical reasoning that ends in a belief about what someone (even perhaps someone other than the person doing the reasoning) should do, and practical reasoning done by the agent that somehow is acted on. So we will need to return to this point.

A third thing to notice about Audi's schema is that, as mentioned, explicitly basing one's reasoning about what to do on what one wants is not the only possible form of deliberation. However plausible it is to think that we sometimes deliberate about how to get what we want, it is not very plausible to think that is the only thing we ever use as a basis of deliberation. Such a claim would suppose a level of self-absorption that seems beyond all but the most solipsistic. So whatever we decide about the idea that desires figure into deliberation that starts from a motivational premise about what the agent wants, we will eventually need to consider other schemas as well.

## 3. Two Puzzles

The fourth thing to notice about Audi's schema will bring us to the problem on which I want to focus. The question we are asking here is how desires fit into the explanation of actions where the agent has a desire that moves her but also deliberates and acts on the basis of that deliberation. According to Audi's schema, the agent simply starts with the realization that she wants something and then reasons about what action she can take that will "contribute to realizing" what she wants. On its face this seems plausible. But there is something puzzling here. According to

Audi's schema, the desire that is supposed to motivate the action isn't, strictly speaking, part of the deliberation on which the agent acts at all. This desire is required to make the motivational premise true, of course, but reasoning can take place whether or not the premises on which it is based are true. All the mental states that constitute the deliberation are conscious thoughts, one of which will be about what the agent wants (i.e., will have the content "I want phi"). So if the agent acts *on the basis* of her deliberation, it is *these* mental states, presumably conscious beliefs, that explain her action, not her desire. On this story the desire itself doesn't seem to have any work to do in the explanation. Deliberation using the motivational premise involves a conscious belief that one wants something, but that is not the same thing as the actual desire which, if one has it, makes this belief true.

This won't be a problem as long as we consider Audi's schema as representing the content of some theoretical reasoning about what I should do, whether you do this reasoning or I do it. In either case to say that this is theoretical reasoning is at least to say that no action or intention results (or, perhaps, is supposed to result), i.e. that the series of mental states of which these propositions are the content simply ends with a conscious belief that I should phi. This belief is its "conclusion" not in the logical sense (of a proposition supported by other propositions that are premises) but in the sense of being the last state in the process. But at the same time this is a process of reasoning. So the *content* of this final belief, the proposition believed, is also intended to be a conclusion, in the logical sense, of the propositions believed to support it. Reasoning of this sort can go wrong in at least two distinct ways: either one or more of the premises used in the reasoning might be false, or the structure of reasoning itself might be fallacious. I will argue that the structure of reasoning represented in Audi's schema is indeed fallacious, but let's set that issue aside here. We are really interested in any reasoning that uses what Audi calls the motivational premise, whether the subsequent reasoning goes as Audi describes it or in some other way.

Suppose you are the one doing the reasoning, on my behalf, and the question on which you are advising me is the question of whether I should get on the bus that has just pulled up at the bus stop at which we are waiting. You engage in some theoretical deliberation about what I should do. "Well, you want to go to campus," you say. "And since this bus goes right there, getting on this bus will get you to campus. So you should get on this bus." Clearly you could be mistaken in either of the two premises you use in your reasoning here. Perhaps this bus doesn't actually go to campus. Or perhaps I don't really want to go there. If you are wrong about either of these things, then however good the form of reasoning you are using, your premises don't support the conclusion that I should get on this bus. And since we are speaking of theoretical reasoning here (about what I should do) and since either of us could do this reasoning, I might do the same reasoning and, like you, make either of these two mistakes. Of course I am less likely than you to be misinformed about what I want. But that doesn't mean I am infallible.[13] In any case, though, desires are different mental states than beliefs. And reasoning about how to get what I want involves the conscious belief that I want phi, not the actual desire for phi. So I might have the belief without the desire.

None of this is problematic as long as we think of ourselves, either you or me, as doing theoretical reasoning about what I should do. As with any reasoning, such reasoning can go wrong. If it is based on false premises, then there is no assurance that the judgment arrived at, that I should get on this bus, is correct. This possibility is a feature of any reasoning. The puzzle here is created when I act on my deliberation. If the motivational premise I use in deliberation is false, the desire referred to in that premise won't exist. So if I act, and don't merely judge, on the basis of this reasoning, then my (non-existent) desire can have no role in explaining my action. So, contrary to what we first thought, Audi's schema could not be used to include the desire described in the motivational premise in the explanation of the action done on the basis of the deliberation described in this schema. If I act "on the basis" of my deliberation, then it doesn't matter whether the desire described in the motivational premise is there or not. I would reason, and act, the same way in either case. This is the first puzzle.

Here is a second one: Suppose that I do in fact use this same reasoning as practical deliberation and on the basis of this reasoning I get on the bus. Since this reasoning has as its motivational premise "I want to go to campus," doesn't it simply *follow* that I wanted to go to campus? That is what I would say if someone asks me why I was getting on the bus, because that is what I would believe. Plus, my action was clearly intentional. It therefore had a purpose. And it was done on the basis of my deliberation, deliberation that took as its main premise my thought that I wanted to go to campus. So what other possible goal could my action have? If someone acts *on the basis* of a conscious belief that the goal of her action was phi, then surely the goal of her action was phi.

So, contrary to what the first puzzle indicated, when we consider this same piece of reasoning as practical deliberation on which the agent acts, it is hard to see how the motivational premise could possibly be false. In sharp contrast to theoretical reasoning involving the motivational premise, this premise is *made true*, apparently, when the person doing the deliberation acts on the basis of that very premise. So we have two puzzles here. My belief, that I want to go to campus, could of course be false when you or I use it to try to figure out what I should do. But even when that premise is false you or I, the ones doing the reasoning, might still come to believe, on the basis of this reasoning, that I should go to campus. And similarly, when the motivational premise is false, my action on the basis of the reasoning in which it is contained doesn't require the existence of the desire to which it refers. But at the same time this belief looks like it cannot possibly be false *if I act on it*. It is made true by the very fact that I acted on it. How can this be?

So far as I can tell neither of these puzzles is explained by the fact that Audi's schema, when considered as the content of theoretical reasoning to the conclusion that "I should phi," is fallacious, which it seems to be. How could the mere fact that I have some goal, just by itself, make it the case that I *should* do what I can to achieve that goal? What if this goal is evil or just wacky? It seems true that it is irrational not to try to achieve goals you have. But Audi's schema says that if you have some goal it follows that you should try to achieve it. That would mean that merely having the goal gives you a reason to try to achieve it. But that is a different and more problematic claim. As John Broome and others have pointed out, unless we consider the claim that we "should avoid irrationality" here to use a "should" of "wide scope," we will find ourselves with a "bootstrapping" problem that lets absolutely any goal I have give me a reason to work toward achieving it, no matter how crazy or evil that goal is.[14]

To avoid that implausible result we will need to say that the "should" conclusion here is "not detachable" in the way Audi's schema seems to allow, that is, that it is not the case that merely having a goal supports a conclusion to the effect that I should do what I can to achieve it, or that I have reason to try to achieve it. What is true, according to Broome, is not that if I want phi and see that my A-ing would contribute to realizing phi, I should A. Rather we should take the "should" here as being of wide scope and say that I should make it the case that if I want phi and see that my A-ing would contribute to realizing phi, I perform act A. So I can do what I should either by doing A or by abandoning my desire for phi. So if Broome is right, this shows, or at least strongly argues, that Audi's schema, when considered as the content of theoretical reasoning that ends in a proposition about what I should do, is not good reasoning.[15]

But it is not obvious that the fallaciousness of Audi's schema precludes use of its motivational premise. This premise might still be used in some perfectly valid reasoning even if the particular schema in which Audi proposes to use it is not valid. To the question of the role of her desire in the explanation of an action in which the agent acts on the basis of her deliberation, the motivational premise seems a natural answer since it registers the recognition on the part of the agent that she has the desire in question. And it is hard to see how someone could include a desire in her deliberation unless she realizes she has it. This fact is simply not touched by the fallaciousness of the schema in which Audi uses it. Still, as we have seen, this motivational premise, however it is used, gives rise to the two apparently conflicting puzzles just described.

## 4. Two Forms of Practical Reasoning

We can see what is happening here if we notice that two different sorts of "reasoning about what to do" get included under the generic label "practical reasoning." Suppose I am working in my office when a friend texts me that she is on her way to the coffee house and I should join her. When she texts, though, I am trying to meet a deadline. So it is not a good time for me to stop for coffee. Some practical deliberation seems called for, weighing the potential enjoyment of meeting my friend for coffee against the need to finish my project. Presumably both are things I want to do, in the sense of "being in favor of" each. And of course I might just ask myself which I like more, that is, which I "want" to do more in the "favoring" sense. But I might also think each of these things has something to be said for it (i.e. has some value in itself), independently of my liking it or being in favor of it. So I might base my deliberation on these perceived values, the enjoyment of seeing my friend for coffee and the value of finishing my project. And of course I might weigh how much I liked either of these activities against how valuable I thought they were. But these bases for deliberation will be different from that envisioned in Audi's schema since my reasoning here will not involve anything analogous to his motivational premise, which we decided was the agent's thought that she has some goal. Now I am trying to decide whether to adopt a new goal, meeting my friend for coffee. So, let's suppose I reason from judgments about the value of working versus the value of having coffee with my friend and come to a conclusion that I should meet my friend for coffee.

I then form the intention to do that. That means that a second sort of reasoning is now called for, how to actually carry out that intention. This one looks a lot like Audi's schema.

> I want to meet my friend for coffee.
> I can do that by walking north across campus to the coffee house.
> So I'll walk north.

If this really were just an instance of Audi's schema, then the same two puzzles would of course arise here as well. But this is not the same as Audi's schema. In Audi's schema the conclusion was a belief or "judgment" (that "I should do A"), and the motivational premise ("I want phi") appeared in my practical deliberation as a conscious belief that I had a certain goal or aim, just as it did in my (or your) analogous theoretical deliberation. One puzzle that this view raised is that the reasoning on which my action was based could apparently proceed and lead to my action, even if the conscious beliefs that it involved were false, including my belief that I want phi, i.e., that I have that goal. But the analogous mental state in my coffee reasoning above, with the content "I want to meet my friend for coffee," is not a conscious belief about what I want and in fact could not be. It is the expression of my intention to meet my friend for coffee. And since intentions are neither true nor false, the possibility that I might base my action on a false belief does not arise.[16]

Why do I think this premise must be an expression of my intention, and how can an intention itself, as opposed to a conscious belief on my part that I have this intention, be part of my reasoning? Though it may be misleading to call what I am doing "deliberation," I think it has to be true that we can and do reason about what to do on the basis of our own intentions.[17] Think about any complex action governed by some intention, e.g. walking across campus to join my friend for coffee. The coffee house is roughly two blocks away. To get there I need to get up from my desk, leave my office, cross a street, walk north to the far end of the central green, turn right onto another street, etc. And of course each of these things involves numerous "smaller" actions. Leaving my office, for instance, involves walking around my desk and over to my office door. I do all these things with the intention of meeting my friend for coffee.

Through all this I am perfectly aware that I am going to join my friend for coffee. So of course I believe that this is what I am doing. The various things I am doing together constitute going to join my friend for coffee. But turning left at a particular point, for instance, is not done as a result of deliberation "based on my belief" that I want to meet my friend for coffee. Putting it that way leaves open the possibility that my belief could be false, and as we have seen it is hard to make sense of that thought. Rather all these things *constitute* "meeting my friend for coffee" because they are part of what I realize is involved in carrying out my intention.

Here is a way of seeing the difference. Suppose that you, knowing the way to the coffee house better than I do, were to walk along with me and offer your advice as to how I should proceed at each point, where I should turn left, etc. Your reasoning would be based on your beliefs about how to get to the coffee house, plus your belief that I wanted to join my friend for coffee, that that was my goal. And, as was argued above, any of those beliefs might be mistaken, including your belief about what I want to do. In any case, though, you would engage in some theoretical reasoning, based on premises about what I want and how I can best get it, that concluded with a judgment about what I should do at each particular point in the journey, which you would then convey to me. But though of course I could utter the same words you utter and indeed form the same beliefs you do, and so engage in the same theoretical reasoning that you do, this cannot be how I myself actually perform the actions involved, forming an opinion about what I want and how I can get it and then giving myself advice as to what I should do. To say that was the way I performed the action of going to meet my friend for coffee would mean understanding "acting on an intention" as coming to believe I have the intention, figuring out how best to act on it, and then advising myself to so act, i.e. doing exactly what you would do if you were walking along with me. But that can't be right. It would be as if the best I can do when trying to perform some action is to give myself advice about how to do it, in the way that you can give me such advice. But clearly this can't be the whole story. Someone has to actually perform the action, not merely offer advice about how to perform it. And that someone is the agent. So we have to say that when I act on an intention it must be the intention itself that guides me, not merely my belief that I have this intention.

So this second sort of reasoning, though it looks like Audi's schema, is actually quite different. In Audi's schema the motivational premise was something I believed and used in my reasoning to come to a conclusion (i.e. a new belief) about what I should do. (The conclusion was the "judgment" that "I should do A.") According to that schema I would be reasoning just as you would be in giving me advice. But when I actually act, it is my intention itself, not my belief that I have this intention, that enters my reasoning. So there is no question of my motivational premise being false.

Intentions are neither true nor false. So, strictly speaking, my intention to join my friend for coffee, even if we say it contains a proposition, should not be thought of as containing a premise in the way premises are used in theoretical reasoning. It is not a belief about what I want. It is part of my understanding of what I am doing, or even part of the actual doing of it.[18] Likewise, and for the same reason, the "conclusion" here is not my belief that I should do something. It too is part of the actual doing of it, perhaps a further, more specific intention, such as an intention to head north, or perhaps just a physical movement, actually walking.

So perhaps we should not call what I am doing here "deliberation," though it is certainly a form of reasoning. Paradigm examples of theoretical reasoning involve proceeding from thoughts containing propositions that have truth values to a conclusion that is supposed to be made likely or even entailed by the truth of those propositions.[19] That is not what is happening when I am carrying out one of my intentions. In that case I am performing an action that involves the employment of some of my beliefs and the formation and execution of more specific intentions. But I am not forming judgments *about* these intentions, as might happen when deliberating about what I should do. When I perform some action, my beliefs and intentions will be employed in the control of my movements. So there will be lots of beliefs involved, about for example such things as how to get out of my office. And there will be lots of intentions involved, such as my intention to turn my office doorknob, which arises because I intend to leave my office and believe that requires opening my office door. And in virtue of all this it will be true that I want to leave my office and so want to turn my office doorknob. But employing my beliefs and intentions in this way when I act, though it involves this sort of "reasoning," is not the same as deliberating, where I start with some claims and try to use them to support some conclusion. In the examples we have been using, the sentence "I want to meet my friend for coffee," when used in actual deliberation, records the content of a belief and is true or false. But that same sentence, if it represents the expression of an intention on which I am acting, gives the purpose guiding my action. So it is neither true nor false.[20]

This suggests that the two puzzles to which Audi's schema gives rise result from conflating these two forms of reasoning. Both puzzles came from trying to understand the role of desire in explaining an action done on the basis of deliberation as involving a conscious belief by the agent that she has the desire, combined with reasoning about how to satisfy it. If the agent then acts on the basis of this deliberation, it wouldn't matter whether or not she had this desire. That was the first puzzle. And yet if she acted on the basis of her belief that she wanted phi, it would follow that she did want phi. That was the second puzzle.

If we understand Audi's motivational premise as an expression of the agent's intention involved in her action (and change the conclusion to an action, as was done in the coffee example), then, since intentions are not beliefs, there is no issue of possibly acting on the false belief that she has this desire. So the first puzzle doesn't arise. And if there is no belief about what is wanted included in the agent's reasoning, then there is no question of her making that belief true by acting on it. So neither puzzle arises.

But we need to be careful here. Clearly there are two distinct processes: deliberation using beliefs that both the agent and anyone else might have and ending in a judgment about what the agent should do, and the reasoning involved in performing the action in question, reasoning that starts from the agent's intention to do something and ends in the completion of that action. This second sort of reasoning, which is of course confined to the agent who has the intention in question, might be very complex and can extend over a long time, as would have been the case, for instance, had my intention to join my friend for coffee been formed a few days in advance,[21] or if the action itself extended over a long time and involved lots of sub-actions.[22] And one might perform the first, deliberative process without then engaging in the second one. Weakness of will, absent-mindedness, or even death might intervene.

But from the fact that we have these different processes and that they can come apart, does it follow that "when things go as intended, practical deliberation involves making up my mind *twice*," as Gary Watson says?[23] That seems to imply that after I have deliberated and concluded what I should do, there is a further issue on which I have to make up my mind and so a further decision to make (whether to do it). Of course there is a difference between deciding that I should do something and forming the intention to actually do it. But it would be a mistake to think we could have reasons for or against forming this intention to act that were distinct from the ones that bore on the question whether we should perform the act. How can that make sense? It would mean that I could have reasons for or against doing something that were not reasons for or against thinking I should do it. How could that be?

It seems clear that I can have reasons for doing the things I do intentionally. In figuring out what I should do, though, I am figuring out what reasons I have for doing the thing in question. So even though we can distinguish two different "processes," deliberating about what I should do and actually forming the intention to do it, and each of these processes involves steps that are themselves intentional, these two processes still have a deep conceptual link. The reasons I am trying to evaluate in deliberating about whether I should do something just are the reasons that support the action that begins with an intention to do that thing. So even though forming the intention to perform an action is something I can do after deliberation leads me to conclude I should do that action, it is not something for which I could have reasons that were not also reasons to think I should do it. Someone who deliberates and comes to the conclusion that she should phi, but then thinks she needs some further reason to "make up her mind" for or against doing it, will find no further reasons because there are none left to find.

## 5. The Role of Desire in Deliberation

This paper began with the question of how an agent's desire, that is, what an agent wants, figures into the explanation of her action when this action is done on the basis of deliberation. Audi's schema suggested an answer to this question, but the plausibility of that answer was only apparent. When an agent acts on the basis of her deliberation, no "desire" (in the "purpose" sense) of hers can be referred to or described in that deliberation. But it does not follow from this that what the agent wants does not figure into the explanation of actions done on the basis of deliberation or even that agents don't sometimes deliberate about how to achieve what they want.[24] The question is how to understand these things in light of the problem with Audi's motivational premise that we have been discussing.

I suggest:

> It is a sufficient condition for acting for a reason that one acts on the basis of some deliberation, whatever its content.

That seems plausible if we assume that the purpose or goal of an action just is (the same thing as) the agent's reason for performing the action. Under this assumption the suggestion here makes sense of the claim that the fact that an agent acted on the basis of deliberation about how to achieve phi entails that she wanted phi. If she acted on the basis of some deliberation, then her purpose in acting was given in the content of that deliberation and so that is what she wanted. On this view the mistake involved in Audi's schema would be to understand "acting on the basis of deliberation about how to achieve phi" as meaning that one's deliberation included, or even could include, the conscious belief "I want phi" (in the "purpose" sense).

How are we to understand deliberation on this suggested view? It is worth remembering that even had we accepted the idea that Audi's motivational premise is a conscious belief that forms the basis of some deliberation, it is not plausible that desires are the basis of all deliberation. Some deliberation surely proceeds from the agent's evaluation of what would be good or worthwhile or just something the agent would like (and so "wanted" in that sense). So even if someone were to hold that some deliberation proceeded from Audi's motivational premise about the agent's goal, considered as the content of a conscious belief, she would still have to make sense of deliberation where that was not the case. Of course one could claim that in such cases no desire figured into the explanation of the action done on the basis of that deliberation. But that would leave the problem of explaining away the plausibility of the claim that if I act on the basis of deliberation about how to achieve phi it follows that I want phi.

So the straightforward thing to do is to accept the suggestion above. When I deliberate from the thought that, for example, "It would be a good thing if phi" and conclude that "I should A," *and* then perform act A *on this basis*, that *just is* having phi as my goal. Likewise, deliberation might proceed from the thought that "Phi would be in my interest" or "I would enjoy phi" or even that "I want phi" (in the "favoring" sense). If I act on the basis of deliberation that starts from one of these thoughts, it follows that I want phi in the "purpose" sense of "want." None of these premises would be subject to the objection made to using "I want phi" (in the "purpose" sense) in deliberation because acting on the basis of the thought that "It would be a good thing if phi," for instance, though it entails that I want phi, does not entail that phi would be a good thing. I could just be mistaken about that, just as I could be mistaken in thinking that phi would be in my interest or that I would enjoy phi or even that I favor phi. For a similar reason, no bootstrapping would occur if my deliberation was based on the thought that phi would be a good thing or in my interest. Bootstrapping would result if I could simply give myself a reason to do something by intending to do it. But if deliberation works on the basis of one's beliefs about what would be good or enjoyable or the like, then since one can be wrong about these things, no bootstrapping results.

Beyond the fact that the reasoning it described was fallacious, there were two issues with the attempt to put a desire into deliberation in the way Audi's schema proposed. Since the desire was merely referred to in the motivational premise, deliberation could proceed even if the agent's belief that she had this desire proved false. So it would seem that if she acted on the basis of her deliberation, then it was her belief that she had this desire, rather than the desire itself, that played the essential role in explaining her action. On the other hand, since it follows from the fact that I acted with the aim of getting phi that I wanted phi, if I deliberate using Audi's motivational premise and then act on the basis of this deliberation, then it follows that I wanted phi and thus this motivational premise couldn't be false. (It is perhaps worth repeating that all this applies to "wanting" in the "purpose" sense. That is the only kind of wanting that actually serves to explain action.)

I have argued that while it is plausible that deliberation on which an agent acts is a source of goals or purposes, that is of what she wants in the purposive sense, I have also argued that it is very problematic to think that reference to such a desire appears in practical deliberation itself. So the answer to the question with which we started, about where what the agent wants figures into the explanation of actions when the agent acts on the basis of her deliberation, must be this. The purpose an agent has, that is, what she wants in the purposive sense, does indeed explain actions in which the agent acts on the basis of her deliberation, but not because such wants are referred to or described in the agent's reasoning. They are constituted by the fact that the agent acted on the basis of that deliberation.[25]

## Notes

1. See Arpaly and Schroeder 2012.

2. This particular puzzle is at least in part created by the fact that desires are usually held to be propositional attitudes, i.e. to have propositional content. But it is not clear that this works for intentions, at least in those cases where the intention in question is guiding an action. See e.g. Lycan (2012). But this, as was said, is an issue on which this paper can remain neutral.

3. Talking only about "wants" allows me to remain neutral as to whether there are desires that have goals as their objects, i.e. in the way intentions do. It is hard to see how that could be since having a purpose seems to involve having an intention. See n17. In any case, nothing in this paper turns on deciding this issue. The argument of this paper at least suggests, however, that the two phenomena covered by "X wants Y" are just what are commonly referred to as desires and intentions.

4. At the risk of belaboring the point, I don't mean here to deny the possibility that this "favoring" sort of desire can be analyzed further, e.g. into a counterfactual claim about what the agent would do under certain circumstances. My point is simply that this sort of case provides a perfectly acceptable use of "want" whether or not such a further analysis is possible.

5. Thanks to Jeff Jordan for this example.

6. Anscombe 1963: 68.

7. The agent's reason is what in fact led the agent to act as she did, i.e. what some philosophers have called the "motivating reason" for the action.

8. See Nagel 1970: 29.

9. I was recently at a college graduation at which one of the student speakers (whose name I never got) admonished her fellow graduates by saying, "Every day, do something you don't want to do." In the "goal" sense of "want" it is not clear this is logically possible, but in the "liking" sense of course it is.

10. Putting it this way leaves open the question of what to call deliberation that ends in a belief that one should act in a certain way, since sentences of the form "X should do Y" can presumably be true and obviously are about whether one should do something. We will return to this issue below, but for clarity for the moment I will refer to the process that ends in a belief about what one should do as a form of "theoretical" reasoning.

11. Audi 2006: 96.

12. So, with Döring and Eker (*this volume*), I would reject any strong version of the "guise of the good" thesis. As will be clear, however, acting on the basis of your evaluations is completely compatible with doing what you want.

13. Some are better than others at knowing their own wants, but anyone who remembers her own childhood can probably recall situations where her parents knew better than she did what she wanted.

14. See Broome 2005. The term *bootstrapping* comes from Bratman 1987. See also Dancy 2002.

15. There may still be a puzzle here, though. On Broome's view it is irrational not to act on an intention one has and has not given up, just as it is irrational not to believe something that follows from a premise one has not rejected. But though it is possible to (irrationally) fail to believe something entailed by premises one fully accepts, it is not so clear that it is possible to fail to act on an intention one has (assuming one is aware of the relevant facts, not paralyzed, etc.). If I am not glued to the chair, am in control of my legs, etc., then doesn't the fact that I don't stand up show that I did not intend to do so?

16. Could we defend Audi's original schema, or at least his original motivational premise, which I argued was a belief about the agent's own desire, by saying here that in his schema the thought "I want phi" *expresses* a desire of the purposive sort (i.e., rather than, as I claim for this new schema, an intention)? One problem with this idea is that since desires can unproblematically conflict, it is hard to see how such a desire could lead to going to meet my friend. I also have a desire to stay in my office, after all. So there would be an exactly parallel motive, and deliberation, leading to my staying put. There cannot be such conflicting intentions. Could we perhaps say Audi's premise expresses an "all-in" or "de toto" desire of the purposive sort? One might think that in any case it is hard to see much difference between the expression of an intention and an all-in expression of a desire for some purpose. So saying that the new premise "I want to meet my friend for coffee" expresses an all-in (purposive) "desire" would hardly be more than a change in terminology. But this would be worse than misleading because an intention involves a decision or commitment to pursue the goal in question, while a desire, even an all-in desire, does not. That is why desires can unproblematically conflict while one

cannot knowingly have intentions that conflict. I can still decide not to pursue a desire, even my strongest one. But if I have an intention, the decision has already been made. (Thanks to Federico Lauria for raising this question.)

17. As has of course been argued by Michael Bratman (1987), as well as by many others. We will return to this issue below.

18. This is another reason for not construing the premise here ("I want to meet my friend for coffee") as the expression of any sort of desire.

19. See Davidson 2004.

20. I am in essence claiming here that my intention to join my friend for coffee constitutes what has sometimes been called an "intention-in-action," roughly, the intention that constitutes the purpose of the action.

21. See Bratman (1987) and subsequent works.

22. Such actions have been discussed under the label "vague projects." See Tenenbaum and Raffman 2012.

23. Watson 2003: 176.

24. In the "purpose" sense, which is the relevant one. I hope it is clear by this point that deliberation that ends in a judgment about what I should do made on the basis of what one wants in the "liking" or "in favor of" sense is no more problematic than anything else one might take as supporting some action. I might try to figure out what I should do based on what I like (want), what is morally required, what is in my interest, or anything else that seems relevant to this question.

25. Very helpful comments on an earlier version of this paper came from members of the conference on the nature of desire at the University of Geneva in June 2012: Daniel Friedrich, Alex Gregory, Federico Lauria, Ronald DeSousa, Graham Oddie, Peter Railton, Tim Schroeder, and David Wall. A later version got a lot of help during a faculty seminar from several of my colleagues at Delaware: Jeff Jordan, Joel Pust, Kai Draper, Richard Hanley, Jeremy Cushing, Kate Rogers, Mark Greene, Tom Powers, Alan Fox, and Seth Shabo. The present version was greatly improved by the editorial comments of Federico Lauria and Julien Deonna.

## References

Anscombe, G. E. M. (1963). *Intention*, 2nd ed. Ithaca, N.Y.: Cornell University Press.

Arpaly, N., and Schroeder, T. (2012). 'Deliberation and Acting for Reasons', *Philosophical Review*, 121 (2), 209–239.

Audi, R. (2006). *Practical Reasoning and Ethical Decision*. Abington, UK: Routledge.

Bratman, M. (1987). *Intentions, Plans and Practical Reason*. Cambridge, Mass.: Harvard University Press.

Broome, J. (2005). 'Does Rationality Give Us Reasons?', *Philosophical Issues*, 15, 321–337.

Dancy, J. (2002). *Practical Reality*. Oxford: Oxford University Press.

Davidson, D. (2004). 'Objectivity and Practical Reason', in *Problems of Rationality*. Oxford: Oxford University Press.

Lycan, W. G. (2012). 'Desire Considered as a Propositional Attitude', *Philosophical Perspectives*, 26 (1), 201–215.

Nagel, T. (1970). *The Possibility of Altruism*. Oxford: Oxford University Press.
Tenenbaum, S., and Raffman, D. (2012). 'Vague Projects and the Puzzle of the Self-Torturer', *Ethics*, 123 (1), 86–112.
Watson, G. (2003). 'The Work of the Will,' in S. Stroud and C. Tappolet (eds.), *Weakness of Will and Practical Irrationality*. Oxford: Oxford University Press.

# CHAPTER 12 | Introspection and the Nature of Desire

LAUREN ASHWELL

AT LEAST SOMETIMES, I know what I want. And at least sometimes, I know what I want in a way that seems quite different from how I know what *you* want—I can *introspect* my desires. To know what you want, I observe how you behave and infer your desires from that information. In general, to know another's mind, I need to infer her mental states from her behavior. In order to know whether or not my students are enjoying class, I have to look to see if they seem interested or bored, if they are paying attention or checking their email on their phones, and if they are participating eagerly or are half asleep. But in my own case, I know right now that I want another cup of coffee, that I want to qualify for the Boston Marathon, and that I want to build a house someday. I don't usually need to wait to observe myself going over to the espresso machine, or to see myself looking up qualifying times, or wait to see myself doodling floor plans in my notebook. I know these desires *before* I make any of these observations.[1] Yet how do I do this?

One might think that this question will be easy to answer once we know what desires *are*. Surely introspecting a desire just involves looking for whether you have that desire! If desires are evaluative beliefs, then wouldn't introspection of desire just involve looking for whether you have a particular evaluative belief? If they are beliefs about normative reasons, then you'd look for those. If they are appearances of value, then you'd introspect by working out what appears valuable to you. And so on. And, for similar reasons, it might seem like looking to the ways in which we make introspective judgments about desire could give us very good reason for accepting a particular view of the nature of desire. If we introspect by judging what is valuable, then desires might just be beliefs about value. And so on.

These thoughts suggest that there is an extremely close match between desire's metaphysics and epistemology. Yet there isn't always such a close match between metaphysics and epistemology for just any kind of subject matter. Of course, if the subject matter is something that we *can* know about, it has to be something that we are *able* to know about, through some method or other. But often all this requires is that the object of knowledge is involved in a causal chain that includes something that we can experience and that we can appeal to as evidence, together with beliefs about why what we observe counts as evidence.

If we know about something only via its causal interaction with other things in the world and with our experiences, then the epistemic method used need not reveal all that much about the *nature* of the thing, and the nature of the thing need not tell us all that much about the way we know about it. For example, you might know that a solution is acidic by observing that it turns blue litmus red, yet it is not as if the redness that you observe reveals the *nature* of the acid. While the disposition *to turn blue litmus red* may be part of the nature of acid, the redness of the paper—the *sign* of the presence of acid—does not mirror anything about the essential nature of the acid. If introspection were like this, then we might introspect our desires via attending to signs that are quite different from what desires really are. If, say, we knew about desire by attending to a chill that the desire causes in the left knee whenever we think about its object, this would show us only that desire is the kind of thing that causes chills in the left knee; it would not show that desire is, by its nature, chilly and located in the left knee.

It is generally thought that introspection cannot be like this. First, introspective knowledge is thought to be especially epistemically privileged in relation to our knowledge of other minds or the rest of the external world. Our knowledge of our own minds is more secure, in some sense, than our knowledge of the world outside our mind.[2] To account for this epistemic privilege, we should prefer a view of the introspective method as sensitive to the nature of the mental state introspected rather than one that does so by detecting something distinct from that state.[3] Second, introspection seems not to involve inference from evidence. While we might often find out about something in the external world by inferring its existence from something distinct from that thing, as we do when we infer the existence of others' mental states from their behavior, this does not seem to happen with introspective knowledge of our own minds.[4] We take the existence of smoke as evidence of fire; we infer from the existence of smoke that there is fire. But this kind of inferential reasoning doesn't seem to be present when we introspect.[5]

I will argue that a theory of the nature of desire that claims that desire is a kind of belief cannot take account of these features of desire introspection, because it does not accurately account for our actual introspective judgments and so must claim that our introspective judgments about our desires are systematically mistaken. Neither could desire consist only in appearances of value; such an account would have the consequence that we often introspect our desires indirectly, by looking to something distinct from desire: our feelings of motivation.

To account for our actual introspective judgments, we need an account of introspection that includes attention to motivation. Thus if introspection is privileged because of its directness, then desire at least partially consists of a motivational component. I should note, however, that I am not arguing for this account of epistemic privilege in introspection. And so while I do think that desires are themselves motivational—it is not just that desires *produce* motivation, although they do produce motivated action—I am not arguing directly for this here. My purpose instead is to highlight a tension between the separation of motivation from desire and a popular view of the privileged nature of introspection. I aim to call attention to the way in which awareness of motivation figures in introspection and also to possible relationships between the epistemology and metaphysics of desire.

## The Distinctive Nature of Introspection

Discussions of introspection usually start by pointing to the special features of introspection: its epistemic distinctiveness, privilege, and especially first-personal nature. Whatever knowledge others have of your mental states, it seems to be through a quite different method. Furthermore, your knowledge of your own mental states is thought to be better than others' knowledge of these states, and it is also thought that you can be more certain of the deliverances of introspection than of your senses. Moreover you, and only you, can introspect your own mental states.

Following Alex Byrne (2005), we can distinguish the claim that introspection involves an epistemically distinctive method[6] and the claim that introspection is particularly epistemically privileged. One way in which first-personal introspective knowledge seems to involve an epistemically distinctive method, relative to our third-personal knowledge of others' mental states, is that such third-personal knowledge involves reasoning from evidence for the existence of those mental states, whereas first-personal introspective knowledge seems not to. When I form the belief that you are angry, in the usual case, it is because I see how you act—perhaps because I see your clenched jaw and hear your raised voice—and from that I work out that you're angry. Such inference may, of course, be very swift (it may have to be, depending on the degree of your anger and how it is directed). And although on rare occasions I might use similar reasoning in my own case (Goodness, I'm clenching my fist and yelling—I must be angry. Calm down), I usually know I'm angry in quite a different way, which doesn't seem to rely on this sort of evidence. Introspective knowledge is thought to have *immediate justification*, in the sense that the justification for an introspective belief doesn't depend on the justification for any other belief.[7] On the other hand, the justification of beliefs reached by reasoning from evidence depends in part on how justified your evidential beliefs are.

The privileged nature of introspection is generally taken to be a desideratum for a theory of introspection.[8] If your account of how introspection works isn't able to explain why introspective knowledge is so privileged, then so much the worse for your account. For example, one historically popular explanation of the difference between introspective and non-introspective knowledge was that we each have a special mechanism for finding out about our own mental states; perhaps we use something like an inner eye, or a kind of internal scanner, to introspect.[9] But this kind of account fails to explain privilege; a mechanism like an inner eye or internal scanner can be more or less reliable, so it does not explain why your introspective knowledge of your own mind is epistemically better off than your knowledge of other minds and the rest of the external world. If your "inner eye" is blind, or even just shortsighted, or if your internal scanner is malfunctioning, then introspection would not be privileged relative to other kinds of knowledge.[10]

If we assume that introspection is highly privileged, we can also note that if a theory of the *nature* of an introspectable mental state would have the consequence that our introspective judgments about that state are systematically mistaken, so much the worse for that theory. In the following section, I will argue that this assumption of privilege means that desire cannot be belief-like.

## Desires as Beliefs

One common version of the view that desires are beliefs holds that desires are *evaluative* beliefs. We might motivate such a view as follows: If, for example, Jo wants to live in Philadelphia, it would be very odd if Jo doesn't see anything good about living in Philadelphia. So, in desiring to live there, Jo must believe that there is something good about living in Philadelphia. Moreover, desires are states that rationalize intentional action. What could make Jo's moving to Philadelphia understandable as a rational action? Well, a belief that moving there would be good or valuable.[11] So, desires are evaluative beliefs. Alternatively, we might hold the view that desire is a *normative* belief—perhaps a belief that the content of the desire ought to be the case, or that you have a reason to bring about the content of the desire.[12]

However, it is not news that our beliefs about goodness, reasons, and value appear to fail to match up with our desires. This experience of weakness of will is all too commonplace. We can believe that something would be good, or valuable, or that there is good reason to do it, but in the same breath say "But I don't want to." I might judge that exercising is a good thing to do, that it is valuable, or that I have reason to do it, yet recognize that I do not want to do it. Moreover, we can usually tell from the first-person perspective that we're being weak-willed. In these kinds of cases, there is a *mismatch* between our judgments of value, or normative reasons, or goodness, and our introspective judgments about our desires.[13]

Given the ubiquity of this kind of experience, these kinds of cases are no surprise to the desire-as-belief theorist. But they do need to be explained away. Perhaps when I judge that exercising is something I have reason to do but also judge that I don't want to do it, I really *do* have the desire—I simply lack the corresponding *motivation.*[14] Now, it is plausible that the reason I judge in cases of weak will that I don't have a corresponding desire is that I just don't feel the right kind of motivation. This lack of motivation is something that is apparent to me from the first-person perspective; I can tell through introspection that I'm not motivated to get up off the couch. I don't have to wait to *observe* myself failing to go and lace up my running shoes to know that I don't want to exercise. Detecting motivation, or lack thereof, is at least sometimes part of making a first-personal judgment about whether or not you want something.

While this kind of explanation allows that desires are evaluative or normative beliefs even though we have these apparent cases of weakness of will, it does so at the cost of the directness and privilege of desire introspection. If desires really are just beliefs about value, or goodness, or reasons for action, then we must be *systematically mistaken* in judging in these cases of apparent weakness of will that we don't have the relevant desire.[15]

Not only can you believe that something is valuable and yet judge introspectively that you don't want it; you can also believe that something is not particularly valuable, yet introspectively judge that you strongly desire it.[16] I might really, really want to stay in bed all morning; however, I get out of bed, despite this desire, because I judge that it really isn't a good idea to laze around for several more hours. Similar things can be said for any of the versions of the desire-as-belief theory. The reasons I have for staying in bed are much weaker than the desire to stay in bed *feels*, and I have to fight against this strong desire to be lazy. Now, the desire-as-belief theorist might claim that, despite appearances, this is not a case where I have a strong desire to stay in bed; what is strong is only the *motivation* to stay in bed. In putting forward this explanation, the desire-as-belief theorist can reject the idea that the judgment of strength of reasons comes apart from the strength of the desire in this kind of case. Yet once again, this move has the consequence that introspection cannot be privileged in the way often assumed. My introspective experience would then *misrepresent* the state of my desires. I judge, through introspection, that I have a strong desire to stay in bed, but if desires are these types of belief, I am just wrong: my desire is weak, and I am only fighting against my motivation, not my desire.

So desire cannot be a belief about goodness, or value, or reasons for action, if we are to hold on to the direct, privileged nature of introspection. The desire-as-belief theorist must claim that we are systematically mistaken about our desires and, moreover, that we make judgments about our desires on the basis of motivational states that are distinct from the desires themselves.

## Desires as Appearances

Once we notice that desire appears not to line up with our evaluative or normative beliefs, we might be tempted to shift to a view on which desires are evaluative *appearances*.[17] In cases of weak will, you judge something to be valuable although it does not *appear* to you to be valuable or good. So you can judge that something is valuable or good but *fail* to desire it. Such a view allows that your introspective judgments in cases of weakness of will are correct: you correctly attribute a lack of desire. While you might *believe* that exercise, for example, is valuable, it does not *appear* to you to be so. This view also allows for space between our evaluative beliefs and our introspective judgments about desire in the other direction. You can take your value appearances to be *value illusions*; something might appear to you to be valuable although you do not judge it to be. Another glass of wine might *appear* to you to be a very good idea, while at the same time you might believe that it would not be such a good idea at all.

However, while this view fares better than the various desire-as-belief views in terms of matching up with our actual introspective judgments,[18] note again that in self-attributing desire we often pay attention to feelings of motivation. When I judge that I really want another glass of wine even though I believe doing so would be a terrible idea, having another glass of wine might appear to me to be a good. But my introspective judgments aren't based just on such appearances; I also feel *drawn* to the wine, and I might feel that I'm about to begin to initiate the action of reaching for the bottle, even if, in the end, I stop myself from doing so. Such feelings are feelings of *motivation* rather than just evaluative appearances.[19]

If desires are value appearances, then *even if* our introspective judgments concerning desire are always in fact correct, they are still misleading in another sense: the method by which we come to these beliefs involves attending to something assumed to be distinct from the desire itself. But yet in feeling motivated—in feeling *drawn* to action—it seems like we are experiencing the desire itself, and not just mere effects of the desire. The *action*, of course, is an effect of the desire; what we experience in feeling motivation is not the performance of the appropriate action.[20] Instead, it is the disposition we have *toward* acting, whether or not we in fact end up acting on it.

## But Is Desire Introspection Really Privileged in This Way?

Given my arguments, we have a choice to make: either desire introspection is systematically mistaken, or desires are neither evaluative beliefs, nor normative beliefs, nor appearances of value. I have argued that we ought to conclude that desires are not identical to these beliefs or appearances. But perhaps we ought to take the other option. Perhaps the assumption that we began with was mistaken; maybe introspection, when applied to desire, isn't all that epistemically privileged. After all, don't we also find cases where we think at some time that we want something, only to realize later that we don't, or that we don't want it as much as we originally thought we did? We might also think that we really *don't* want something, only to realize later that we wanted it all along; many romantic comedies are built on the plausibility of just this kind of case. Maybe, *even if* the assumption of privilege is plausible for belief introspection (where those beliefs are not of the kind that desire consists in), it just doesn't hold for introspection of desire. When writing about introspection, philosophers have a habit of disregarding desire—as they often do when writing about the mind. The most influential arguments in this literature tend to consider just belief, with a secondary focus on pain or perceptual experience, as the central example of an introspectable mental state. Only recently has desire introspection started to gain some attention in its own right.[21] Because of this, we might wonder whether these general claims made about introspection really carry over to desire. Perhaps we have direct epistemic access to our beliefs, but not to our desires.

My discussion here is complicated somewhat by the fact that I do not think a complete story about self-knowledge should involve the assumption that desire introspection is as highly privileged as is usually claimed; I am also not unsympathetic to views of self-knowledge that have a place for inference from evidence in introspection. Unfortunately, I am arguing to a claim that I take to be true—that desire is not separate from motivation—from a premise that I suspect might be false, at least as an account of how desire introspection works in general. So it remains that those who want to hold desire and motivation as separate may simply reject the premise that desire introspection is direct in these cases.

However, note that the kind of mistakes that might motivate a rejection of privilege for desire introspection are quite different from the ones that are required for a doxastic theory of desire to address my arguments, as these aren't like the cases of weakness of will considered earlier. When we are weak-willed it seems all too obvious that we know what we want and that it doesn't line up with our judgments about value or reasons. The kinds of cases that call into question the privileged nature of desire introspection are ones where we judge that our desires *do* line up with our judgments of value or reasons, but where we act in ways that suggest our self-attributions of desire are incorrect, either through direct action or through later retraction of that self-attribution.

When the romantic comedy's heroine realizes that she has wanted to be with her love interest all along, although she fervently denied that before, it isn't that she realizes that she *always believed this person was the one for her.* If desires *are* beliefs like this, then we will have to say that not only did she fail realize at the time that she desired her love interest but that she was also mistaken about her beliefs. She *did* in fact believe that this potential relationship was good for her, despite her protestations to the contrary.

In order to not attribute contradictory beliefs here, the desire-as-belief theorist will have to claim that the heroine believes that her love interest is not right for her (he is *so* infuriating, and her family wouldn't approve), but also believes that he is right for her for other reasons. She is aware of the first belief and not the second, which is why she denies that she desires to be with her love interest. However, a better account of what is going on here is that this heroine has good introspective access to her evaluative beliefs but not to her desires. When she asks herself if getting together with her supposed love interest is a good idea, she *thinks* she is introspecting but is not. The deliverances of introspection are drowned out by her beliefs about value. When we theorize about our own mind, we often rely on an assumption that we are much more rational than we in fact are, so that we use our beliefs about what is good or what we have reason to do as a way to figure out what we want. We can also use these beliefs to try to control and strengthen recalcitrant desires to get them in line with our evaluative and normative beliefs, by focusing on these beliefs.

This kind of case shows, at the very least, that our folk-psychological theory about desire does not equate desire with normative or evaluative belief. Certainly, beliefs about value or reasons are not motivations, though they can motivate us. But they are also not desires.

## Notes

1. Of course, not all one's beliefs about one's own mental states are formed through introspection; you might work out, for example, that you really want to become an accountant by noticing that taxation and finances are all you ever talk about. Such a method is third-personal—it is a method that someone else could use to work out what you want—while introspection seems to be distinctively *first*-personal.

2. This kind of thought has a long philosophical tradition. See Alston (1971) for historical examples. Here are some more recent statements of this claim of epistemic privilege: "Philosophical tradition has it that one's own mental life enjoys a privileged epistemic standing. I know my own states of mind immediately and with confidence. You may discover what I am thinking, of course, but you are liable to err in your assessment of my thoughts in ways that I cannot" (Heil 1988: 238). "At least sometimes, while you reflect on an occurrent thought, you know what it is that you are thinking with more certainty than anyone else could have regarding your thought. Moreover, at times you know this without using evidence about the so-called external world; and your knowledge does not depend on contingent fact about that world" (Gertler 2000: 125). "Subjects have the ability to acquire beliefs about their own mental states in a way that makes them especially justified in holding those beliefs" (Fernández 2003: 352).

3. Hume, for example, seems to be claiming that introspection must reveal the nature of mental states when he says, "For since all actions and sensations of the mind are

known to us by consciousness, they must necessarily appear in every particular what they are, and be what they appear. Everything that enters the mind, being in reality as the perception, tis impossible anything should to feeling appear different" (quoted in Alston 1971: 224).

4. "[Independent of a Cartesian picture of self-awareness] there remains a set of basic asymmetries between self-knowledge and the knowledge of others. . . . The type of access we ordinary take ourselves to have [to our own mental states] is special in at least two basic ways. First, a person can know of his belief or feeling without observing his behavior, or indeed without appealing to evidence of any kind at all. And second, rather than this nonreliance on evidence casting doubt on the reliability of such reports, judgments made in this way seem to enjoy a particular epistemic privilege not accorded corresponding third-person judgments that *do* base themselves on evidence" (Moran 2001: 9–10).

5. See Carruthers (2011) and Lawlor (2009), however, for recent statements of views on which introspection involves reasoning from evidence. Carruthers argues that knowledge of mental states generally involves reasoning from evidence; Lawlor argues this particularly for some cases of desire, although she allows that perhaps not all first-personal knowledge of desire is like this. Byrne (2005, 2012) argues that introspection involves something akin to inference, but still quite distinct from reasoning from evidence.

6. Byrne (2005, 2012) calls this being epistemically "peculiar."

7. Note that privilege isn't explained simply by introspective knowledge being immediately justified; a belief could be immediately justified but not highly justified, or particularly secure.

8. Introspection's privileged nature is generally agreed upon, although it isn't clear that everyone in the debate means the same thing in attributing this privilege. Sometimes this is taken to mean that beliefs formed by introspection are more likely to be true than other beliefs, or that they can't be rationally doubted, or that they can't be false, among other things. For a discussion of some of the different things that have been meant by "privilege" in these debates, see Alston (1971).

9. For more recent versions of this kind of view, see Armstrong 1968; Nichols and Stitch 2003.

10. This is not the only objection to inner-eye or inner-scanner views; for example, Brie Gertler (2000) argues that this kind of view can't account for the essentially first-personal nature of introspection. This objection, and the objection discussed above, however, may simply mean that *reliability* is not the way to understand privilege. This is a problem for causal theories of introspection if reliability is the only way to understand the epistemic quality of the process.

11. Although see Döring and Eker *this volume*. They argue that beliefs about goodness or value don't rationalize in the way they are assumed to, so a key motivation for the view that desires are beliefs does not hold. See Oddie, Friedrich, Schroeder (*this volume*) for other concerns about the thesis that desires are beliefs.

12. See Gregory *this volume*.

13. See Ashwell (2013) for arguments that these kinds of mismatch cause problems for so-called transparency accounts of desire introspection: that we introspect our desires by making evaluative judgments.

14. See Gregory's contribution to this volume for this kind of explanation.

15. Moreover, if you're particularly weak-willed, and vocal about it, then someone who is versed in this kind of theory of the nature of desire could have more reliable knowledge of your desires than you do. While it is not clear that introspection's epistemic privilege involves such relative reliability, it would be odd for us to be less reliable than others in *this* way. Alternatively, we might be wrong that we believe that we have the relevant belief, but again this would have to be counted as an introspective mistake.

16. I think, in fact, that you can also believe that something is not valuable *at all*, while judging that you desire it. However, here I only need a less controversial case where the judged *strength* of your desire is out of line with how valuable you judge the object of desire to be.

17. See, for example, Stampe 1987; Oddie 2005, *this volume*.

18. See Ashwell 2013.

19. I have not here considered the view that the relevant appearances are instead normative appearances (see Lauria, Massin *this volume*). If appearances of reasons for action do not involve motivations, then the same objection applies to these views. However, I find it plausible that appearances of reason for action do consist, at least in part, in feelings of motivation. Since, however, motivations seem to be dispositions toward action (see Ashwell *forthcoming*), this would be, in effect, a partially dispositional view of the nature of desire.

20. If this was the case, then we would not feel motivated to take the last cookie on the plate when we refrain from acting on this desire.

21. See Ashwell (2013), Byrne (2012), Fernández (2007), Lawlor (2009), and Moran (2001) for recent discussions of the introspection of desire.

## References


Alston, W. (1971). 'Varieties of Privileged Access', *American Philosophical Quarterly,* 8 (3), 223–241.

Armstrong, D. M. (1968). *A Materialist Theory of the Mind*. London: Routledge and Kegan Paul.

Ashwell, L. (2013). 'Deep, Dark, ... or Transparent? Knowing Our Desires', *Philosophical Studies,* 165 (1), 245–256.

———. (*forthcoming*). 'Conflicts of Desire: Dispositions and the Metaphysics of Mind', in J. Jacobs (ed.), *Causal Powers*. Oxford: Oxford University Press.

Byrne, A. (2005). 'Introspection', *Philosophical Topics*, 33, 79–104.

———. (2012). 'Knowing What I Want', in J. Liu and J. Perry (eds.), *Consciousness and the Self: New Essays*. Cambridge, UK: Cambridge University Press.

Carruthers, P. (2011). *The Opacity of Mind: An Integrative Theory of Self-Knowledge*. Oxford: Oxford University Press.

Fernández, J. (2003). 'Privileged Access Naturalized', *Philosophical Quarterly*, 53 (212), 352–372.

———. (2007). 'Desire and Self-Knowledge', *Australasian Journal of Philosophy*, 85 (4), 517–536.

Gertler, B. (2000). 'The Mechanics of Self-Knowledge', *Philosophical Topics*, 28, 125–146.

Heil, J. (1988). 'Privileged Access', *Mind*, 97 (386), 238–251.
Lawlor, K. (2009). 'Knowing What One Wants', *Philosophy and Phenomenological Research*, 79 (1), 47–75.
Moran, R. (2001). *Authority and Estrangement*. Princeton, N.J.: Princeton University Press.
Nichols, S., and Stitch, S. (2003). *Mindreading: An Integrated Account of Pretence, Self-Awareness, and Understanding Other Minds*. Oxford: Oxford University Press.
Oddie, G. (2005). *Value, Reality, and Desire*. Oxford: Oxford University Press.
Stampe, D. (1987). 'The Authority of Desire', *Philosophical Review*, 96 (3), 334–381.

# INDEX